The African American Encyclopedia

Second Edition

The African American Encyclopedia

Second Edition

Volume 6
Lee-Nat

Editor, First Edition
Michael W. Williams

Consulting Editor, Supplement to First Edition
Kibibi Voloria Mack

Managing Editor, Second Edition
R. Kent Rasmussen

Marshall Cavendish
New York • London • Toronto • Sydney

Project Editor: McCrea Adams
Production Editor: Cindy Beres
Assistant Editor: Andrea Miller
Research Supervisor: Jeffry Jensen
Photograph Editor: Philip Bader
Page Layout: William Zimmerman

Marshall Cavendish Corporation
99 White Plains Road
Tarrytown, New York 10591-9001

Printed in the United States of America
09 08 07 06 05 04 03 02 01 5 4 3 2 1

Library of Congress Cataloging-in-Publication Data

The African American encyclopedia.—2nd ed. / managing editor, R. Kent Rasmussen.
p. cm.
Includes bibliographical references and index.
1. Afro-Americans—Encyclopedias. I. Rasmussen, R. Kent.
E185 .A253 2001
973'.0496073'003—dc21
ISBN 0-7614-7208-8 (set) 00-031526
ISBN 0-7614-7214-2 (volume 6) CIP

∞ This paper meets the requirements of ANSI/NISO Z39.48-1992 (R1997)
Permanence of Paper for Publications and Documents in Libraries and Archives

Contents

The African American Encyclopedia

Second Edition

Lee, Spike (b. March 20, 1957, Atlanta, Georgia): FILM DIRECTOR, screenwriter, and actor. Shelton Jackson Lee, nicknamed "Spike" by his mother because he was a tough baby, was the oldest child of Bill Lee, an accomplished JAZZ bassist and composer, and Jacquelyn Shelton Lee, a black literature and art teacher. Lee grew up in the Fort Greene section of Brooklyn, New York, with his sister, Joie, and three brothers, David, Cinque, and Chris. His mother died of cancer in 1976.

A fourth-generation college graduate, Lee received his bachelor's degree in 1979 from Morehouse College in Atlanta, where he majored in mass communications. That fall, he began working on his master's degree in filmmaking at the New York University (NYU) Institute of Film and Television, Tisch School of the Arts.

Early Films

In his first year at NYU, Lee put together a ten-minute film called *The Answer*, about a black screenwriter assigned to remake D. W. Griffith's 1915 masterpiece THE BIRTH OF A NATION. Lee's film, which criticized the racism in Griffith's, put him at odds with several professors and faculty members, and he was almost expelled. His next attempt at filmmaking was a piece called *Sarah*, about a Harlem family's Thanksgiving Day celebration.

In 1982, his last year at NYU, Lee received artistic recognition for his master's thesis film project, *Joe's Bed-Stuy Barbershop: We Cut Heads*. Produced, written, and directed by Spike Lee, the film featured an original jazz score by his father, Bill Lee. The film told the story of a barber in the Bedford-Stuyvesant section of Brooklyn whose shop was really a front for the neighborhood numbers racket. *Joe's Bed-Stuy Barbershop: We Cut Heads* won Lee critical acclaim and a student Academy Award from the Academy of Motion Picture Arts and Sciences. The picture also became the first student production selected for the New Directors/New Films series at New York's Lincoln Center.

After receiving his master's degree in filmmaking, Lee was signed by the ICM and William Morris talent agencies. Unfortunately, neither firm was able to present Lee with employment opportunities. He supported himself by cleaning and shipping film at a film distribution house, earning a weekly salary of only two hundred dollars.

In 1984, resolving to produce his own films, Lee attempted to make a picture about a New York City bike courier entitled *Messenger*. Working with a limited budget, Lee applied for a waiver from the Screen Actors Guild to use nonunion actors, but the guild claimed that the project was too commercial and refused to grant the waiver. By then, the picture was in its eighth week of preproduction, and Lee had $40,000 invested in it. Attempts to recast the film using union actors failed, and he had to discontinue the entire project.

First Success

Lee had his first commercial success in 1986. The film *She's Gotta Have It* was made on a shoestring budget of $175,000. The only funding Lee had to begin the filming was an $18,000 grant from the New York State Council on the Arts. Determined to make the picture, he financed the rest of the film himself by soliciting money and help from family and friends and using credit cards to their limit to buy whatever he needed.

She's Gotta Have It centered on Nola Darling, an independent, self-assured, attractive, single young woman who, because she cannot find everything she wants in one man, has three different lovers with very diverse personalities. Lee wrote, produced, directed, and acted in the picture, which was shot in only twelve days during the summer of 1985.

The film featured Lee in his debut acting role as the streetwise Mars Blackmon, one of Nola's lovers. Lee's sister, Joie, had a small

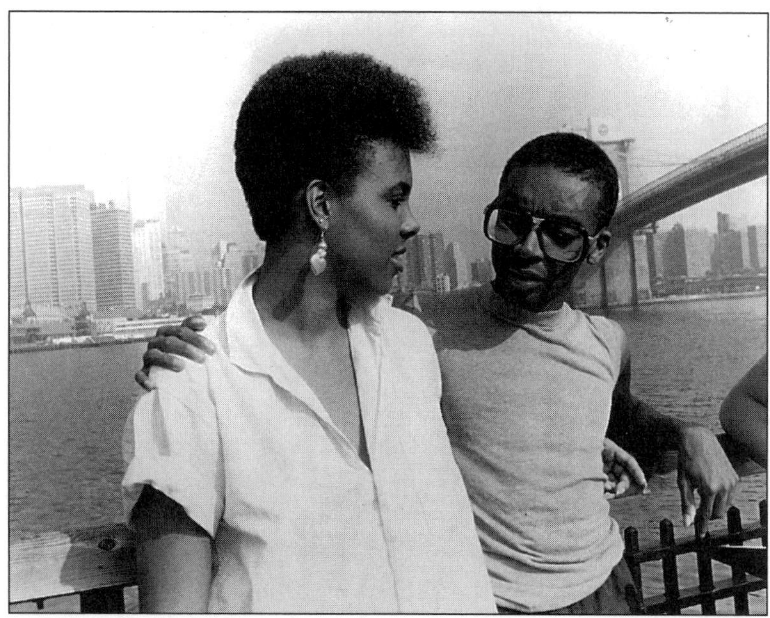

Spike Lee (right) made his acting and directorial debuts in *She's Gotta Have It*, in which he plays one of the three lovers juggled by Nola Darling (Tracy Camila Johns). *(Museum of Modern Art, Film Stills Archive)*

part in the picture, and *She's Gotta Have It* again boasted a jazz score by father Bill. Spike Lee's Blackmon persona became one of his most commercial characters, reappearing in several Nike athletic shoe advertising campaigns. *She's Gotta Have It* was a major success, grossing more than $7 million and winning the Cannes Film Festival award for best new film.

Lee put together his own film company, 40 Acres and a Mule Filmworks. The company was named for the never-realized idea that, after the EMANCIPATION PROCLAMATION, freed slaves in the South would be given FORTY ACRES AND A MULE so they would not begin their free lives empty-handed.

Tackling Taboo Issues

She's Gotta Have It was such a success that Island Pictures, the distributors for the film, budgeted $4 million for Lee's next film, a 1988 musical entitled *School Daze*. The script, originally entitled *Homecoming*, was written by Lee after he graduated from film school. With it, he attempted to highlight several issues facing African Americans. The film focused on black students on an all-black college campus; according to Lee, the film was based on his own experiences at Morehouse College. The basic problem touched on in *School Daze* was the very real but often taboo issue of the color lines drawn between light-skinned blacks and dark-skinned blacks.

Before preproduction on *School Daze* was finished, Island Pictures pulled out of the deal. Executives at the studio feared that the film would go over the budgeted $4 million. Lee, by then with considerable influence and contacts, was able to get a deal with Columbia Pictures within days. In addition to the new deal, Columbia also contributed an additional $2 million to the project, raising the existing budget to $6 million.

Controversy continued to surround the film. Lee, who was on his third week of filming at Morehouse, was asked to leave because officials at the school felt the film would be a negative portrayal of black colleges and people. Filming was completed at ATLANTA UNIVERSITY. Lee received mixed reviews for *School Daze*, with many critics saying that the film touched on too many issues, never concentrated on any one problem, and offered no solutions.

Provocative Exploration of Racism

Lee's third and most provocative commercial film, *Do the Right Thing*, was released in 1989. He wrote, produced, directed, and starred in the picture. This film also featured an original score by Bill Lee and starred sister Joie. Lee completed *Do the Right Thing* for Universal Pictures for $6 million.

The film presents the viewer with several questions, including how one can best combat racism and stereotypes—with nonviolence, as advocated by Martin Luther KING, Jr., or by any means necessary, as suggested by MALCOLM X. Which is the right thing to do? *Do the Right Thing* ends with quotations from the two men, whose messages, Lee felt, were both valid.

The film takes place on the hottest day of the year in Brooklyn's Bedford-Stuyvesant neighborhood and explores the racial tensions that exist and build among the African, Korean, Hispanic, and Italian Americans who live and work there. The tension builds to a crescendo when, in the end, a young black man is killed by white police, and a riot ensues.

Do the Right Thing won lavish praise from many critics, who saw it as a very honest and important piece of work, but it was passed over at the Academy Awards. Lee considered this a blatant attempt to discount his work and appeared on the television news program *Nightline* to criticize the Academy's process of picking winners.

Without stopping to rest, Spike Lee began shooting his next picture, originally entitled *Love Supreme*. The movie, eventually retitled *Mo' Better Blues*, told the story of a jazz musician with two women in his life, whose only real loves are himself and his music. The 1990 picture, which Lee wrote, produced, and directed, starred Oscar winner Denzel WASHINGTON as the main character and Lee as his manager.

Lee got his next film idea straight from the headlines. In 1989 an African American teenager named Yusuf Hawkins was attacked and killed by Italian youths in the Bensonhurst section of Brooklyn because the youths thought Hawkins was dating an Italian girl from their neighborhood. Lee used the idea of interracial romance in the explosively charged *Jungle Fever*. The film, released in 1991, explored myths and stereotypes surrounding race, sex, and class.

Wesley Snipes portrayed an African American architect having an affair with his Italian secretary, played by Annabella Sciorra. The relationship receives strong emotional and sometimes violent responses from family and friends as well as from the black and white communities. In the film, Lee also tackled the topic of drugs and their destructive effects on the main character's family and the black community. Once again, he stirred up controversy and made the public think. The hostile attitudes and intolerance caused by interracial relationships caused debate across the country.

In 1992 Lee's largest undertaking to date, *Malcolm X*, was released. Adapted from Alex HALEY and Malcolm X's *The Autobiography of Malcolm X* (1965) and newsworthy because of its multimillion-dollar budget, *Malcolm X* and Lee received much publicity and stirred controversy even prior to the film's November opening. Denzel Washington starred as the Black Muslim civil rights leader, and Angela Bassett starred as Betty SHABAZZ. Lee also had a role in his film, which was shot on location in the United States, Saudi Arabia, and Egypt.

Other Professional Ventures

In addition to directing feature films, Lee directed music videos for several artists and groups, including Miles DAVIS, Anita Baker, EU, Phyllis Hyman, and PUBLIC ENEMY; film shorts for MTV and *Saturday Night Live*; commercials for Nike (starring his good friend, basketball great Michael JORDAN) and Levi Strauss; and advertisements for the 1988 presidential campaign of Jesse JACKSON. Lee also lectured and headed a film workshop at Long Island University in New York. In the 1993-1994 academic year, he served as a lecturer-in-residence at Harvard University.

In July, 1990, Lee officially opened Spike's Joint, a corner storefront on DeKalb Avenue in Brooklyn, to sell merchandise associated with his films. In 1991 Lee started his own record company, 40 Acres and a Mule Musicworks, which featured some of the artists who appeared on the sound tracks of his movies as well as new and established artists from many musical genres. In 1997 he established an advertising agency as a joint venture with DDB Needham; called Spike/DDB, it was launched to specialize in selling to urban and ethnic consumers.

Having six commercially successful feature films to his credit by age thirty-five, Lee took time off in 1993 to marry New York attorney Tonya Linette Lewis. Lee and Lewis had met the previous year at a Congressional Black Caucus conference in Washington, D.C. The couple became the proud parents of a baby girl, Satchel Lewis Lee, in December of 1994. Their daughter was named for the legendary pitcher Satchel Paige, who played in the Negro Leagues before appearing in major league baseball.

Spike Lee in 1991. *(Universal City Studios, Inc.)*

Crooklyn and Clockers

Lee's next film project was a collaboration with his sister Joie Lee and his brother Cinque Lee. Together, they wrote and produced *Crooklyn* (1994), which tells the story of a Brooklyn family of five siblings growing up in the 1970's with their jazz-musician father (played by Delroy Lindo) and their schoolteacher mother (portrayed by Alfre Woodard). Despite similarities to the circumstances of the Lee family, the filmmakers said that the work was based only loosely on their own lives.

Lee's eighth film, *Clockers* (1995), broadened the director's vision of African American life in Brooklyn. Based on a novel by Richard Price and starring Harvey Keitel and Delroy Lindo, the film focuses on a murder mystery among drug dealers in a Brooklyn housing project. Mekhi Phifer made his acting debut as a teenage drug dealer named Strike whom the police believe is responsible for the murder. *Clockers* received critical acclaim greater than Lee's previous work. In an interview on NBC's *Today* show, Lee attributed this critical success to the fact that, unlike some of his earlier work, *Clockers* places most of the responsibility for some problems within the African American community on the community itself and not solely on racism or some other external or uncontrollable factor.

Lee's films in the late 1990's included the documentary *Four Little Girls: Bombing of the Sixteenth Street Baptist Church, Birmingham, Alabama* (1998), which was shown on the HBO cable network and was nominated for an Academy Award; *He Got Game* (1998); and *Summer of Sam* (1999).

—Gwen Sparks
—Updated by Timothy Tee Boddie

Suggested Readings:
Bambara, Toni Cade. "School Daze." In *Deep Sightings and Rescue Missions: Fictions, Essays and Conversations*. Edited by Toni Morrison. New York: Pantheon Books, 1996.
Chrisman, Robert. "What Is the Right Thing? Notes on the Deconstruction of Black Ideology." *The Black Scholar* 21 (March/May, 1990): 53-57.
Lee, Spike. *Spike Lee's Gotta Have It: Inside Guerrilla Filmmaking*. New York: Simon & Schuster, 1987.
_______, and Ralph Wiley. *The Best Seat in the House: A Basketball Memoir.* New York: Crown, 1997.
McKelly, James C. "The Double Truth, Ruth: *Do the Right Thing* and the Culture of Ambiguity." *African American Review* 32 (February, 1998): 215-227.
McMillan, Terry, et al. *Five for Five: The Films of Spike Lee*. New York: Stewart, Tabori & Chang, 1991.
Moore, Suzanne. "You Can't Do the Right Thing All the Time." *New Statesman and Society* 3 (September 21, 1990): 31-32.
Reid, Mark, ed. *Spike Lee's "Do the Right Thing."* New York: Cambridge University Press, 1997.

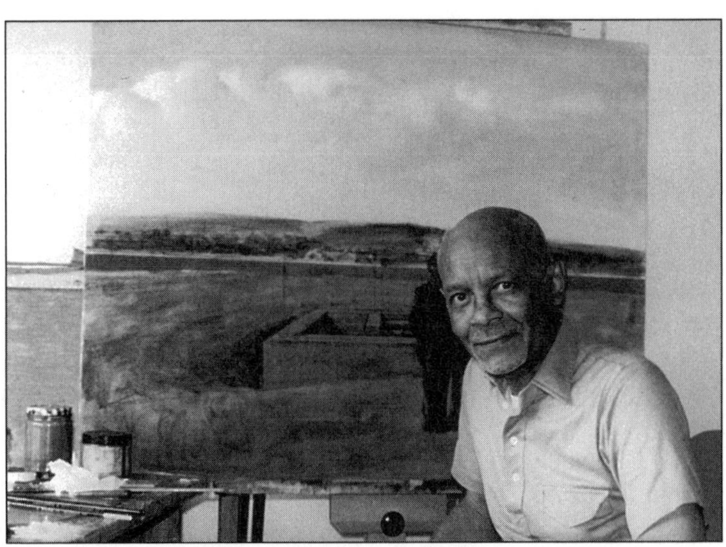
Painter Hughie Lee-Smith in 1992. *(Patricia Lee-Smith)*

Lee-Smith, Hughie (September 20, 1915, Eustis, Florida—February 23, 1999, Albuquerque, New Mexico): Painter. Lee-Smith studied at the Cleveland Institute of Art and at Wayne State University. His work is known as being technically mature and eloquent; its settings are spare, even bleak; its figures—people dressed in normal street clothes, sometimes wearing exotic masks—are graceful.

Born in Florida, Lee-Smith went to live with his grandmother, Queenie Victoria Williams, in Atlanta, Georgia, after his parents divorced. At age ten he moved to Cleveland, Ohio, to live with his mother, Alice Williams Smith, who enrolled him in local art school classes. He later taught art at what later became the Cleveland Museum of Art and at the Karamu House, a center for African American artists. During the Great Depression, he did paintings and drawings on political and patriotic themes for the Works Progress Administration. While serving in the Navy during World War II, he painted a mural titled "History of the Negro in the U.S. Navy."

In 1958 Lee-Williams moved to New York to teach at the Art Students League. In 1967 he was named a member of the National Academy of Design. Among his numerous prizes are the Emily Lowe Award (1957) and the Founders Prize of the Detroit Institute of Arts (1953). His paintings can be seen in numerous public galleries, including New York's Metropolitan Museum of Art, the Detroit Institute of Art, Washington's National Gallery of Art, and New York's Schomburg Center for Research in Black Culture, where his work was featured in a special exhibition on New York City artists mounted in 1999-2000. Despite the proliferation of his work in public collections,

no career retrospective was organized for him until 1988, when the New Jersey State Museum put together an exhibition that also traveled to several other sites.
See also: Painters and illustrators.

Legal professions: By the beginning of the twenty-first century, African Americans were involved in the legal professions at all levels: from maintaining private law practices to serving as prosecutors and JUDGES to serving on the U.S. SUPREME COURT. Many others also served in support roles, working in the court system as bailiffs and other officials and working for attorneys as assistants and legal secretaries.

For most of American history, however, few African Americans were involved in the legal professions. As was true in most other professions, they faced nearly insurmountable discrimination until the mid-twentieth century. Nonetheless, there were black lawyers even in the nineteenth century, and hundreds of black lawyers practiced between the 1840's and the mid-twentieth century.

The Nineteenth Century

Black lawyers were practicing in the United States even before the CIVIL WAR. The bars of Maine, Massachusetts, New York, and Ohio admitted a handful of black lawyers in the 1840's and 1850's. Macon Allen, admitted to the MAINE bar in 1844, was probably the first practicing African American lawyer. He was sponsored and tutored by a prominent white lawyer, Samuel Fessenden. Before the twentieth century, it was common practice for aspiring lawyers to "read law" with mentors and sponsors rather than to go to law school. African Americans hoping for a law career had to find the unusual white lawyer interested in teaching them. Allen was later admitted to the MASSACHUSETTS bar as well. His appointment as a justice of the peace in 1847 made him the first black lawyer in the United States to be named to a judicial post.

Robert Morris, admitted to the Massachusetts bar in 1847, was sponsored by abolitionist and attorney Ellis Gray Loring. In *Roberts v. City of Boston* (1849), Morris became the first black lawyer to be involved in a case that went before a state supreme court. Morris became known for his criminal defense work, and he frequently represented Irish immigrant defendants. In a case that carried considerable symbolic importance, Morris represented a black client who sued a white man for payment for "services rendered." The verdict was in favor of Morris's client; Morris later wrote that "my people [African Americans observing the trial] in the courtroom acted as if they would shout for joy."

John Mercer LANGSTON, who was a slave in VIRGINIA as a boy, attended OBERLIN COLLEGE in Ohio but was denied admission to a number of law schools. In 1853 he apprenticed with Philamon Bliss, a white lawyer and former judge. Langston was subsequently admitted to the OHIO bar. He won a reputation for successfully representing both black and white criminal defendants in rural Ohio.

After the Civil War

The most significant development regarding African Americans and the legal professions in the post-CIVIL WAR era was the founding of black universities and law schools. The HOWARD UNIVERSITY Law School was founded in 1869, and in the 1870's John Mercer Langston was a professor and the first dean of law there. By 1900 Howard had trained between two hundred and three hundred lawyers.

Another historically black university, FISK UNIVERSITY, also established a school of law, as did a handful of other black institutions, including LINCOLN UNIVERSITY, Shaw University, and Central Tennessee University. Some of these law schools were short-lived, unable to maintain adequate funding and resources.

In the late nineteenth and early twentieth centuries, a number of northern black lawyers won reputations in criminal law. As Robert Morris did, many defended white immigrants as well as African Americans. Although by far most of the country's black population lived in the South, most black lawyers practiced in the North because it was difficult to overcome southern racism, both inside and outside the courtroom. Those lawyers who did manage to practice in the South performed a particularly valuable service because almost no white lawyers were willing to defend a black man accused of an offense against a white person. Whether in the North or South, black attorneys were often expected by the black community to represent African Americans accused of serious crimes even if there was no money available to pay their fees, and most lawyers accepted this responsibility.

Among those lawyers who began their careers after the Civil War were John Rock and John Roy LYNCH. In 1865 U.S. senator Charles Sumner sponsored Rock as the first black lawyer admitted to practice before the U.S. Supreme Court. Lynch, born a slave, had a unique career—or series of careers. He was named a justice of the peace by the RECONSTRUCTION-era governor of MISSISSIPPI in 1869. Lynch went on to serve two terms in the U.S. Congress in the 1870's. He later passed the Mississippi bar in 1896 and went on to practice law in Washington, D.C., and Illinois.

The Early Twentieth Century

The American Bar Association, founded in 1878, routinely refused to admit black applicants. Moreover, the private clubs to which white lawyers and judges belonged also barred blacks. African American lawyers therefore faced difficulties in establishing connections with others within the legal profession. A group of African American lawyers founded the National Negro Bar Association in 1909. Then, in 1925, the NATIONAL BAR ASSOCIATION was founded. The National Bar Association quickly became the largest and most significant national organization of black lawyers.

In 1921 black lawyers served on university law reviews for the first time. There were three that year: Jasper Atkins at Yale, William Taylor at the University of Iowa, and Charles Hamilton Houston at Harvard. In 1924 Clara Burrill Bruce, at Boston University, became the first African American woman on a law review; the next year she was the review's editor-in-chief.

Black Lawyers and the Civil Rights Movement

To some extent, simply to be a practicing black lawyer was to be an agent of social change and to embody an implicit challenge to racism and segregation. By the third decade of the twenti-

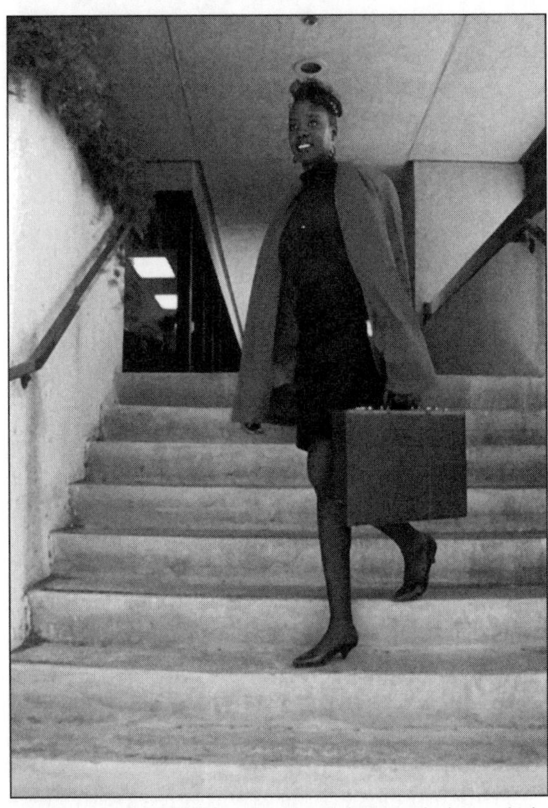

Women and minorities have made steady inroads in legal careers, but attorneys in the United States have remained predominantly middle- to upperclass white males. *(Gerold Lim/Unicorn Stock Photos)*

Thurgood Marshall was the most renowned African American jurist of the twentieth century. *(AP/Wide World Photos)*

eth century, black lawyers were taking a more directly activist role in the struggle for CIVIL RIGHTS, particularly in working with the NATIONAL ASSOCIATION FOR THE ADVANCEMENT OF COLORED PEOPLE (NAACP). The NAACP and its lawyers won crucial court victories in the early Civil Rights movement.

Before the 1930's, the NAACP relied largely on white lawyers to argue its major cases. In the 1930's, however, Charles Hamilton Houston and a number of his colleagues began to change that situation, and black lawyers were soon in the forefront of legal battles regarding segregation.

Houston earned his law degree from Harvard in 1922 and the next year was the first African American to earn a Harvard doctorate in law. Between 1929 and 1935 he headed—and transformed—the Howard University Law School, hiring a number of top-level law professors for the faculty. Houston believed that black lawyers must be activists and social engineers; if they were not, he insisted, they were "parasite[s] on society." Houston later became the first full-time paid special counsel of the NAACP, serving from 1935 to 1938. Houston's primary efforts were directed toward legal battles for school desegregation. Among the cases in which he was involved were *University of Maryland v. Murray* (1936) and MISSOURI EX REL GAINES (1938).

Thurgood MARSHALL was the most renowned African American jurist of the twentieth century. Marshall attended Howard University Law School, where he was strongly influenced by Charles Hamilton Houston. After Houston began working full-time for the NAACP, he appointed Marshall his assistant in 1933. Marshall replaced him as chief counsel in 1938. Marshall argued thirty-two cases before the U.S. Supreme Court for the NAACP, and he won twenty-nine of them. The best known is the Court's landmark 1954 *Brown v. Board of Education* decision outlawing segregation in public schools. President John F. Kennedy appointed Marshall to a federal judgeship in 1961. President Lyndon B. Johnson named him U.S. solicitor general in 1965 and then nominated him to the U.S. Supreme Court in 1967. Marshall served with distinction until 1991.

Pauli MURRAY graduated at the top of her class from Howard University Law School in 1944; she was the only woman in her class. She served as a deputy attorney general of CALIFORNIA in 1946. Murray wrote *States' Law on Race and Color* (1951), praised by Thurgood Marshall as an invaluable reference in the struggle for desegregation, and she taught law at Brandeis and Boston Universities. A staunch activist, Murray also led SIT-INS in Washington, D.C. She later helped found the National Organization for Women (NOW). Murray, like another lawyer and civil rights crusader, Oliver W. Hill, had gone to law school largely so she could fight against segregation.

Spottswood ROBINSON received his law degree in 1939 from the Howard University Law School. He became a practicing attorney, and he served as an active NAACP member and counsel for the NAACP Legal Defense and Education Fund as well as on the U.S. COMMISSION ON CIVIL RIGHTS.

Black Women Lawyers

African American women have been active in the field of law since the late nineteenth century. They were among the first female law students in the United States. Most attended the Howard University Law School—as did some early white female law students, since women were denied admission to most law schools. In 1872 Charlotte Ray was the first woman to graduate from Howard's law school. Lutie A. Lytle, who was admitted to the TENNESSEE and KANSAS bars in 1897, became the first female law professor of any race in the United States when she began teaching at Central Tennessee College of Law.

Pauli Murray, as noted previously, was active in the legal fight against segregation in the 1940's and 1950's. In 1970 Elaine JONES was the first black woman to earn a law degree from the University of Virginia. She became head of the NAACP Legal Defense and Education Fund in 1993.

Judges

Muffin Wistar Gibbs is said to have been the first black judge in America's history. He was named a judge in California during its early years as a state in the mid-nineteenth century. Nearly a century later, William Henry HASTIE became the first African American federal judge. He was appointed to the Third Circuit Court of Appeals in 1949. Thurgood Marshall was appointed a federal judge in 1961 and named to the U.S. Supreme Court in 1967. Spottswood Robinson served as a district court judge before he was appointed a circuit court judge in 1966. Benjamin HOOKS, a lawyer and a Baptist minister, served as a public defender in MEMPHIS, TENNESSEE, from 1961 to 1964 and as a criminal court judge in Shelby County, Tennessee, from 1966 to 1968.

Leon HIGGINBOTHAM was appointed a U.S. court of appeals circuit judge in 1977. In 1978 President Jimmy Carter appointed Michigan assistant attorney general Julian Abele COOK to serve as U.S. district judge for the Eastern District of Michigan. Cook was promoted to chief judge of the Eastern District in 1989. Florida lawyer Alcee Lamar HASTINGS was named a U.S. district court judge in 1979; Hastings was later elected to the U.S. Congress in 1992. Archibald J. CAREY was appointed an Illinois Supreme Court judge in 1989. In 1991 President George Bush nominated Clarence THOMAS to replace the retired justice Marshall on the U.S. Supreme Court; Thomas was sworn in in 1991.

The 1960's to the 1990's

The number of black lawyers and judges increased dramatically after the Civil Rights movement. In 1930 there were about twelve hundred African American lawyers; in 1950 there were about seventeen hundred. After the Civil Rights movement, their numbers grew more rapidly—to forty-six hundred in 1970, sixteen thousand in 1983, and slightly under twenty-four thousand in 1997. Although these numbers undeniably reflect progress, the 1997 figure also indicates that blacks composed only 2.7 percent of the country's lawyers. The number of African Americans holding judgeships also increased; in 1983 there were about sixteen hundred black judges, and in 1997 there were about two thousand.

African American lawyers were prominent in the most highly publicized criminal case of the late twentieth century, the 1994-1995 murder trial of former football star O. J. SIMPSON. Johnnie COCHRAN was a leader of Simpson's successful team of defense lawyers, and Los Angeles County prosecutor Christopher DARDEN led the prosecution team along with Marcia Clark.

—*McCrea Adams*

Suggested Readings:

Goldman, Roger. *Thurgood Marshall: Justice for All*. New York: Carroll & Graf, 1992.

Smith, J. Clay, Jr. *Emancipation: The Making of the Black Lawyer, 1844-1944*. Philadelphia: University of Pennsylvania Press, 1993.

Tushnet, Mark V. *The NAACP's Legal Strategy Against Segregated Education, 1925-1950*. Chapel Hill: University of North Carolina Press, 1987.

Ware, Gilbert. *William Hastie: Grace Under Pressure*. New York: Oxford University Press, 1984.

Washington, Linn. *Black Judges on Justice: Perspectives from the Bench*. New York: New Press, 1994.

Welch, Susan. *Affirmative Action and Minority Enrollments in Medical and Law Schools*. Ann Arbor: University of Michigan Press, 1998.

Wright, Bruce. *Black Robes, White Justice*. New York: Carol, 1993.

Leland, George "Mickey" (November 27, 1944, Lubbock, Texas—August 7, 1989, near Fugnido refugee camp, Ethiopia): TEXAS politician. Leland was born into poverty. He graduated from Texas Southern University in 1970, was a clinical pharmacy instructor at that university for one term, and then entered politics. He was a member of the Texas legislature from 1973 to 1978 and was elected to the U.S. Congress in 1978. He was reelected continuously by his district and served until his death. His commitments were global, and he challenged Congress to reorder its priorities to include funds and programs for refugees, the homeless, and the hungry in Africa and throughout the world.

Leland was well known to the communications industry of the United States for authoring the equal employment opportunity language in the Cable Act of 1984. His particular concern was that the media be responsible as they related to children, women, and minorities. He was more widely recognized by the general public, however, as the main congressional advocate of defeating world hunger. It was Leland's idea to create the House Select Committee on Hunger, which he later chaired. He also initiated intercultural programs between African Americans and Jews in Israel, visited CUBA and Vietnam to gain the release of political prisoners and binational children, and traveled to Ethiopia and the Sudan on six occasions to aid refugees from regional wars. Leland died in a plane crash en route to an Ethiopian refugee camp in mountainous territory. He was prominent in movements to erase world hunger, and he frequently noted that he was a citizen of the world as well as of the United States.

Leland's passionate commitment to saving lives throughout the world was bolstered by his diligent manner, his ability to relate to political adversaries, and his capacity to represent his interests in established political circles. He was chairman of the CONGRESSIONAL BLACK CAUCUS as well as of various congressional committees. He was clearly an internationalist. He remained popular in his Texas district and was reelected with large majorities five times. He attributed his powerful advocacy on behalf of oppressed groups to his religious background, an orientation shared with many fellow African Americans.

See also: Congress members; Politics and government.

Lew, Barzillai (November 5, 1743, Groton, Massachusetts—1793): Revolutionary war soldier. Lew served for six years during the AMERICAN REVOLUTION. He was the fife player with the Twenty-seventh Massachusetts Regiment at the Battle of Bunker Hill on June 17, 1775. He served with that unit for eight months, then with a different infantry regiment. He had also fought in the French and Indian War. Some accounts give his date of death as January 19, 1821.

Lewis, Delano (b. November 12, 1938, Arkansas City, Kansas): Attorney and corporate executive. Born to a father who worked for the Santa Fe Railroad and a mother who worked as a domestic while studying to become a beautician, Lewis grew up in Kansas City and attended segregated public schools. He majored in history and political science at the University of Kansas and earned his bachelor's degree in 1960. Lewis went on to complete his J.D. degree from the Washburn School of Law in 1963 before moving to WASHINGTON, D.C., and launching his legal career as an attorney for the Justice Department.

During his stay in the federal capital, Lewis also worked in the Office of Analysis and Advice for the EQUAL EMPLOYMENT OPPORTUNITY COMMISSION (EEOC). In 1966 he began serving as a volunteer associate director for the Peace Corps in Nigeria and then in Uganda. After returning from AFRICA in 1969, Lewis worked as a legislative assistant to Senator Edward Brooke of MASSACHUSETTS and later for congressional representative Walter Fauntroy from 1971 to 1973. Lewis soon made his own bid for public office, campaigning for a seat on the Washington, D.C., city council, but was defeated by Marion BARRY, the city's future mayor.

Leaving public service, Lewis joined the staff of the Chesapeake and Potomac Telephone Company as public affairs manager in 1973. He began to rise through the company ranks and helped improve the company's minority hiring efforts. Lewis was promoted to company vice president in 1983, and went on to become president in 1988. Earning a reputation as a principled executive with a strong sense of corporate responsibility, Lewis was tapped to serve as the company's chief executive officer in 1990. During his tenure at the company, Lewis used his business connections to assist in fund-raising efforts for the United Way and other important charities

In October of 1993, Lewis accepted a post as president and chief executive officer of National Public Radio (NPR), the nation's largest public broadcasting network. His decision to move to NPR was considered unusual, since the company was only one-tenth the size of Chesapeake and Potomac Telephone. Nevertheless, Lewis stated his interest in pursuing new challenges at NPR, and he used his fund-raising skills to enlarge the network's operating budget. He also worked to improve NPR's record of minority recruitment and promotion. In 1994 President Bill Clinton appointed Lewis to serve on the newly formed National Information Infrastructure advisory council, proposed by Vice President Al Gore to help shape government policies that would apply to the telecommunications industry as revolutionized by the Internet and other communications services.

See also: Business and commerce.

Lewis, Edmonia (July 4, 1845, Albany, New York—c. 1900): Believed to be the first female African American sculptor. Mary Edmonia Lewis was a product of mixed parentage: Her father was an African American and her mother was a Chippewa Indian. Lewis, whose Indian name was Wildfire, was raised with her mother's tribe. The awareness of her own racial origins fueled her desire to expose the inequalities of American society toward

African Americans and Native Americans.

With the help of one of her brothers and the patronage of a number of abolitionists, she entered Oberlin College in 1859. The school was one of the first to admit women on an integregated basis. While at Oberlin, she was accused falsely of fatally poisoning two white classmates. Although she was not found guilty of the crime, it was difficult for her to remain at Oberlin. With the help of William Lloyd Garrison, who had defended her, she relocated to Boston, Massachusetts, in 1862.

In Boston, she began to develop her unique talent by training with Edmund Brackett and opening a studio. Specializing in portrait busts and symbolic groups, usually sculpted in marble, her work portrayed the plight of Native Americans and the racial hatred endured by African Americans. One of her earliest pieces was a bust of Robert Gould Shaw, commander of the first all-black regiment in the Union Army. Sales of copies of it financed a trip to Rome, Italy, in 1865.

Many of Lewis's most recognized pieces show the will and strength of an oppressed people struggling to be free. These pieces include *Forever Free*, *Hagar*, the *Hiawatha* series, *Freedwoman*, *Medallion Head of John Brown*, *Abraham Lincoln*, *Henry Wadsworth Longfellow*, *Madonna and Child*, *Old Indian Arrow Maker and His Daughter*, *William Lloyd Garrison*, *Baby's Waking*, *Asleep*, and *Poor Cupid*.

Lewis returned to the United States several times. She brought *The Death of Cleopatra* to the 1876 American Centennial Exposition in Philadelphia, Pennsylvania. It won an award and brought Lewis a brief period of fame. A self-confident and determined woman, Lewis used her neoclassical art style to aid in the struggle for equality and civil rights by making the world aware. She eventually faded from the public art scene and is believed to have died in Rome.

See also: Sculptors.

Lewis, James B. (b. November 30, 1947, Roswell, New Mexico): State official. Lewis grew up in New Mexico and received his B.S. degree in education from Bishop College in 1970. After graduation, Lewis served in the U.S. Army for two years, attaining the rank of E-4 specialist. He worked as an administrator and instructor in Afro-American studies at the University of Albuquerque from 1974 to 1977. At the same time, Lewis pursued graduate studies at the University of New Mexico and earned a master's degree in public administration in 1977.

Lewis's career in public service began when he worked as an investigator and purchasing director for the district attorney's office in Albuquerque from 1977 to 1983. During this time, he also pursued an additional college degree, graduating magna cum laude with a B.S. in business from the National College of Business in 1981. Lewis became treasurer for Bernalillo County, serving from 1983 to 1985. In 1984 he was elected treasurer for the state of New Mexico. Upon taking office in 1985, Lewis became the first African American in New Mexico's history to hold a major statewide office. While he was treasurer, Lewis served as a member of the New Mexico State Board of Finance and was a member of the National State Treasurers Association.

See also: Politics and government.

Lewis, John Robert (b. February 21, 1940, Troy, Alabama): Georgia politician. Lewis, one of ten children born to a sharecropping family, grew up on a farm in Alabama. He graduated from public high school and attended the American Baptist Theological Seminary in Nashville, Tennessee. Lewis received his bachelor of arts degree from the seminary in 1961, then enrolled at Fisk University, where he studied religion and philosophy and graduated in 1967.

During his student years in Nashville, Lewis became a prominent leader in the Civil

Rights movement. He organized sit-ins at segregated lunch counters and led freedom ride demonstrations to challenge segregation in bus terminals and on cross-country bus rides. He was beaten severely during bus ride demonstrations held in Rock Hills, South Carolina, and in Montgomery, Alabama.

SNCC chair John Lewis (left) and Hosea Williams of the Southern Christian Leadership Conference planning a campaign in Georgia in 1965. *(Library of Congress)*

Lewis also helped establish the Student Nonviolent Coordinating Committee (SNCC) and became its first chairman. He was one of the key speakers at the March on Washington in 1963. He participated in the Selma to Montgomery march and helped organize the Mississippi Freedom Summer in 1964 to encourage registration of black voters in the South. As a result of his activism, Lewis was appointed by President Lyndon Johnson to serve on the White House conference entitled "To Fulfill These Rights" in 1966.

After leaving SNCC when Stokely Carmichael was elected chairman, Lewis continued his civil rights activism in Atlanta. Among his other activities, Lewis headed up the Voter Education Project, an organization responsible for spearheading voter registration drives and assisting black elected officials in the South. Lewis's enthusiasm brought him to the attention of Georgia's Democratic governor, Jimmy Carter. After Carter was elected president in 1976, he invited Lewis to Washington to serve on the staff of ACTION, the government agency responsible for coordinating the volunteer activities of organizations such as Volunteers in Service to America (VISTA). When Carter was defeated in the 1980 election, Lewis returned to Atlanta.

Upon his return, Lewis was elected as a member-at-large on the Atlanta city council and served from 1981 to 1986. He decided to run as a candidate for Georgia's Fifth Congressional District seat after Congressman Wyche Fowler declared his intention to run for the U.S. Senate in 1986. Lewis challenged his good friend Julian Bond, who had worked as SNCC communications director with Lewis and was serving as state senator, for the Democratic nomination. In a closely fought race, Lewis won 52 percent of the vote in the Democratic primary before going on to win easily in the November election. Lewis took his seat in Congress in 1987 and was appointed to serve on the Committee on Interior and Insular Affairs and the Committee on Public Works and Transportation.

See also: Congress members; Politics and government.

Lewis, Julian Herman (May 26, 1891, Shawneetown, Illinois—March, 1989, Dyer, Indi-

ana): Physician. Lewis was the first African American to earn a Ph.D. in physiology, from the University of Chicago in 1915. He earned an M.D. from Rush Medical College in 1917 and taught pathology at the University of Chicago from 1917 to 1943. His *The Biology of the Negro* was published in 1942.
See also: Health care professionals; Medicine.

Lewis, Reginald F. (December 7, 1942, Baltimore, Maryland—January 19, 1993, New York, New York): Business executive. Lewis began his professional life as an attorney in 1968, after graduation from Harvard Law School. He served at several firms and from 1970 to 1973 was a partner at Murphy, Thorpe, and Lewis, the first black law firm on Wall Street. He was a corporation lawyer in private practice from 1973 to 1989. He then became president and chief executive officer of TLC Beatrice International Holdings, Inc.
See also: Business and commerce.

Reginald F. Lewis, chairman and chief executive officer of Beatrice International Holdings. *(Greg Heisler)*

Lewis, W. Arthur (January 23, 1915, Castries, St. Lucia, British West Indies—June 15, 1991, Bridgetown, Barbados): Economist. William Arthur Lewis shared the 1979 Nobel Prize in Economic Sciences with Theodore W. Schultz. Both economists were honored for their work in the problems of developing nations. Lewis also was a student of economic growth and economic history, and he was the first black person to win a Nobel Prize in the sciences. He used the public stature gained from that award to express his opinions on problems of black people, both in the mainstream press and in black periodicals.

Lewis was the fourth of five children born to his parents, both of whom were schoolteachers. He finished high school at the age of fourteen. As he was too young to take the examination necessary to attend a British university, he worked as a civil service clerk for three years. He won a university scholarship in 1932 and attended the London School of Economics, earning a Bachelor of Commerce degree in 1937. The school granted him a scholarship to continue his studies, and he earned his Ph.D. in industrial economics in 1940. He had begun lecturing there in 1938 and continued to work as a lecturer until 1948, when he was made a full professor at the University of Manchester. In 1959 he was named vice chancellor of the University of the West Indies, where he served until 1963. He was knighted in 1963, and in that same year accepted a position at Princeton University as a professor. He taught there until his retirement in 1983.

Lewis's most famous work is probably his "Economic Development with Unlimited Supplies of Labour," published in 1954 in the journal *The Manchester School of Economics and Social Studies*. That article was expanded into *The Theory of Economic Growth* (1955). In addition to his academic work, Lewis traveled extensively in the Third World during the 1950's. His experiences led him to write *Politics in*

Nobel Prize-winning economist W. Arthur Lewis. *(Nobel Foundation)*

West Africa (1965). He worked with the United Nations as economic consultant for Asia and the Far East in 1952 and as economic adviser to the prime minister of Ghana in 1957 and 1958. He took a leave of absence from Princeton from 1970 to 1974 to work with the Caribbean Development Bank, which he helped establish. He also was chair of the Caribbean Research Council from 1985 to 1991. Lewis served as president of the American Economic Association in 1982 and was a consultant to the NATIONAL ASSOCIATION FOR THE ADVANCEMENT OF COLORED PEOPLE (NAACP) in 1979, when he won his Nobel Prize.

Liberia: Tropical West African country. Covering an area roughly equivalent to the state of OHIO, Liberia had a population of a little more than 2.6 million people in 1991. Its capital city, Monrovia, was named after James Monroe, the U.S. president at the time Liberia was established in 1822. The official language of Liberia is English; other languages spoken in Liberia include Kpelle, Bassa, Vai, Gio, Mano, Loma, Kru, Krahn, Kissi, Gola, Mende, Belle, and Dei. About 60 percent of the population of Liberia is Christian. Muslims make up about 15 percent of the population; the remaining 25 percent of its population practice indigenous African religions.

Historical Background

Liberia was established in 1822 by the African American leaders of the AMERICAN COLONIZATION SOCIETY (ACS). Samuel J. Mills and Ebenezer Burgess, two white New Englanders, were sent to West Africa in 1817 by the ACS to find an appropriate location where African Americans could be settled. Mills and Burgess arrived in West Africa in 1818 after a stay in England. William Wilberforce and Earl Bathurst, prominent English crusaders against the SLAVE TRADE, provided help to the ACS representatives, because the objective of the mission was similar to what the English had already accomplished in West Africa. The colony of Sierra Leone, which had been established by the English in 1787 for blacks from England, Nova Scotia, and JAMAICA, was similar to what the ACS was working to accomplish in West Africa.

Additional assistance was given to Mills and Burgess in Sierra Leone by Governor Charles MaCarthy and John Kizell, an African returnee who had been a slave in America but who had won his freedom by fighting for the English during the AMERICAN REVOLUTION. Much of Mills's and Burgess's information was provided by Kizell. Sherbro, an island several miles from Freetown, the chief town of Sierra Leone, was recommended to the two ACS representatives by Kizell as a possible site for the colonization scheme; Kizell also volunteered to travel with Mills and Burgess to Sherbro Island.

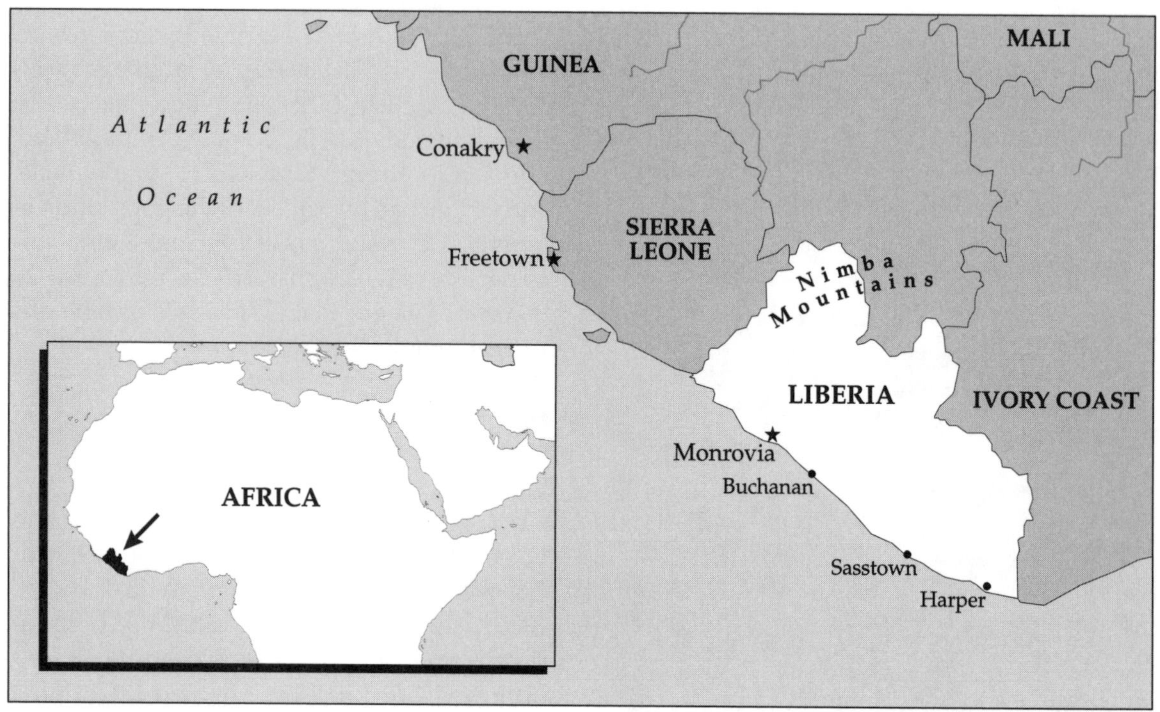

The reports gathered and passed on to the ACS by Mills and Burgess were to have a tremendous impact on the effort to establish a colony on the West African coast. The information influenced the unanimous decision of the leaders of the ACS to establish without delay the anticipated colony in West Africa. The position of the ACS was enhanced as a result of an authorization given to President James Monroe by the U.S. government to use $100,000 indirectly on behalf of the ACS.

The ACS leased a ship, the *Elizabeth,* for the transportation of eighty-eight free African Americans to West Africa. The voyage began at the harbor of New York on January 31, 1820. Most of the emigrants were children and women from the District of Columbia, New York, Pennsylvania, Virginia, and Maryland. The group included both newly freed African Americans and some who had been free for years. Nearly all were devout Christians. The group was led by John Bankson, Samuel Crozer, and Samuel Banon, all of whom were white. Another group of emigrants was sent to West Africa on the ship *Nautilus* in March, 1821. The third group, composed of some thirty-five people, left the United States for West Africa on the ship *Alligator* in April, 1821.

Despite the many problems the colonists had with indigenous Africans, diseases, and leadership, they succeeded in accomplishing their main goal. They founded the settlement that became known as Liberia on April 28, 1822, at Cape Montserrado on the coast of West Africa. The objective was accomplished in large part because of the excellent leadership provided by prominent African Americans such as Daniel Coker, Elijah Johnson, and Lott Carey.

The Colony Under the ACS

From 1822 to 1847, the Liberian colony was led by the ACS through its governors. Eli Ayres, a white physician from Baltimore, served as the first governor of the colony. He was succeeded by Jehudi Ashmun; it was during Ashmun's leadership, from 1822 to 1828, that the colonists defeated the indigenous Africans who lived in the Cape Montserrado area. Ashmun personally led the colonial militia during the war, in which more than eight hundred indigenous Africans were killed. The colonists' losses were tiny in comparison. Another war was fought between the two groups in 1823, and again the colonists were victorious. The result of the wars was that the original residents of Cape Montserrado were forced to give up their land to the colonists, a development that was followed by the expansion of the colony.

The administrative system introduced in Liberia by the ACS was not democratic. The governor, who was the chief executive of the colony, was not elected but was appointed by the ACS; governors chosen during the early colonial period were exclusively white men. Although the constitution of the colony allowed the settlers to elect the vice governor and the members of the Colonial Council, or legislature, the constitution also stipulated that the final decision concerning who would occupy such offices would be decided by the governor. The army and the judiciary were placed directly under the control of the governor, who treated the colonists paternalistically. Not surprisingly, there was continued tension between the colonists and their leaders throughout most of the colonial period. In 1823 the colonists attempted to overthrow Governor Ashmun for what they described as his tyrannical behavior. Stability was brought to the colony only because the ACS threatened to withhold basic necessities designated for the colony.

Despite such problems, the population of the colony continued to increase, from fewer than one hundred persons in 1824 to nearly seven hundred persons in 1828. This trend continued up to the beginning of the American Civil War in 1861. Commercial and agricultural activities, especially those associated with the production of cash crops, also intensified throughout the colonial period.

Monrovia during the period the American Colonization Society administered Liberia. *(Library of Congress)*

One of the purposes of the American Colonization Society, which founded Liberia, was to promote the spread of Christianity in West Africa. Missions such as this Episcopal Station played a major role in early Liberia. *(Library of Congress)*

The Movement for Self-Rule

Because the white-dominated colonial government was tyrannical, the colonists decided to demand self-rule in 1839. Fearing that the colonists would rebel if the demand was not met, the colonial leadership tried to neutralize the potential for rebellion by appointing in 1841 Joseph J. Roberts, a light-skinned African American, to lead the colony. Although the appointment helped to ease tension in the colony, it did not stop the colonists from demanding self-rule. Moreover, the colony was becoming too expensive for the ACS to operate; the colonists were thus told by the ACS to help to pay for the costs of running the colony. Roberts decided to levy customs duties on all ships that traded in the ports of the colony, but Europeans involved with the Liberian trade refused to pay the newly imposed customs duties on the grounds that Liberia was not a sovereign nation.

On July 26, 1847, however, the Liberian colonists declared their independence. A new constitution and flag, which were similar to those of the United States, were developed and adopted. Independence, though, did not mean that the country's problems were over. Although their countries recognized the independence of Liberia, English and French merchants still refused to honor Liberia's customs laws. Liberia protested the refusal, but such protests were not taken seriously, because Liberia did not have a navy or army to back its diplomacy.

Another problem independent Liberia continued to face was rising tension among its population. The dispute that had existed between the white leadership and the black colonists during the colonial era took political form after independence. Light-skinned blacks governed the colony through its independence until 1869. Like the white leaders during the colonial period, the members of the mulatto ruling class supported the paternalistic and aristocratic social orders that had been introduced in Liberia by the ACS. Light-skinned black colonists were at the top of the new social scale; dark-skinned colonists were lower on the scale, and indigenous Liberians were at the bottom.

Such a social arrangement turned out to be one of the main sources of tension and violence in Liberia. A violent confrontation between the light- and dark-skinned Liberians in 1869 led to the mysterious death of E. J. Roye, the first dark-skinned president of Liberia. Although a new political alliance was formed in the 1870's, the colonists and their descendants failed to accommodate the indigenous African population. This failure not only undermined the interests of the indigenous Liberians but also slowed Liberia's social and political development.

Liberian Politics

Liberia's two leading political parties, the Republican Party and the National True Whig Party, competed until the time of the administration of President H. R. Johnson, who served from 1883 to 1892. During the administration of President Johnson, the Whigs succeeded in making Liberia a one-party state. This political unity was a manifestation of a social alliance that had been formed as a result of the seizure of half of Liberia by Great Britain and France in the 1880's and 1890's. The international economic depression of the 1880's also reinforced the desire for political unity. The depression disrupted Liberia's reliance on international trade, and as a result, heavy taxes were imposed by the government on the indigenous Liberians. This action precipitated revolts by indigenous Liberians in the 1880's and 1890's, in 1912, 1915, and in the 1920's and 1930's. These revolts, though, only reinforced the ruling classes' inclination toward political and social unity.

Foreign Investment

The United States and American companies became increasingly interested in Liberia, especially in the period from 1926 to 1980. The Firestone Rubber Company, an American company, decided to invest in Liberia in 1926. The company bought large tracts of land from the Liberian government in order to grow a kind of tropical tree that produced latex. Other American companies became involved with the mining of iron ore in Liberia. Against this background, the United States became increasingly interested in Liberia; American troops were sent to Liberia, for example, during World War II to protect Firestone's holdings. The United States also made substantial material investments in Liberia during and after the war. The seaport of Monrovia and Liberia's main international airport were built with American funds. In the 1960's and early 1970's, massive investments were made in Liberia not only by American but also by German, Italian, and Swedish companies.

The economy of Liberia grew rapidly as a result of the investments. The national annual budget increased, for example, from $37 million in 1960 to more than $300 million in 1972. New roads, schools, hospitals, and other public projects were constructed as a consequence of the economic growth. The growth also created jobs for more than one-third of the working adult population in the 1960's and the early 1970's.

Challenging the Status Quo

The economic growth helped to preserve the dominant social standing of Liberians of American descent. Opposition to the Liberian status quo, however, was becoming evident by the early 1970's. Economic troubles in the 1970's intensified the grievances of the indigenous population, and tensions erupted in a riot in Monrovia on April 14, 1979, that resulted in the death of some 140 protestors. One year later, a military coup led by indigenous Liberians violently overthrew the National True Whig Party government of President William R. Tolbert, Jr., on April 14, 1980, and assassinated Tolbert.

Samuel K. Doe took control of the government. By the late 1980's, severe economic problems were leading to turmoil. Charles Taylor began a revolution in late 1989. Doe was assassinated by a separate rebel group led by Yormie Johnson a year later. Johnson's and Taylor's forces then battled each other during the early 1990's. In 1995 a peace accord was signed, and an uneasy peace prevailed under a ruling "council of state." In 1997 elections, Charles Taylor was elected president of Liberia. The civil war had seriously damaged Liberia's economy and disrupted food production, making the country dependent on food aid even during the late 1990's.

The history of Liberia manifests a serious and sad contradiction. The motto on the national seal maintains that "Love of Liberty Brought Us Here." Yet African American Liberians failed to extend their newly acquired liberty to most indigenous Liberians until the twentieth century. In this sense, the liberty of many Liberians was obtained at the expense of the indigenous population. Liberia has paid a heavy and painful price for this contradiction, as illustrated by the brutal civil war that plagued the country in the 1990's.

—*Amos J. Beyan*

See also: Africa; Garvey, Marcus; Universal Negro Improvement Association.

Suggested Readings:

Beyan, Amos J. *The American Colonization Society and the Creation of the Liberian State: A Historical Perspective, 1822-1900*. Lanham, Md.: University Press of America, 1991.

Campbell, Penelope. *Maryland in Africa: The Maryland Colonization Society, 1831-1857*. Urbana: University of Illinois Press, 1971.

Harris Katherine. *African and American Values: Liberia and West Africa*. Lanham, Md.: University Press of America, 1985.

Liebenow, J. Gus. *Liberia: Quest for Democracy*. Bloomington: Indiana University Press, 1987.

Moses, Wilson J., ed. *Liberian Dreams: Back-to-Africa Narratives from the 1850's*. University Park: Pennsylvania State University Press, 1998.

Shick, Tom. *Behold the Promised Land: A History of Afro-American Settler Society in Nineteenth Century Liberia*. Baltimore: Johns Hopkins University Press, 1980.

Staudenraus, P. J., *The African Colonization Movement, 1816-1865*. New York: Columbia University Press, 1961.

Liberty Party: First antislavery political party in the United States. The Liberty Party was founded on November 13, 1839, in Warsaw, New York, by a group of egalitarian abolitionists that included Gerrit Smith and Lewis Tappan. Henry Highland GARNET and Samuel Ringgold WARD were among the party's leading supporters. Rejecting the nonpolitical stance of William Lloyd GARRISON, the party adopted a platform of social and political equality for blacks and pledged to fight any inequality of rights and privileges based on color. Former slaveholder turned abolitionist James Gillespie Birney garnered the party's presidential nomination for the 1840 election. Birney received slightly more than seven thousand votes, 3 percent of the total.

After that election, the party split into factions, with a radical element promoting the view that the Constitution gave the federal government the power to abolish SLAVERY in all the states. Leading the more conservative faction, Ohioan Salmon P. Chase, who joined the party in 1841, became dominant in party theory and platform writing. Chase believed in abolition but focused on the more immediate, and reachable, goal of keeping slavery from expanding into the territories. Chase wanted the party to merge with antislavery

Whigs and Democrats so as to concentrate political power into a position more palatable to a broader range of Northerners.

In 1844 Birney again carried the party banner and received more than sixty thousand votes. Still more of a religious crusade than a political organization, the Liberty Party held up the Bible as the guideline for change, offered scripture as moral suasion, and tried to infuse Christian ethics into government.

In 1848 the party convention nominated Senator John Parker Hale of NEW HAMPSHIRE for president. Hale withdrew his candidacy as the party voluntarily dissolved and merged with antislavery Whigs and Democrats to form the FREE SOIL PARTY at the new party's first convention in Buffalo, New York. Although the Liberty Party surrendered its plank of equality to unite with more conservative elements, the rise of the REPUBLICAN PARTY in 1854 and the election of Abraham Lincoln in 1860 can be attributed in large part to Liberty Party roots.

Life insurance companies: The first large business enterprises organized and managed by African Americans were banks and life insurance companies. Managing these companies helped blacks obtain experience in managing large enterprises and enabled them to amass capital for financing other enterprises. Life insurance companies provided much of the capital financing for early black entrepreneurs and encouraged BLACK CAPITALISM.

Life insurance protects the insured person's family, creditors, and others from financial loss resulting from the death of the insured person. Life insurance is provided through assessment associations, burial associations, FRATERNAL SOCIETIES, and legal reserve insurance companies. (Legal reserve companies sell stock and accumulate and invest a pool of surplus premium payments and capital reserves.)

Life Insurance During Slavery

During the era of SLAVERY, African Americans were insured by slaveowners under chattel contracts much as horses and livestock are insured by farmers. However, many slaves also insured themselves. As early as the 1840's, sick-benefit and burial insurance for slaves was provided by voluntary assessment and benevolent societies organized in nearly every community with a sizable slave population. A slave who could read and write was designated as secretary. Because it was illegal for slaves to assemble in any numbers, members would come by ones and twos to pay weekly or monthly dues to the secretary or to pay assessments levied to pay claims. The president of the benevolent society was usually a privileged slave who had the confidence of his or her master and could come and go at will and was thus able to organize the society and arrange funerals and burials. In the event of the death of a member, the benevolent society provided funds for a decent burial, and all members attempted to obtain permits to attend the funeral. Life insurance was a matter of self-help, and insurance procedures were conducted by these fraternal and secret societies with little regard for business or actuarial principles.

Life Insurance After Emancipation

Fraternal societies grew rapidly in the decades following the end of the CIVIL WAR in 1865; they rivaled the black church in numbers and members. Societies such as the Sons and Daughters of Samaria, Galilean Fishermen, United Order of the True Reformers, Knights of Pythias, and Grand United Order of Odd Fellows provided sick benefits and burial insurance as membership benefits. Members paid the same joining fee regardless of age, and all paid the same weekly or monthly fees. These societies lacked a system for maintaining and investing financial reserves and were exempt from state regulation. Their leaders knew nothing of scientific insurance principles. Most societies soon encountered financial difficulties when the number of claims exceeded dues income. Because fraternal societies also served as a medium for black self-expression and social dignity, members often remained loyal in spite of failures to pay insurance claims.

Both blacks and whites relied heavily on fraternal societies and mutual-benefit assessment organizations to provide insurance coverage, but whites also organized state-chartered legal reserve insurance companies to provide insurance benefits. Blacks gradually began seeking insurance coverage from the white insurance companies. In 1881 the Prudential Life Insurance Company decided that insuring African Americans was not profitable because of higher death rates for blacks at each age, lower life expectancies, and lower policy-renewal rates. The average death rate for blacks was 50 to 80 percent higher than that for whites, and life expectancy at various ages ranged from three to six years less for blacks.

White insurance companies responded to the greater risk posed by black policyholders by no longer actively soliciting black policyholders, by reducing the benefits on all black policies to two-thirds the benefits granted white policyholders for the same premium, by increasing the premiums to be paid by blacks for all categories of benefits, and finally simply by refusing to issue policies to blacks.

As late as 1940, 42 percent of the 238 insurance companies then operating in the United States refused to accept black policyholders, and another 22 percent did not seek black business or refused to pay commissions on sales to black policyholders. Eighteen percent charged higher premiums, provided lower benefits, or limited the types of coverage available to African Americans. Only about 18 percent of all insurance companies accepted black policyholders on the same basis as white policyholders.

As white insurance companies withdrew insurance coverage from African Americans, members of black communities responded by forming new fraternal, assessment, and mutual-benefit societies. Gradually the black community began chartering legal reserve insurance companies of their own. Most states required about $100,000 of capital for legal reserve insurance companies in their state jurisdictions. Because of POVERTY, unemployment, low wages, and lack of accumulated capital in the black community, it was difficult for any black company to raise the $100,000 reserve requirement. The Mississippi Life Insurance Company became the first black legal reserve insurance company when it began operating in 1902 under a MISSISSIPPI reserve requirement of a mere $25,000. The Standard Life Insurance Company of Georgia, launched in 1913, was the first black insurance company to meet a $100,000 reserve requirement.

Many fraternal and mutual-benefit companies became legal reserve companies in the twentieth century. These included the North Carolina Mutual Life Insurance Company, founded in 1898; in 1913 it became the first mutual-assessment association to convert to a legal reserve basis. By 1939 North Carolina Mutual Life was the United States' largest black-owned company. The number of black insurance companies grew rapidly until 1929, when economic decline during the GREAT DEPRESSION began to reduce the number of black companies from fifteen to eleven through mergers, receivership, and failures. The decline reduced the dollar value of insurance in force by 44 percent.

Threats to Solvency

During the early twentieth century, black fraternal, assessment, mutual, and legal reserve companies all suffered similar threats to their solvency. The organizations performed inadequate investigations for confirming the ages, character, habits, finances, mental competency, and health of applicants. Medical screening examinations were inadequate, as were charts of mortality rates, needed for determining premiums. Increased risk factors were posed by black policyholders because of inferior health facilities, poverty, hazardous working conditions, and ignorance of disease. Moreover, the proprietorship attitude of some company executives limited their companies' ability to expand, innovate, and adopt new technology and new business practices.

Finally, the insurance companies had difficulty making the quality investments necessary to increase their assets. Many black insurance companies invested in black businesses, each operating in a segregated economic system in which some white businesses sold to both white and black customers, but most black businesses had difficulty selling to white customers. Most of these black businesses were also in service industries, where the possibility of profit and the accumulation of capital were limited and where the negative effects of economic cycles were most severe.

Desegregation and After

Black life insurance companies recovered and expanded after World War II, but they went into decline in both profitability and stature after 1960. Desegregation from the early 1960's to the 1980's increased interaction between white-controlled businesses and black consumers. Most black leaders emphasized integrating predominantly white institutions rather than strengthening black institutions and increasing black economic independence. The number of black-owned insurance companies declined from forty-two in 1973 to thirty-nine in 1975, twenty-three in 1993, and thirteen in 1998.

The remaining companies faced increased competition from white companies, escalating operating costs associated with technological change, and the need to provide innovative insurance and financial products. They were also damaged by negative press coverage following some high-profile insolvencies, and the black unemployment rate remained more than double the white rate. The surviving black insurance companies benefited from consolidation with weaker companies. The remaining companies in the late twentieth century included North Carolina Mutual Life Insurance Company, the nation's largest black insurance company, and the Atlanta Life Insurance Company. However, the total value of the assets of black insurance companies and the value of policies in force remained stagnant in the 1990's.

—*Gordon Neal Diem*

See also: Business and commerce; Cemeteries and funeral customs.

Suggested Readings:

"B.E. Financial Overview: A New Day for Black Financial Institutions." *Black Enterprise* (June, 1993): 143-148.

Bryson, Winfred Octavus, Jr. *Negro Life Insurance Companies: A Comparative Analysis of the Operating and Financial Experience of Negro Legal Reserve Life Insurance Companies*. Philadelphia: University of Pennsylvania Press, 1948.

McCoy, Frank. "Life-Sustaining Measures." *Black Enterprise* (June, 1998): 182-189.

Mitchell, James B. "The Collapse of the National Benefit Life Insurance Company: A Study in High Finance Among Negroes." *The Howard University Studies in the Social Sciences* 2 (1939): 1-150.

Riley, Jason L. "The Quota Culture's Slow Demise—Return to Self-Reliance." *Wall Street Journal* (August 13, 1997): A14.

Scott, Matthew S., Rhonda Reynolds, and Cassandra Hayes. "Twenty-five Years of Blacks in Financing." *Black Enterprise* (October, 1994): 146-151.

Weems, Robert E., Jr. "A Crumbling Legacy: The Decline of African American Insurance

Companies in Contemporary America." *Review of Black Political Economy* 23, no. 2 (1994): 25-37.

Lincoln, Abbey (Gaby Lee; August 6, 1930, Chicago, Illinois): Singer and composer. She began to perform locally as a singer in the 1950's under the names Gaby Lee, Anna Marie, and Gaby Woolridge. In 1956 she took the name Abbey Lincoln, and soon afterward made her first recording, with the Benny CARTER Orchestra. She also performed occasionally with the Sonny Rollins/Max ROACH Quartet. She was married to Roach from 1962 to 1970. Although always known as a competent JAZZ performer, Lincoln's reputation grew during the 1960's, when she became known as a CIVIL RIGHTS activist and actor. In the 1980's and 1990's, she returned to her roots as a jazz and ballad singer.

Lincoln, C. Eric (June 23, 1924, Athens, Alabama—May 14, 2000, Durham, North Carolina): PRESBYTERIAN minister, scholar, and university teacher. Charles Eric Lincoln enjoyed a deserved reputation as one of America's leading black theologians and sociologists of religion. He earned his B.A. from LeMoyne College in TENNESSEE in 1947, his M.A. from FISK UNIVERSITY in 1954, his B.D. from the University of Chicago in 1956, and his M.Ed. and Ph.D. from Boston University in 1960.

His ensuing career shifted in its principal roles and venues. Lincoln was pastor of John Calvin Presbyterian Church in Nashville, Tennessee (1953-1954); assistant professor in the fields of religion, philosophy, and social relations at Clark College (1954-1965); resident chaplain of the Boston University School of Theology (1958-1959); professor of sociology at Portland State University (1965-1967); professor of sociology and religion at Union Theological Seminary in New York City (1965-1973); chair of religious studies and professor of sociology and religion at Fisk (1973-1976), where he had taught, briefly, in the 1950's; and professor of religion and culture at Duke University.

A veteran civil rights activist and member of the NATIONAL ASSOCIATION FOR THE ADVANCEMENT OF COLORED PEOPLE (NAACP), Lincoln was a frequent international conference speaker while maintaining a formidable output of both academic and popular writing. His full-length works especially won him acclaim for their depth and incision. They include *The Black Muslims in America* (1961), a pioneering analysis of the NATION OF ISLAM that contains a groundbreaking interview with Elijah MUHAMMAD; *The Black Experience in Religion* (1974), an edited compilation which examines black church culture and belief from a sociological vantage point; *The Black Church Since Frazier* (1974), an analytical history; and *Race, Religion, and the Continuing American Dilemma* (1984), an insider's update of Gunnar Myrdal's epochal *An American Dilemma: The Negro Problem and Modern Democracy* (1944). Lincoln's other contributions range from journalism and articles to compilations of essays and articles.

Lincoln administration: In 1860 Abraham Lincoln was elected sixteenth president of the United States. Southern states, interpreting his election as signaling the imminent end of SLAVERY, seceded from the union to form the Confederate States of America, also known as the CONFEDERACY. These states, in their order of secession from the union, were SOUTH CAROLINA, FLORIDA, GEORGIA, ALABAMA, MISSISSIPPI, LOUISIANA, TEXAS, VIRGINIA, ARKANSAS, NORTH CAROLINA, and TENNESSEE. This secession led directly to the CIVIL WAR.

From 1861 to 1865 the Lincoln administration guided a divided nation through the trials of civil war. Key policies of the administration that had consequences for African American

President Abraham Lincoln. *(Library of Congress)*

lives were two Confiscation Acts, a bill abolishing slavery in the District of Columbia, a preliminary Proclamation of Emancipation, the EMANCIPATION PROCLAMATION, the Conscription Act, a bill granting African Americans in the armed forces equal pay with whites, and the THIRTEENTH AMENDMENT to the Constitution.

The first Confiscation Act was passed by Congress in 1861. According to this act, runaway slaves who had been used to aid the Confederate states could be granted freedom once they were under the Union army's control. On April 16, 1862, Lincoln signed a bill that abolished slavery in the District of Columbia and provided compensation to the slaveholders. Congress passed a second Confiscation Act on July 17, 1862, granting freedom to all slaves held by slaveholders endorsing the Confederacy.

On September 22, 1862, Lincoln issued his preliminary Proclamation of Emancipation. In this document, Lincoln announced that on January 1, 1863, all slaves residing in Confederate states would be free. With this warning, Lincoln gave the Confederate states an opportunity to rejoin the union with slavery intact. Shortly after the preliminary proclamation, the United States authorized its first African American combat units; the First Regiment Louisiana Heavy Artillery and the FIFTY-FOURTH MASSACHUSETTS COLORED and Fifty-fifth Infantry Regiments were established.

On January 1, 1863, President Lincoln issued the Emancipation Proclamation, stating that slaves in the Confederacy were free. The Emancipation Proclamation did not affect slave states that had not left the union or areas in the Confederate states under Union control. For these states and areas, Lincoln encouraged willing, compensated liberation of slaves.

On March, 1863, Congress passed the Conscription Act, which brought into existence a full-scale national draft enforced by federal authority. With this national draft act, active recruitment of African American soldiers into the Union army began under the designation United States Colored Troops, or USCT. In 1864 Congress passed a bill granting African American soldiers the same pay as white soldiers. By the end of the Civil War, 200,000 African Americans had served in the Union army, of whom more than 38,000 had given their lives. Twenty-two African Americans were awarded Congressional Medals of Honor.

On January 31, 1865, Congress passed the Thirteenth Amendment to the Constitution, abolishing slavery in the United States. The amendment was ratified on December 18, 1865. The Civil War officially ended at Appomattox Courthouse in central Virginia on April 9, 1865, with the surrender of Confederate general-in-chief Robert E. Lee. Days later, on April 15, President Lincoln was assassinated. The abolition of slavery throughout the United States and the defeat of the Confederacy, ending the Civil War and preserving the

Abraham Lincoln's signing of the Emancipation Proclamation and leading the Union to victory in the Civil War forever linked his name to African American freedom. *(James L. Shaffer)*

union, were the major accomplishments of the Lincoln administration.

—Louis Gesualdi

Lincoln Motion Picture Company: First black FILM company. Formed in 1916 by brothers Noble M. and George P. Johnson, the company was based in LOS ANGELES, CALIFORNIA, and at first distributed its films through Omaha, NEBRASKA. The company gradually expanded, placing agents in the black ghettos of many major cities. During WORLD WAR I, it produced films about black sports and Westerns. Noble Johnson left the company in 1920 to work for Universal Studios. Lincoln made its last film in 1923, a documentary about the Tenth Cavalry.

See also: Ninth Cavalry and Tenth Cavalry.

Lincoln University (Oxford, Pennsylvania): First secondary school in the United States established expressly for African Americans. Founded in 1854 as Ashmun Institute, Lincoln University is the oldest continuously operating HISTORICALLY BLACK COLLEGE in the United States.

John Miller Dickey, Lincoln's founder, was the pastor of the Oxford Presbyterian Church and a supporter of the AMERICAN COLONIZATION SOCIETY, which proposed settling free blacks in LIBERIA, West Africa. Dickey envisioned Lincoln as an institution where black men could receive training as missionaries to

Lincoln University president David Henson in 1999. *(AP/Wide World Photos)*

work in West Africa. Accordingly, he named the school Ashmun Institute in honor of Jehudi Ashmun, an agent of the colonization society and first governor of Liberia. In keeping with his vision, all three students in the institution's first graduating class sailed for West Africa as missionaries in 1859.

Lincoln's mission changed after the Civil War, when slavery ended. Freedom created a need for educated blacks to uplift the race. The school's mission changed to that of training these leaders. Fittingly, the school's name was changed to Lincoln University, in honor of Abraham Lincoln, the Great Emancipator. Moreover, the college was reorganized, with a liberal arts college and schools of medicine, law, and theology. The medical and legal branches, however, were short-lived. By the early twentieth century, Lincoln had attained a favorable reputation, and its graduates were certified to teach in the public school systems. Several graduates had entered graduate and professional schools. However, no African Americans taught at Lincoln itself until 1932.

Even though its mission changed, Lincoln's African connection continued over the years. Many West Africans studied at the college, and some of them became outstanding statesmen in their homelands. Nnamdi Azikiwe (1930) became Nigeria's first post-independence president, and Kwame Nkrumah (1939) became the first president of an independent Ghana. During the 1960's, the school inaugurated an African language and area-studies program. In addition, the U.S. Department of State has sponsored several projects in African studies at Lincoln.

In 1953 Lincoln's charter was amended to allow admittance of female students. In 1972, during the presidency of Herman Branson, the school became state-related and eligible for state funding. In 1986 Lincoln inaugurated its eleventh president and first female head, Niara Sudarkasa, a noted anthropologist and educator.

Lindy hop: Dance popularized at the Savoy Ballroom in Harlem during the late 1920's. Taking its name from aviator Charles Lindbergh ("Lucky Lindy") after he flew the first solo trans-Atlantic crossing in 1927, this dance remained popular through the 1930's. Synthesizing many forms of African American popular dance, it included the shimmy, shuffling steps, and improvisation time during which dancing couples competed for attention. It became more acrobatic as dancers added steps done in the air to those done on the floor. The

Lindy dance contest at Harlem's Savoy Ballroom in 1953. *(AP/Wide World Photos)*

Lindy hop led to the development of the jitterbug.

Literature: The history of African American writing began a century and a half after the first Africans landed in Jamestown, Virginia, in 1619. During the period before the Civil War, African Americans—whether enslaved or free—were forced into an inferior social position. Although history indicates that African Americans responded to slavery and the denial of their humanity in many ways, a survey of their early literature suggests three basic responses—accommodation, protest, and escape.

Historical Background

It is natural that the early literature produced by African Americans had a serious tone, reflecting their intense struggle to break the physical, intellectual, and spiritual bondage that had been imposed upon them. The earliest black poets included Jupiter Hammon, Phillis Wheatley, and George Moses Horton, all of whom produced verses dealing with solemn and religious themes. Another early literary form was the slave narrative, a genre that included notable works by Olaudah Equiano, Harriet Jacobs (Linda Brent), Mary Prince, and Frederick Douglass. After the Civil War, African American writers expanded the scope of their work to include other genres such as novels, short stories, drama, essays, and literary criticism.

POEMS

ON

VARIOUS SUBJECTS,

RELIGIOUS AND MORAL.

BY

PHILLIS WHEATLEY,

NEGRO SERVANT to Mr. JOHN WHEATLEY,
of BOSTON, in NEW ENGLAND.

LONDON:
Printed for A. BELL, Bookſeller, Aldgate; and ſold by
Meſſrs. COX and BERRY, King-Street, *BOSTON.*

M DCC LXXIII.

Phillis Wheatley's 1773 book is believed to have been the first volume of poetry published by an African American. *(Library of Congress)*

Early Poetry

One of the first African American poets to be identified was Lucy Terry, who is credited with a verse account of a 1745 Indian raid on Deerfield, Massachusetts, entitled "Bars Fight." Although a fragment was included by George Sheldon in an 1893 article published in *New England Magazine*, the full version of the original verse has not been recovered. Jupiter Hammon, a slave poet from Long Island, New York, produced "An Evening Thought: Salvation by Christ with Penitential Cries" (1760), the first full literary work by an African American to be published in the United States.

Hammon's contemporary, Phillis Wheatley, was an intensely moralistic and religious poet whose works were first published in England. Wheatley absorbed much of the late Puritan culture of her owners, who, after recognizing her talent and genius, educated her and encouraged her writing career. Wheatley modeled her work on such classic English poets as John Milton and Alexander Pope, evidenced by her use of the heroic couplet and her inclusion of classical allusions. With the help of friends in England, she published her 1773 collection, *Poems on Various Subjects, Religious and Moral.*

George Moses Horton was a considerably more complex poet than either Hammon or Wheatley. From the publication of his poetry collection *The Hope of Liberty* (1829), he hoped to earn enough money to purchase his freedom and buy passage to Africa, but the money never materialized. Instead, Horton contented himself for more than thirty years with the reputation he acquired in Chapel Hill, North Carolina, where his knack for composing verses on a variety of subjects earned for him a tidy income from university students who wished to send poems to young women they were courting. Horton dealt lightly with subjects such as love, women, fortune, and fame, and he possessed great imaginative powers.

The post-Civil War era did not alter greatly the social status of African Americans, yet more of them were able to attain an education by attending newly founded free schools and missionary schools financed through the activities of the Freedmen's Bureau. Greater access to education was accompanied by an increase in the literary output of African Americans.

Paul Laurence Dunbar is perhaps the best known African American poet of this postwar period. He wrote dialect poems, which were acclaimed in his own time, and lyric poems, which have received literary acclaim from critics in the late twentieth century. The son of former slaves, Dunbar was elected editor of his school paper during his senior year, but was too poor to attend college. He became an elevator operator, writing verses on the job and peddling them to his riders. In 1893 Dunbar published his first volume of poetry, *Oak and Ivy,* followed by *Majors and Minors* (1895) and *Lyrics of Lowly Life* (1897), which was sponsored by noted white author and critic William Dean Howells.

An accommodationist in his poetry, Dunbar almost completely avoided any mention of racial injustice in his work. In his dialect poetry, he focuses on two aspects of black life—its pathos and its humor—yet his works also show a deep insight into black life. His lyric poems are written in Standard English, and some, such as "We Wear the Mask" and the often-anthologized "Sympathy," demonstrate his poetic excellence.

Among poets of this period who chose to write solely in standard English rather than dialect, William Stanley Braithwaite emerged as one of the most accomplished writers. A staff writer on the Boston *Transcript* as well as a critic and nationally known anthologist, Braithwaite was an assimilationist who rejected racial themes, preferring to compete with white writers on their own terms rather than addressing his works to black readers only. Three volumes of his poetry were published—*Lyrics of Life and Love* (1904), *The House of Falling Leaves* (1908), and *Selected Poems* (1948)—and he was also known for annual anthologies of magazine verse, which he compiled for many years.

The Slave Narrative

African Americans used the experience of bondage as raw material for their literary works, thereby documenting their own enslavement. In literacy lay the true freedom for black slaves, since it allowed them to indict those who enslaved them as well as the system used to justify their enslavement. African Americans accomplished this goal with the weapon of the printing press. Talented and articulate former slaves such as Frederick Douglass published narrative accounts of the times and the often-brutal facts of their enslavement. These narratives were extraordinarily popular texts and sold extremely well, while at the same time serving as extensions of their authors' speeches. Many narratives sold more than twenty-five thousand copies in their first two years of publication; examples include *Twelve Years a Slave* (1853), the narrative of free black New Yorker Solomon Northup and his harrowing experiences after being kidnapped into slavery in 1841, and *A Narrative of the Adventures and Escape of Moses Roper, from American Slavery* (1838), which went into ten editions.

Literary critic Henry Louis GATES, Jr., noted that the slave narrative forms the foundation upon which most African American literature, both fiction and nonfiction, subsequently has been based. There are hundreds of documented slave narratives, but four of the most famous examples include *The Interesting Narrative of the Life of Olaudah Equiano, or Gustavus Vassa, the African* (1789), *The History of Mary Prince, a West Indian Slave* (1831), *Narrative of the Life of Frederick Douglass: An American Slave* (1845), and Harriet Jacobs's *Incidents in the Life of a Slave Girl* (1861).

Olaudah Equiano's narrative became the standard among early nineteenth-century slave narratives. Equiano gives a cultural account of the Igbo people of eastern Nigeria, relates the details of his own capture and his fascinating maritime adventures, and provides valuable observations on slavery in the Caribbean and the United States. His life story documents the freedom and social customs of blacks in Africa, the degradation of enslaved Africans at the hands of European owners, and the experience of freed slaves in England. Equiano's narrative also demonstrates a sophisticated command of narrative devices.

Mary Prince's narrative broke the silence of the slave woman. Prince's twenty-three page narrative, which appeared in London in 1831 in two editions, quickly alerts readers that hers is a tale that has not been told before with such accuracy or immediacy. Slaves such as Equiano before her and Douglass after her provided accounts of sexual abuse and violence against black women slaves, but Prince's account makes readers acutely aware of the brutalization of black women under slavery—including the violation of a woman's natural relationship with her children and her spouse. Harriet Jacobs's *Incidents in the Life of a Slave Girl* has been cited as the preeminent example of women's autobiography in the slave narrative tradition.

The most famous of all slave narratives was written by the brilliant abolitionist orator and writer, Frederick Douglass. Douglass demonstrates how a man was made a slave and how a slave was made a man, brilliantly employing the same rhetorical devices that served him well in his career as a speaker and activist.

Novels and Short Fiction

African American fiction writers reacted in various ways to racism. Many early novelists and short story writers chose to emphasize racial issues and exhibit the methods of abolitionist propaganda written before the Civil War. In the tradition of the slave narratives, these authors used fiction to illustrate the condition of black Americans, in freedom and in slavery. Such writers included William Wells BROWN, Frank J. Webb, Martin DELANY, and Frances E. W. HARPER.

Though first published in England, William Wells Brown's *Clotel: Or, The President's Daughter: A Narrative of Slave Life in the United States* (1853) was the first novel written by an African American. The novel deals with the theme of the tragic mulatto as well as the protest theme. Frank Webb repeated the theme of the tragic mulatto in *The Garies and Their Friends* (1857), which was also published in London. Martin Delany's *Blake: Or, The Huts of America* was published serially in seven installments in *The Anglo-African Magazine* in 1859. Delany sympathized with the plight of the black masses in the South and chose to highlight their struggles by portraying idealized characters in his novel. Frances E. W.

Harper's short story "The Two Offers" was the first story by an African American to be published in *The Anglo-African Magazine,* in 1859. Her transitional novel, *Iola Leroy* (1892), was the first African American novel to be set in the era of RECONSTRUCTION.

Some later authors chose to give little or no attention to controversial racial issues and wrote narratives about white people or plantation tales about blacks. The majority, however, undertook to defend the race and to make a case for social justice. Three of Paul Laurence Dunbar's novels—*The Uncalled* (1896), *The Love of Landry* (1900), and *The Fanatics* (1901)—dealt with white characters, as did his series of five short stories entitled "Ohio Pastorals," which appeared in *Lippincott's Monthly Magazine* between August and December, 1901. Dunbar's fourth novel, *The Sport of the Gods* (1902), illustrates the plantation-tale concept in that the black man becomes homesick and demoralized in the urban North. *Folks from Dixie* (1898), Dunbar's first book-length collection of short stories, contains twelve tales set in the periods before and after the Civil War. *The Strength of Gideon and Other Stories* (1900), another collection of Dunbar's short fiction, also shows the imprint of the plantation tradition. Dunbar's wife, Alice Dunbar Nelson, tended to avoid racial issues in her fiction, included in *Violets and Other Tales* (1895) and *The Goodness of St. Rocque and Other Stories* (1899).

Like Paul Laurence Dunbar, Charles Waddell CHESNUTT also dealt with characters of both races in his fiction. His short story "Baxter's Procrustes," which appeared in *The Atlantic Monthly* in June of 1904, focuses on white characters. Chesnutt deals with black life in *The Conjure Woman* (1899), a collection of stories that use the plantation motif while downplaying the cruelty and oppression that was also the lot of enslaved African Americans. Other short collections by Chesnutt in the same romanticized vein were *Folks from Dixie* (1898), *The Strength of Gideon* (1900), *In Old Plantation Days* (1903), and *The Heart of Happy Hollow* (1904).

In contrast with the novels and stories of the Dunbars and Chesnutt, the works of novelist Sutton E. Griggs contain militant protests against racial violence and oppression. A writer who shared many of the social concerns of W. E. B. DU BOIS and Marcus GARVEY, Griggs incorporated the theme of racial pride in works such as *Imperium in Imperio* (1899), *Overshadowed* (1901), *Unfettered* (1902), *The Hindered Hand: Or, The Reign of the Repressionist* (1905), and *Pointing the Way* (1908).

The Harlem Renaissance

The HARLEM RENAISSANCE was an unprecedented creative upsurge among African American artists that was brought about by literary and social influences between 1900 and 1925. The Harlem Renaissance was specifically influenced by a group of African American writers and intellectuals that included W. E. B. Du Bois, James Weldon JOHNSON, Claude MCKAY, Jean TOOMER, and Alain Leroy LOCKE. Their novels, short stories, poems, and essays appeared during one of the most significant periods of African American writing in the United States. The beneficiaries of the creative genius of these writers were such well known literary artists as Langston HUGHES, Arna BONTEMPS, Zora Neale HURSTON, Nella LARSEN, Jessie FAUSET, and Countée CULLEN. According to Arthur P. DAVIS, one of its foremost students, the Harlem Renaissance was not a closely knit, monolithic movement, but rather a diverse blending of many literary themes and forms, ranging from the sonnets of McKay, to the sociological works of Du Bois, and the folk themes employed by Hughes in his novels, short stories, and dramas.

W. E. B. Du Bois was among the most gifted and influential scholars who prepared the groundwork for the Harlem Renaissance. Du Bois was a journalist, novelist, short-story writer, poet, and essayist. One of the primary founders of the National Association for the Advancement of Colored People (NAACP), he was also the editor of its journal, The Crisis. As early as 1915, Du Bois predicted the themes of the Renaissance in a *Crisis* editorial in which he stated the need for African Americans to resurrect ancient African art and history and set people of African descent before the world as creative artists and subjects for artistic treatment. *The Souls of Black Folk* (1903), perhaps his most successful literary work, is a miscellany of fourteen essays and sketches describing the status and opportunities of African Americans of that period. Du Bois also published five novels during his lifetime, as well as essays, short stories, poems, sketches, and three autobiographies—*Darkwater: Voices from Within the Veil* (1920), *Dusk of Dawn: An Essay Toward an Autobiography of a Race Concept* (1948), and *The Autobiography of W. E. B. Du Bois: A Soliloquy on Viewing My Life from the Last Decade of Its First Century* (1968).

Two other literary figures achieved fame with poetry. James Weldon Johnson—educator, songwriter, novelist, diplomat, and secretary of the NAACP—was a rare combination of creative artist and man of public affairs. Among his publications are an anthology of African American literature entitled *The Book of American Negro Poetry* (1922), the novel *The Autobiography of an Ex-Coloured Man* (1912), and a collection of poems entitled *God's Trombones* (1927). Countée Cullen was a scholar and lover of traditional literature. Cullen confessed that his poetry primarily addressed the joys and sorrows of African Americans and was inspired by racial themes. One of his most popular sonnets, "Yet Do I Marvel," reveals his concerns with racial prejudice. In other poems, such as "Heritage," Cullen implies that the African American is and ever will be an alien in the United States and an exile from his African homeland. Cullen's verse forms, like those of Claude McKay, are traditional: quatrains, couplets, and sonnets, as well as poems with stanzas of varying lengths.

Of all the literary artists of the Harlem Renaissance, Langston Hughes stands as perhaps the most popular and widely read. Poet, fiction writer, dramatist, newspaper columnist, autobiographer, anthologist, compiler of children's works, and translator, Langston Hughes was a highly versatile author and was considered by many to be the greatest literary artist of the period. African American writing is indebted to Hughes for his example of incorporating black popular culture into literature through the use of the blues, spirituals, ballads, jazz, and folk speech and themes. He gave African American drama a boost and broke away from the stereotypical portrayals that pervaded literature by and about African Americans. His poems are among the most memorable in American literature and his urban folk character, Jesse B. Semple, serves as the black Everyman of Harlem. Hughes collaborated with his contemporary and good friend, Arna Bontemps, on several important anthologies throughout the years. Bontemps was himself a gifted poet, novelist, anthologist, and short-story writer. His most significant work of the Harlem Renaissance was the historical novel *Black Thunder* (1936), which documents the abortive slave rebellion of Gabriel Prosser in Virginia in 1800.

African American Drama

A combination of economic and cultural circumstances combined to limit the chances for the development of African American dramatists. In the United States, establishing a reputation in drama is more costly than in other literary fields because a dramatist needs a cast of actors, an auditorium with a stage, and an audience. The earliest-known play by an African American was *The Escape: Or, A Leap for Freedom* (1858) by William Wells Brown. Even though Brown gave public readings from his drama, there is no evidence that it was ever staged. It was not until 1925 that the first full-length serious drama written by an African American was produced on Broadway.

Most popular theatrical works written and performed by African Americans prior to the 1920's fell within the minstrel tradition. These musical variety revues, often termed "coon" shows, emphasized comedy, singing, and dancing rather than a story line, and black poets and authors pandered to the expectations of white audiences, writing about buffoons and carefree primitives. Musical comedy remained popular in the American THEATER; thus, *Shuffle Along* (1921), an all-black musical written and directed by blacks, is frequently praised as a work which revived American interest in African American talent and culture during the 1920's.

The first African American play to be produced on Broadway was *The Chip Woman's Fortune* (1923), a one-act play by Willis Richardson. Three years later, Frank Wilson created *Meek Mose*, which opened in February of 1928. The end of the 1920's marked the Broadway debut of *Harlem*, a dramatic collaboration between Wallace THURMAN, a talented black novelist, and William Jordan Rapp, a white playwright. During the 1930's, the GREAT DEPRESSION prompted writers to question all aspects of life and to protest against the condition of poor people in the United States. *Legal Murder*, a dramatization of the SCOTTSBORO CASES, was written by black playwright Dennis Donoghue in 1934. In 1935 Langston Hughes's *Mulatto* began its Broadway run, the longest of any play by an African American dramatist until the 1960's.

Literature Since 1945

The course of African American literature has been influenced by the social and political crises that affected the socioeconomic status of African Americans. The efforts of African Americans to assert their equality, culminating in the U.S. SUPREME COURT's 1954 decision in BROWN V. BOARD OF EDUCATION and the rise of the Civil Rights movement led by Martin Luther KING, Jr., affected the course of African American writing between 1940 and 1960.

Throughout WORLD WAR II, African American literature was characterized by such protest and problem novels as Richard WRIGHT's *Native Son* (1940), William Attaway's *Blood on the Forge* (1941), Ann Petry's *The Street* (1946), and Chester HIMES's *If He Hollers Let Him Go* (1945). Poets such as Margaret WALKER, Langston Hughes, and Gwendolyn BROOKS wrote in a similar vein; their works had strong protest elements and dealt with the fight against segregation and discrimination. With the gradual realization of their struggle, African American writers were faced with the probable loss of their cherished protest tradition and were forced to seek fresh themes and material. Many shifted their attention to the problems and conflicts within the black community. In *The Third Generation* (1954), Chester Himes focuses on the conflict within a black family caused by complexion differences and other problems. Owen Dodson, in *Boys at the Window* (1950), and Gwendolyn Brooks, in *Maud Martha* (1953), also focus on divisive issues within the African American community.

During the 1960's, many writers shifted their attention to the protests raised by the BLACK NATIONALIST and Black Power movements. The resulting return to protest themes is evident in the works of Amiri BARAKA (LeRoi Jones), Haki R. MADHUBUTI (Don L. Lee), Angela DAVIS, Ed BULLINS, Nikki GIOVANNI, and Sonia SANCHEZ.

As nationalist fervor waned in the late 1970's, a new black literary tradition emerged. Black writers such as Alice WALKER, John Edgar WIDEMAN, Toni MORRISON, Gloria NAYLOR, and Charles JOHNSON began to focus on themes and subjects that reflected larger social and political concerns of the times, such as poverty, feminism, self-realization, the environment, and world peace. They also maintained their unique vision as African Americans by borrowing more freely from older traditions such as folk themes and the slave narrative.

Poetry

Beginning in the 1940's, poets such as Sterling Brown, Margaret Walker, Gwendolyn Brooks, Robert Hayden, and Langston Hughes began to focus on sociological topics related to conflict.

Margaret Walker's collections of poetry include *For My People* (1942) and *Prophets for a New Day* (1970). In *For My People*, there is a subdued strain of militance, far less than that found in other protest poetry. In the title poem, Walker suggests that African Americans will not always remain quiet and acquiescent, and she demonstrates great compassion for the oppressed and misled black masses. The theme of brotherhood runs through Walker's poetry and she deals with folk material as well. In *Prophets for a New Day*, Walker focuses on the African American heritage using images and subjects from the Civil Rights movement in poems such as "Street Demonstration" and "Girl Held Without Bail." Other poems in the collection deal with liberation and treat historical figures such as Nat Turner, Gabriel Prosser, and Toussaint-L'Ouverture.

Langston Hughes's influence as a writer extended beyond the period of the Harlem Renaissance. Critics have placed Hughes's poems in several thematic categories: those focused on protest and social commentary, those dealing with Harlem, those treating folk themes, those incorporating African and Negritude themes, and those with miscellaneous themes. Although protest and social commentary run through the entire body of Hughes's poetry, his first two poetic works—*The Weary Blues* (1923) and *Fine Clothes for the Jew* (1927)—contain few protest poems. There are many more, however, in *One Way Ticket* (1949), and from then on the protest theme remains prominent in his poetry. Hughes, like many other black writers, used lynching as the supreme symbol of American injustice, and he devoted an entire section of *One Way Ticket* to this subject. While he never became a communist, Hughes, like many other young poets of the 1930's and 1940's, did see hope for the oppressed in Marxist teachings. Unlike some others, however, Hughes retained the ability to see both sides of an issue.

As a result of his focus on African American life, Hughes became known as the poet laureate of Harlem. Hughes's fullest treatment of Harlem is found in *Montage of a Dream Deferred* (1951), which also incorporates popular folk themes found in blues music. His experimentation with folk themes in this collection and *Ask Your Mama: Twelve Moods for Jazz* influenced many younger poets. His fascination with Africa and the Negritude movement changed and deepened throughout his lifetime. These themes were prominent in several poems, including his "Lament for Dark Peoples."

Sterling A. Brown—poet, critic, folklorist, scholar, and teacher—was another poet who served as a transitional figure from the themes of the Harlem Renaissance to the postwar literary scene. His first publication, *Southern Road*, appeared in 1932. *The Last Ride of Wild Bill and Eleven Narrative Poems* was published in 1974, and *The Collected Poems of Sterling A. Brown* was edited by Michael S. Harper and appeared in 1980. Brown's poetry is imbued with the folk spirit and culture of African Americans and reflects his deep understanding of the multitudinous aspects of the African American personality and soul. His poems are primarily set in the South, where he traveled and listened to the folktales, songs, wisdom, sorrow, and frustrations of his people. The recurring themes of endurance, tragedy, and survival found in much of Brown's poetry are best delineated in his poem "Strong Men."

(continued on page 1532)

Notable Poets

Angelou, Maya. *See main text entry.*

Baraka, Amiri. *See main text entry.*

Braithwaite, William Stanley Beaumont. *See main text entry.*

Brooks, Gwendolyn. *See main text entry.*

Brown, Sterling A. *See main text entry.*

Cortez, Jayne. *See main text entry.*

Cotter, Joseph Seamon, Jr. (Sept. 2, 1895, Louisville, Ky.—Feb. 3, 1919, Louisville, Ky.). After contracting TUBERCULOSIS while still in college, Cotter died at the age of twenty-three. The death of his sister Florence Olivia, also from tuberculosis, inspired his first poem, "To Florence," written in December, 1914. The poem appeared in his book *The Band of Gideon, and Other Lyrics* (1918). His poetry makes use of traditional and free verse forms.

Cotter, Joseph Seamon, Sr. (Feb. 2, 1861, Nelson County, Ky.—Mar. 14, 1949, Louisville, Ky.). Taken to Louisville, TENNESSEE, at an early age by his freeborn mother, Cotter wrote poetry, fiction, drama, tales, short plays, and prose. His poetry is diverse in form (from the ballad to the sonnet) and content. His works include *Links of Friendship* (1898) and the *Collected Poems of Joseph S. Cotter, Sr.* (1938).

Cullen, Countée. *See main text entry.*

Cunard, Nancy. *See main text entry.*

Dove, Rita. *See main text entry.*

Dunbar, Paul Laurence. *See main text entry.*

Dunbar Nelson, Alice Moore. *See main text entry.*

Evans, Mari. *See main text entry.*

Giovanni, Nikki. *See main text entry.*

Grimké, Angelina Weld. *See main text entry.*

Hammon, Jupiter (Oct. 17, 1711, Oyster Bay, N.Y.—1806?, Hartford, Conn.). Born a slave, is the first African American poet known to have had his work published. "An Evening Thought: Salvation by Christ, with Penitential Cries," one of his most representative poems, was dated December 25, 1760. Hammon refused to accept the widespread notion that African Americans had been cursed by God, believing that God's grace was available to everyone.

Harper, Frances E. W. *See main text entry.*

Harper, Michael S. *See main text entry.*

Hayden, Robert. *See main text entry.*

Hemphill, Essex (Apr. 16, 1957, Chicago–Nov. 4, 1995). Hemphill's poetry and prose spoke of the alienation caused by being a black HOMOSEXUAL. His first collection, *Earth Life*, was published in 1985, and his second, *Conditions*, in 1986. The major collection *Ceremonies* followed in 1992. The next year, Hemphill became an artist-in-residence at the Getty Museum in Los Angeles.

Horton, George Moses. *See main text entry.*

Hughes, Langston. *See main text entry.*

Johnson, Fenton. *See main text entry.*

Kaufman, Bob. *See main text entry.*

Knight, Etheridge (Apr. 19, 1931, Corinth, Miss.—Mar. 6, 1991, Indianapolis, Ind.). Knight began writing in prison. His collections include *Poems from Prison* (1968), *Black Voices from Prison* (1970), *Belly Song and Other Poems* (1973), and *Born of a Woman: New and Selected Poems* (1980). He received a Guggenheim Fellowship in 1974 and held writer-in-residence positions at several universities.

Marable, Manning. *See main text entry.*

Randall, Dudley (b. Jan. 14, 1914, Washington, D.C.). Known for his contributions to the Black Arts movement, Randall founded Broadside Press, an independent publishing house in DETROIT, and edited

(continued)

Black Poetry: A Supplement to Anthologies Which Exclude Black Poets (1969). He published several volumes of his own poetry, including *Poem, Counterpoem* (1966).

Redmond, Eugene (b. Dec. 1, 1937, East St. Louis, Ill.). A critic, journalist, playwright, and educator, as well as poet, Redmond helped form the Black Arts movement. His work emphasizes his pride in his cultural heritage and the history of African Americans, and its themes are often informed by folktales. His poetry includes *Songs from an Afro/Phone* (1972) and *In a Time of Rain and Desire* (1973). His critical survey, *Drumvoices: The Mission of African American Poetry* (1976), examines African American poetry from 1746 to 1976.

Rivers, Conrad Kent (1933, Atlantic City, N.J.—1968). Rivers was educated at Wilberforce University, where he met Langston Hughes, a lifelong influence on his poetry. His first book of poetry, *Perchance to Dream, Othello*, was published in 1959. Other publications include a play, *Dusk at Selma* (1965), and a book of poetry, *The Still Voice of Harlem* (1968). His poetry emphasizes sadness, loneliness, and isolation and evinces a preoccupation with death.

Rodgers, Carolyn M. (b. Dec. 14, 1945, Chicago, Ill.). Mentored by Hoyt Fuller and Gwendolyn Brooks, Rodgers wrote poetry and short fiction on the subjects of revolution, love, religion, African American male-female relationships, and feminism. In 1970 she received an award from the National Endowment for the Arts. Her publications include *Songs of Black Bird* (1969) and *Eden and Other Poems* (1983).

Sanchez, Sonia. *See main text entry.*

Terry, Lucy. *See main text entry.*

Tolson, M. B. *See main text entry.*

Weaver, Michael S. (b. Nov. 26, 1951, Baltimore, Md.). Weaver's poetry collections include *Water Song* (1985), *My Father's Geography* (1992), *Stations in a Dream* (1993), and *Timber and Prayer: The Indian Road Poems* (1995). Weaver received numerous awards and fellowships, including a Pennsylvania Arts Council Fellowship in 1994 and a National Endowment for the Arts Fellowship in 1985. His plays *Elvira and the Lost Prince* and *Rosa* were produced professionally.

Wheatley, Phillis. *See main text entry.*

Wright, Jay (b. May 25, 1934 or 1935, Albuquerque, N.Mex.). Wright's intellectually demanding poetry is informed by his studies in history, anthropology, and primitive religions. It is also infused with allusions to early Christian and Renaissance writers such as Saint Augustine and Dante Alighieri. His publications include *The Homecoming Singer* (1971), *Dimensions of History* (1976), *The Double Invention of Komo* (1980), *Elaine's Book* (1988), and *Boleros* (1991).

Gwendolyn Brooks published her first collection of poetry, *A Street in Bronzeville*, in 1945. Later collections include the Pulitzer Prize-winning *Annie Allen* (1949) and *The Bean Eaters* (1960). These works fall into the category of protest poetry. In her first three collections, Brooks wrote with understanding and compassion about the experiences of the inhabitants of America's black urban ghettos. Her poems are subtly ironic and sometimes quietly humorous, as in her poem "Beverly Hills Chicago," which depicts a group of blacks driving through an upper-class white section of Chicago. With the publication of *In the Mecca* (1968), Brooks focused on new interests and themes. The Mecca is more than a run-down apartment house; it is a microcosm of all urban ghettos imbued with the blight that results from being black and poor, thus revealing a new, more militant and nationalistic viewpoint of the poet.

African American poetry in the later decades of the twentieth century was characterized by both excellence and diversity. The outspoken poetry of protest and urban desolation continued to find a voice in the work of writers such as Sonia Sanchez and Etheridge Knight. The evolution of poet Haki Madhubuti reflected that of many African Americans who turned to Islam; in addition to writing poetry and nonfiction, Madhubuti founded the Third World Press, which became an important outlet for books on African American and Afrocentric themes.

Other significant and highly individual voices in African American poetry from the 1960's to the 1990's include Ai, Rita Dove, Nikki Giovanni, Robert Hayden, Audre Lorde, Essex Hemphill, Yusef Komunyakaa, and Jay Wright. Dove won a Pulitzer Prize for her 1986 collection of narrative poems, *Thomas and Beulah*, and held the post of poet laureate of the United States from 1993 to 1995.

African American poetry enjoyed a resurgence in the 1990's, with the emergence of important new poets including Elizabeth Alexander, Jabari Asim, Thomas Sayers Ellis, Esther Iverem, Karl Phillips, Natasha Trethewey, Kevin Powell, and Ras Baraka. Collections featuring these young poets' work include *In the Tradition: An Anthology of Young Black Writers* (1992), edited by Baraka and Powell, and *On the Verge: Emerging Poets and Artists* (1993), edited by Ellis and Joseph Lease. At the same time, older, established poets continued to publish collections, including Rita Dove's *Through the Ivory Gate* (1992) and *Mother Love* (1995) and Sonia Sanchez's *Wounded in the House of a Friend* (1995), and to receive awards and honors. West Indian poet Derek Walcott received the Nobel Prize for Literature in 1992. In 1993 poet Maya Angelou read at the inauguration of President Bill Clinton. Gwendolyn Brooks was named the Jefferson Lecturer for 1994 by the National Endowment for the Humanities.

Novels and Short Fiction

African American fiction writers became both prolific and popular after World War II. Richard Wright, Ralph Ellison, Chester Himes, Ann Petry, and James Baldwin produced their most important novels from the 1940's through the 1960's. Charles Johnson, Toni Morrison, Ishmael Reed, Alice Walker, and John Edgar Wideman are some of the leading figures in the next generation of African American novelists, who gained national recognition during the 1970's, 1980's, and 1990's.

Richard Wright was a prolific and multitalented writer, as demonstrated in such works as *Uncle Tom's Children* (1938), *Native Son* (1940), *Black Boy* (1945), *The Outsider* (1953), *The Long Dream* (1958), *Eight Men* (1961), and *Lawd Today* (1963). *Uncle Tom's Children* contains four novellas that portray the bleakness, barrenness, and violence of black life in the United States. The novellas are written in the naturalistic tradition, as seen in "Big Boy Leaves Home." Wright's novel *Native Son* jolted the nation in 1940 by pointing out the brutal and dehumanizing effects of American racism. The novel's protagonist, Bigger Thomas, became a symbol of the violence and fatalism that resulted from being born black in a racist society. Wright's autobiography, *Black Boy*, is an example of excellence

Ann Petry in 1946. *(AP/Wide World Photos)*

in American autobiography. It, too, demonstrates the dehumanizing and violent effects of American racism.

Ralph Ellison and James Baldwin, like Wright, emphasized the effects of racism on black life in their novels and short stories. Ellison's novel *Invisible Man* (1952) is one of the most artistically structured and profound explorations of the meaning of African American experience. It concerns the protagonist's search for individual identity and racial meaning in his passage from innocence to experience. Ellison's long-in-process second novel, *Juneteenth,* was unfinished when he died. It was edited by John F. Callahan, working from Ellison's partially finished draft, and published in 1999.

James Baldwin was not only a master of the essay form but also a talented novelist and playwright. During a sojourn in Paris, he finished his autobiographical novel *Go Tell It on the Mountain* (1953). Baldwin's other publications include *Another Country* (1962), *Giovanni's Room* (1956), *Tell Me How Long the Train's Been Gone* (1968), *If Beale Street Could Talk* (1974), and *Just Above My Head* (1979). Baldwin also published numerous short stories and several essay collections, including *Notes of a Native Son* (1955), *Nobody Knows My Name: More Notes of a Native Son* (1961), *The Fire Next Time* (1963), and *No Name in the Street* (1972).

Many significant African American women have made important contributions to American letters during the 1960's through the 1990's. Some of the most notable include Alice Walker, Gloria Naylor, June JORDAN, Paule MARSHALL, Toni Morrison, Sherley Anne Williams, and Terry McMillan.

Alice Walker burst onto the literary scene with her works of poetry in the 1960's. She went on to publish many essays, a collection of short stories entitled *In Love and Trouble: Stories for Black Women* (1973), and several novels, including *The Third Life of Grange Copeland* (1970), *Meridian* (1976), *The Color Purple* (1982), *The Temple of My Familiar* (1990), and *Possessing the Secret of Joy* (1992).

Pulitzer Prize-winning author Alice Walker in 1983. *(AP/Wide World Photos)*

Toni Morrison's first novel was *The Bluest Eye*, published in 1970. She continued with *Sula* (1973), *Song of Solomon* (1977), *Tar Baby* (1981), the Pulitzer Prize-winning *Beloved* (1987), *Jazz* (1992), and *Paradise* (1997). Morrison said that she wants her novels to clarify roles of African Americans that have been obscured and to identify black historical and cultural traditions that are useful as well as those that are not. Her novels have been called fabulistic, since Morrison relies freely on African and African American FOLKLORE and mythology. This is especially true of *Song of Solomon*, which won the National Book Critics Circle Award for fiction, and her internation-

(continued on page 1542)

Notable Works of Fiction

Baldwin, James. *Another Country* (1962). Exploration of issues confronting a loosely knit group of New Yorkers of varied races, genders, and sexual identities. *Another Country* sold more than four million copies. Although most early reviews of the novel were unfavorable, later critics have reassessed it as among BALDWIN's best works.

Baldwin, James. *Giovanni's Room* (1956). This bleak account of a young American expatriate's futile search for his sexual identity was one of the first books by an African American that dealt openly with the topic of HOMOSEXUALITY.

Baldwin, James. *Go Tell It on the Mountain* (1953). This semiautobiographical work, set in 1935 in HARLEM, deals with the isolation and frustrating limitations facing NEW YORK CITY's African Americans and with their desire to change their condition. Baldwin shows that religion, one of the escapes within their reach, may be a dangerous alternative.

Baraka, Amiri. *The System of Dante's Hell* (1965). Mixture of autobiography and fiction drawing on BARAKA's life experiences to describe Western culture's impact on African Americans. Educating African Americans according to Western traditions, Baraka believes, produces ambivalence and confusion, alienating African Americans from their roots and causing feelings of racial inferiority.

Bontemps, Arna. *Black Thunder* (1936). Fictionalized account of the abortive 1800 rebellion of Virginia slaves led by GABRIEL Prosser and the ensuing reprisals by Virginia whites. The largely unknown work received considerable attention after it was reprinted in 1968 and was compared to William Styron's 1967 best-seller *The Confessions of Nat Turner.*

Bradley, David. *The Chaneysville Incident* (1981). John Washington, a black Philadelphia university professor, attempts to come to terms with his origins in the wild Pennsylvania mountain country. He travels back through time in an examination of records, relics, and family and oral histories. The novel, BRADLEY's second, received the prestigious PEN/Faulkner Award as the best novel of 1981.

Brown, Claude. *Manchild in the Promised Land* (1965). Autobiographical novel set in Harlem, portraying a young black man's tragic struggle against drugs, CRIME, and racial unrest. BROWN dramatizes the tension between the suffocating social restrictions of the city and the lead character's desire to control his life and escape poverty and destruction. In the end, he uses education as a path out of Harlem.

Brown, William Wells. *Clotel: The President's Daughter, a Narrative of Slave Life in the United States* (1853). Examination of the tragic fate of a MULATTO mother and her two quadroon daughters, who are the offspring of Thomas Jefferson, after the family is separated. It examines slavery's effect on family bonds, the sexual exploitation of mulatto females, interracial relationships between white men and mulatto women, and the issue of slaveholding Christianity.

Campbell, Bebe Moore. *Your Blues Ain't Like Mine* (1992). Incorporating various narrative strands as different verses of a blues song, CAMPBELL recounts episodes in the lives of a white man acquitted of the killing of a young black man, in Hopewell, MISSISSIPPI, during the early days of integration, and the parents of the slain teenager. The legacy of fear and racism in the southern town start to be erased when the liberal white son of plantation owner Stonewall Pinochet agrees to share the plantation's wealth with his black half-sister.

Chesnutt, Charles Waddell. *The House Behind the Cedars* (1900). Tragic story of Rena Walden, a beautiful, light-skinned mulatto woman who "passes" for white and becomes engaged to an aristocratic white man. When Walden's fiancé discovers her racial identity, he rejects her, and she dies of a broken heart. CHESNUTT's first novel-length work, the book generated controversy over its unambiguous condemnation of RACIAL PREJUDICE.

Childress, Alice. *A Hero Ain't Nothin' but a Sandwich* (1973). A thirteen-year-old black boy troubled by his father's abandonment of the family, his mother's love for another man, and his increasing alienation from family and friends becomes addicted to heroin. When his life is saved by his stepfather, he comes to understand his mother's feelings and realizes that he does have a father.

(continued)

Colter, Cyrus. *A Chocolate Soldier* (1988). This account of the life of a highly distraught and restless African American, "Cager" Lee, as narrated by his preacher friend, Meshach Barry, is an engrossing and disturbing tale of black power and powerlessness. Meshach's narration of his own colorful and troubled life is skillfully interwoven with Cager's agitated life as a murderer of a high-class white woman and as a paramilitary leader seeking salvation.

Cooper, J. California. *Some Love, Some Pain, Some Time* (1995). Cooper's usual themes of romance and struggle are evident in these ten short stories about WOMEN and their loves. The women described include a self-described femme fatale seeking a husband, a forty-year-old widow who tries to make a new start, and an elderly woman describing her three MARRIAGES. Cooper offers intimate, involving portrayals of simple, direct people who manage to enjoy life.

Cooper, J. California. *Some Soul to Keep* (1987). Cooper's third story collection consists of five tales told in monologue form and featuring the unhappy lives of each of the troubled female protagonists. Among the story's memorable characters are an orphaned girl, a blind girl who becomes an unwed mother as the result of a traumatic rape experience, a deserted wife, a prosperous homeowner, and the friendly rivals. All of the women experience hardship, but they eventually find personal contentment within their souls.

Danticat, Edwidge. *Breath, Eyes, Memory* (1998). Twelve-year-old Sophie leaves her native HAITI to join her mother in New York. There she learns painful secrets that are healed only after she returns to Haiti to the woman who reared her. Danticat, a twenty-four-year-old Haitian American woman, explores the bonds of duty and love that link Sophie to her mother and grandmother.

Dumas, Henry. *Goodbye, Sweetwater* (1988). Posthumously published short stories depicting the lives of rural and urban African Americans confronting racial cruelty, familial love, loss, and displacement. The subjects of the stories range from the plight of a young boy devastated by a flood in the South of the 1930's, to the death of a black soldier in the KOREAN WAR of the early 1950's, to the complexity of political activism in the 1960's. The collection reflects Dumas's renowned flair for combining poetry and prose, evoking poignant human scenes, and conveying the diverse knowledge and life experiences of African Americans.

Dunbar, Paul Laurence. *The Sport of the Gods* (1901, serial; 1902, book). Set around 1900, this racial protest work portrays a middle-class family of southern blacks who are the victims of racial prejudice. Having served a wealthy white businessman for twenty years, the family is torn apart following the father's sentencing by the white employer to ten years of hard labor for a theft he did not commit. When the truth comes out one year later, he is released from jail and the family is reinstated on the employer's estate.

Ellison, Ralph. *Invisible Man* (1952). Set in the late 1930's, ELLISON's novel depicts a nameless protagonist's attempt to reach spiritual freedom amid repeated failures and painful humiliations at the hands of both whites and blacks. After experiencing several absurd situations, he retreats into a coal cellar in New York City, where he is manipulated by religious and political groups. He begins to see the world as a comical mad dream full of possibilities and realizes that the only way human beings can be rescued from oppression is by liberating their minds. *Invisible Man* won the National Book Award in 1953.

Everett, Percival L. *Suder* (1983). Zany adventures of professional BASEBALL player Craig Suder are interjected between flashbacks to his formative youth. Suder runs away from a failed career and marriage only to find himself in the very act of flight. Thus, peopled by quirky characters and propelled by unpredictable plot twists patterned after the complex rhythms of bebop jazz, the novel is essentially a comic affirmation of the supremacy of the individual and the necessity for self-definition.

Fauset, Jessie Redmon. *The Chinaberry Tree: A Novel of American Life* (1931). A community of middle-class African Americans is burdened by denial, customs, and pretensions. Fauset examines how such group attitudes can have negative consequences on the community, arouse enmity among its members, and ruin hopes for a better life.

Fauset, Jessie Redmon. *Plum Bun* (1929). Examination of the life of the fictional Angela Murray, a light-skinned black woman who leaves her childhood home in Philadelphia to attend college in New York City, where she chooses to "pass" and live as a white woman. Murray's decision estranges her from her darker-skinned relatives, and she eventually is forced to confront her own racial consciousness.

Forrest, Leon. *There Is a Tree More Ancient Than Eden* (1973). Weaving together black history, American ideas about democracy, and ROMAN CATHOLIC and BAPTIST religious beliefs, FORREST's novel tells the story of a young man's search for meaning in life within a family at odds over its racial identity. The family is descended from Jericho Witherspoon, a former slave who was the illegitimate child of a white slave master and an unknown black woman. Two other novels, *The Bloodworth Orphans* (1977) and *Two Wings to Veil My Face* (1983), complete the Witherspoon family saga.

Gaines, Ernest J. *The Autobiography of Miss Jane Pittman* (1971). Southern history is related from the perspective of the fictional Miss Jane Pittman, a black woman born into slavery who lives to see the dawning of the Civil Rights movement a century later. In 1974, the book was made into a popular and highly acclaimed television film starring Cicely TYSON.

Gaines, Ernest J. *A Lesson Before Dying* (1993). Schoolteacher Grant Wiggins is commissioned by Emma Glenn to bring the gift of humanity to her twenty-one-year-old godson, Jefferson, who was sentenced to die in an electric chair for a robbery and murder that he only witnessed. He initially resists Wiggins's efforts but is eventually transformed. Two weeks after Easter of 1948, Jefferson dies and, in his apparent resurrection to humanity, makes it seem possible that his people might also rise above the tragedy of their past and reach their full potential.

Greenlee, Sam. *The Spook Who Sat by the Door* (1969). Dan Freeman becomes the first black agent in the Central Intelligence Agency (CIA), a token known as "the spook who sat by the door." Returning to Chicago, he uses his CIA training to reshape a street gang, the Cobras, into a highly disciplined band of urban guerrillas who begin a war of liberation against the white authorities. Made into a film in 1973, the novel typifies its era in its satirizing of white liberals and the black bourgeoisie, its flamboyant action scenes, and its call for armed revolution by African Americans.

Holman, John. *Squabble: And Other Stories* (1990). The eleven stories in Holman's collection deal with the lives of young African Americans in the South. Holman writes clearly and simply, in the minimalist tradition of Raymond Carver, his mentor and teacher. The stories give the reader a fresh perspective on the complex and precarious conditions facing young African Americans. In many of the stories, especially the title story and "Scuff," the young characters demonstrate a remarkable emotional and spiritual resilience in the face of all kinds of adversities.

Hopkins, Pauline. *Contending Forces* (1900). The book's first part, set in the 1790's, depicts the ill effects of SLAVERY on a Bermuda planter who flees the island with his family and slaves. Its second part, set one hundred years later, portrays the lives of African Americans in the northern United States in the aftermath of the CIVIL WAR.

Hurston, Zora Neale. *Moses, Man of the Mountain* (1939). HURSTON's fictional Moses is a combination of the biblical Moses, who led the enslaved Hebrews out of Egypt into the promised land of Canaan, and the Moses of African folklore. The work can be read as an allegory of the American slaves' struggle for emancipation.

Library of Congress

Hurston, Zora Neale. *Their Eyes Were Watching God* (1937). A strong and romantic black woman tells her life story to a close woman friend. She explains how she struggled through three marriages in order to find fulfillment and a sense of purpose in her life. She finally finds happiness by rejecting her society's attitudes toward security, materialism, and hierarchies, and by making her own decisions and controlling her own life. The novel is a vital account of the life of uneducated and rural African Americans in the South during the period and of black gender roles.

(continued)

Johnson, Charles Richard. *Middle Passage* (1990). A well-educated and self-centered twenty-one-year-old ex-slave, in order to escape a forced marriage to a schoolteacher and debts to a black underground leader, sails on a ship bound for Africa. The *Republic* becomes the stage of his philosophical debates, of his search for meaning in his life, and of his coming-of-age. *Middle Passage* won the National Book Award for fiction in 1990.

Johnson, James Weldon. *The Autobiography of an Ex-Coloured Man* (1912). Loosely based on events in JOHNSON's own life, the novel recounts the odyssey of an anonymous light-skinned black man who discovers that he can "pass" and who opts to live as a white man. The book, Johnson's first, broke new ground with its subject matter and laid the foundation for his championing of the black aesthetic during the HARLEM RENAISSANCE.

Kelley, William Melvin. *A Different Drummer* (1966). The action takes place in a fictional state in the Deep South. Told in flashbacks interspersed with events in 1957, the novel explores the impact of Tucker Caliban's decision to destroy the PLANTATION that represents the burden of his slave ancestry and lead the state's African American population in a northward exodus. KELLEY received the Rosenthal Foundation Award from the National Institute of Arts and Letters for the work.

Kenan, Randall. *A Visitation of Spirits* (1989). Story of the fictional Cross family, an African American family living in NORTH CAROLINA, is told from various perspectives in a lively mixture of different voices. The main focus is on Horace, the youngest family member, and his struggle with personal and societal "demons," including his homosexuality, and on his cousin Jimmy Greene, a Baptist minister and elementary school principal. Widely praised by critics for its experimental style, the novel shifts between realism and fantasy in its portrait of a rural black community in the South.

Kincaid, Jamaica. *The Autobiography of My Mother* (1996). Xuela, a seventy-year-old West Indian woman reflects on her life. An independent woman whose mother died in childbirth and whose father was always distant, Xuela aborts the child she conceives at age fourteen and determines never to have another. The alienated Xuela examines the power and powerlessness in the world around her and in her relations with other people.

Larsen, Nella. *Passing* (1929). The lives of two light-skinned black women, Clare, who enjoys risk and danger and "passes" for white, and Irene, who prefers security, are compared and contrasted. Contemporary critics praised the novel's psychology, but some considered the book's rather melodramatic ending to be contrived.

Larsen, Nella. *Quicksand* (1928). Helga Crane, a young mulatto woman leaves her job as a small-town TEXAS schoolteacher to search for happiness in Chicago, New York, and Denmark. Her social and sexual adventures lead her to a nervous breakdown, and she returns to the South to recover. Both *Quicksand* and LARSEN's novel *Passing* (1929) have been rediscovered and reread as significant precursors of later fiction by black female writers.

Lee, Andrea. *Sarah Phillips* (1984). Reared in an affluent Philadelphia suburb and educated at a private school and at Harvard, Sarah Phillips has been insulated from racial strife despite her father's position as a prominent African American minister and civil rights activist. While she is traveling in Europe, Sarah finds her mind flooded with memories of childhood that force her to come to terms with her family beliefs and her racial heritage. Originally published in *The New Yorker* as a series of short stories, the novel was criticized by some as being too episodic. Other critics, however, praised Lee for her perceptiveness and the quality of her prose.

Lester, Julius. *Do Lord Remember Me* (1984). The Reverend Joshua Smith, Sr., born in Mississippi in 1900 and now an old man, emotionally recalls his past. Divided into four sections, "Afternoon," "Morning," "Night," and "Evening," the novel depicts one generation's struggle for dignity, identity, freedom, and survival.

McKay, Claude. *Home to Harlem* (1928). Account of the experiences of Jake Brown, a black man who has deserted from the U.S. Army in France during WORLD WAR I and returned to New York City. Back in the United States, Brown meets a wide assortment of black characters, including prostitutes, gamblers, nightclub singers, waiters, and philosophers. McKay's depiction of Harlem's seamier side drew harsh criticism from such prominent African Americans as W. E. B. Du Bois and Alain Locke; however, the book was praised by white critics and received the medal of the Institute of Arts and Sciences.

McMillan, Terry. *How Stella Got Her Groove Back* (1996). Forty-two-year-old Stella, newly divorced and working, is trying to put her life together with the help of her two sisters. While on vacation in Jamaica, Stella gets her "groove" back when she falls in love with a young man in his twenties. The best-selling novel, which, like McMillan's earlier works, focuses on relationships between women and their families and their men, was made into a 1998 film starring Angela Bassett.

McMillan, Terry. *Waiting to Exhale* (1992). Four women in their mid-thirties find themselves holding their breath, anticipating the arrival of the men who will make their lives whole. Savannah and Robin explore new and old relationships, while Bernadine fights her way through a messy divorce. Gloria, an overweight single mother, fears that her life will continue to be defined solely by her son, her work, her appetite for food, and her addiction to television. As they learn to cope with the advent of new boyfriends, an unplanned pregnancy, and a huge divorce settlement, the four women exhale as they become more aware of their own self-worth. In 1995, the novel was adapted into a film directed by Forest Whitaker and starring Whitney Houston and Angela Bassett.

Morrison, Toni. *Beloved* (1987). A woman who escapes from slavery with her children but is pursued by her former master kills her baby girl rather than have her experience the horrors of slavery. The mother later is haunted by the baby's ghost. This explicit work shows how slave women often became pregnant at an early age, how they were used for their childbearing capabilities, how their rights as mothers were denied, and how a mother's love for a child carried grave consequences. It won the Pulitzer Prize for Literature in 1988 and was made into a 1998 film starring Oprah Winfrey and Danny Glover.

Maria Mulas

Morrison, Toni. *The Bluest Eye* (1970). Claudia MacTeer reminisces about events of her childhood. The story revolves around Claudia's eleven-year-old friend, Pecola Breedlove, who is raped by her father and driven insane, and Pecola's resulting impossible desire to have blue eyes. *The Bluest Eye* was Morrison's first book.

Morrison, Toni. *Jazz* (1992). Joe and Violet, a middle-aged couple living in Harlem in the 1920's, strike up a relationship with a young woman named Dorcas. The woman becomes Joe's mistress and is eventually killed by him. This work is particularly interesting for its writing style, which is reminiscent of jazz improvisations.

Morrison, Toni. *Paradise* (1997). In the 1970's, nine men from Ruby, a small black town in Oklahoma, travel to the nearby town of Convent, where they assault the women who live in what was once a Catholic retreat. Morrison begins this plea for tolerance and understanding between the races with the scene of a white woman lying dead on the street and traces the history of Ruby to its founding in 1890.

Morrison, Toni. *Song of Solomon* (1977). A selfish and spoiled black man in his early thirties is dissatisfied with his financial and emotional dependence on his wealthy parents and goes in search of a store of gold left by his aunt. His search, inspired and guided by his fearless aunt, turns instead into a discovery of his past, his heritage, his identity, and finally his freedom. *Song of Solomon* won the National Book Critics Circle Award in 1977.

Morrison, Toni. *Sula* (1973). Exploration of the lives, families, and strong friendship ties of two black women who are separated for ten years. Sula goes to the city to get an education, while Nel gets married and remains in the small town. Their friendship turns to hatred after Sula seduces Nel's husband.

Morrison, Toni. *Tar Baby* (1981). An African American model orphaned at the age of twelve and educated at the Sorbonne is torn between white society, of which she is part, and black society, from which

(continued)

she feels cut off. She struggles to find her identity and assert her individuality amid pressure from each side to subscribe to its culture.

Mosley, Walter. *Devil in a Blue Dress* (1990). Easy Rawlins, fired from his job, reluctantly becomes a private detective and searches for a missing woman wearing a blue dress. His search in the jazz clubs of postwar Los ANGELES soon uncovers murder. This mystery was the first in a popular series featuring Rawlins. President Bill Clinton named Mosley as his favorite writer.

Murray, Albert. *The Spyglass Tree* (1991). Scooter, a young African American attending a HISTORICALLY BLACK COLLEGE in the 1930's, finds himself growing apart from his childhood friend Little Buddy Marshall after being singled out as one of the "talented tenth" by his teacher. He navigates the treacherous waters between his rural origins and the sophisticated outside world. In the improvisational elements of juke joint blues and jazz music, Scooter finds a useful means of coping with the conflict not only between black and white cultural practices but also between the different modes of discourse employed within these cultures.

Naylor, Gloria. *Mama Day* (1988). Two lovers, Ophelia and George, discover new truths during their stay with Miranda Day, an elderly black midwife and conjure woman, on Willow Springs, a fictional SEA ISLAND located off the Georgia-South Carolina coast. Modeled on William Shakespeare's play *The Tempest*, the work describes a kind of Eden, untainted by racism but threatened by human malice and natural disaster. Although portions of the story set in Manhattan were considered somewhat weak, critics admired NAYLOR's female characters for embodying the heroic strength of black women and praised the novel's lyrical celebration of African American folk history.

Naylor, Gloria. *The Women of Brewster Place: A Novel in Seven Stories* (1982). Portrayal of the lives of seven dauntless black women who live in an urban ghetto in a northern American city. It accurately depicts the reality of African American women in the United States who are victims of emotional and physical abuse by men. It won the American Book Award and was made into a television miniseries.

Petry, Ann. *The Street* (1946). After her divorce, an ambitious, self-reliant African American mother moves into a run-down Harlem apartment with her son. Her hopes of improving her situation are shattered when she is manipulated by those around her. She ends up killing a man and fleeing Harlem, leaving her son behind.

Pinckney, Darryl. *High Cotton* (1992). An unnamed man from a college-educated black family searches for authenticity as he moves from his extended family into the white world and, eventually, into historical movements for civil rights and black cultural nationalism. Although he is conscious of his privileges and elite position within the African American community, he is haunted by the differences between that community and the larger white community. The man's emptiness and detachment from life raise key questions about racial identity. PINCKNEY's book received the 1992 Art Seidenbaum Award for first fiction from the *Los Angeles Times*.

Porter, Connie. *All-Bright Court* (1991). Although it is structured like a collection of short stories, Porter's book is unified by the figures of Samuel Taylor, his wife Mary Kate, and their children, particularly their intelligent and ambitious son Michael (Mikey). It is also unified by its setting, a steel mill ghetto near Buffalo, N.Y., where southern blacks have come in hopes of finding a better life. Unlike Mikey, most of the characters will never escape from poverty and disease. While PORTER describes her characters' misery in realistic terms, she also shows their strength, most notably their capacity for compassion and love.

Reed, Ishmael. *Flight to Canada* (1976). This satire set in a bizarre Civil War era in which slaves escape to freedom in airplanes and the assassination of Abraham Lincoln is televised revolves around the conflict between Raven Quickskill, a famous writer and runaway slave, and Arthur Swille, Quickskill's reprehensible vengeful former master. In this, as in his other works, Reed debunks legends and offers a new perspective on history.

James Lerager

Reed, Ishmael. *Mumbo Jumbo* (1972). Reinterpretation of history, art, and religion presented in the form of a mystery story centering around PaPa LaBas, a private investigator, and his search for the original text that records the secrets of Jes Grew, an ancient religious cult. Reed expresses his faith in a non-Western spiritual tradition that will be the West's salvation.

Reed, Ishmael. *Yellow Back Radio Broke-Down* (1969). Parody of the Western dime novel. This work portrays, in a mixture of epic, fantasy, and myth, the supernatural characters Loop Garoo Kid, a black circus cowboy who is the hero of the story, and Drag Gibson, a wealthy rancher and Loop's nemesis.

Schuyler, George S. *Black Empire* (1991). An African American genius directs a bold scheme to retake AFRICA from its European colonizers in this book, which was formed by combining two serials originally published in the PITTSBURGH COURIER under the pen name Samuel I. Brooks, "The Black Internationale" (1936-1937) and "Black Empire" (1937-1938). Written during the depths of the GREAT DEPRESSION, when black American pride was reeling from seeing Ethiopia fall to Fascist Italy, the serials served as a symbolic tribute to African American intelligence and courage in a spectacular fantasy triumph over white racism.

Schuyler, George S. *Black No More.* (1930). Satire about what happens when a well-meaning black doctor develops a process that physically transforms black people into white people. The first person to undergo the process is a streetwise New York hustler, who immediately goes off to the South, where he marries a white belle and becomes the spokesman for her father's white racist organization. The book satirizes both the KU KLUX KLAN and black leaders such as Marcus GARVEY (depicted as "Santop Licorice") and W. E. B. DU BOIS ("Dr. Shakespeare Agamemnon Beard").

Toomer, Jean. *Cane* (1923). Mixture of short stories, sketches, and poems that portray various aspects of black life and black social problems in rural Georgia and the urban North. The work concerns African Americans living in an indifferent society, attempting to fulfill their dreams but being held back by their past and failing to communicate with whites and with each other.

Tyree, Omar. *Flyy Girl* (1995). Follows Tracy Ellison, the "flyy girl" of the title, from her sixth birthday party through high school. The popular novel, self-published by Tyree before being reissued by a major publisher, examines the young, sometimes selfish girl's dealings with her parents and her pursuit of boys as she grows up in the 1980's.

Wade, Brent. *Company Man* (1992). Billy Covington is a black corporate executive who is a confused mixture of ambition and deepening alienation. While convalescing, Bill writes a journal addressed to Paul, a long-estranged friend. Billy examines his successes as a token African American in an overwhelmingly white world of power and affluence and despairs as sexual impotence produces marital discord. He finds hope in the life-affirming Caribbean nurse who cares for him, and through his writing, for a reconciliation with Paul, the homosexual friend whose ability to embrace and move past his own otherness stands as a model for Billy's desperately needed self-acceptance.

Walker, Alice. *The Color Purple* (1982). The letters of Celie, a poor, uneducated southern black woman, chronicle her transformation from an abused young wife into a self-confident agent of healing. Walker's book received both the Pulitzer Prize and the American Book Award for fiction and was made into a successful 1985 film. Many African Americans criticized the film for depicting black men too negatively.

Walker, Alice. *Meridian* (1976). Traces the moral and psychological development of Meridian Hill, the daughter of a middle-class southern black family, during the civil rights struggles of the 1960's. Although the book drew scant attention when first published, it became the object of much critical praise after WALKER's *The Color Purple* won both the Pulitzer Prize and the American Book Award for fiction.

Walker, Alice. *The Third Life of Grange Copeland* (1970). Examines three generations of the family of a black sharecropper as he searches for identity and dignity. The work depicts the realities of racism in the South and deals with the frustrations of black men, the deterioration of the family, domestic violence, and adultery.

West, Dorothy. *The Wedding* (1995). The daughter of a wealthy black doctor who lives in a black enclave

(continued)

in Martha's Vineyard in the 1950's intends to marry a white jazz musician. Her plans cause consternation and tension within her family and draw the attentions of an unwanted black suitor who wants to wed her to gain social acceptance. West, a Harlem Renaissance writer, examines race and family in her first novel in forty-five years.

Williams, John A. *Captain Blackman* (1972). Novel following Captain Blackman, a heroic black U.S. Army soldier in the Vietnam War, through a number of dream sequences as he lies unconscious after receiving a severe wound. In his dreams, Blackman participates in virtually every major American military action since the American Revolution. His bravery and intelligence, however, are undercut continually by the actions of incompetent and hostile white superiors.

Williams, Sherley Anne. *Dessa Rose* (1986). Set in Alabama in the late 1840's, Williams's first novel deals with the struggle of a fearless black woman to free herself and her friends from bondage. She befriends a white woman who helps her and her friends escape.

Wilson, Harriet E. *Our Nig* (1859). A mulatto abandoned by her white mother at the age of six becomes the servant, for twelve years, of the Bellmonts, a middle-class white family. Freed at the age of eighteen, she marries a black man who leaves her when she becomes pregnant. She writes her story hoping that its sale will help support her and her little boy.

Wright, Richard. *Native Son* (1940). A twenty-year-old black man, full of hate for white people, accidentally kills his white employer's daughter, Mary, and later murders his own girlfriend to protect himself. Mary's killing gives him a sense of freedom and equality, and his impending death sentence teaches him the meaning of life. Wright's powerful novel was the first best-seller by an African American writer.

Wright, Richard. *The Outsider* (1953). The work portrays a black postal worker, influenced by existential philosophy and disappointed with his existence, who decides to change his life and be free of his past, including his estranged wife and his fifteen-year-old pregnant lover. He pretends to have died in an accident, assumes a new name, and begins a life of crime and lies.

Wright, Sarah E. *This Child's Gonna Live* (1969). Mariah is a young black mother striving to rear a family on Maryland's Eastern Shore during the Depression. Although she is hopeful of a better day, Mariah must first survive the sting of death that claims the lives of two of her children and a best friend. Convinced that she is married to a useless man in a death-ridden town, Mariah makes plans to move north but runs into a series of roadblocks. Praised for its brilliant blend of folk dialect and humorous tales expressed from the perspective of an African American woman, the novel enjoyed renewed popularity when it was reissued by the Feminist Press in 1986.

ally acclaimed novel *Beloved*, which in 1998 was made into a film starring Oprah Winfrey and Danny Glover.

In the 1990's, the African American novel appeared to shift away from direct political commentary on racism and integration and instead to let these issues shape the lives of characters and the situations that develop. In addition to semiautobiographical novels such as Edwidge Danticat's *Breath, Eyes, Memory* (1998), writers such as Terry McMillan and J. California Cooper produced popular novels that focus on African American women and their relationships with men and families. McMillan's best-selling *Waiting to Exhale* (1992) and *How Stella Got Her Groove Back* (1996) were made into films in 1995 and 1998.

Popular black male writers include Omar Tyree, whose *A Do Right Man* (1997) and *Single Mom* (1998) portray modern black men in their roles as fathers and lovers, and Eric Jerome Dickey, whose somewhat lighthearted works include *Milk in My Coffee* (1998) and *Friends and Lovers* (1997). Walter Mosley produced a series of best-selling detective novels featuring Easy Rawlins, a reluctant private eye, beginning with *Devil in a Blue Dress* in 1990.

(continued on page 1548)

Notable Prose Writers

Andrews, Raymond. *See main text entry.*

Ansa, Tina McElroy (b. 1949, Macon, Ga.). Ansa can be described as a southern writer for her use of GEORGIA settings and southern customs. Her fiction depicts a close-knit African American community whose strength wards off the worst effects of racism. *Baby of the Family* (1989) and *Ugly Ways* (1993) portray middle-class African American women dealing with family issues.

Anthony, Michael (b. Feb. 10, 1932, Mayaro, Trinidad and Tobago). Anthony is best known for his novels and short stories describing life in the Caribbean. Often told from a child's viewpoint, such novels as *Green Days by the River* (1967) tell seemingly simple stories offering insights into human relationships. The optimism in Anthony's writing contrasts with the alienation expressed in much West Indian fiction.

Baldwin, James Arthur. *See main text entry.*

Bambara, Toni Cade. *See main text entry.*

Bell, Derrick Albert, Jr. *See main text entry.*

Bennett, Lerone, Jr. *See main text entry.*

Bonner, Marita. *See main text entry.*

Bontemps, Arna. *See main text entry.*

Bradley, David. *See main text entry.*

Braithwaite, William Stanley Beaumont. *See main text entry.*

Briscoe, Connie (b. Dec. 31, 1952, Washington, D.C.). Born with a hearing loss that developed into complete deafness, Briscoe began writing as a way of coping. *Sisters and Lovers* (1994), her novel about the lives and relationships of three middle-class African American sisters, made the *Quarterly Review of Black Books* best-sellers list. In 1996 Briscoe published the novel *Big Girls Don't Cry*.

Brown, Claude. *See main text entry.*

Brown, Les. *See main text entry.*

Brown, William Wells. *See main text entry.*

Bullins, Ed. *See main text entry.*

Butcher, Philip. *See main text entry.*

Butler, Octavia E. *See main text entry.*

Campbell, Bebe Moore. *See main text entry.*

Chesnutt, Charles Waddell. *See main text entry.*

Child, Lydia Maria. *See main text entry.*

Childress, Alice. *See main text entry.*

Christian, Barbara T. (b. Dec. 12, 1943, St. Thomas, U.S. Virgin Islands). Christian began teaching at the College of the City University of New York and moved to the University of California, Berkeley, in 1972 to teach African American studies. Her books include *Black Women Novelists: Development of a Tradition, 1892-1976* (1980) and *Black Feminist Criticism: Perspectives on Black Women Writers* (1985).

Cleage, Pearl (b. 1948, Detroit, Mich.). Cleage, whose father was a black Christian nationalist, created highly polemic works that focus on African American women. Her works include *We Don't Need No Music* (1971), *Hospice* (1983), *Deals with the Devil and Other Reasons to Riot* (1993), *Flyin' West* (1994), and *What Looks Like Crazy on an Ordinary Day* (1998), which was featured on the television book club created by Oprah Winfrey.

Coleman, Wanda (b. Nov. 13, 1946, Los Angeles, Calif.). A self-described West Coast writer, Coleman created short stories and poetry that use Los Angeles images. During the 1970's, she worked as a scriptwriter and was a staff writer for the NBC soap opera *Days of Our Lives* from 1975 to 1976, earning an Emmy Award for her work. Her books include *Mad Dog Black Lady* (1979), *African Sleeping Sickness: Stories and Poems* (1990), and *Hand Dance* (1993).

Cliff, Michelle. *See main text entry.*

(continued)

Cooper, J. California (b. Berkeley, Calif.). Alice Walker praised Cooper's portrayals of a woman's life as believable. Although some critics have found her narrators too similar, they admired her colloquial style and her use of humor to suggest her characters' endurance. Cooper's books include *A Piece of Mine: A New Short Story Collection* (1984), *Homemade Love* (1986), *Some Soul to Keep* (1987), *The Matter Is Life* (1991), and *Some Love, Some Pain, Some Time* (1995).

Delany, Samuel R. *See main text entry.*

Demby, William. *See main text entry.*

Du Bois, Shirley Graham. *See main text entry.*

Du Bois, W. E. B. *See main text entry.*

Dumas, Henry Lee (July 20, 1934, Sweet Home, Ark.—May 23, 1968, New York, N.Y.). Shot to death by a New York City policeman in a case of mistaken identity, Dumas produced a large body of work that was published posthumously. His books include three volumes of short stories, *Ark of Bones and Other Stories* (1970), *Rope of Wind and Other Stories* (1979), and *Goodbye Sweetwater: New and Selected Stories* (1988); one volume of poems, *Play Ebony, Play Ivory* (1974; first published in 1970 as *Poetry for My People*); and an unfinished novel, *Jonoah and the Green Stone* (1976).

Ellis, Trey. *See main text entry.*

Ellison, Ralph. *See main text entry.*

Everett, Percival L. (b. Dec. 22, 1956, Fort Gordon, Ga.). Attracted to the spaciousness of the American West, Everett populated his books with offbeat black and white characters whose personal desires were paramount and whose social consciousness was marginal. Works include the novels *Suder* (1983), *Walk Me to the Distance* (1985), *Cutting Lisa* (1986), *For Her Dark Skin* (1990), *Zulus* (1990), and *God's Country* (1994). Everett also published a short-story collection, *The Weather and Women Treat Me Fair* (1987), and a children's book, *The One That Got Away* (1992).

Fair, Ronald L. *See main text entry.*

Fauset, Jessie Redmon. *See main text entry.*

Fisher, Rudolph. *See main text entry.*

Forrest, Leon. *See main text entry.*

Gaines, Ernest J. *See main text entry.*

Gayle, Addison, Jr. *See main text entry.*

Gloster, Hugh (b. May 11, 1911, Brownsville, Tenn.). Gloster served as president of Morehouse College from 1967 to 1987. He founded the College Language Association in 1937 and was a contributing editor for *Phylon: The Atlanta University Review of Race and Culture* from 1948 to 1953. He received Fulbright fellowships to travel to Hiroshima, Japan (1953-1955), and Warsaw, Poland (1961-1962). He wrote *Negro Voices in American Fiction* (1948).

Greenlee, Sam (b. July 13, 1930, Chicago, Ill.). A former officer for the U.S. Information Agency, Greenlee wrote *The Spook Who Sat by the Door* (1969), which earned the British Press book of the year award and was made into a film. His other works include *Blues for an African Princess* (1970) and a four-volume autobiography: *D'jokarta Blues*, *Bagdad Blues*, *Mykonos Blues*, and *Babylon Blues* (1988-1989).

Guy, Rosa (b. Sept. 1, 1928, Trinidad). Author of young adult fiction, such as *The Disappearance* (1979) and *And I Heard a Bird Sing* (1987), as well as adult fiction, such as her first novel, *Bird at My Window* (1966). Her other works include *Caribbean Carnival: Songs of the West Indies* (1992) and *The Sun, the Sea, a Touch of the Wind* (1995). In addition to writing about urban American life, she explored the fables and folklore of West Indian culture.

Haley, Alex. *See main text entry.*

Hansberry, Lorraine. *See main text entry.*

Haskins, James S. (b. Sept. 19, 1941, Demopolis, Ala.). Haskins's works include political literature and biographies of African Americans for children and young adults. His early years as an educator inspired his first book, *Diary of a Harlem Schoolteacher* (1969), and much of his subsequent writing. His work focused on "great persons" of African American history as well as broader social, cultural, and political issues.

Himes, Chester Bomar. *See main text entry.*

Holland, Endesha Ida Mae. *See main text entry.*

Holman, John (b. Aug. 24, 1951, Durham, N.C.). Holman's debut collection, *Squabble: and Other Stories* (1990), coolly probes the lives of African Americans in the south. Holman studied writing with short-story writers Raymond Carver and Frederick Barthelme, whose minimalist style he mastered. Holman also contributed stories to *The New Yorker.* He was nominated for the Pushcart Prize for fiction in both 1983 and 1984, and in 1991, he received the Whiting Writer's Award.

Holman, M. Carl. *See main text entry.*

Hopkins, Pauline. *See main text entry.*

Hunter, Kristin Elaine Eggleston (b. Sept. 12, 1931, Philadelphia, Pa.). The bulk of Hunter's work deals with relations among black and white people. Her children's novels include *The Soul Brothers and Sister Lou* (1968) and *Lou in the Limelight* (1981). Her adult fiction includes *God Bless the Child* (1964). The former advertising copywriter and newspaper columnist and feature writer won the 1968 National Council on Interracial Books for Children award.

Hurston, Zora Neale. *See main text entry.*

Johnson, Charles Richard. *See main text entry.*

Johnson, Georgia Douglas. *See main text entry.*

Johnson, James Weldon. *See main text entry.*

Jones, Gayl. *See main text entry.*

Jordan, June. *See main text entry.*

Kelley, William Melvin. *See main text entry.*

Kenan, Randall G. *See main text entry.*

Kennedy, Adrienne. *See main text entry.*

Killens, John Oliver. *See main text entry.*

Kincaid, Jamaica. *See main text entry.*

Komunyakaa, Yusef. *See main text entry.*

Larsen, Nella. *See main text entry.*

Lee, Andrea (b. 1953, Philadelphia, Pa.). Lee worked as a staff writer for *The New Yorker* magazine in the 1980's. The experiences she recorded in her diary while with her husband, who was studying in the Soviet Union from 1978 to 1979, became the basis for her best-known work, *Russian Journal* (1981). Lee's semiautobiographical novel *Sarah Phillips* (1984) focused on the life of an upper-class black woman and the conflicts she faces in reconciling her own secure status in society with her sense of obligation toward African Americans who share her cultural heritage.

AP/Wide World Photos

Lester, Julius (b. Jan. 27, 1939, St. Louis, Mo.). Lester was famous for his militant politics and for his confrontations with other African American activists. His writings include *Lovesong: Becoming a Jew* (1988), *This Strange New Feeling* (1982), *All Is Well* (autobiography, 1976), *To Be a Slave* (1968), and numerous politically oriented works. Lester converted to Judaism and focused his academic career on Judaic studies.

Lorde, Audre. *See main text entry.*

Lovelace, Earl (b. 1935, Trinidad). Lovelace's novels, short stories, and plays are often set in Trinidadian slums and villages, where characters try to overcome the confusion and injustices of life. Lovelace pointed to the need for social change and suggested that a combination of individual responsibility and community identity would help diverse peoples live together in harmony. His works include *The Dragon Can't Dance* (1979) and *Salt* (1997).

Madhubuti, Haki R. *See main text entry.*

Major, Clarence (b. Dec. 31, 1936, Atlanta, Ga.). A poet, novelist, and essayist, Major is known for his experimentation with syntax, narrative structure, and characterization. His novels include *Reflex and*

(continued)

Bone Structure (1975), *Painted Turtle: Woman With Guitar* (1988), and *Dirty Bird Blues* (1995).

Marshall, Paule. *See main text entry.*

Mayfield, Julian. *See main text entry.*

McCall, Nathan Jerome (b. Nov. 25, 1954, Portsmouth, Va.). McCall's autobiography, *Makes Me Wanna Holler: A Young Black Man in America,* appeared on *The New York Times* best-seller list in 1994. McCall's book describes the people and books that influenced him. The book earned a National Black Image Award for McCall in 1995.

AP/Wide World Photos

McKay, Claude. *See main text entry.*

McMillan, Terry. *See main text entry.*

McPherson, James Alan. *See main text entry.*

Meriwether, Louise. *See main text entry.*

Mitchell, Loften. *See main text entry.*

Morrison, Toni. *See main text entry.*

Mosley, Walter. *See main text entry.*

Motley, Willard Francis (July 14, 1912, Chicago, Ill.—Mar. 5, 1965, Mexico City, Mexico). Because Motley wrote mostly about poor white people on the West Side of CHICAGO, relatively few readers realized that he was black. His first novel, *Knock on Any Door* (1947), was made into a 1949 film starring Humphrey Bogart. That book, as well as its sequel, *Let No Man Write My Epitaph* (1958), concerned juvenile delinquency. The latter book also was made into a film, in 1960.

Mowry, Jess (b. Mar. 27, 1960, Mississippi). Educated only through the eighth grade, Mowry began his writing career at age eighteen. In 1990 his short story collection *Rats in the Trees* appeared. Mowry also wrote novels, including *Children of the Night* (1989), *Way Past Cool* (1992), and *Six Out Seven* (1993). He won praise for the authenticity of his dialogue and for his unflinching view of inner-city life, particularly the lives of street children.

Murray, Albert (b. June 12, 1916, Nokomis, Ala.). Murray served as a major in the U.S. Air Force and later as visiting professor and lecturer at several universities. He wrote *The Omni-Americans: New Perspectives on Black Experience and American Culture* (1970), *South to a Very Old Place* (1971), *The Hero and the Blues* (1973), *Trainwhistle Guitar* (1974), *Good Morning Blues: The Autobiography of Count Basie* (1985), *The Spyglass Tree* (1991), and *The Blue Devils of Nada* (1996).

Myers, Walter Dean (b. Aug. 12, 1937, Martinsburg, W.Va.). Myers worked as a teacher, publisher, and editor, but he is best known as the author of more than twenty-five books for children and young adults. His works for young people include *Won't Know Till I Get There* (1982), a novel about Harlem residents, and *Crystal* (1987), about a dissatisfied young fashion model.

Naylor, Gloria. *See main text entry.*

Neal, Larry. *See main text entry.*

Pinckney, Darryl. *See main text entry.*

Polite, Carlene Hatcher (b. Aug. 28, 1932, Detroit, Mich.). Beginning her career as a dancer, Polite turned to political activism in the 1960's and organized the Northern Negro Leadership Conference. In 1964 she moved to Paris and published her first novel, *Les Flagellents* (1966); the novel was published in the United States as *The Flagellants* (1967) and was reissued in 1987. Polite returned to the United States in 1971 and accepted a teaching post at the State University of New York, Buffalo. In 1975 she published her second novel, *Sister X and the Victims of Foul Play.*

Redding, Jay Saunders (Oct. 13, 1906, Wilmington, Del.—Mar. 2, 1988, Ithaca, N.Y.). In addition to teaching at the university level, Redding wrote several important books exploring the African American experience. Among them are *The Negro* (1967), *The Lonesome Road: The Story of the Negro's Part in America* (1958), *They Came in Chains: Americans from Africa* (1950), and *To Make a Poet Black* (1939).

Reed, Ishmael. *See main text entry.*

Sanders, Dori (b. c. 1935, near Filbert, S.C.). Sanders's first novel, *Clover* (1990), received the Lillian Smith Award for Outstanding Writing about the South and an award for the best book for young adults given by the American Library Association. *Clover* and her second novel, *Her Own Place* (1993), were drawn from people Sanders met while working at a produce stand at which she and her family sold peaches and other produce they grew in rural South Carolina.

Schuyler, George Samuel. *See main text entry.*

Scott, Nathan Alexander, Jr. (b. Apr. 24, 1925, Cleveland, Ohio). An Episcopal priest, Scott was a professor of religious studies and English at the University of Virginia. Among his numerous scholarly publications are *Samuel Beckett* (1965), *The Broken Center: Studies in the Theological Horizon of Modern Literature* (1966), *Ernest Hemingway* (1966), *Negative Capability: Studies in the New Literature and the Religious Situation* (1969), *The Poetry of Civic Virtue: Eliot, Malraux, and Auden* (1976), and *Mirrors of Man in Existentialism* (1978).

Shange, Ntozake. *See main text entry.*

Silverstein, Shel. *See main text entry.*

Smith, Barbara. *See main text entry.*

Steele, Shelby. *See main text entry.*

Tarry, Ellen. *See main text entry.*

Taylor, Theodore (b. June 23, 1921, Statesville, N.C.). Taylor is best known for his children's novel, *The Cay* (1969), about a boy on a life raft in the Caribbean. *The Cay* won numerous major awards, including the Jane Addams Children's Book Award and the Lewis Carroll Shelf Award. In 1974 *The Cay* was produced for television, starring James Earl Jones. The book subsequently came under fire as presenting a racist depiction of black people.

Tyree, Omar (b. 1969). A reporter for a weekly newspaper, Tyree self-published his first book, *Colored, on White Campus*, in 1992 (republished in 1995 as *BattleZone: The Struggle to Survive the American Institution*). With the funds it generated, he published *Flyy Girl* in 1993. The next year, he published *Capital City: The Chronicles of a D.C. Underworld*. In August, 1995, a commercial publisher picked up Tyree and re-issued *Flyy Girl*. Tyree's next works were *A Do Right Man* (1997) and *Single Mom* (1998). His novels generally depict young black men and their relationships with women.

Thurman, Wallace Henry. *See main text entry.*

Toomer, Jean. *See main text entry.*

Walker, Alice. *See main text entry.*

Walker, Margaret Abigail. *See main text entry.*

Walrond, Eric. *See main text entry.*

West, Dorothy. *See main text entry.*

Whitfield, James. *See main text entry.*

Wideman, John Edgar. *See main text entry.*

Wiley, Ralph. *See main text entry.*

Williams, John Alfred. *See main text entry.*

Williams, Patricia J. (b. 1951). Williams joined the ranks of premier writers with her autobiographical work *The Alchemy of Race and Rights: Diary of a Law Professor* (1991). This seminal text captured varied instances of racial, gender, and class injustices. Using powerful allegories and personal experiences, Williams critically documented conflicting legal theories and practices. Other works by Williams include the shorter pieces "Hate Radio" and "Inside the Black Middle Class."

Wilson, August. *See main text entry.*

Wolfe, George C. *See main text entry.*

Wright, Richard. *See main text entry.*

Wright, Sarah Elizabeth. *See main text entry.*

Yerby, Frank. *See main text entry.*

Young, Al. *See main text entry.*

(continued)

Angela Bassett and Taye Diggs in the 1998 film adaptation of *How Stella Got Her Groove Back. (Museum of Modern Art, Film Stills Archive)*

The 1990's also saw the rise of a group of southern black women writers, including Dori Sanders (*Her Own Place*, 1993), Marita Golden (*And Do Remember Me*, 1992), and Tina McElroy Ansa (*Ugly Ways*, 1993). These women writers affirm African American culture, seeing black women as politically aware, positive, and strong in their relationships with other human beings. In 1995 Dorothy West, active in the Harlem Renaissance, published her first work in forty-five years, *The Wedding*, the story of an upper middle-class black woman who is about to marry a white jazz musician.

African American literature's popularity grew when talk-show host Oprah Winfrey launched an on-air reading club in September of 1996. Although Winfrey's aim was to interest people in reading, rather than to promote African American literature specifically, she featured a number of works by black writers, including Toni Morrison's *Song of Solomon* and *Paradise*, Maya Angelou's *The Heart of a Woman* (1981), Ernest J. Gaines's *A Lesson Before Dying* (1993), Edwidge Danticat's *Breath, Eyes, Memory*, and Pearl Cleage's *What Looks Like Crazy on an Ordinary Day* (1998). Winfrey's popular club established a Web site and tie-ins with major bookstore chains that discounted and featured her selections, many of which became best-sellers.

Drama

Professional drama by African Americans came of age in the 1950's. In addition to dramatic works of playwrights, many dramas debuted which were created by writers known primarily for their fiction, poetry, and essays. A notable production from 1953 was Louis Peterson's *Take a Giant Step*, which told the story of educated African Americans in the urban North who are neither primitive nor pathetic but who have universal human problems. During this period, Langston Hughes's *Simply Heavenly* (1957), a musical based on his Jesse B. Semple character, also reached Broadway.

One of the most notable playwrights of the postwar period was Lorraine Hansberry. Her first play was *A Raisin in the Sun*, the title of which was taken from a poem by Langston Hughes. A huge hit on Broadway when it opened in 1959, the play won the New York Drama Critics Circle Award. Hansberry observed that while the play was unabashedly focused on the upward mobility of African Americans, it also contained universal themes about people everywhere. *The Sign in Sidney Brustein's Window* (1964) was Hansberry's second Broadway play and was followed by the posthumous production of *To Be Young, Gifted, and Black* in 1969.

James Baldwin contributed to the growing reputation of African American drama with his plays *Blues for Mister Charlie* (1964) and *The Amen Corner* (1968). Young dramatists of the Black Arts movement included Amiri Baraka, whose plays *Dutchman* and *The Slave* appeared in 1964; Charles Gordone, who received a Pulitzer Prize for his absurdist play, *No Place to Be Somebody* (1969); and Ed Bullins, known for his Obie Award-winning drama, *The Taking of Miss Janie* (1975).

Women playwrights whose dramas were produced nationally in the 1970's, 1980's, and 1990's included Adrienne KENNEDY and Ntozake SHANGE. George C. Wolfe's *The Colored Museum* (1986) satirized mainstream misconceptions of black culture, and Charles Fuller's Pulitzer Prize-winning drama, *A Soldier's Play* (1982), was made into the popular film *A Soldier's Story*. Another Pulitzer Prize-winning dramatist is August WILSON, whose works include *Ma Rainey's Black Bottom* (1984), *Joe Turner's Come and Gone* (1985), *Fences* (1985), *The Piano Lesson* (1988), *Two Trains Running* (1991), and *Seven Guitars* (1996).

Criticism

African American critics, many of whom are also distinguished writers in other genres, have done notable work in documenting the literary contributions of fellow African Americans. Early critics of the 1920's through 1940's include James Weldon Johnson, Alaine Leroy Locke, Sterling Brown, Langston Hughes, and Arna Bontemps. Later critics include Hugh Gloster, Arthur P. Davis, J. Saunders Redding, Blyden Jackson, Addison GAYLE, Houston BAKER, and Henry Louis Gates, Jr. Critics and anthologists such as Barbara Christian, Mary Helen WASHINGTON, Trudier Harris, Thadious Davis, and Claudia Tate have highlighted the important contributions of black women writers to American letters.

—*Betty Taylor-Thompson*
—*Updated by Rowena Wildin*

See also: Afrocentricity; Children's literature; Detective fiction; Juvenile and young adult fiction; Science fiction.

Suggested Readings:

Bruce, Dickson D., Jr. *Black American Writing from the Nadir: The Evolution of a Literary Tradition, 1877-1915*. Baton Rouge: Louisiana State University Press, 1989.

Callahan, John F. *In the African-American Grain: The Pursuit of Voice in Twentieth Century Black Fiction*. Urbana: University of Illinois Press, 1988.

De Jongh, James. *Vicious Modernism: Black Harlem and the Literary Imagination*. New York: Cambridge University Press, 1990.

Gabbin, Joanne V., ed. *The Furious Flowering of African American Poetry*. Charlottesville: University Press of Virginia, 1999.

Gates, Henry Louis, Jr. *The Signifying Monkey: A Theory of Afro-American Literary Criticism*. New York: Oxford University Press, 1988.

Jackson, Blyden. *The Long Beginning, 1746-1895*. Vol. 1 in *A History of Afro-American Literature*. Baton Rouge: Louisiana State University Press, 1989.

Jones, Gayl. *Liberating Voices: Oral Tradition in African American Literature*. Cambridge, Mass.: Harvard University Press, 1991.

Kostelanetz, Richard. *Politics in the African-American Novel: James Weldon Johnson, W.E.B. Du Bois, Richard Wright, and Ralph Ellison*. New York: Greenwood Press, 1991.

Nelson, Emmanuel S. *Contemporary African American Novelists*. Westport, Conn: Greenwood Press, 1999.

Petesch, Donald A. *A Spy in the Enemy's Country: The Emergence of Modern Black Literature*. Iowa City: University of Iowa Press, 1989.

Sundquist, Eric J. *The Hammers of Creation: Folk Culture in Modern African-American Fiction*. Athens: University of Georgia Press, 1992.

_______. *To Wake the Nations: Race in the Making of American Literature*. Cambridge, Mass.: Harvard University Press, 1993.

Little, Joanne (b. May 8, 1954, Washington, North Carolina): Victim of attempted rape. While in custody at the Beaufort County Jail in NORTH CAROLINA, Little killed Clarence Alligood, a white male prison guard. Little, who was in jail pending appeal of a conviction for breaking and entering, claimed that she was defending herself against sexual advances by Alligood when she stabbed him with an ice pick. Alligood's partially unclothed body was found in Little's cell on August 27, 1974. After stabbing Alligood, Little fled from the prison. She later stated her reason for escaping as a fear that as a black woman, she would be unable to prove her innocence in a legal system dominated by white people and men. She surrendered eight days after her escape.

Little's case gained national attention and support from various feminist and CIVIL RIGHTS organizations. Thousands of dollars were raised for her legal defense. Attorneys Jerry Paul and Karen Galloway fought unsuccessfully for a change of venue and a delay of Little's trial, arguing that racist feelings in the area and extensive pretrial publicity would prevent a fair trial. Representative Shirley CHISHOLM of New York called on U.S. Attorney General Edward Levy to intervene in the case, citing the fact that few black people served on juries in the area of North Carolina where Little was scheduled to be tried.

On June 5, 1975, while Little's case was awaiting trial, the SOUTHERN POVERTY LAW CENTER of MONTGOMERY, ALABAMA, sponsored a million-dollar damage lawsuit on her behalf against Alligood's estate. A class-action portion of the lawsuit asked for protection for female prisoners against sexual abuse by male attendants at the prison, who could see the prisoners undress, bathe, and use the bathroom.

At her trial on a charge of second-degree murder (reduced from first-degree), Little testified that she had acted in self-defense. Prosecutors charged that she had lured Alligood to her cell with promises of sex. Little's case was strengthened by the testimony of three former female inmates who told of Alligood's unwanted sexual advances toward them while they were in custody. Six black and six white jurors acquitted Little in August of 1975 after deliberating for only one hour and eighteen minutes.

See also: Jury selection.

Little Anthony and the Imperials: Singing group popular from the late 1950's into the 1970's. The group was organized in 1955 around Anthony Gourdine and included Ernest Wright and Clarence Collins. All three were natives of Brooklyn. The group originally performed as the Chesters but reorganized in 1958 under the name Little Anthony and the Imperials at the suggestion of disc jockey Alan Freed. Others singing with the group included Tracy Lord, Glouster Rogers, and Sammy Strain.

The group got its start playing for school dances and at nightclubs in the mid-1950's. Their first successful record, "Tears on My Pillow," appeared in 1958 and was followed by "Shimmy, Shimmy, Ko-ko-Bop" in 1960. The group appeared on *American Bandstand* and other television shows and established itself as a significant rock-and-roll presence. In 1960 the group broke up, with Gourdine undertaking a solo career and the Imperials performing on their own. Neither effort was overly successful, and the group reunited in 1964, with the three core members and Strain.

The mid-1960's proved to be the group's most successful period. In 1964, it made the top ten with "Goin' Out of My Head," following with another top-ten hit, "Hurt So Bad," the following year. Although Little Anthony and the Imperials never returned to the top ten, they did produce a number of lesser hits over the next decade: "Hurt" and "It's Not the Same" (1966), "Out of Sight, Out of Mind" (1969), "Help Me Find a Way" (1971), and "I'm Falling in Love with You" (1974). The group broke up and reformed several times in the 1970's, increasingly making its living from

Anthony Gourdine, better known as "Little Anthony." *(Archive Photos)*

club and casino dates. It also proved popular on the nostalgia circuit. Gourdine also enjoyed some success as an actor.

Little Anthony and the Imperials began as a DOO-WOP group in the 1950's, but adapted its style to changing musical tastes. "Tears on My Pillow" was a ballad, and "Hurt So Bad" was more soulful. Gourdine's was the dominant voice, an imploring tenor capable of rendering a shrill falsetto. That the group maintained its popularity over many years in the ever-changing world of rock music is testimony to its ability to adapt.

See also: Music.

Little Richard (Richard Penniman; b. December 25, 1935, Macon, Georgia): One of the most influential early rock-and-roll musicians. Richard Penniman was one of twelve children in a Seventh-day Adventist family in GEORGIA. He often played piano and sang in church services, but he had turned to secular music by the time he signed his first recording contract with RCA Victor in 1951. Little Richard's early records were recorded in a jump-blues style similar to that of Louis Jordan and achieved little commercial success.

Between 1952 and 1955, Little Richard recorded with various combos (including the Johnny Otis Orchestra) for Houston's Peacock Records, but he did not find his artistic niche until, at the urging of RHYTHM-AND-BLUES singer Lloyd Price, he submitted a recording of his composition "Tutti Frutti" to Specialty Records in Los Angeles. The song reached number seventeen on the charts in 1956 and marked the beginning of three years of commercial success for Little Richard, with hit rock-and-roll songs including "Long Tall Sally" (1956), "Lucille" and "Jenny, Jenny" (1957), and "Good Golly Miss Molly" (1958).

Little Richard's music was marked by his energetic piano playing, which reflected an up-tempo boogie-woogie style, and his wildly expressive vocals, which included squeals, shrieks, and howls, influencing many later rock performers including Paul McCartney and John Fogerty. Both the Beatles and Fogerty's group, Creedence Clearwater Revival, recorded cover versions of Little Richard's songs. Additionally, his early performances exhibited the emotional and physical fervor of his early church training. Little Richard almost always appeared in outrageous costumes, with a high pompadour hairstyle and heavy eye makeup, suggesting sexual ambiguity as well as a rejection of mainstream American norms. Rolling Stones singer Mick Jagger and funk-rock musician Prince later used similar tactics with much the same effect.

Little Richard renounced rock-and-roll music in 1957 to return to the church, and he was ordained as a Seventh-day Adventist minister soon after. Beginning in the mid-1960's, he alternated between secular and spiritual music, but he never regained the commercial success he enjoyed in the late 1950's. Nevertheless, he continued to perform regularly through the 1990's and appeared occasionally in films, such as *Down and Out in Beverly Hills* (1986).

Little Rock crisis: The best-known and perhaps most significant school-desegregation incident in U.S. history occurred in September, 1957, in Little Rock, ARKANSAS. Before 1954 it was legal for public school districts in the United States to maintain separate schools for separate races, so long as such schools were ostensibly equal. Most schools that African Americans attended, however, were inferior as the result of inadequate supplies, extreme overcrowding, dilapidation, and poor financial support.

The May 17, 1954, U.S. SUPREME COURT decision in BROWN V. BOARD OF EDUCATION, declaring segregation in public schools to be unconstitutional, was a major victory for the NATIONAL ASSOCIATION FOR THE ADVANCEMENT OF COLORED PEOPLE (NAACP) and for others who had worked to end segregation. The Court ordered that public schools were to be desegregated with "all deliberate speed," and in 1955, Little Rock's school board adopted a plan to integrate the city's schools. The decision was made to enroll nine African American students at Little Rock's Central High School in the fall of 1957, to the dismay of many whites in Arkansas, including Governor Orval Faubus.

The First Day

Rumors and threats of violence by whites escalated as the first day of school drew near. Because of the mounting tension, Governor Faubus ordered the National Guard to Central High to prevent violence. The school board asked the parents of the African American students not to let them attend the school until the conflict was resolved; however, a U.S. District Court Judge, Ronald N. Davies, directed the school board to ignore the troops and permit the students to attend school.

White students taunt Elizabeth Eckford as she attempts to enter Central High School before National Guardsmen turn her away. *(AP/Wide World Photos)*

On September 4, 1957, the "Little Rock Nine," as the nine brave students were called, were to start school. They were Carlotta Walls, Jefferson Thomas, Elizabeth Eckford, Thelma Mothershed, Melba Patillo, Terrance Roberts, Gloria Ray, Minnie-Jean Brown, and Ernest GREEN, the only

Daisy Bates (standing, second from right) with the "Little Rock Nine." *(Library of Congress)*

senior. They planned to meet at the home of Little Rock NAACP leader Daisy BATES, who had suggested that the students all arrive at school together on the first day.

While eight of the students met at Bates's home the first morning of school, the ninth student, Elizabeth Eckford, did not. Because she did not have a telephone, she was unaware of the plan to meet together, and she thus arrived at the school alone. A large, angry crowd of whites had already gathered outside the school in protest of the integration.

When Eckford arrived, National Guard troops raised their bayonets to prevent her from entering the school as she approached the door. After she again unsuccessfully attempted to enter the school, she walked away to sit on a bench to wait for the bus. A mob of two hundred white hecklers immediately surrounded her, jeering and taunting her. A sympathetic white man sat next to her to soothe her, and a white woman, Grace Lorch, ventured from the crowd to rescue the frightened girl from the mob, placing her on a bus for home. The National Guard then prevented the rest of the Little Rock Nine from entering the school.

During the following weeks, President Dwight Eisenhower and Governor Faubus conferred by telephone and telegram and in special meetings to resolve the crisis. Eisenhower mandated that the governor follow the Supreme Court's decision to integrate the schools, reminding him that the matter was a federal issue. Faubus, on the other hand, argued that integration should be a decision of each state, and not the federal government. While both were adamant in their arguments regarding integration, the Little Rock Nine were not attending school. On September 14, Eisenhower and Faubus met in Rhode Island, and each issued a statement expressing support for the law. Under a court order, Faubus then removed the National Guard from the school on September 20.

Federal Intervention

On September 23, the Little Rock Nine entered the school from another entrance. When the crowds discovered this, they attempted to charge past the police barricades guarding the entrances. While some white students walked out of their classes in protest, the majority remained in their classrooms.

Irate parents telephoned the school all morning, requesting the removal of their children from school. By noon, the mob had become so chaotic and violent that the nine children were dismissed and escorted home by police. Twenty-five protesters were arrested.

President Eisenhower held an emergency press conference on the Little Rock situation in which he reaffirmed his commitment to implementing the 1954 Supreme Court decision. The next day, Eisenhower issued an executive order directing federal troops to aid Little Rock in enforcing the ruling of the Court.

On the morning of September 24, Central High School was surrounded by U.S. Army troops, who barricaded the streets around the school in an attempt to prevent the angry crowds from forming. Whenever a group of people gathered, troops immediately forced them to scatter. The soldiers that surrounded the school were armed with bayonets and rifles; such extreme measures were necessary to enable the black students to enter the school unharmed and to prevent the forming of the angry mobs they had confronted in the past.

Continuing Standoff

During the following two months, the nine students, under armed protection, attended school with almost two thousand white students. When students entered the school, they passed by lines of armed soldiers. Once school started, troops wearing steel helmets and carrying bayonets patrolled the hallways. The federal troops continued to escort the black students inside the school as well as to escort them to and from school in a military convoy to protect them from harassment.

During the day, there were few racial incidents within the school, largely because of the presence of the troops. While both African American and white students shared the school's facilities, there was little social interaction between the two groups. There were some subtle disruptions, with most of them occurring after the troops withdrew from the school in November.

One incident culminated when one of the African American girls, Minnie-Jean Brown, threw a bowl of chili on a white boy who had badgered her one day in the cafeteria. As a result, she was suspended. A white girl was later suspended for pushing Elizabeth Eckford. In May, 1958, Ernest Green graduated from Central High School in the midst of public protest.

Further Opposition

During the summer of 1958, a district court granted the school board a two-and-a-half-year deferment from the desegregation process until the tensions subsided. The NAACP worked expeditiously to appeal the decision, and as a result, a Supreme Court decision ordered the continuation of the integration process. Governor Faubus immediately ordered the entire public school system in Little Rock to close for the upcoming school year of 1958-1959 and was hailed by the state's white community as a hero.

Temporary schools were established to educate the white children once the public schools closed. Other white parents sent their children to schools in other cities or counties. Most blacks had no such options, however, and after the closing of the African American public schools, the majority of black students remained out of school. Public pressure and further federal legal action led to the reopening of the public schools in August, 1959, and the gradual integration of the schools continued under waning protests.

Consequences

The Little Rock incident in 1957 was a major victory for school desegregation. By focusing international attention on the state of race relations in the South, moreover, the incident had effects that went beyond the integration of classrooms. The courage of the Little Rock Nine inspired many and encouraged others to continue fighting for equality, both in education and in society in general.

—*Kibibi Mack-Williams*

See also: Segregation and integration.

Suggested Readings:

Bates, Daisy. *The Long Shadow of Little Rock: A Memoir.* New York: D. McKay, 1962. Reprint. Fayetteville: University of Arkansas Press, 1987.

Beals, Melba. *Warriors Don't Cry: A Searing Memoir of the Battle to Integrate Little Rock's Central High.* New York: Pocket Books, 1994.

_______. *White Is a State of Mind: A Memoir.* New York: G. P. Putnam's Sons, 1999.

Berry, Mary F., and John W. Blassingame. *Long Memory: The Black Experience in America.* New York: Oxford University Press, 1982.

Blossom, Virgil T. *It Has Happened Here.* New York: Harper, 1959.

Huckaby, Elizabeth. *Crisis at Central High, Little Rock, 1957-1958.* Baton Rouge: Louisiana State University Press, 1980.

Murphy, Sara A., and Patrick C. Murphy. *Breaking the Silence: Little Rock's Women's Emergency Committee to Open Our Schools, 1958-1963.* Fayetteville: University of Arkansas Press, 1997.

Record, Wilson, and Jane C. Record, eds. *Little Rock, U.S.A.* San Francisco, Calif.: Chandler, 1960.

Little Walter (Marion Walter Jacobs; May 1, 1930, Marksville, Louisiana—February 15, 1968, Chicago, Illinois): Harmonica player. Born Marion Walter Jacobs, Little Walter taught himself to play the harmonica when he was eight years old. He later ran away from home and formed his own group, playing on the streets and in small clubs. His earliest known recording was made in 1947.

In 1950 Little Walter recorded in CHICAGO with Muddy WATERS's band. He became part of some of the most exciting postwar CHICAGO BLUES. He had developed a harmonica style that seemed to come out of no tradition, and he may have been the first to amplify a harmonica electrically. He soon left Waters. In 1952 he recorded "Juke," an instrumental piece, and "Can't Hold You Much Longer." The two were released by Checker records, a subsidiary of the Chess label. "Juke" was a number-one hit on the RHYTHM-AND-BLUES charts. Little Walter formed his own group, the Jukes.

Little Walter had been performing since he was a child, and had hardened quickly. He was said to drink too much and to be bitter, aggressive, and moody. His death in 1968 was a result of injuries suffered in a fight.

Little Walter was responsible for developing the harmonica as a lead BLUES instrument. He was the first to mimic the sound of saxophone players such as Louis Jordan with the harmonica. He was also a powerful singer with a warm, mournful voice. One component of the postwar blues was the electric ensemble. Little Walter was a highly organized bandleader with a new innovative sound. He recorded about one hundred titles for Chess, and his music helped to redefine blues. His sense of tonal distance and timing allowed his songs to range from lamenting melodies to whooping boogie rhythms. His harmonica solos have been described as eerie and mournful, broken by stabbing notes that seem to come from out of the distance.

L.L. Cool J (James Todd Smith; b. 1969?, Queens, New York): RAP singer. L.L. Cool J. (Ladies Love Cool James) was reared by his grandparents in Queens. His grandfather, a JAZZ saxophonist, wanted to encourage his interest in MUSIC and paid $2,000 for some turntables and other stereo equipment when L.L. was eleven years old. By 1982 L.L. was performing with other neighborhood rappers at local roller rinks and block parties. He also sent homemade demo tapes of his raps to various record companies. Rick Rubin and Russell Simmons were forming their Def Jam production company in 1984 when they received L.L.'s rap song "I Need a Beat." They agreed to produce L.L.'s song, and the single became Def Jam's first rap record when it was released later that year, selling more than one hundred thousand copies.

With the success of his first recording, L.L. decided to drop out of high school in order to devote all of his time to his music. L.L.'s second album, *Radio*, was released in 1985 and went platinum (selling more than one million copies). The album contained the rap ballads "I Want You" and "I Can Give You More," along with the anthem "I Can't Live Without My Radio." That same year, L.L. had a cameo role in the rap film *Krush Groove* (1985). In 1987 L.L.'s third album, *Bigger and Deffer*, was released. Its sales were so strong that the album remained on *Billboard*'s Top Ten list for two months. L.L.'s popularity led to the inclusion of his single "Goin' Back to Cali" on the sound track of the film *Less Than Zero* (1987).

Def Jam sponsored a tour of rap artists headlined by L.L. Cool J., who appeared along with PUBLIC ENEMY, Stetsasonic, Eric B. and Rakim, Whodini, and Doug E. Fresh. *Walkin' with a Panther*, L.L.'s third album, was released in 1989, and his fourth album, *Mama Said Knock You Out*, appeared in 1990.

Rapper L.L. Cool J in 1991. *(AP/Wide World Photos)*

L.L. Cool J.'s music is known for its boasting lyrics, its depiction of street life, and its sly parodies of the obsession with wealth and self-glorification practiced by both headlining rappers and the public at large. At the same time, his songs did not follow later rap trends of promoting a political message or glorifying the criminal image promoted by some hard rappers. L.L.'s bragging persona is not merely an act. He became involved in a back and forth "dissin'" war with Kool Moe Dee, trading insults in public and on their records. Their animosity spilled over into their other activities.

Although he was invited to participate and eventually helped M.C. LYTE compose her rap lyrics for the project, L.L. Cool J. did not record music or appear in the video for the song "Self-Destruction," part of the Stop the Violence project involving several popular rap groups in an effort to raise money for the NATIONAL URBAN LEAGUE and to make rap audiences aware of the devastating effects of BLACK-ON-BLACK VIOLENCE.

Locke, Alain Leroy (September 13, 1886, Philadelphia, Pennsylvania—June 9, 1954, New York, New York): Educator and author. Locke's parents, Pliny Ishmael Locke and Mary Hawkins Locke, met as school founders in LIBERIA. As the custodial spirit of the 1920's HARLEM RENAISSANCE, a HOWARD UNIVERSITY teacher and philosopher, and a major essayist and anthologist, Locke continues to rank as a leading African American intellectual.

His own brilliance and his favored Philadelphia birth and education led Locke to Harvard University, where he won the Bowdoin Prize for an English essay, earned his B.A. magna cum laude in 1907, and was elected to

Phi Beta Kappa. From 1907 to 1910, he studied Greek and philosophy at Oxford University as the first black Rhodes Scholar. He was appointed as an assistant professor of philosophy and education in 1912 at Howard University, where, with intermissions, he would serve as chair of the philosophy department until the 1950's. He received his Ph.D. in 1918 from Harvard University for a thesis on *The Problem of Classification in the Theory of Value: Or, an Outline of a Genetic System of Values*.

A patron of the arts, a proponent of cultural pluralism, and an early stalwart of the NATIONAL ASSOCIATION FOR THE ADVANCEMENT OF COLORED PEOPLE (NAACP), he was also an inveterate chronicler and explainer of black American culture. Given the pan-African range of his output and his great clarity of presentation, prizes and commendations were quick to come his way.

Locke's greatest fame derives from *The New Negro: An Interpretation* (1925), his anthology and manifesto which proclaimed an African American cultural and spiritual "coming of age," with HARLEM, New York as its "race-capital." He included as the vanguard of this new age the likes of Langston HUGHES, Zora Neale HURSTON, Jean TOOMER, Countée CULLEN, James Weldon JOHNSON, Claude MCKAY, and graphic artist Aaron DOUGLAS. His lifetime's essays and volumes such as *The Negro and His Music* (1936), *The Negro in Art: A Pictorial Record of the Negro Artist and of the Negro Theme in Art* (1940), and the study unfinished at his death in 1954, *The Negro in American Culture*, made Locke a ranking presence in the history of black American achievement.

See also: Intellectuals and scholars; Pan-Africanism.

Logan, Rayford Whittingham (January 7, 1897, Washington, D.C.—November 4, 1982, Washington, D.C.): Historian and author. Logan received his B.A. (1917) and M.A. (1929) from Williams College and his Ph.D. from Harvard University (1936). He taught history at Virginia Union University (1925-1930), at ATLANTA UNIVERSITY (1933-1938), and at HOWARD UNIVERSITY from 1938 until his retirement in 1965. He was editor of the JOURNAL OF NEGRO HISTORY and the author or editor of several books, including *The Betrayal of the Negro: From Rutherford B. Hayes to Woodrow Wilson* (1965). He was also the historian for the centennial history of Howard University.

See also: Historiography.

Long, Jefferson Franklin (March 3, 1836, Knoxville, Georgia—February 4, 1901, Macon, Georgia): U.S. representative from GEORGIA during RECONSTRUCTION. Born into SLAVERY, Long became a successful tailor in Macon by the end of the CIVIL WAR. He was an organizer of the Georgia REPUBLICAN PARTY and worked to increase voter registration among African Americans. Georgia's readmission to the Union was delayed after a coalition of white legislators expelled twenty-eight black members of the state legislature in 1868. The state finally was readmitted after the black legislators were reinstated and the state legislature ratified the FIFTEENTH AMENDMENT.

In 1870 Long was nominated to run for the remaining term of the Forty-first Congress as a representative from Georgia's Fourth District. He won the election but was ineligible for immediate reelection because another candidate had won the seat for the Forty-second Congress in the election that had been held simultaneously. After taking office, Long became the first black representative ever to deliver a speech on the floor of Congress, on February 1, 1871. Less than a month after that historic occasion, Long's term expired. He returned to Georgia to resume his tailoring business and to campaign for Republican candidates. Frustrated by white Republicans' treatment of black party members, Long later encouraged

African Americans to support sympathetic independent DEMOCRATIC PARTY candidates.
See also: Congress members; Politics and government.

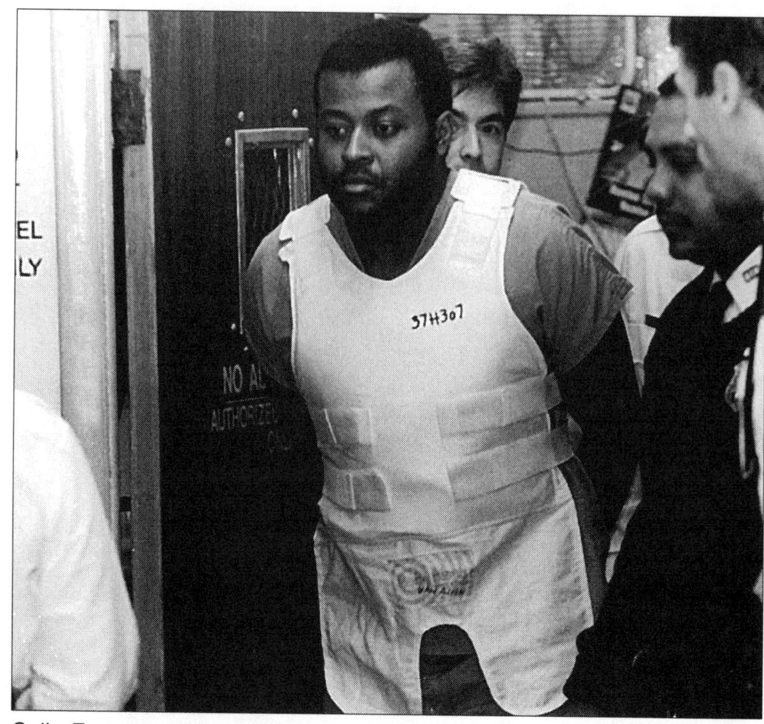

Colin Ferguson being led into court for a pretrial hearing in December, 1993. *(AP/Wide World Photos)*

Long Island Railroad murder case: Murder trial. Colin Ferguson, a Jamaican-born immigrant of African descent, was found guilty of murdering six white passengers on a New York commuter train. The trial garnered national attention because attorneys argued that Ferguson was driven to his crime out of rage caused by white racism.

The son of an influential Jamaican businessman, Ferguson attended private school in JAMAICA and lived in an exclusive neighborhood as a child. The family's fortunes declined after the death of his parents, so Ferguson emigrated to the United States in 1982 at the age of twenty-four. He married Audrey Warren in 1986, and qualified for permanent residency in the United States. After settling with his wife on Long Island, Ferguson attended classes at a local community college. In 1988, however, his wife sued for divorce and won custody of their child. Employed by a burglar-alarm manufacturer, he injured his back at work in 1989, and was fired. He successfully sued for worker's compensation, receiving more than $26,000. Nevertheless, Ferguson was dissatisfied with the ruling. Charging that he was the victim of RACIAL PREJUDICE, he demanded that the compensation board reopen his case. His constant telephone calls and letters alarmed board officials, who placed his name on a list of potential troublemakers.

Ferguson enrolled at New York's Adelphi University in 1990. At school, he accused white students of racism and derided black students as "Uncle Toms." His disruptive behavior resulted in suspension from the university in 1991. A 1993 trip to CALIFORNIA in search of employment failed—a friend reported that Ferguson disliked competing with immigrants. He returned to New York in May of 1993. On December 7, when Ferguson learned that the compensation board had not reopened his case, he boarded a Long Island commuter train and shot twenty-five people, killing six. Three passengers grabbed him as he was reloading his gun and held him until police arrived.

Ferguson's attorneys, William Kunstler and Ronald Kuby, announced that they would plead insanity because Ferguson had been driven insane by white racism and was not responsible for his actions. This "black rage" defense sparked intense debate. Advocates hoped the plea would bring attention to the destructive effects of racism on African Americans. Critics argued that the black rage defense would allow African Americans to engage in violent acts without accepting responsibility for their behavior. In an unusual move, Ferguson chose to fire his attorneys before they could make their case. After he passed competency exams, the court allowed him to exercise his right to act as his own attorney.

Although Ferguson surprised observers with his courtroom abilities, his argument that a white man had taken his gun and done the shooting proved untenable. Fifteen witnesses testified that Ferguson was the gunman. Because Ferguson acted as his own attorney, he had the right to question the witnesses, which included several people he had shot. Despite Ferguson's contention that he was innocent, the jury found him guilty of six counts of murder. Judge Donald Belfi permitted victims and relatives to make statements to the court prior to the sentencing, a controversial move intended to give victims an opportunity to face their attacker. On March 22, 1995, Belfi sentenced Ferguson to two hundred years in prison. Ferguson hired attorneys who hoped to appeal his conviction on the grounds that Ferguson had made technical errors while acting as his own attorney, a defense that many legal experts questioned.

Longview, Texas, riot: On June 17, 1919, an African American man was murdered vigilante-style in Longview, Texas, for the alleged rape of a local white woman. On July 5, an article concerning the murder appeared in the Chicago Defender, a prominent African American newspaper that was regularly delivered to the Longview area. This article asserted that the black man had actually been the white woman's lover. Outraged white citizens of Longview accused a local African American schoolteacher, Samuel L. Jones, of being the author of the article.

On July 10, Jones was beaten on a local street. Longview businessman and physician C. P. Davis became involved when Jones sought medical treatment in Davis's office. That evening, an angry white mob surrounded Jones's home but was repelled in a thirty-minute gun battle with a group of African Americans organized by Davis. Several white men were wounded in the fighting, and a larger white mob retaliated the next day by setting fire to several black homes and businesses, including those of Jones and Davis, who had managed to escape Longview.

On July 12, the National Guard and Texas Rangers restored order in the town. This riot, along with several other racial disturbances during the summer of 1919, helped focus attention on white racism in the United States. It also showed that African Americans were willing to fight back and even die in order to turn the democratic ideals that emerged from World War I into reality.

—*Terry Nienhuis*

See also: Hate crime.

Lorde, Audre (February 18, 1934, New York, New York—November 17, 1992, St. Croix, Virgin islands): Poet, orator, and writer. Lorde was an outspoken activist against various forms of oppression, and her powerful position as a black lesbian feminist poet earned her international fame. Lorde was a founding member of Women of Color Press and received many honors, including the 1991 Walt Whitman Citation of Merit and honorary doctorates from Hunter, Haverford, and Oberlin colleges.

Born the third and youngest daughter of West Indian parents in the Virgin Islands, Lorde grew up in Harlem and eventually graduated from Hunter College High School. After publishing her first poem in *Seventeen* magazine, Lorde went on to develop her writing talents. Lorde attended the University of

Audre Lorde left the Harlem Writer's Guild because of the homophobic tendencies of some of its members. *(Ingmar Schullz/W. W. Norton)*

Mexico for a year before transferring to NEW YORK CITY's Hunter College, where she received her undergraduate degree in 1959. Two years later, Lorde earned a master's degree in library science from Columbia University. In 1962 Lorde married Edwin Ashley Rollins; together, they had two children before obtaining a divorce in 1969.

While employed as a librarian in three New York libraries, Lorde wrote her first book of poetry, *The First Cities* (1968). In 1968 she lectured at City University of New York and served as poet-in-residence at Tougaloo College in MISSISSIPPI, where she met her future companion, Frances Clayton. After a brief tenure at Tougaloo, Lorde returned to New York City and taught writing and racism courses at Lehman College and John Jay College. She also worked as an English professor at Hunter College.

For a short time, Lorde was involved with the Harlem Writers' Guild. Her connections with this respected organization, however, were short-lived. The homophobic attitudes of the group isolated Lorde. In Lorde's search for acceptance, her relationship with life partner Frances Clayton helped to establish her identity as a black lesbian poet. *Zami: A New Spelling of My Name* (1982) captured the crux of Lorde's alienating experiences as a child and a lesbian. Her lesbian, racial, and gender identifications would serve as the subjects of many of her later works. Lorde went on to publish other prominent books of poetry such as *Cables to Rage* (1970), *From a Land Where Other People Live* (1973), *New York Head Shop and Museum* (1975), and *Between Ourselves* (1976).

Lorde attracted national attention when *From a Land Where Other People Live* was nominated for a National Book Award in 1974. After publishing two more books, Lorde signed a contract with W. W. Norton. *Coal* (1976) and *The Black Unicorn* (1978) were two of Lorde's most significant poetry works. In 1980 she published *The Cancer Journals*, a chronicle of her struggle with breast CANCER and the aftermath of her mastectomy. Examining her experience from her own vantage point as a black lesbian feminist, Lorde encouraged other female cancer patients to consider the ramifications of choosing to be silent and hiding their condition.

Lorde's connections with her publisher afforded her the opportunity to meet other poets, including Adrienne Rich, who was also under contract with W. W. Norton. In 1981 Lorde published an interview with Rich in *Signs: Journal of Women in Culture and Society*. Her relationship and work with Rich significantly expanded her pool of readers. Lorde gained national fame and attracted many white readers with the publication of *Sister*

Outsider (1984). An important work of prose, this book was best known for its strong feminist message and became a standard text for women's studies courses across the country.

In *A Burst of Light* (1988), Lorde chronicled her struggle with liver cancer without surgical treatments. Despite her failing health, Lorde continued to travel and present inspiring speeches. On November 17, 1992, Audre Lorde died on the island of St. Croix in the U.S. Virgin Islands. In August of 1993, W. W. Norton published her last book of poetry, *The Marvelous Arithmetic of Distance*.

—*Phyllis Michelle Jones*

See also: Health; Homosexuality; Literature; West Indian heritage.

Los Angeles, California: Largest city in CALIFORNIA and second-largest city in the United States. In 1998 an estimated 3.6 million people lived in the city of Los Angeles. In Los Angeles County, within which the city is located, there were about 10 million residents. In 1999 14 percent of the people of the city of Los Angeles were of African descent. In the county of Los Angeles, 10 percent of the population were African Americans. These figures may be compared to the 44 percent of the county's population who identified themselves as Hispanic, the 33 percent who were white, and the approximately 12 percent who were of Asian background.

In its South Central section, Los Angeles has one of the largest concentrations of African Americans found in any city in the United States. While some residents of this area of Los Angeles are of lower socioeconomic status, African Americans in Los Angeles, on average, have higher per capita incomes than do African Americans nationwide. About 40 percent of all African American households in Los Angeles fall within the middle income bracket. This statistic is about 10 percent higher than the national average for African Americans.

About 25 percent of middle-class African Americans living in Los Angeles work at some sort of government job. This statistic is much higher for middle-class African Americans than it is for middle-class Asians, 14 percent of whom have this sort of job, or middle class Hispanics, 10 percent of whom are employed by government. About 20,000 Los Angeles businesses are owned by African Americans, compared to 220,000 businesses owned by Asians and Hispanics.

In 1925 there were about twenty-five thousand African Americans living in Los Angeles. Many were recent arrivals who had come by railroad from Texas and Oklahoma to work as service personnel in the growing movie industry and the other businesses that it had spawned.

From 1940 to 1945, the African American population of Los Angeles increased dramatically as people from throughout the United States moved to Los Angeles to work in war industries. Many of these African American newcomers settled in South Central Los Angeles and further south in the WATTS district.

After WORLD WAR II, African Americans were largely segregated from white Americans, and there were growing racial tensions. In 1964 California voters passed Proposition 14, which was later declared unconstitutional by the U.S. Supreme Court. Proposition 14 was an attempt to validate RACIAL DISCRIMINATION in the rental and sale of housing. In August, 1965, a traffic arrest precipitated five days of rioting in Watts. The WATTS RIOTS, which yielded thirty-four deaths, thousands of arrests, and $40 million in property damage, served as a catalyst for civil unrest among African Americans in other major cities. After the riots, the Los Angeles city government worked to improve conditions for African Americans. Jobs were created, bus service was improved, and a hospital was built in the Watts area.

During the 1970's and 1980's, African Americans in Los Angeles gained both economically and politically. In 1973 Tom BRADLEY was elected the first African American mayor of the city, and he remained in office until 1993. Bradley ran unsuccessfully for the California governor's office in 1982 and 1986.

In 1992 riots broke out again in Los Angeles. Residents of South Central took to the streets after four white police officers, whose actions had been videotaped during the arrest of African American Rodney King, were acquitted when they were tried for police brutality. The 1992 LOS ANGELES RIOTS caused fifty-eight deaths, thousands of arrests, and about one billion dollars in property damage. After the riots, a commission was established to improve community relations and to make recommendations for improving African American life in Los Angeles.

Many famous African Americans associated with the TELEVISION, music, and FILM industries and with athletic teams make their homes in Los Angeles. Two past Los Angeles residents among many African Americans who have contributed much to American history and culture were Jackie ROBINSON, the first African American elected to the National Baseball Hall of Fame (Robinson played ball at the University of California at Los Angeles before joining the Brooklyn Dodgers), and Nat "King" COLE, the first African American to have his own television show.

—*Annita Marie Ward*

See also: Waters, Maxine.

With a legacy of five thousand buildings damaged or ruined, the 1992 Los Angeles riots destroyed a billion dollars worth of property and killed more than fifty people. *(AP/Wide World Photos)*

Los Angeles riots: Civil disturbance following 1992 acquittal of police officers accused of beating Rodney King, an African American motorist. On March 3, 1991, King was stopped by police, following a high-speed automobile chase during which his car reached speeds up to 115 miles per hour. King refused to lie down on the ground as ordered by the officers. The officers used force to subdue King, force which resulted in a broken leg and several broken facial bones for King.

A portion of King's beating at the hands of four police officers was videotaped by a bystander. Television networks later broadcast the tape. The segments most often televised appeared to show a flagrant case of police brutality against King. The four officers involved were brought to trial on charges of police brutality.

Legal maneuvering brought a change of venue in the case to Simi Valley, a largely white and middle-class town. The JURY SELECTION process for the trial produced a panel that included ten white people, one Mexican American, and one Filipino. Evidence presented at the trial indicated that King had been legally intoxicated at the time of his arrest, and the officers on trial testified that they thought he may have been on the drug PCP, which can give a user unusual strength. The officers also explained their behavior as reasonable in light of circumstances. Sergeant Stacey Koon and officers Timothy Wind and Theodore Briseno were found not guilty, and a mistrial was declared for officer Laurence Powell. President George Bush would later ask the Justice Department to press civil rights charges against Powell.

The jury verdicts were announced at about 3:00 P.M. on Wednesday, April 29, 1992. Within hours, crowds had gathered at various locations in Los Angeles in protest of the verdicts. Police officials had discussed in advance the possibility of rioting following the trial's conclusion, should any or all of the officers be found not guilty. No formal contingency plans, however, had been made. Police chief Daryl Gates claimed to have plans, but they did not appear to have been implemented. Some reports identified these plans as generic ones meant more to apply to police mobilization following an earthquake. Gates himself was out of his office for several hours immediately following the verdict, driving to a fund-raiser.

By 5:30 P.M. a crowd had gathered at the corner of Florence and Normandie, in South Central Los Angeles. About twenty-five officers tried to restrain the crowd but were forced to leave. Most of the subsequent riot activity took place within the approximately 50 square miles of South Central. Large-scale police mobilizations did not take place until about 7:30 P.M. By 10:00 P.M. about twenty-five square blocks were on fire. Shortly before midnight, CALIFORNIA governor Pete Wilson announced plans to send 750 highway patrol officers and 2,000 members of the National Guard to Los Angeles. These reinforcements took about a day to reach the city. In the meantime, secondary riots of smaller scale took place in San Francisco, Seattle, Atlanta, and other urban centers.

The rioting in Los Angeles spread north to Hollywood and as far as the San Fernando Valley, south to Long Beach, and west to Culver City. More than a thousand fires were set, and looting was widespread. Store owners attempted to protect their stores by posting signs announcing ownership by African Americans, but looters often ignored them. Attacks against stores owned by Asian Americans were particularly prevalent, reflecting longstanding animosity between the African American and Asian American (especially Korean-descent) communities.

Ironically, considering the videotape evidence presented at the King beating trial and in advance of it, videotaping and cameras

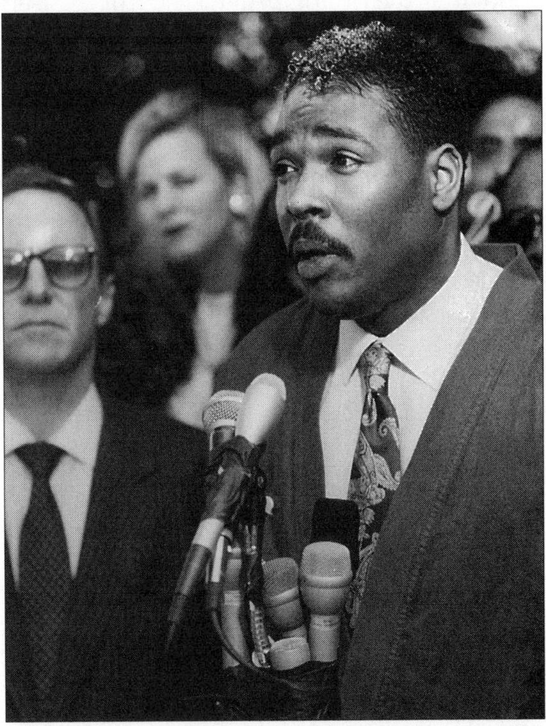

In the midst of the rioting, Rodney King made a moving public appeal to stop the violence, asking, "Can we all just get along?" *(AP/Wide World Photos)*

played an important part in the riots. Airborne television cameras captured the scene of several black youths dragging Reginald Denny, a white man, from his truck and beating him. Five black youths later were arrested for the crime. Several area residents who saw the beating on television rushed to the scene and took Denny to the hospital. Television news cameras captured numerous scenes of looting, and reporters even conducted interviews with looters.

President Bush eventually put the U.S. Army at Fort Ord into service to control the riots, along with a thousand federal officers trained in riot control. A total of about forty-five hundred federal troops became involved. By Friday, May 1, most of the rioting had stopped. More than fifty people had been killed and almost four hundred injured. Seventeen thousand people were arrested, many on charges of violating the curfew imposed soon after the rioting began. The riots caused an estimated billion dollars of property damage, with five thousand buildings damaged by fire or looting. More than six thousand insurance claims eventually would be filed for amounts totaling $775 million, but much of the property in the poverty-stricken South Central area was not insured. Many of the businesses in the area were barely surviving, and an estimated 30 percent did not carry insurance because of the expense.

Peter Ueberroth was named as chairman of Rebuild L.A., a task force created by Mayor Tom BRADLEY and Governor Pete Wilson. The task force was intended to be a clearinghouse for assistance and volunteers to help repair damage caused by the riots. Black unemployment in the South Central area reached 40 percent following the riots, and area residents pressured the city to provide jobs for them in the rebuilding. The riots destroyed an estimated forty thousand jobs throughout the city.

See also: King, Rodney, arrest and beating; Korean-African American relations.

Louis, Joe (Joseph Louis Barrow; May 13, 1914, Lafayette, Alabama—April 12, 1981, Las Vegas, Nevada): World heavyweight BOXING champion from 1937 to 1949, Joe Louis came to symbolize both race pride and American strength and virtue. Beginning his career when racist theories of black inferiority reigned and boxing was largely a white sport, Louis became a hero to blacks for his ability to knock out white contenders. When the German Max Schmeling knocked Louis out in the twelfth round at Yankee Stadium on June 19, 1936, African Americans cried openly in the streets of Harlem. By the time of their rematch on June 22, 1938, however, news of Nazi persecutions had politicized the bout. The fight's symbolic importance shifted from black against white to Americans versus Nazis. Sportswriters characterized Schmeling as "Moxie" and "the Nazi-man." Seventy thousand people watched Louis knock out the thirty-two-year-old Schmeling in the first round, making Louis the representative not only of black power but also of national greatness. No African American had ever before gained such wide acceptance in America.

Beginnings

Born Joseph Louis Barrow, Joe was the seventh of eight children of SHARECROPPERS Lillie and Munroe Barrow. When Louis was twelve, the family moved to Detroit. Because of inadequate schooling, Louis was placed in classes with younger students and then in vocational school. Quitting at seventeen, he worked at a factory and learned to box from Atler Ellis at Brewster Center, a recreation facility. After losing his first amateur match to Johnny Miler, a member of the 1932 Olympic team, Joe dropped the name Barrow, quit his job, and concentrated on boxing. He fought fifty-four bouts during the next year, winning fifty—forty-three by knockouts. A few months after winning the national amateur light heavyweight championship, Louis turned professional, knocking out Jack Kracken, a white man, in the first round on July 4, 1934, in Chicago for a purse of fifty-nine dollars.

Boxing Career

In less than six months, under the guidance of managers Julian Black and John Roxborough and trainer Jack Blackburn, all African Americans, Louis was rated the number-nine contender for the heavyweight title. His defeat of former heavyweight champion Primo Carnera on June 25, 1935, in Yankee Stadium made him the most famous African American in the country. Louis downed Carnera three times before referee Arthur Donovan stopped the fight in the sixth round. Louis's previous twenty-two straight wins, eighteen by knockouts, plus the curiosity engendered by a black fighter had drawn sixty thousand spectators.

Louis's next big fight was with another former champion, Max Baer, on September 24, 1935, in Yankee Stadium for a $240,000 purse. Billed as a fight between the world's best heavyweights, the Louis-Baer fight received tremendous publicity. Louis battered Baer to one knee and knocked him out in the fourth round.

Since James Braddock was not anxious to defend his world heavyweight title, Louis signed to fight the number-one contender, Schmeling, in 1936. After almost continuous training for two years, Louis enjoyed celebrity life before returning to camp. He did not train as hard as usual. Consequently, Schmeling floored Louis in the fourth round, the first time in his professional career that he had been knocked down. In the fifth, Schmeling landed a right when Louis dropped his hands just as the bell rang, but Louis hung on until he was knocked out in the twelfth. His managers quickly scheduled another fight, and Louis defeated former champion Jack Sharkey on August 18 with a third-round knockout.

Attracted by financial concessions, Braddock finally agreed to defend his world championship. On June 22, 1937, in Chicago's Comiskey Park, fifty thousand fans (almost half of them African Americans) saw Braddock knock Louis down for an instant, but Louis got up to batter Braddock to a knockout in the eighth. At twenty-three, Louis became the youngest person to hold the heavyweight title.

Although there had been only eight title fights between August, 1928, and June, 1937, Louis's managers felt the country would not accept an African American who did not fight, so he defeated Tommy Farr, the British champion, and two other fighters before his June 22, 1938, rematch with Schmeling, whom he quickly dispatched to become a national hero. His best opponent after Schmeling was Billy Conn, who nearly beat him in June, 1941, but Louis rallied to knock out Conn with two seconds to go in the thirteenth round.

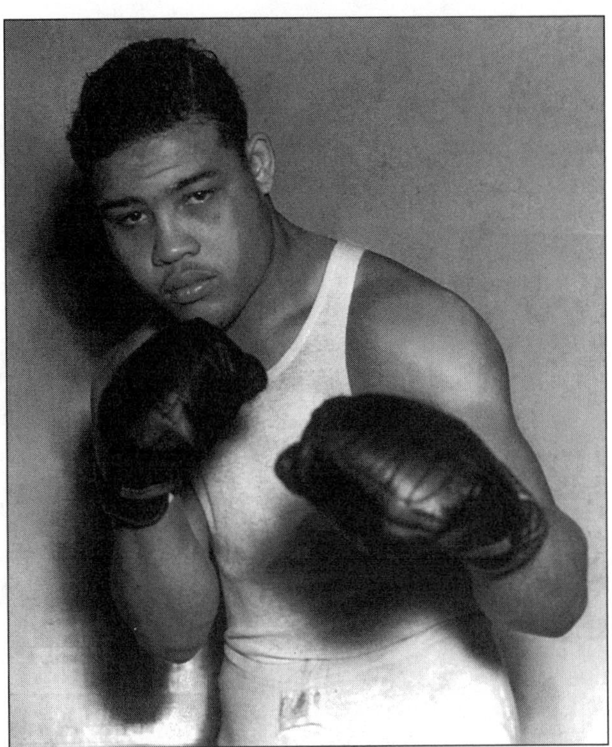

Joe Louis in 1937. *(AP/Wide World Photos)*

African Americans in Washington, D.C., celebrating news of Joe Louis's victory over Max Schmeling in June, 1938. *(AP/Wide World Photos)*

Louis's wife, entertainer Marvis Louis, visiting a training base for African American soldiers during World War II. *(National Archives)*

World War II

Louis successfully defended his title fifteen times (thirteen by knockouts) from June, 1938, to September, 1941. He agreed to fight a title match against Buddy Baer on January 9, 1942, for the Navy Relief Society, privately hoping to embarrass the Navy into giving African Americans more than menial positions. Louis knocked out Baer in the first round and then volunteered to serve in the Army. In his forty-six months of duty, Louis fought ninety-six exhibition matches. He also appeared in *This Is the Army*, a 1943 film featuring Ronald Reagan. Although he did not speak out publicly against segregation, Louis refused to follow Jim Crow policies on military bases.

Career's End

Returning to civilian life, Louis knocked out Conn in the eighth round of a 1946 rematch after Conn's strategy of avoiding Louis in the ring failed. Louis then went on an exhibition tour. When Jersey Joe Walcott emerged as a title contender, Louis beat him in a split decision on December 5, 1947, even though Walcott had floored Louis twice. Walcott again floored Louis in a rematch on June 25, 1948, but Louis managed to put Walcott down for the count in the eleventh round. After some exhibition bouts, Louis relinquished the title on March 1, 1949.

A 1950 Internal Revenue Service audit showed that Louis owed the federal government hundreds of thousands of dollars in unpaid taxes, leaving him no choice but to return to boxing. Ezzard Charles had defeated Walcott for the vacated title and agreed to fight Louis in September, 1950. Charles was declared the winner, and Louis's purse of $100,458 was insufficient to pay his debts. Rocky Marciano, who had won thirty-seven fights in the previous five years, thirty-two by knockouts, guaranteed Louis $300,000 for a fight. On October 26, 1951, at the age of thirty-seven, Louis fought his last fight. When Marciano knocked him through the ropes in the eighth round, the referee stopped the fight.

Louis sews the sergeant stripes he has earned on his uniform. *(National Archives)*

Louis's career spanned more than a quarter of a century, during which he fought 129 amateur and professional fights, winning 54 of 58 amateur bouts (31 by knockouts) and 68 of 71 professional fights (54 by knockouts). Louis himself was knocked out twice. He held the title eleven years, defending it twenty-five times.

Financial Difficulties

Louis was generous, supporting siblings, buying his mother a house, turning unemployed Detroit pals into the touring Brown Bomber Softball Team, and contributing to black causes. He borrowed against future fights to maintain a large entourage. Illegal tax deductions made by his promoter, Mike Jacobs, left him indebted to the government and forced him to become a professional wrestler in 1956. Finally, in the early 1960's, the Internal Revenue Service permitted him to keep a percentage of his income.

Louis married Marva Trotter in 1935. She divorced him on grounds of desertion in 1945; they were remarried and again divorced in 1948. They had a daughter in 1943 and a son in 1947. With no money or possessions, Louis traveled, staying with friends until he married Rose Morgan, a successful Harlem beautician, in 1955; they were divorced two years later. In 1959 he married Martha Malone Jefferson, the second black woman admitted to the CALIFORNIA bar.

In 1970 Louis underwent court-ordered psychiatric treatment. He spent his remaining days as a greeter at Caesars Palace in Las Vegas. In 1977 he was confined to a wheelchair as a result of an aortic aneurysm, and he died on April 12, 1981, of a heart attack. Jesse JACKSON gave the eulogy, and Louis was buried in Arlington Cemetery.

Different Perceptions of Louis

Joe Louis arrived in the shadow of Jack JOHNSON, the first African American world heavyweight champion, who flouted Jim Crow conventions. Louis's managers countered with a public-relations image of humility and reticence. They urged Louis never to say anything negative about an opponent or smile after beating him. Louis did not smoke or drink, nor did he appear publicly with white women, although he had numerous affairs with women of both races.

Tagging Louis the "Brown Bomber," sportswriters portrayed his success as the result of racial differences. Joe was depicted as a natural athlete who did not think in the ring—a jungle man—whereas his white opponents were described as methodical, hardworking, and courageous. African Americans identified with him, although some were ambivalent, approving of Louis's strong, clean-living image but disapproving of his apparent ignorance. Ironically, although Louis was considered inarticulate, he is remembered for a remark about Conn, "He can run, but he can't hide," and for his assessment of WORLD WAR II, "We will win because we're on God's side."

By the 1940's, Louis was no longer unique, as more African Americans broke into big-time SPORTS, and by the 1960's his reticence gave him an "Uncle Tom" image. Nevertheless, Louis remained one of boxing's all-time greats and an African American folk hero.

—*Christie Farnham*

See also: Ali, Muhammad; Robinson, Jackie; Tyson, Mike.

Suggested Readings:

Bak, Richard. *Joe Louis: The Great Black Hope*. Dallas, Tex.: Taylor, 1996.

Barrow, Joe L., and Barbara Munder. *Joe Louis: Fifty Years an American Hero*. New York: McGraw-Hill, 1988.

Dupont, Jill. "Joe Louis." In *The Twentieth Century: Great Athletes*. Pasadena, Calif.: Salem Press, 1992.

Edmonds, A. O. *Joe Louis*. Grand Rapids, Mich.: Wm. B. Eerdmans, 1973.

Fleischer, Nat. *Black Dynamite: The Story of the Negro in the Prize Ring from 1792 to 1938*. 5 vols. New York: C. J. O'Brien, 1938-1947.

Louis, Joe, Edna Rust, and Art Rust. *Joe Louis, My Life*. New York: Harcourt Brace Jovanovich, 1978.

Mead, Chris. *Champion: Joe Louis, Black Hero in White America*. New York: Charles Scribner's Sons, 1985.

Nagler, Barney. *Brown Bomber: The Pilgrimage of Joe Louis*. New York: World, 1972.

Vitale, Rugio. *Joe Louis: Biography of a Champion*. Los Angeles: Holloway House, 1981.

Louisiana: According to the CENSUS OF THE UNITED STATES, in 1997 there were about 1.4 million African Americans in the state of Louisiana; about one of every three people in the state was of African ancestry. Therefore, Louisiana, a slave state before the CIVIL WAR, proportionately had one of the largest African American populations in the United States.

Louisiana was originally established as a French colony, and its laws regarding race and slavery were somewhat different from those of the English colonies of North America. In 1724 Louisiana's colonial government published the *code noir*, or "black code." This set of laws required that slaves be instructed in Roman Catholicism and be baptized. It also required that they be allowed ownership of property and have the right to marry. These laws were changed when the French ceded

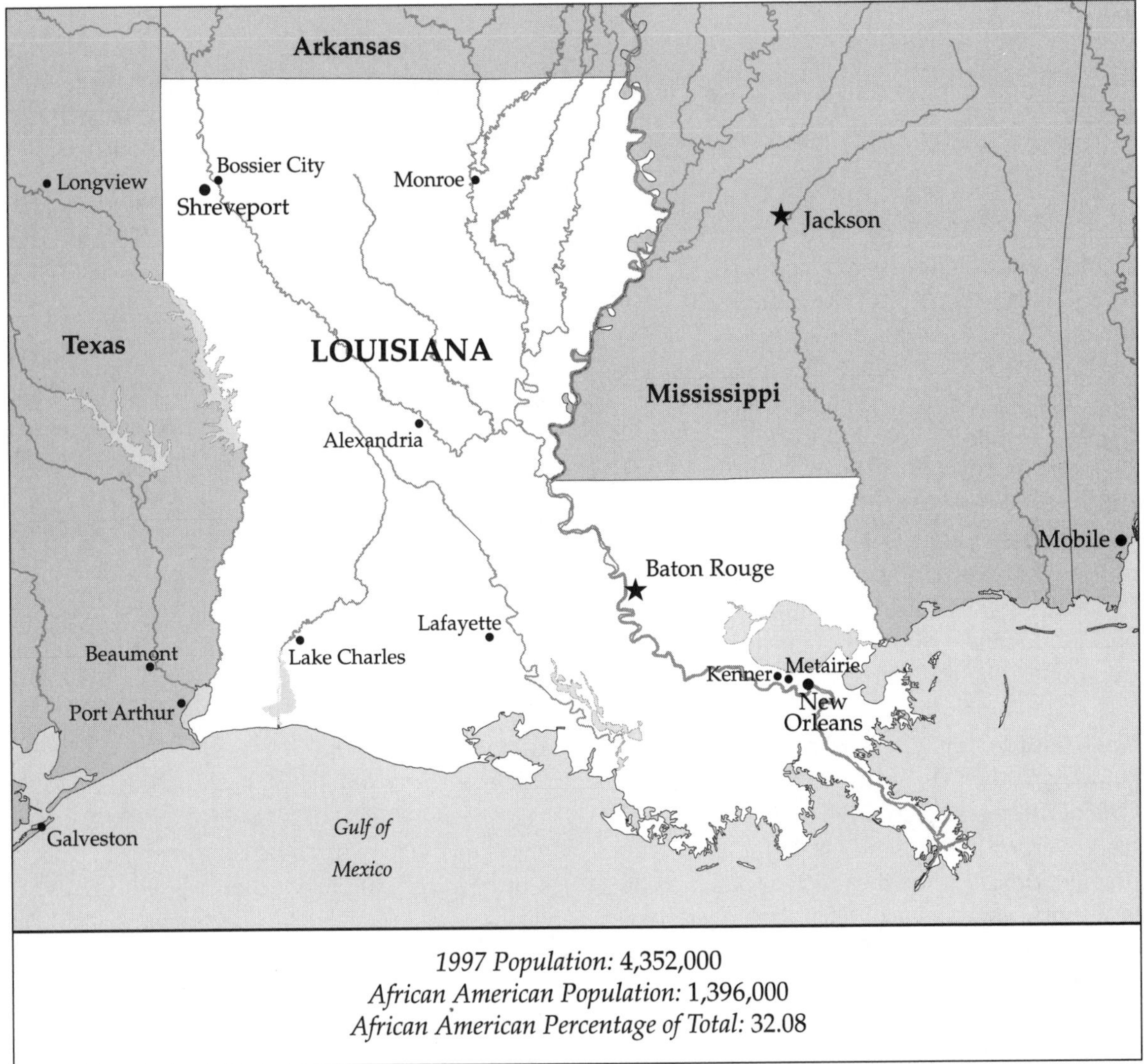

1997 Population: 4,352,000
African American Population: 1,396,000
African American Percentage of Total: 32.08

Louisiana to Spain in 1763, but by that time the unique situation of black people in Louisiana had allowed the development of a class of people in a social situation between the slaves and the whites. These were the *gens de couleur libres*, or free people of color, nonslaves of mixed race. In the 1800's, mixed-race immigrants from Haiti, fleeing the Haitian revolution, became part of the class of the free people of color. This fact contributed a Haitian cultural element to Louisiana black culture.

Despite some of the comparatively liberal elements of race relations in early Louisiana, slavery in the state was still harsh. This was particularly true in the southwestern part of the state, where large numbers of slaves were employed in the hard work of growing sugar cane. After the United States purchased Louisiana in 1803, legal restrictions on slaves became more stringent, and the rights of free people of color were increasingly limited.

Louisiana still had a large population of people of mixed race after the Civil War, and many of them were well educated. They formed the core of Louisiana's black political leadership during Reconstruction (1866 to

1877), when about one-third of the state's governmental leaders were black. In 1872 Louisiana's P. B. S. PINCHBACK became the first black governor in the United States.

After the withdrawal of Union troops in 1877, whites in the state reacted against Reconstruction violently. Taking control of the government, whites systematically excluded African Americans from many areas of public life. Legal segregation and the prevention of voting and political organization by African Americans continued until the 1960's, when Louisiana became a focal point of the CIVIL RIGHTS movement.

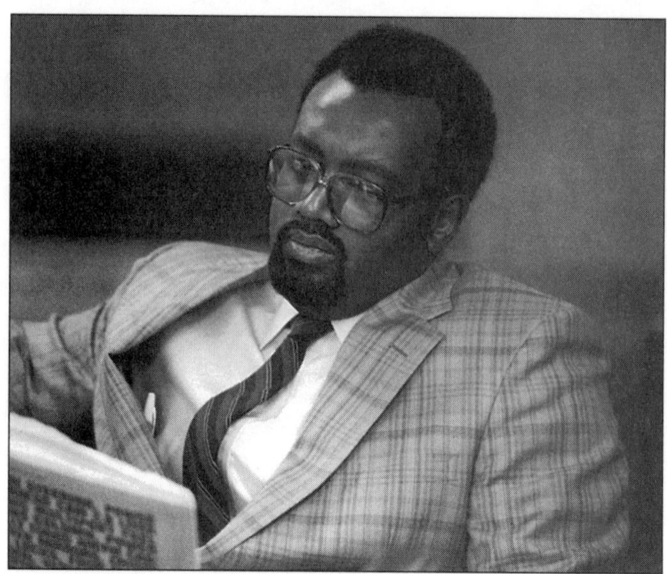
Glenn C. Loury in 1987. *(AP/Wide World Photos)*

By the 1990's, African Americans had made substantial progress toward political equality in Louisiana. During this decade, the state legislature was about 16 percent black, and by 1992 there were two black Louisianians in the U.S. House of Representatives. One of these representatives, Cleo FIELDS, ran for governor in 1996 and got as far as the runoff elections. Despite these advances, incomes and living conditions of African Americans in Louisiana lagged far behind those of whites. It also appeared that racism was still prevalent. David Duke, a former leader of the KU KLUX KLAN, won a majority of white votes in the 1990 election for governor. Duke was defeated largely because black voters turned out in record numbers.

—*Carl L. Bankston III*

Loury, Glenn C. (b. September 3, 1948, Chicago, Illinois): Political economist and educator. Loury earned a B.A. in mathematics from Northwestern University and a Ph.D. in economics from the Massachusetts Institute of Technology. His work challenges assumptions about costs of AFFIRMATIVE ACTION programs to the African American community. Loury became a strong advocate of self-reliance among the African American community, and his writings argue that the problems of the GHETTO cannot be reversed effectively by CIVIL RIGHTS policies. He is critical of civil rights leaders and others who turn to government as the primary source of empowerment. Loury taught at Harvard and Boston Universities.

Love, Nat (June, 1854, Davidson County, Tennessee—1921, Los Angeles, California): Cowboy. Love was known as "Deadwood Dick," a skilled gun handler and range rider who pursued criminals and fought Indians. Love grew up on a farm, then left for the West at the age of fifteen. He worked in TEXAS and ARIZONA, then gave up trail herding upon his marriage in 1889. He worked as a railroad Pullman porter and published his autobiography in 1907. *See also:* Cowboys.

Lovejoy, Elijah (November 9, 1802, Albion, Maine—November 7, 1837, Alton, Parish, Illinois): Abolitionist publisher. PRESBYTERIAN minister, Elijah Parish Lovejoy was a bitter foe of SLAVERY. His views and his courage in publishing them ultimately cost him his life.

A product of largely abolitionist New England, Lovejoy was educated at Waterville College before moving to St. Louis in 1827 and becoming a schoolteacher. While living in MISSOURI, he attended Princeton Theological Seminary and published both a religious journal and a political newspaper. Despite his training in education and theology, it was the print medium that most attracted him. Lovejoy became controversial because of his open hatred of human bondage, a dangerous belief to espouse in slave-owning Missouri. He also criticized what he saw as the undeserved influence and intrusion of the Vatican in American political affairs, thus angering the growing Catholic population found in most river communities.

Contemporary silhouette of Elijah Lovejoy. *(Library of Congress)*

In 1836 Lovejoy fled Missouri by crossing the Mississippi River into Illinois, where he settled in the community of Alton. Even in this free midwestern state, however, his strident opinions soon led to trouble. An armed mob threw his press into the river, and he was condemned at public meetings. On the evening of November 7, 1837, Lovejoy was killed by an attacking mob while he tried to protect a newly purchased press. To his enemies he was an agitating abolitionist who received only what he richly deserved. To his supporters, Lovejoy was an honorable martyr to the twin causes of constitutional rights and moral courage.

—*Thomas W. Buchanan*

See also: Abolitionist movement; Hate crime.

Loving v. Virginia: Case argued before the U.S. SUPREME COURT in 1967 that legalized marriages between blacks and whites. In June of 1958, two residents of Virginia—Mildred Jeter, a woman of black and Indian ancestry, and Richard Perry Loving, a white man—were married in the District of Columbia. Soon after their marriage, the couple returned to Virginia and established residence in Caroline County. In October of that year, a grand jury indicted the newlyweds for violating Virginia's ban on interracial marriages. At the time, Virginia was one of sixteen southern states that had antimiscegenation laws.

On June 6, 1959, the Lovings stood before Judge Leon M. Bazile and confessed that they were indeed married and had willingly broken the Virginia law prohibiting blacks and whites from living together as marriage partners. Judge Bazile sentenced the couple to one year in jail; he suspended the sentence for twenty-five years on the condition that the Lovings leave Virginia and not return for that period.

After their convictions, the Lovings moved to the District of Columbia; there, they began the legal battle to have their convictions overturned. For nine years, they and their lawyers challenged Virginia's ban on interracial marriages. Finally, in 1967, the U.S. Supreme Court, in a surprising, unanimous vote, ruled that laws which forbade blacks and whites marrying were "repugnant" to the equal protection clause of the FOURTEENTH AMENDMENT and therefore unconstitutional. The lawyers for the state of Virginia had argued that the so-called MISCEGENATION statutes were constitutional because they applied to blacks and whites equally. In delivering the opinion of the High Court, Chief Justice Earl Warren countered: "The fact that Virginia only prohibits interracial marriages involving white persons demonstrates that the racial classifications must stand on their own justification, as measures designed to maintain White Supremacy."

Mildred and Richard Loving, whose challenge to Virginia's antimiscegenation law led to a landmark decision by the U.S. Supreme Court. *(AP/Wide World Photos)*

Laws barring black-white marriages in the United States were first enacted during the 1600's. These antimiscegenation laws were originally intended to stop black and white indentured servants from forming sexual unions. Despite legal and social prohibitions, many white men had sexual relations with black women; sometimes the women were concubines, sometimes, nonconsenting partners, but rarely were they marriage partners.

For centuries mainstream American society accepted the belief that interracial marriages were harmful to the nation in general (because they promoted "mongrelization"), and to whites in particular (because the "superior" race would be polluted). As a result, antimiscegenation sentiments undergirded patterns of segregation. Integrated schools and parks, for example, were opposed because they would bring blacks and whites together, where they might meet and form intimate friendships. Marriage implied equal status, and such "social equality" was opposed by many Americans, particularly before the advent of the CIVIL RIGHTS movement and the women's liberation movement.

Although aware of the history of antimiscegenation sentiments in America, Richard Loving was more practical than political when he heard the Supreme Court's ruling on his case. He said, "For the first time, I could put my arm around her and publicly call her my wife."

See also: Interracial marriage; Segregation and integration.

Civil rights leader Joseph E. Lowery. *(© Roy Lewis Archives)*

Lowery, Joseph E. (b. October 6, 1924, Huntsville, Alabama): Civil rights leader and Methodist cleric. In 1952 Lowery was ordained as pastor of the Warren Street Church, a United Methodist congregation in Mobile, Alabama. As one of the coordinators of the 1955 Montgomery bus boycott, Lowery helped operate the Montgomery Improvement Association (MIA) and was a founding member of the Southern Christian Leadership Conference (SCLC) in 1957. Lowery was elected vice president of the organization and was known as chief adviser to Martin Luther King, Jr.

While continuing to maintain a high profile in the Civil Rights movement, Lowery was an active minister and received appointments as pastor of St. Paul's Church in Birmingham, Alabama, from 1964 to 1968; as pastor of Central United Methodist Church in Atlanta, Georgia, from 1968 to 1986; and as pastor of Cascade United Methodist Church in Atlanta from 1986 to 1992. In 1977 Lowery became president of the SCLC, succeeding Ralph Abernathy. As president, Lowery worked to combat the effects of drugs, poverty, and violence in the black community by developing programs such as "Liberation Lifestyles." He fought the dumping of toxic waste near predominantly black neighborhoods and worked diligently to locate corporate sponsors to participate in joint-venture programs with black-owned businesses and black colleges to help train and educate future black business leaders.

In 1995 Lowery led the celebrations commemorating the thirtieth anniversary of the Selma to Montgomery march. Among his various honors and awards, Lowery was given two notable awards in 1990: the Martin Luther King, Jr., Nonviolent Peace Prize from the Martin Luther King, Jr., Center for Nonviolent Social Change and the Martin Luther King, Jr., Medal for Outstanding Professional Service from George Washington University.

See also: Environmental hazards and discrimination; Methodists.

Lowery, Robert O. (b. April 20, 1916, Buffalo, New York): Government official. Lowery was the first African American fire commissioner of any major American city when appointed on January 1, 1966, to that position in New York City. He represented new administrative emphases, such as the recruiting of minority personnel, which would characterize the programs of later black government officials across the United States.

Lowery attended City College in New York, Michigan State University, and the National Institute on Police and Community Relations. He began working in the New York Fire Department in 1941, was made a deputy commissioner in the department in 1963, and was its chief administrator from 1966 to 1973. He was a prototype for African Americans who successfully have sought promotions within governmental institutions and ultimately have secured highest-ranking posts.

Lowery's success was not achieved without expressions of independence. When appointed as fire commissioner by Mayor John Lindsay of New York, a Republican-Liberal politician, Lowery acknowledged that he had not voted for the mayor. When Lowery resigned as chief, he actively worked for the election of Mayor Lindsay's opponent and successor. While fire commissioner, Lowery gained national attention by assertively attempting to enlist African American and Latino recruits. He established tutoring programs for minorities that would help them to qualify, and he disseminated recruitment information through media that specifically targeted minority populations, acts that some considered controversial in the 1960's. In addition, his administration was known for its educational programs that attempted to inform

Robert O. Lowery at the time he was named New York City's fire commissioner in 1965. *(AP/Wide World Photos)*

the larger society about fire prevention and for its innovative programs to establish better relations between fire fighters and the public.

Lowery resigned from the New York Fire Department in 1973, at the age of fifty-seven. His administrative legacy includes his concerted attempts to educate, qualify, and recruit large numbers of African Americans for governmental positions and to establish positive relationships between minority communities and government agencies.
See also: Employment and unemployment.

Lucas, William (b. January 15, 1928, New York, New York): Political appointee. Lucas graduated from law school at Fordham University before joining the Department of Justice in 1961. While in WASHINGTON, D.C., Lucas worked as an agent for the FEDERAL BUREAU OF INVESTIGATION (FBI). He served as a CIVIL RIGHTS investigator in Tuskegee, ALABAMA, to help the U.S. government in its efforts to desegregate that city's public school system. Lucas also worked as a teacher, as a social worker, and as a policeman with the New York Police Department. He then served as a county executive and as sheriff of Wayne County, MICHIGAN, which includes DETROIT.

In 1986 Lucas switched his political allegiance and ran as the Republican candidate for governor of Michigan with the active support of President Ronald Reagan. Although Lucas had received generous support from the African American community in his previous political campaigns, he was opposed in his pursuit of the governorship by prominent black Democrats who disliked his ties to Reagan. Lucas was defeated in the election. In 1989 President George Bush nominated him to serve as assistant attorney general for civil rights. Lucas's nomination was controversial because he had spoken out as an opponent of QUOTAS as a method of advancing the career opportunities of minority groups.

William Lucas during his Senate confirmation hearings in 1989. *(AP/Wide World Photos)*

Since most of his work in the area of civil rights enforcement dated from the 1960's, Lucas also was criticized as being out of touch with contemporary civil rights issues. On August 1, 1989, the Senate Judiciary Committee was deadlocked in a seven-to-seven vote on the question of confirming Lucas's nomination. As a result of the tie vote, his nomination was rejected. Lucas later served as the director of the Office of Liaison Services in the Office of Legislative Affairs of the Department of Justice.

See also: Politics and government.

Lunceford, Jimmie (June 6, 1902, Fulton, Missouri—July 12, 1947, Seaside, Oregon): Bandleader and instrumentalist. James Melvin "Jimmie" Lunceford was one of the preeminent bandleaders of the big band era. He spent his early years in Warren, Ohio, where his father was a musician and choir master, but he later moved to Denver, Colorado. During his childhood and teen years, Lunceford learned to play several instruments, including guitar, trombone, saxophone, and flute. In high school, he studied music with Wilberforce Whiteman (father of musician Paul Whiteman). In 1922 he played alto saxophone in the George Morrison band. He received a bachelor's degree in music from Fisk University in 1926 and studied further at City College in New York. He then taught music at a high school in Memphis, Tennessee. In 1927 he formed a jazz ensemble among his students, the Chickasaw Syncopators. After several local successes, including radio broadcasts, the group turned professional in 1929 with the addition of Edwin Wilcox, Willie Smith, and Henry Wells, also Fisk alumni. The following year, the group made its first recording.

After touring mostly in the Midwest, the group went to New York City in 1933. It continued to record as it began an important residency at the Cotton Club in Harlem. Some of the important recordings from this period include "White Heat," "Jazznocracy," "Rhythm in Our Business," and Duke Ellington's "Mood Indigo," all recorded in 1934. By the mid-1930's, Lunceford's group was among the most sought-after big bands. Lunceford ranked with Count Basie and Ellington as a leader of a big band. Although Lunceford's facility with various instruments allowed him to stand in for other musicians when necessary, his real strengths were in conducting and ensemble playing. One of his trumpeters, Sy Oliver, was also the arranger for many works that the band performed. Several other well-known recordings that Lunceford made were "Organ Grinder's Swing," "For Dancers Only," "Margie," "Lunceford Special," and "Yard Dog Mazurka."

By the mid-1940's, as the United States discovered bebop, Lunceford's organization still enjoyed success. In 1947 he suffered a heart attack and died in Seaside, Oregon, while signing autographs at a music store. The band continued under the leadership of Eddie Wilcox and Joe Thomas, but it was not as successful.

Lymon, Frankie, and the Teenagers: Doo-wop vocal group. The group consisted of Frankie Lymon on lead vocals, Herman Santiago as first tenor, Jimmy Merchant as second tenor, Joe Negroni as baritone, and Sherman Garnes as bass. All of the members were indeed teenagers except Lymon, who was only twelve at the time the group was formed in 1954. They all attended the same New York City school and had been singing together for years prior to their first recordings.

Once formed, the Teenagers (as they were first called) pursued their goals relentlessly, often rehearsing in junkyards and on street corners. They were discovered by former Valentine Richard Barrett, who rehearsed them in

Frankie Lymon performing in London in 1957. *(AP/ Wide World Photos)*

a local junior high school music room until he thought they were ready to audition for a record label. When Barrett took them to Gee Records in late 1955, George Goldner and John Kilsky of Gee were amazed at the group's sound as well as by the fact that its members could write songs such as its first hit, "Why Do Fools Fall in Love?" (1956). The song actually had been rehearsed with Santiago on lead, but a sore throat thrust young Lymon into the lead role. The response to the single made him an instant star.

Toward the end of 1956, the group released its other hit single, "I'm Not a Juvenile Delinquent." The group appeared in promoter/disc jockey Alan Freed's film *Rock, Rock, Rock* (1956). Its success, however, was to be short-lived.

By 1957 Lymon had gone out on his own as a solo act, but puberty caused such a change in his voice that he quickly lost his fan support. The group did not stay together long without its star, and the members all quickly faded from the limelight. Three of its members were dead by the late 1970's, Negroni of a brain aneurysm, Gates during open heart surgery, and Lymon of a heroin overdose on the eve of signing a new recording deal after spending years fluctuating between rehabilitation and relapses. In 1992 Frankie Lymon and the Teenagers were elected to the Rock and Roll Hall of Fame.

See also: Music.

Lynch, John Roy (September 10, 1847, near Vidalia, Louisiana—November 2, 1939, Chicago, Illinois): Mississippi politician. Lynch was born a slave, the third son of plantation manager, Patrick Lynch, who was from Dublin, Ireland, and Catherine White, a slave. The elder Lynch's plan was to move his wife and family to New Orleans after purchasing them, but he took ill and died before this plan could be realized. The family was sold to an-

Born into slavery, John Roy Lynch became a member of Congress and lived ninety-two years. *(Associated Publishers, Inc.)*

other plantation owner. John Roy Lynch remained a slave until Union forces liberated the plantation near Natchez, Mississippi, in 1863, during the Civil War.

Displaying an eagerness to learn, Lynch was employed in a photography studio in 1866. He parlayed his knowledge of the trade into a thriving business. His only formal schooling lasted four months in late 1865, but by reading newspapers and books, and by listening to an array of oral discourse, he had become quite literate and a fine public orator at a young age.

His activities in a Natchez Republican Party club came to the attention of Mississippi governor Adelbert Ames, a radical supporter of Reconstruction, who appointed Lynch local justice of the peace in 1869. The same year, Lynch was elected to the state's House of Representatives, where he became a member of the military affairs and elections committees. In his second term, he was elected Speaker of the House and recognized as one of the most effective and influential Mississippi statesmen of his time. In 1872 Lynch was elected to the U.S. House of Representatives, where he served until 1877. He was defeated in the 1876 election by James R. Chalmers. He contested that decision, but it was upheld. He ran against Chalmers again in 1880, and again Chalmers initially was proclaimed the winner. This time, however, Lynch's protest was upheld, and he was seated on April 29, 1882. He lost a reelection bid and two subsequent attempts to regain a congressional seat.

Lynch by then had become one of the most prominent Republicans in the country. He accepted various government appointments from Presidents Benjamin Harrison and William McKinley in the late 1890's and the early 1900's. After passing the Mississippi bar in 1896, he practiced law in Washington, D.C., until he entered the Army in 1898 as a major and paymaster of volunteers. He later was appointed to the regular Army and retired in 1911 with the rank of major. Lynch then entered into a law practice in Chicago, Illinois.

Lynch's first marriage to Ella Sommerville, by whom he had a daughter, ended in divorce in 1900. In 1911 he married Cora Williams, who remained with him until his death. From the time he settled in Chicago, Lynch began to write prolifically, publishing papers in the Journal of Negro History in 1917 and 1918, writing his account of the role of African Americans during Reconstruction (*The Facts of Reconstruction*, 1913), and compiling his autobiography, which was published under the title *Reminiscences of an Active Life: The Autobiography of John Roy Lynch* (1970).

See also: Politics and government.

Lynching: The concept of lynching and lynch law are thought to have originated in colonial Virginia, where Colonel Charles Lynch, a

In 1935 thirty-two-year-old Rubin Stacy was hanged in Fort Lauderdale, Florida, by a group of masked men, who had seized him from sheriff's deputies who had arrested him for allegedly attacking a white woman. *(AP/Wide World Photos)*

wealthy planter and justice of the peace, headed an extralegal court and led an organization of patriots that meted out punishment to outlaws and Loyalists for their presumed crimes during the AMERICAN REVOLUTION. Lynch and his followers justified their actions on the grounds that no other form of law was immediately available during the period of upheaval brought on by the war. In later periods, lynching spread to other frontier regions where formal legal provisions for punishing crime were nonexistent or thought to be inadequate. Not until Reconstruction begin in the South did lynching become widespread as a traditional method of summary execution in which mobs punished African Americans who were believed to have transgressed against the law.

While carried out in the name of justice, the lynching of African American victims was a cruel and unjust means by which whites maintained the racial status quo, inducing and reinforcing fear in the hearts and minds of other members of the black community.

Historical Background

Early examples of lynching ranged from incidents involving Loyalists who were tarred, feathered, and ridden out of town on a rail to incidents involving frontier horse thieves or cattle rustlers who were hanged by vigilante groups. During times of economic hardship in the nineteenth century, mob violence often came to be directed at members of identifiable immigrant groups—such as the Irish and the Chinese—who were thought to be depriving native-born Americans of employment opportunities.

While violence against slaves and free blacks was widespread before the CIVIL WAR, it was not until Reconstruction that mobs of frustrated southerners used lynching to wage a campaign of terror and intimidation against African Americans, whose political and economic status had been improved in relation to that of their defeated former masters. The KU KLUX KLAN, the Knights of the White Camellia, and other secret organizations were formed around this time; members of these marauding groups sought to destroy the rights of black citizens by conducting nighttime raids, setting fire to black-owned houses, assaulting black families, and murdering black individuals who spoke out against them.

Escalation of Mob Violence

By the 1890's, lynch mobs had begun to employ brutal and sadistic tactics against black victims. These victims were hunted down, beaten, tortured, and burned at the stake. Sometimes, lynching victims were dismembered in order to provide souvenirs for onlookers. While still serving as a symbol of entrenched racial hatred, lynching was transformed into a recreational spectacle in which white residents brought their families to view the hangings. It was not uncommon for newspapers to carry advanced publicity for some lynchings, and railroads chartered special excursions to transport large crowds to these events. State laws that were designed to prosecute lynch mobs were not enforced, and white officials conspired to ignore evidence of lynching by declining to apprehend or prosecute known lynch mob participants and by attributing the deaths of lynching victims to unknown causes. By the early twentieth century, lynching became even more difficult to prosecute as the mob's access to automobiles made possible the transportation of lynching victims to remote locations where corpses might easily be hidden.

Contrary to general assumptions, most lynching victims were not black men accused of rape or attempted rape of white women. The overwhelming majority of those lynched between 1890 and 1900 were accused of social offenses—disputing with white shopkeepers, using offensive language, failing to address whites respectfully—or of challenging white authority by attempting to vote in elections, testifying against white citizens in court, and seeking jobs considered to be above their social station. While many black lynching victims were men, black women were not exempt. In 1918 a particularly barbaric lynching occurred in Valdosta, GEORGIA, when Mary Turner, a pregnant black woman, was hanged, burned, and eviscerated.

Crusade Against Lynching

Black journalist Ida B. WELLS was one of the leaders in the fight to eliminate lynching. On March 9, 1892, three black businessmen in MEMPHIS, TENNESSEE, were lynched on the pretext of having raped white women. Wells, who was a columnist and part-owner of the Memphis *Free Speech and Headlight*, was well acquainted with the three victims and denounced the lynchings as having been committed in order to eliminate the men as successful competitors to white Memphis storekeepers. After mobs destroyed the newspaper's offices, Wells left Memphis to continue her antilynching crusade in editorials in northern newspapers. Her determination to uncover the facts of the Memphis lynching led her to investigate lynchings in other locales and to

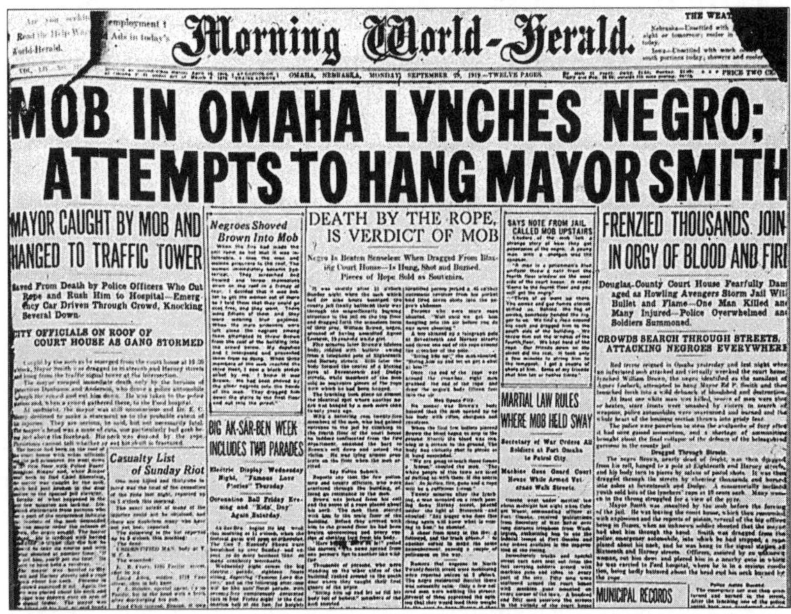
Morning World-Herald.

OMAHA, NEBRASKA, MONDAY, SEPTEMBER 29, 1919—TWELVE PAGES

MOB IN OMAHA LYNCHES NEGRO: ATTEMPTS TO HANG MAYOR SMITH

MAYOR CAUGHT BY MOB AND HANGED TO TRAFFIC TOWER

Saved From Death by Police Officers Who Cut Rope and Rush Him to Hospital—Emergency Car Driven Through Crowd, Knocking Several Down.

CITY OFFICIALS ON ROOF OF COURT HOUSE AS GANG STORMED

Negroes Shoved Brown Into Mob

DEATH BY THE ROPE, IS VERDICT OF MOB

Negro Is Beaten Senseless When Dragged From Blazing Court House—Is Hung, Shot and Burned. Pieces of Rope Sold as Souvenirs.

SAYS NOTE FROM JAIL CALLED MOB UPSTAIRS

FRENZIED THOUSANDS JOIN IN ORGY OF BLOOD AND FIRE

Douglas County Court House Fearfully Damaged as Howling Avengers Storm Jail With Bullet and Flame—One Man Killed and Many Injured—Police Overwhelmed and Soldiers Summoned.

CROWDS SEARCH THROUGH STREETS, ATTACKING NEGROES EVERYWHERE

MARTIAL LAW RULES WHERE MOB HELD SWAY

BIG AK-SAR-BEN WEEK INCLUDES TWO PARADES

Casualty List of Sunday Riot

MUNICIPAL RECORDS

Every article on the front page of this 1919 Omaha newspaper relates to a lynching incident that exploded into a white race riot. *(Great Plains Black History Museum)*

publish the facts of these cases. Her findings, supported by the statistical records on lynchings kept by TUSKEGEE INSTITUTE beginning in 1882, were published in a pamphlet entitled *Red Record: Tabulated Statistics and Alleged Causes of Lynchings in the United States, 1892-1894* (1895).

Between 1893 and 1897, six states—Georgia, KENTUCKY, NORTH CAROLINA, OHIO, SOUTH CAROLINA, and TEXAS—enacted laws prohibiting lynching, largely as a result of Wells's efforts. She later estimated that approximately ten thousand people were lynched in the United States between 1878 and 1898. Wells was secretary of the National Afro-American Council from 1898 to 1902 and used her influence with its members to increase efforts to sponsor antilynching legislation.

After the NATIONAL ASSOCIATION FOR THE ADVANCEMENT OF COLORED PEOPLE (NAACP) was formed in 1910, James Weldon JOHNSON was elected as its first executive secretary and was instrumental in supporting Wells's crusade for antilynching legislation. He persuaded L. C. Dyer, a member of the House of Representatives from MISSOURI, to introduce such legislation in 1921. Although the proposed DYER ANTILYNCHING BILL was passed by the House in 1922, it was defeated in the Senate by a filibuster engineered by southern senators. In 1935 and again in 1940, similar antilynching legislation was introduced through the lobbying efforts of NAACP executive secretary Walter WHITE, but these bills also failed in the face of proposed Senate filibusters. Despite these setbacks, NAACP lobbyists did gain national attention for the problem of lynching, and their efforts helped consolidate the political influence they later wielded in the emerging CIVIL RIGHTS movement of the 1950's and 1960's.

Decline in Lynching Atrocities

During the 1950's, the incidence of lynching steadily declined. No lynchings were recorded in 1952—the first year that this was the case since systematic records were first kept in 1882. However, not all lynchings were ever recorded. Improved law enforcement and the threat of federal intervention helped account for the decline. The last recorded lynching incident occurred in 1964, when the bodies of black civil rights worker James Chaney and two white workers, Michael Schwerner and Andrew Goodman, were discovered on a farm outside Philadelphia, MISSISSIPPI. Although no evidence of hanging or burning was discovered, the brutal beating and shooting of the three men was considered to have the hallmarks of a lynching. Although the FEDERAL BUREAU OF INVESTIGATION (FBI) accused nearly two dozen white segregationists, including Mississippi law enforcement officers, of complicity in the murders, only three perpetrators were ultimately convicted in 1967 of conspiring to violate the civil rights of the three victims.

While lynching incidents subsided, racially motivated violence and hate crimes continued to trouble the black community. During the late 1960's and 1970's, this violence erupted in riots, harassment of black militant radicals, and other forms of hostility. Membership in white supremacist groups such as the Ku Klux Klan grew during the 1970's and 1980's, leading to increased outbreaks of hate crimes and other violence directed against African Americans. In December of 1992, a black Wall Street executive visiting FLORIDA during the Christmas holidays died after being abducted and set on fire by whites. This incident graphically illustrates that while lynching as it was traditionally practiced in the South was no longer tolerated, the violent mentality that spurred white mobs to lash out against African Americans had yet to be totally extinguished.

—*Gervase Hittle*

See also: Homicide; Race, racism, and race relations; Race riots; Racial violence and hatred.

Suggested Readings:
Brundage, W. Fitzhugh. *Lynching in the New South: Georgia and Virginia, 1880-1930*. Urbana: University of Illinois Press, 1993.
_______, ed. *Under Sentence of Death: Lynching in the South*. Chapel Hill: University of North Carolina Press, 1997.
Finkelman, Paul, ed. *Lynching, Racial Violence, and Law*. New York: Garland, 1992.
Ginzburg, Ralph, ed. *One Hundred Years of Lynchings*. Baltimore: Black Classic Press, 1988.
Goldsby, Jacqueline. "The High and Low Tech of It: The Meaning of Lynching and the Death of Emmett Till." *The Yale Journal of Criticism* 9 (Fall, 1996): 245-282.
Moses, Norton H. *Lynching and Vigilantism in the United States: An Annotated Bibliography*. Westport, Conn.: Greenwood Press, 1997.
Perkins, Kathy A., and Judith L. Stephens, eds. *Strange Fruit: Plays on Lynching by American Women*. Bloomington: Indiana University Press, 1998.
Tolnay, Stewart E., and E. M. Beck. *A Festival of Violence: An Analysis of Southern Lynchings, 1882-1930*. Urbana: University of Illinois Press, 1995.
White, Walter. *Rope and Faggot: A Biography of Judge Lynch*. New York: Alfred A. Knopf, 1929.
Zangrando, Robert L. *The NAACP Crusade Against Lynching, 1909-1950*. Philadelphia: Temple University Press, 1980.

Lynk, Miles Vandahurst (June 3, 1871, Brownsville, Tennessee—December 29, 1957, Memphis, Tennessee): Physician. The *Medical and Surgical Observer*, published by Lynk beginning in 1892, was the first medical journal issued by a black person in the United States. Lynk founded the University of West Tennessee and was named as its president in 1900. He was the first to suggest publicly organizing the body of black physicians that became the NATIONAL MEDICAL ASSOCIATION, and he helped establish the group.
See also: Health care professionals; Medicine.

Miles Vandahurst Lynk, the first African American to publish a medical journal. *(National Library of Medicine)*

M

Mabley, Moms (Loretta Mary Aiken; March 19, 1897?, Brevard, North Carolina—May 23, 1975, White Plains, New York): Comedian. As a child, Jackie "Moms" Mabley was interested in show business, especially VAUDEVILLE. While she was still in her teens, the team of Buck and Bubbles discovered her talent and gave her a part in a vaudeville skit entitled "Rich Aunt from UTAH." This opportunity gave her an opening into the world of entertainment.

Mabley's first big success, in 1923, was her performance at the famous Connie's Inn in NEW YORK CITY. Success was the result of many years of developing her own monologue with the help of comedian Bonnie Bell Drew and of her experiences on the vaudeville circuit, performing before large African American audiences. During those years, she had grown to maturity. Following the practice of such groups as Butterbeans and Susie, she had developed her own comic character—that of a worn-out old woman wearing a funny hat and droopy stockings—for which she is best remembered. Her comic material had wide appeal; it ranged from domestic issues to race relations and the battle of the sexes. Her gags combined folk wisdom with sly insights. She performed in concert halls, college auditoriums, theaters, and clubs throughout the United States, often to packed houses.

Mabley performed with such celebrities as Duke ELLINGTON, Benny Goodman, Cab CALLOWAY, Count BASIE, and Louis ARMSTRONG. In 1962 she performed on a bill with Nancy Wilson and Cannonball ADDERLEY in her successful debut at Carnegie Hall. On television, she performed with Harry BELAFONTE, the Smothers Brothers, and Bill COSBY.

Mabley's comedy albums brought her more commercial success and public recognition. Among her enduring albums are *Moms Mabley at the U.N.* and *Moms Mabley at the Geneva Conference*. Her successful career as a comedian encouraged younger women to break into the field of comedy, which was dominated by men. She also proved that comedy record albums can find a place among U.S. audiences. Her first album eventually sold more than a million copies. Her motherly attitude and love for people earned her the nickname "Moms."

See also: Comedy and humor; Comics, stand-up.

Moms Mabley during an appearance on Merv Griffin's television show in 1969. *(AP/Wide World Photos)*

Madhubuti, Haki R. (Don L. Lee; b. February 23, 1942, Little Rock, Arkansas): Writer, cultural critic, and educator. Madhubuti developed a deep concern with the construction of institutions that foster the cultural independence of African Americans. When he began writing poetry in the 1960's under his given name, Don L. Lee, Madhubuti sometimes was grouped with writers such as Sonia SANCHEZ, Etheridge Knight, and Nikki GIOVANNI, whose work also was published by Dudley Randall's Broadside Press. These "Broadside poets" believed poetry to be a means of political and social revolution.

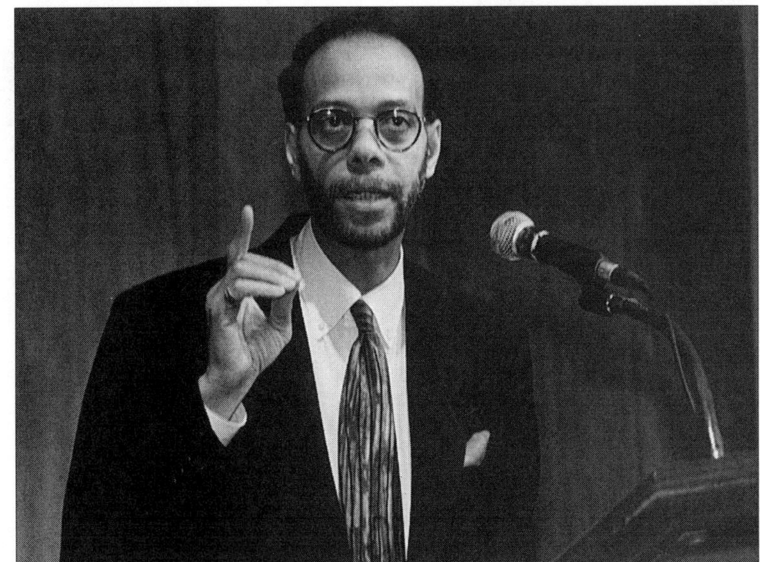
Poet and publisher Haki R. Madhubuti. *(© Roy Lewis Archives)*

Madhubuti wrote critical essays that articulate a black aesthetic; a number were collected in *Dynamite Voices: Black Poets of the 1960's* (1971). Twenty years later, during a 1991 presentation at the national convention of the National Council of Teachers of English, he reaffirmed that, "As a poet, it is my responsibility to change the state, point out contradictions and hypocrisies." That same year he published *Black Men: Obsolete, Single, Dangerous?: Afrikan American Families in Transition: Essays in Discovery, Solution, and Hope* (1991).

Madhubuti considered himself primarily a poet in the African griot tradition. His first book of poetry, *Think Black* (1967), was well received, and within four years of its publication, he had sold more than one-quarter million books of poetry. He was by far the best-selling African American poet to that time. His poetry has been criticized by some as being too bombastic, but he has been defended by Gwendolyn BROOKS and others as artistically representing the black speaking voice. This voice is well represented in *Don't Cry, Scream* (1969). Some of his later work is collected in *Heartlove: Wedding and Love Poems* (1998).

Madhubuti founded the Third World Press in 1967 as a means of bringing writers with a vision for the African American community to the public. In 1969 he founded the Institute of Positive Education in CHICAGO, ILLINOIS. The institute saw the goal of education as being empowerment rather than acculturation. Madhubuti held various teaching positions as well as high posts in various pan-African organizations.

See also: Literature; Pan-Africanism.

Maine: The African American population of Maine has always been quite small. According to estimates of the CENSUS OF THE UNITED STATES, in 1997 about 6,000 Maine residents, fewer than 0.5 percent of the state's entire population, were African Americans, and Maine ranked forty-ninth among the states in terms of the percentage of African American residents.

From 1691 until it became a state in 1820, Maine was part of the MASSACHUSETTS Bay Colony, where SLAVERY was legal. The first

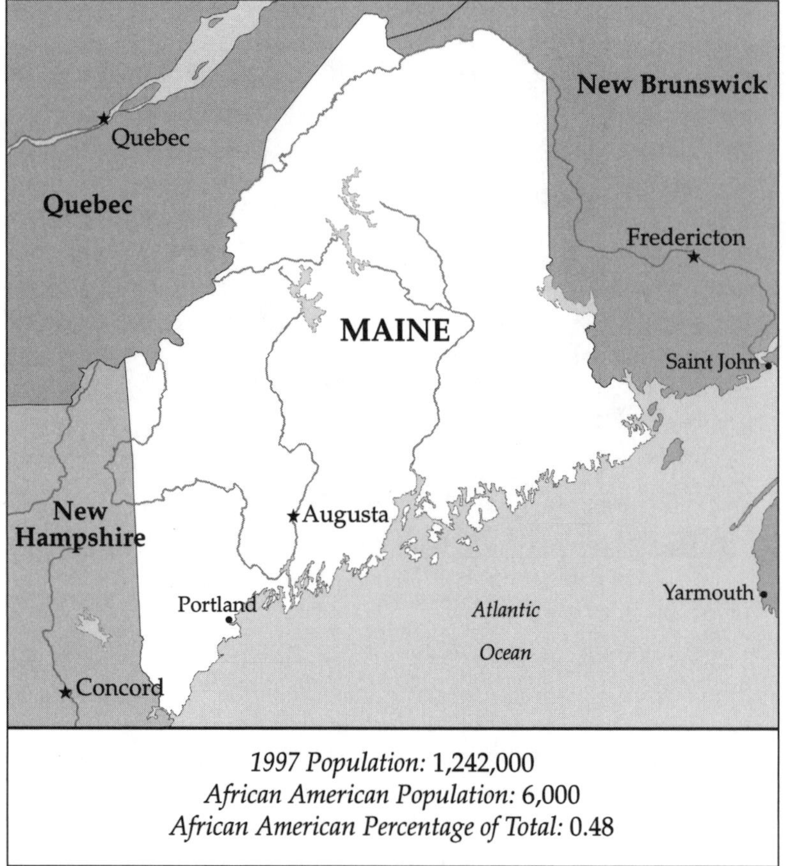

1997 Population: 1,242,000
African American Population: 6,000
African American Percentage of Total: 0.48

written evidence of a black slave in Maine dates to 1663 in York. By 1700 several wealthy Maine families had slaves, who were mostly house servants. By 1776 there were approximately six hundred slaves, mostly in York County. However, the ABOLITIONIST MOVEMENT, begun by Pennsylvania QUAKERS, was gaining momentum, particularly during the AMERICAN REVOLUTION.

When the Massachusetts supreme court in 1783 determined that the new 1780 state constitution made slavery illegal, Maine was included in the ruling. Forty years later, as part of the agreement known as the MISSOURI COMPROMISE OF 1820, Maine was admitted to the union as a free state, balancing the admission of MISSOURI as a slave state. Nonetheless, a Maine law prohibiting INTERRACIAL MARRIAGE existed between 1821 and 1883.

Notable Maine African Americans include Pauline HOPKINS (an editor, novelist, and playwright in the late nineteenth century), John Brown RUSSWURM (one of the first African Americans to graduate from an American college—Bowdoin, in 1826—and a proponent of emigration to LIBERIA), James HEALY (the first African American bishop), and William Burney (in 1988, the first African American mayor in Maine).

Two prominent white figures in the antislavery movement were from Maine: Harriet Beecher Stowe (author of UNCLE TOM'S CABIN, 1852) and Elijah LOVEJOY, an abolitionist publisher martyred for his beliefs in 1837.

—*Thomas L. Erskine*

Malcolm X (Malcolm Little; Muslim name, el-Hajj Malik el-Shabazz; May 19, 1925, Omaha, Nebraska—February 21, 1965, New York, New York): Political activist and religious leader. Malcolm X was a charismatic spokesman during the 1950's and early 1960's for the NATION OF ISLAM, a black separatist religious group, also known as the Black Muslims, under the leadership of Elijah MUHAMMAD.

Malcolm X differed sharply from most CIVIL RIGHTS leaders of his time, notably Martin Luther KING, Jr., who favored integration with whites and nonviolent protest as means for African Americans to gain equal rights. As a Black Muslim minister, Malcolm believed that integration was not an effective route to empowerment. To save themselves, he contended, African Americans needed their own land; they needed to separate from, not integrate into, what Malcolm viewed as a deteriorating and immoral society.

Malcolm's physical energy was matched by his quick mind and incisive wit. He traveled around the country speaking on behalf of the Nation of Islam. Some labeled him a radical and a firebrand, but many who heard his spellbinding oratory, especially African Americans who had become demoralized by the slow pace of racial progress, felt that Malcolm understood and spoke the truth about American problems with race. Through his eloquent speeches, he gave them a newfound sense of pride and won for them a measure of respect. Membership in the Nation of Islam increased dramatically during Malcolm's ministry; one estimate holds that membership increased from four hundred to forty thousand.

Early Life

Malcolm X was born Malcolm Little, the fourth child of Earl and Louisa Little. His father had had three children by a previous marriage. When Malcolm later became a member of the Nation of Islam, he changed his name from Little to the Muslim "X" as a rejection, he believed, of a "slave" name and as a symbol of a lost African name that he was destined never to learn.

Malcolm was tall and light-complexioned, with reddish-brown hair and skin, characteristics he inherited from his mother, who was born in Grenada of a black mother and a Scottish father. Young Malcolm was in awe of his dark-complexioned, solidly built father, who at various times was a BAPTIST preacher, construction worker, businessman, and local organizer for Marcus GARVEY'S UNIVERSAL NEGRO IMPROVEMENT ASSOCIATION (UNIA).

When Malcolm was six years old, his father was found mangled and barely conscious near Lansing, MICHIGAN, lying in a pool of blood beside the tracks of a trolley. He died a few hours later. Malcolm became convinced that his father, like three of his father's brothers, had been murdered by white men. Malcolm's mother then fell victim to the physical and psychological strain of having to provide for eight children alone, and she had to be institutionalized. State workers placed some of the children with relatives and friends; others were placed in foster homes. Malcolm never forgave the state workers for splitting up his family.

Burglary and Prison Experiences

Shortly before his twenty-first birthday, having lived alternately in foster homes and with relatives and then having survived a profligate life on the streets of HARLEM and Boston, Malcolm was arrested for burglary. He and a

Formal portrait of Malcolm X while he was a spokesperson for the Nation of Islam. *(AP/Wide World Photos)*

black friend named Shorty were given concurrent eight-to-ten-year sentences. In prison, Malcolm discovered the religious teachings of Elijah Muhammad, which, he later wrote, completely transformed his life.

Many who later bore witness to Malcolm's graceful manner and polished manner of speaking were surprised to learn that he possessed no university degrees. His formal education, in fact, had stopped at the eighth grade. In prison, he improved his vocabulary by arduously handwriting every word in the dictionary. Malcolm further honed his skills by reading voraciously.

Following his release from prison in 1952, Malcolm intensified his studies with the Black Muslims. Two years later, he was appointed a minister by Muhammad. In 1958 Malcolm married Betty Saunders. The couple had four children.

Black Muslim Ministry

Faithful to the teachings of his mentor, Elijah Muhammad, Malcolm preached that politicians, civil rights workers, and sociologists had all failed to solve America's intractable racial problems. Much as Marcus Garvey had earlier, the Nation of Islam asserted that integration was little more than a fraud: White "devils" had no true intentions of uniting with African Americans. Elijah Muhammad demanded that a separate territory be granted by the U.S. government for the establishment of an all-black society in reparation for SLAVERY and the subsequent exploitation of African Americans.

In the early 1960's, the separatist position taken by the Black Muslims put them at odds with mainstream civil rights groups such as the NATIONAL ASSOCIATION FOR THE ADVANCEMENT OF COLORED PEOPLE (NAACP), led by Roy WILKINS, the NATIONAL URBAN LEAGUE, led by Whitney M. YOUNG, Jr., and the SOUTHERN CHRISTIAN LEADERSHIP CONFERENCE (SCLC), headed by King. To fight discrimination in housing, employment, and education and to end segregation in public facilities, these organizations advocated action in the form of boycotts, FREEDOM RIDES, SIT-INS, and protest marches. The Black Muslims, on the other hand, asked why any proud African American would beg to be integrated with former slaveholders. Furthermore, the Black Muslims argued, white people were not truly interested in integration and equality—they would accept only a token form of integration.

The Nation of Islam taught that the original race of humans was black and that this race had built a glorious civilization with a flourishing culture. Central to Black Muslim teachings was the concept that the white race had been created centuries ago by a defiant black scientist through the use of recessive gene structure. Further, the, Nation of Islam taught that whites had fashioned the religion of Christianity to deceive, subjugate, and enslave people of color around the world. It was now time for blacks to resist the "brainwashing" attempts of the white race, to return to their true religion, Islam, and to claim their rightful heritage.

Malcolm was in great demand as a public speaker. Whether appearing on television shows or in forums at universities, Malcolm passionately voiced the hopes and frustrations of black Americans. Many listeners were deeply moved by his words.

Break with Elijah Muhammad

Shortly after the assassination of President John F. Kennedy on November 22, 1963, Elijah Muhammad summoned Malcolm to speak at the Nation of Islam's Manhattan Center in New York. At the conclusion of his speech, responding to a question, Malcolm commented on the Kennedy assassination: He said that the assassination was a case of "the chickens coming home to roost."

Malcolm believed that the shooting of the president was proof that hatred in some whites went beyond the need to murder blacks. Such hatred, he said, had become so uncontrolled that it had brought down the nation's commander in chief. Malcolm likened the killing to the deaths of civil rights leader Medgar EVERS and African political leader Patrice Lumumba. His comments about the assassination made instant headlines; they outraged many people and provoked a storm of controversy.

Elijah Muhammad, stating that Malcolm's remarks were "ill-timed," officially silenced Malcolm for ninety days. Malcolm later surmised that his own popularity and—perhaps even more important—his recent knowledge of ethical misconduct by Elijah Muhammad had irreparably strained the relationship between the two leaders.

Mecca and Beyond

Shortly thereafter, Malcolm broke from Muhammad and founded the independent Muslim Mosque. Aware of the reaction he would invoke by publicly divorcing himself from the powerful Elijah Muhammad, and needing to prepare himself for his new responsibilities, Malcolm decided to make his first religious pilgrimage, or *hajj*, to the Muslim holy city of Mecca, in Saudi Arabia. The journey proved to be a revelation. He was surprised to learn that orthodox Muslim practices varied greatly with what Elijah Muhammad had taught. Malcolm encountered people with white complexions who treated him like a brother in the faith. No longer, for him, were all people with white skin or blue eyes necessarily devils. The journey to Mecca, he wrote, was "the start of a radical alteration in my whole outlook about 'white' men."

The color-blindness of the Muslim world of Mecca led Malcolm to see Islam as the antidote for America's festering racial problems. Malcolm's devotion to Islam was underscored by the signature that he affixed to a letter he wrote back to the United States and made available to the American press. It contained his new Islamic name: "El-Hajj el-Shabazz (Malcolm X)."

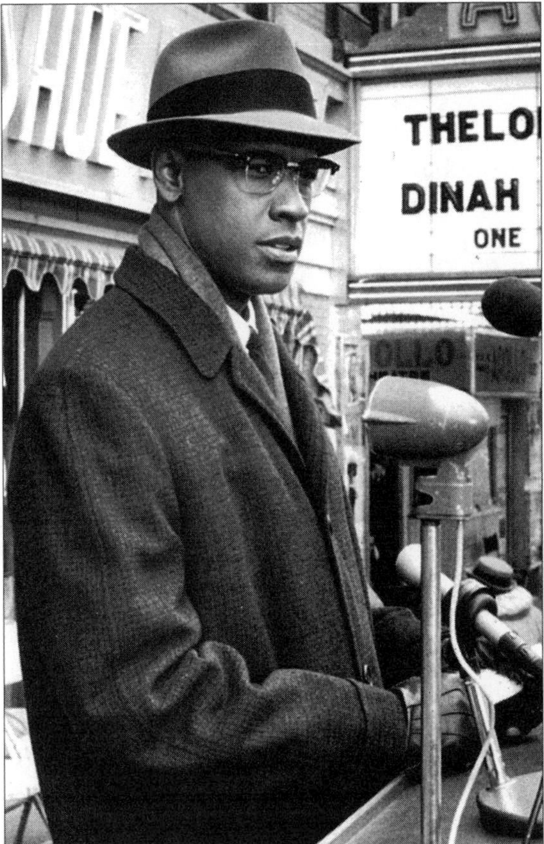

In 1992 actor Denzel Washington played Malcolm X in Spike Lee's film of the same title. *(Museum of Modern Art, Film Stills Archive)*

Following his return to the United States, Malcolm modified his stance on racial separatism. He sought to expand his concern for civil rights to an interest in human rights, and he began to consider the United Nations, rather than the American courts, to be the most appropriate venue for seeking redress. He also sought to explore areas of commonality between African Americans and their African relatives.

Malcolm did not live long enough to make many steps toward his new goals, however. An assassin's bullets ended his life on February 21, 1965, in the Audubon Ballroom in NEW

York City. Malcolm X's memoirs, entitled *The Autobiography of Malcolm X*, written with Alex Haley, were published later that same year. The work stands as one of the most memorable autobiographies in American literature.

—*James E. Walton*

See also: Fard, Wallace D.; Farrakhan, Louis Abdul; Shabazz, Betty.

Suggested Readings:

Bloom, Harold, ed. *Alex Haley and Malcolm X's "The Autobiography of Malcolm X."* New York: Chelsea House, 1996.

Carson, Clayborne, David Gallen, and Spike Lee. *Malcolm X: The FBI File*. New York: Carroll & Graf, 1991.

Collins, Rodnell P., and Peter A. Bailey. *Seventh Child: A Family Memoir of Malcolm X*. Secaucus, N.J.: Birch Lane Press, 1998.

DeCaro, Louis A. *Malcolm and the Cross: The Nation of Islam, Malcolm X, and Christianity*. New York: New York University Press, 1998.

_______. *On the Side of My People: A Religious Life of Malcolm X*. New York: New York University Press, 1996.

Gallen, David, ed. *Malcolm A to X: The Man and His Ideas*. New York: Carroll & Graf, 1992.

Karim, Benjamin, David Gallen, and Peter Skutches. *Remembering Malcolm: The Story of Malcolm X from Inside the Muslim Mosque by His Assistant Minister Benjamin Karim*. New York: Carroll & Graf, 1992.

Malcolm X with Alex Haley. *The Autobiography of Malcolm X*. New York: Ballantine Books, 1965.

Myers, Walter D. *Malcolm X: By Any Means Necessary, a Biography*. New York: Scholastic, 1993.

Perry, Bruce. *Malcolm: The Life of a Man Who Changed Black America*. Barrytown, N.Y.: Station Hill Press, 1991.

Sales, William W., Jr. *From Civil Rights to Black Liberation: Malcolm X and the Organization of Afro-American Unity*. Boston: South End Press, 1994.

Manpower programs: Programs aimed at finding jobs for participants or improving their work skills. The federal Manpower Development and Training Act (MDTA) was passed in 1962 to train the unemployed and the underemployed. It was established because of a national concern that, despite a general high level of prosperity, too many people were unemployed. When experience under MDTA programs revealed that the unemployed often lacked literacy skills required for successful training, the MDTA was amended in 1963 to include basic education skills as part of the training process. Also included as part of this program was a relocation allowance for the acquisition of a new job. The MDTA program provided both on-the-job training and training in the skills needed to secure a job.

In 1968 priority was given to the development of Manpower Training Skills Centers, which served as centralized locations for vocational training and other support skills. This moved the instructional training out of vocational schools. About 230,000 trainees were enrolled in the program in 1966, and about 267,000 were enrolled in 1973. Between 1966 and 1973, 2.3 million persons were enrolled in the program. Funding for this program rose from $70 million in 1963 to $400 million by the mid-1970's. The MDTA was phased out in the early 1980's. African Americans were a significant proportion of program participants. During the late 1960's, more than 40 percent of the participants in New York City were black.

Although a considerable effort was placed on the training of the disadvantaged, the programs also were geared toward resolving the unemployment problem in the long run. Evaluations of the effectiveness of the MDTA programs are mixed. One series of studies reported that the training program resulted in only a small annual increase in the participants' income. Another set of studies suggested that the MDTA was effective, but that white Americans fared better than African Americans. A third set of studies reported that success under MDTA was related to the background of participants. Women who received AID TO FAMILIES WITH DEPENDENT CHILDREN (AFDC) grants and recovering drug addicts fared better under this program than those with criminal records and high school dropouts. This was because the first two groups needed only motivation, while the latter two required more intensive training.

MDTA is probably the best known of the manpower programs. The COMPREHENSIVE EMPLOYMENT AND TRAINING ACT (CETA) OF 1973 allocated funds to communities, which then provided classroom and on-the-job training. The Job Training Partnership Act (1982) replaced CETA with training programs focused on the private sector. Far more of the money under this act was spent on direct training costs.

Manumission: Legal release of a person from SLAVERY. Manumission was generally a private matter, with owners freeing slaves as a reward for meritorious or faithful service. Many colonies, and later states, passed laws regulating manumission. In 1722 SOUTH CAROLINA ordered all freed slaves to leave the state. Northern laws frequently required former owners to post bonds and to bear responsibility for the support of their former slaves. By 1860 several southern states, afraid of insurrections, had outlawed manumission.
See also: Free blacks; Slave resistance.

Marable, Manning (b. May 13, 1950, Dayton, Ohio): Educator and author. Both a scholar in the field of political economy and a poet, Marable won the Third and Fourth International Poetry Prizes from Triton College (1976 and 1977). His books include *From the Grassroots: Essays Toward Afro-American Liberation* (1980), *How Capitalism Underdeveloped Black America: Problems in Race, Political Economy, and Society* (1983), *Race, Reform and Rebellion: The Second Reconstruction in Black America, 1945-1990* (1991), *Beyond Black and White: Transforming African-American Politics* (1995), *Black Liberation in Conservative America* (1997), and *Black Leadership* (1998).

Marable graduated from Earlham College (1971), the University of Wisconsin at Madison (M.A., 1972), and the University of Maryland (Ph.D., 1976). He became an associate professor of political economy at TUSKEGEE INSTITUTE in 1976. In 1979 he became an associate professor of political economy and a senior research fellow at the Africana Studies and Research Center at Cornell University. He moved in 1982 to FISK UNIVERSITY, where he was professor of history and economics as well as director of the Race Relations Institute. Marable also served as executive director of Black Research Associates, was on the executive committee of the National Black Political Assembly, and served as national vice chair of the Democratic Socialists of America.

Marchbanks, Vance Hunter (1905, Fort Washikie, Wyoming—1973): Physician and military officer. Marchbanks received his bachelor's degree from the University of Arizona in 1931 and went on to earn an M.D. from HOWARD UNIVERSITY in 1937. He began his career in MEDICINE on the medical staff of the Veterans Administration hospital in Tuskegee, ALABAMA.

Marchbanks joined the Air Force in 1941 as a member of the TUSKEGEE AIRMEN. Marchbanks was awarded the Bronze Star for his service during WORLD WAR II and later served during the KOREAN WAR. He went on to achieve the rank of colonel and the rating of chief flight surgeon through extensive flight experience and medical research. His work contributed significantly to the Air Force's un-

derstanding of flight fatigue. Marchbanks was assigned to the National Aeronautics and Space Administration (NASA) as part of its Project Mercury program from 1960 to 1963. He served as an aeromedical monitor in the first manned space flights and was responsible for tracking readings from sensor devices on John Glenn during the latter's 1962 orbital mission on *Friendship 7*.
See also: Health care professionals; Military.

March on Washington: On August 28, 1963, more than two hundred thousand demonstrators marched through WASHINGTON, D.C., to lobby Congress to pass CIVIL RIGHTS legislation and to celebrate the centennial of the EMANCIPATION PROCLAMATION. For years, African American leaders had looked toward the centennial; the NATIONAL ASSOCIATION FOR THE ADVANCEMENT OF COLORED PEOPLE (NAACP) had long used the slogan "Free by '63." The African American campaign for freedom drew recognition from many quarters.

Governor Nelson Rockefeller of New York was in attendance on September 22, 1962, when his state opened an exhibit of Abraham Lincoln's preliminary Emancipation Proclamation (which had been delivered on September 22, 1862). Rockefeller reminded his audience that Lincoln's vision of a nation truly fulfilling its spiritual heritage had not yet been achieved. Vice President Lyndon B. Johnson (destined to be remembered as the "civil rights president") echoed Rockefeller's sentiments in 1963 when he addressed a crowd in Gettysburg, Pennsylvania, saying "Until justice is blind, until education is unaware of race, until opportunity is unconcerned with the color of men's skins, emancipation will be a proclamation but not a fact."

As if to endorse the thoughts of such leaders as Rockefeller and Johnson, the U.S. COMMISSION ON CIVIL RIGHTS finished a study in 1963 entitled *Freedom to the Free: Century of Emancipation, 1863-1963*, a report on the history of civil rights in the United States, and delivered it to President John F. Kennedy. *Freedom to the Free* concluded that widespread discrimination and segregation still harmed the African American community. The president added his voice to the call for equal rights, saying, "Surely, in 1963, one hundred years after emancipation, it should not be necessary for any American citizen to demonstrate in the streets for an opportunity to stop at a hotel, or eat at a lunch counter."

Historical Background

Indeed, it was necessary to take to the streets. One of the major early 1960's protests occurred in BIRMINGHAM, ALABAMA, a city where all public facilities were still segregated. Called the "Johannesburg of America" by many leaders, Birmingham was home to Reverend Fred SHUTTLESWORTH, an activist in the SOUTHERN CHRISTIAN LEADERSHIP CONFERENCE (SCLC); in 1962, he demanded an end to segregation and discrimination and organized a black boycott of white merchants, a boycott that lasted for months. Even as the city suffered a local depression, whites resisted change. Police Commissioner Eugene "Bull" Connor eventually cracked down on the protesters, allowing his men to attack them with tear gas, dogs, and water hoses. Authorities arrested more than forty people, including Shuttlesworth, who quickly called for Martin Luther KING, Jr.

After arriving in Birmingham in April, King personally directed more protests. He vowed that he would stay in Birmingham until "Pharaoh lets God's people go." Televised images of peaceful protesters, including children, being beaten, gassed, and hosed by Connor's squad and by outsiders reputed to be members of the KU KLUX KLAN outraged the nation. *The New York Times* commented that the Birmingham "barbarities" were "revoltingly reminiscent of totalitarian excesses." Senator Wayne Morse of Oregon added that the beatings would even "disgrace a Union of South Africa or a Portuguese Angola."

Meanwhile, Connor called the demonstrators "sons of bitches," and King announced that he was at war with Birmingham and its segregation. Relief came only after President Kennedy applied political pressure. City authorities and merchants agreed to desegregate, adopt nondiscriminatory hiring practices, and release all demonstrators.

Murder of Medgar Evers

Yet another of the tragedies of the early 1960's was the murder of Medgar EVERS, a veteran of WORLD WAR II who had helped to defeat racist Nazi Germany and then come home to racist America. Serving as the president of the MISSISSIPPI branch of the NAACP, Evers organized a massive demonstration in Jackson, another segregated southern city. On June 12, 1963, Evers was gunned down by an unknown assailant. In the next ten weeks, hundreds of racial demonstrations occurred in the United States. Outraged and touched by Evers's death, Kennedy sent his civil rights bill to Congress on the day of Evers's funeral.

The protests, the "Birminghams," the murders, Kennedy's final response—all combined to pressure Congress, and several African American leaders believed that a "March on

In July, 1963, leaders of the largest civil rights organizations met in New York City to plan the March on Washington. From left to right: John Lewis (SNCC), Whitney Young (Urban League), A. Philip Randolph (Negro American Labor Council), Martin Luther King, Jr. (SCLC), James Farmer (CORE), and Roy Wilkins (NAACP). *(AP/Wide World Photos)*

Washington" might add yet more pressure, perhaps enough to push the civil rights bill through Congress.

The March

Key organizers of the march included Bayard Rustin, its principal architect, a moderate socialist; Asa Philip Randolph, a longtime African American labor leader and liberal socialist reformer; Martin Luther King, Jr., the Civil Rights movement's greatest national spokesperson; Roy Wilkins, the head of the NAACP; Walter Reuther, a powerful white labor leader; and a host of others. Further, various organizations and groups endorsed the march, including the National Council of Churches, the American Jewish Congress, the American Federation of Labor-Congress of Industrial Organizations (AFL-CIO), and the National Congress of Catholics for Interracial Justice.

On the day of the march, between 200,000 and 250,000 people, including almost 50,000 whites, assembled at the Washington Monument and marched to the Lincoln Memorial. March participants included such notable African Americans as Whitney Young of the National Urban League and John Lewis of the Student Nonviolent Coordinating Committee (SNCC). White leaders included Rabbi Joachim Prinz and fifteen U.S. senators, led by Hubert H. Humphrey of Minnesota and Edward Kennedy of Massachusetts. One of the major leaders of the early Civil Rights movement, however, was notably absent. W. E. B. Du Bois, embittered by his experiences, had renounced America, moved to Ghana, and joined the Communist Party. He died in Ghana on August 27, 1963, on the very eve of the March on Washington.

Although others, such as Randolph and Rustin, played major roles in organizing the march, the man who captured the nation's imagination was Martin Luther King, Jr., who seemed to be the heart of the Civil Rights movement. He accepted the nonviolent philosophy of such historic figures as Henry Da-

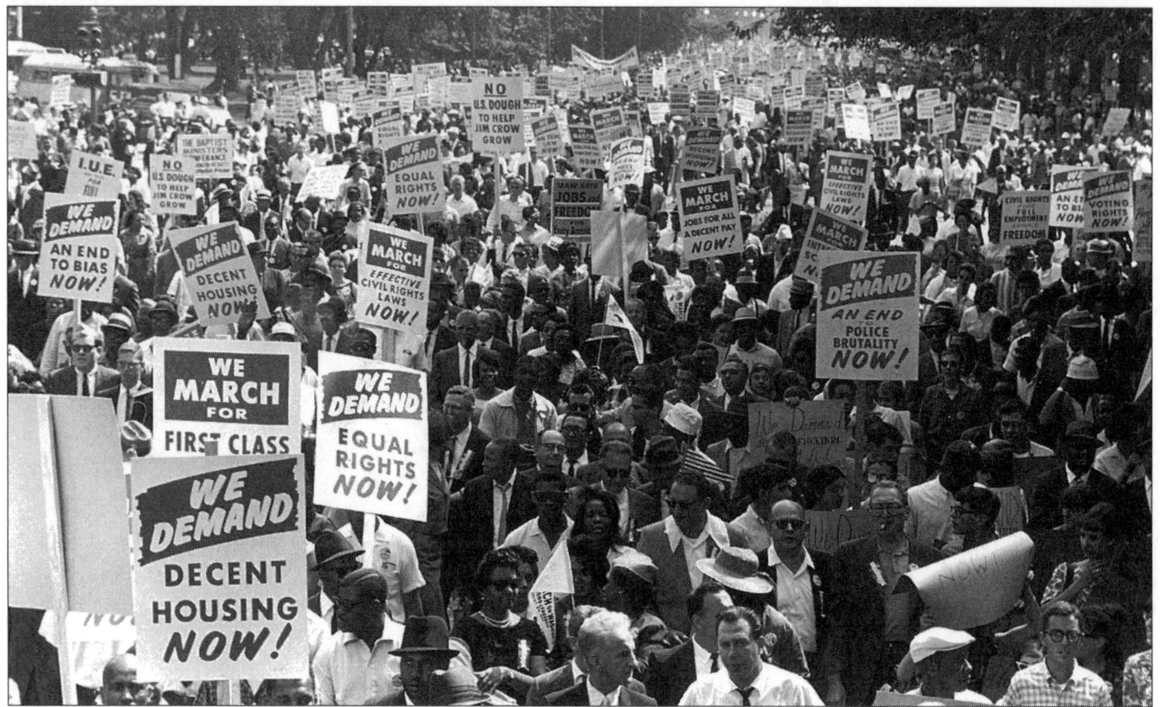

Marchers advance on the Mall on the morning of August 23, 1963. *(AP/Wide World Photos)*

vid Thoreau and Mohandas Gandhi. King believed that African Americans could successfully appeal to the consciences of white Americans and that such an appeal would eventually lead to the end of segregation and discrimination. King proclaimed that

> we will not hate you, but we cannot obey your unjust laws. Do to us what you will and we will still love you. . . . But we will soon wear you down by our capacity to suffer. And in winning our freedom, we will so appeal to your heart and conscience, that we will win you in the process.

From Mass Protest to Celebration

King was at the forefront as the march developed, and he provided the climax of the day with his famous "I Have a Dream" speech, one of the most powerful and eloquent that he ever delivered. Yet King's prominence and that of other black leaders did not hide the fact that the presence of so many whites changed the tone of the march. What Rustin and Randolph originally envisioned as a strong mass protest became instead a mass celebration among "race liberals," and some African American leaders who were going to address the crowd changed strong remarks into mellower statements. Lewis of SNCC modified his speech to expunge sentences such as:

> We will march through the South, through the heart of Dixie, the way Sherman did. We shall pursue our own "scorched earth" policy and burn Jim Crow to the ground—nonviolently.

As historian William O'Neill noted, it appeared that "everyone but racists enjoyed the march." President Kennedy met with a large group of African American leaders, opening the White House to them. Further, the national media, for the most part, praised the march. Russell Baker of *The New York Times* said that the march represented a "vast army of quiet, middle-class Americans who had come in the spirit of a church outing"; *Time* magazine hailed the march as a "triumph."

Combined with later events—some tragic, some positive—the march had a telling effect on the fate of the Kennedy administration's civil rights bill. Kennedy did not live to see the bill's passage, but after Kennedy was killed in November, 1963, Johnson, the country's new president, declared that the bill, stalled by a Senate filibuster, was the first item on his agenda. Although it took many months, Johnson supporters in the Senate broke the filibuster, and the result was the Civil Rights Act of 1964, the provisions of which helped create a true—but not complete—political, economic, and social revolution in the United States.

—*James Smallwood*

See also: Johnson administration.

"I Have a Dream"

"I have a dream that one day on the red hills of Georgia, sons of former slaves and the sons of former slaveowners will be able to sit down together at the table of brotherhood. I have a dream that my four little children will one day live in a nation where they will not be judged by the color of their skin but by the content of their character. . . . [A]nd when we allow freedom to ring, when we let it ring from every state and every city, we will be able to speed up that day when all of God's children, black men and white men, Jews and Gentiles, Protestants and Catholics, will be able to join hands and sing the words of that old Negro spiritual: 'Free at last! Free at last! Thank God almighty, we are free at last!'"

—Martin Luther King, Jr., August 28, 1963

Suggested Readings:

"Black-Led 'March on Washington' Observes Its Thirtieth Anniversary Year." *Jet* (September 13, 1993): 4-13.

Branch, Taylor. *Parting the Waters: America in the King Years, 1954-1963*. New York: Simon & Schuster, 1988.

_______. *Pillar of Fire: America in the King Years, 1963-1965*. New York: Simon & Schuster, 1998.

Forman, James. *The Making of Black Revolutionaries*. New York: Macmillan, 1972.

Garrow, David J., ed. *We Shall Overcome: The Civil Rights Movement in the United States in the 1950's and 1960's*. 3 vols. New York: Carlson, 1989.

Jackson, Jesse, and Elaine Landau. *Blacks in America: A Fight for Freedom*. New York: Julian Messner, 1973.

Pauley, Garth E. "John Lewis's 'Serious Revolution': Rhetoric, Resistance, and Revision at the March on Washington." *The Quarterly Journal of Speech* 84 (August, 1998): 320-340.

Powledge, Fred. *Free at Last? The Civil Rights Movement and the People Who Made It*. Boston: Little, Brown, 1991.

Sitkoff, Harvard. *The Struggle for Black Equality, 1954-1980*. New York: Hill & Wang, 1981.

Markham, Pigmeat (April 18, 1904, Durham, North Carolina—December 13, 1981, Bronx, New York): Comedian. Dewey "Pigmeat" Markham left home at age fourteen to perform in MINSTREL shows, carnivals, and medicine shows. He is best known for the Broadway musical *Hot Rhythm* (1930) and as the originator of the phrase, "Here come de judge," which would be popularized on the television program *Rowan and Martin's Laugh-In* (1968-1973).
See also: Comedy and humor.

Maroons: Bands of runaway slaves who gathered in wilderness areas outside slaveholding communities and often continued to resist SLAVERY by making raids on PLANTATIONS and assisting other fugitive slaves. Maroons existed in the early years of the seventeenth century and continued to exist until the end of institutionalized slavery in both North and South America.

Maroon bands were active especially in JAMAICA and HAITI. England sent troops to control the Maroons in colonial Jamaica. In Haiti, a large outlaw colony was recognized officially by the colonial government in 1784. This colony continued to participate in popular uprisings in Haiti in the late 1700's and early 1800's. Famous Maroon leaders from these regions include Cudgo (Jamaica, 1730's) and Macandal (Haiti, 1750's).

In North America, Maroons also were called "outliers." Sometimes these groups were racially mixed, including Native Americans and whites. Maroon bands, often armed, harassed and raided individual plantations, disregarded local laws in order to help other slaves escape, and provided refuge for those fugitives who chose to join them.

Maroons are best understood as part of the resistance to slavery that occurred in the Americas from slavery's earliest days. Maroon communities mostly comprised African Americans who had fled slavery, an extremely risky act in itself, rather than submit to the authority of white slaveholders. Life in Maroon communities no doubt was harsh, dangerous, and difficult, but Maroons chose this life of active resistance over one of submission on the plantations or of fleeing to safety in a nonslaveholding area. Maroons represent one of the earliest organized and political African American responses to enslavement.
See also: Slave resistance.

Marr, Carmel Carrington (b. June 23, 1923?, Brooklyn, New York): Lawyer, diplomat, and political appointee. Marr graduated from Hunter College in 1945 and received her J.D. from Columbia University Law School in 1948. After gaining experience in international law, Marr was appointed as legal adviser to the U.S. Mission to the United Nations in 1953

by President Harry S Truman. During her term, she served on a number of key committees in the General Assembly. From 1968 to 1971, Marr served as commissioner on the Human Rights Appeal Board of New York State, and from 1971 to 1986 she served on the New York State Public Service Commission. Marr became an energy consultant in 1987 and retired from legal practice.
See also: Diplomats; Legal professions.

Marsalis, Wynton (b. October 18, 1961, New Orleans, Louisiana): Jazz trumpeter and composer. At the age of eight, Marsalis already was performing in a band organized and led by New Orleans musical legend Danny Barker. Marsalis eventually obtained formal musical education at the Berkshire Music Center and the Juilliard School of Music. He debuted professionally and first came to national prominence through performances with Art Blakey's Jazz Messengers in 1980.

Marsalis then toured with musicians Herbie Hancock, Ron Carter, and Tony Williams, with whom he also made his first recordings in 1981. In 1982 he formed a quartet with his brother, saxophonist Branford Marsalis. By 1984 he had become a national force on the music scene, becoming the first musician to win Grammy Awards in both the classical and jazz categories.

By the mid-1980's, Marsalis had left "fusion," the predominant jazz style of the last twenty years, and made a commitment to reinvigorate past styles and continue the modernist revolution. In particular, Marsalis led a movement to revitalize the reputation of Louis Armstrong. Marsalis's work toward that end has been labeled positively as "neo-classic" and negatively as "nostalgic." His goal was to expand the audience for jazz by recovering the music's past audiences, some of whom gave up on the music when it became less involved in the production of what he called "beautiful melodies." On the other hand, Marsalis was critical of jazz musicians participating in the world of pop music and had a public dispute with his brother Branford over the latter's touring with the rock musician Sting.

Wynton Marsalis performing at New York City's Lincoln Center in early 1997. *(AP/Wide World Photos)*

Marsalis became the single most highly recognized jazz musician and composer of the 1980's. With his father, pianist Ellis Marsalis, and brothers Branford, Delfeayo, and Jason, he helped to create a jazz "royal family." He continued to perform in a variety of contexts—with small jazz groups, jazz orchestras, and major symphony orchestras. He also worked on the musical scores of several major Hollywood films. His outspoken views on jazz led to his being called upon often by the media to comment on the politics of African American culture.

Marshall, Paule (b. April 9, 1929, Brooklyn, New York): Novelist and short-story writer. Many of Marshall's novels and short stories

Author Paule Marshall in 1991. *(AP/Wide World Photos)*

portray a young woman growing up within the West Indian African American community and draw on the culture of Barbados and the West Indies. Her novels include *Brown Girl, Brownstones* (1959), *Praisesong for the Widow* (1983), and *Daughters* (1991). Marshall lectured on African American literature at several major universities.

Marshall, Thurgood (July 2, 1908, Baltimore, Maryland—January 24, 1993, Bethesda, Maryland): Civil rights attorney and U.S. Supreme Court justice. In 1930 Thurgood Marshall entered Howard University's law school in Washington, D.C. Howard was not his initial choice; he had planned to attend the University of Maryland, but the institution's law school did not admit African Americans.

Marshall's mentor, Charles Hamilton Houston, had arrived at Howard in 1924 to teach in the school's evening program. The law school elevated Houston to the post of dean in 1929, and he quickly transformed the fledgling law school into a full-time program with special courses in civil rights law. In this setting, Marshall learned that law could be used as a vehicle for social change and that an African American lawyer had a special obligation to participate in the civil rights struggle. (Houston called such participation "social engineering.") Marshall applied these ideas diligently and was largely responsible for the U.S. Supreme Court's Brown v. Board of Education (1954) decision, which launched the dismantling of legal segregation in the United States. However, although *Brown* was a landmark case, winning that case was not Marshall's greatest achievement. In 1967 President Lyndon B. Johnson appointed Marshall as an associate justice of the U.S. Supreme Court.

Background

William C. Marshall, Thurgood's father, worked as a steward at the prestigious Gibson Island Country Club on Chesapeake Bay. His mother, Norma, was an elementary school teacher. The Marshalls were a proud family, and the parents taught their children racial pride. Thurgood, for example, learned his family's legacy and learned that his great-grandfather was a native-born African enslaved and brought to the United States.

Thurgood attended Lincoln University in Oxford, Pennsylvania, with ambitions to study dentistry. He was a precocious student who early recognized that he would pursue a professional career. He quickly became well known on campus for his strong intellect and his ability to remember details. He was also known for his wit, and he pulled more than a few pranks during his undergraduate days. His biology professor was not always amused by such behavior, and because of this conflict, Thurgood decided on a different course of study. A skilled debater, he decided to study law. Segregation limited his choice of law schools; ultimately, he decided on Howard University, where he met Houston.

Marshall's association with Charles Hamilton Houston was a seminal experience. Houston, a Harvard graduate and specialist in constitutional law, had become renowned for his ability as a litigant and for his philosophy of law. He believed that law could be applied to the race problem, and he influenced a generation of African American lawyers to participate in civil rights reform. The NATIONAL ASSOCIATION FOR THE ADVANCEMENT OF COLORED PEOPLE (NAACP), founded in 1909, had early recognized the value of law in the struggle for racial justice, and it called upon Houston to participate in ongoing litigation. Ultimately, Houston rose to become special counsel of the NAACP's Legal Defense Fund. Marshall, his star pupil, became his assistant in 1933.

Precedents Upholding Segregation

Marshall, Houston, and the NAACP had a formidable task. American custom and law had long recognized the validity of segregation. The Supreme Court had made its position clear in PLESSY V. FERGUSON (1896), when it approved segregation in the states. After RECONSTRUCTION, southern states had adopted JIM CROW LAWS that established separate facilities for blacks and whites. Homer Plessy, a Louisiana traveler, tested this policy when he boarded a railroad car reserved for whites. After the conductor removed him from the coach on account of his race, Plessy sued, claiming that the railroad company had violated his civil rights. The Supreme Court denied him relief; instead, it acknowledged the legality of "SEPARATE BUT EQUAL" treatment. With this endorsement, the United States, especially the South, expanded racial separation. By the time Marshall joined the NAACP staff, legal segre-

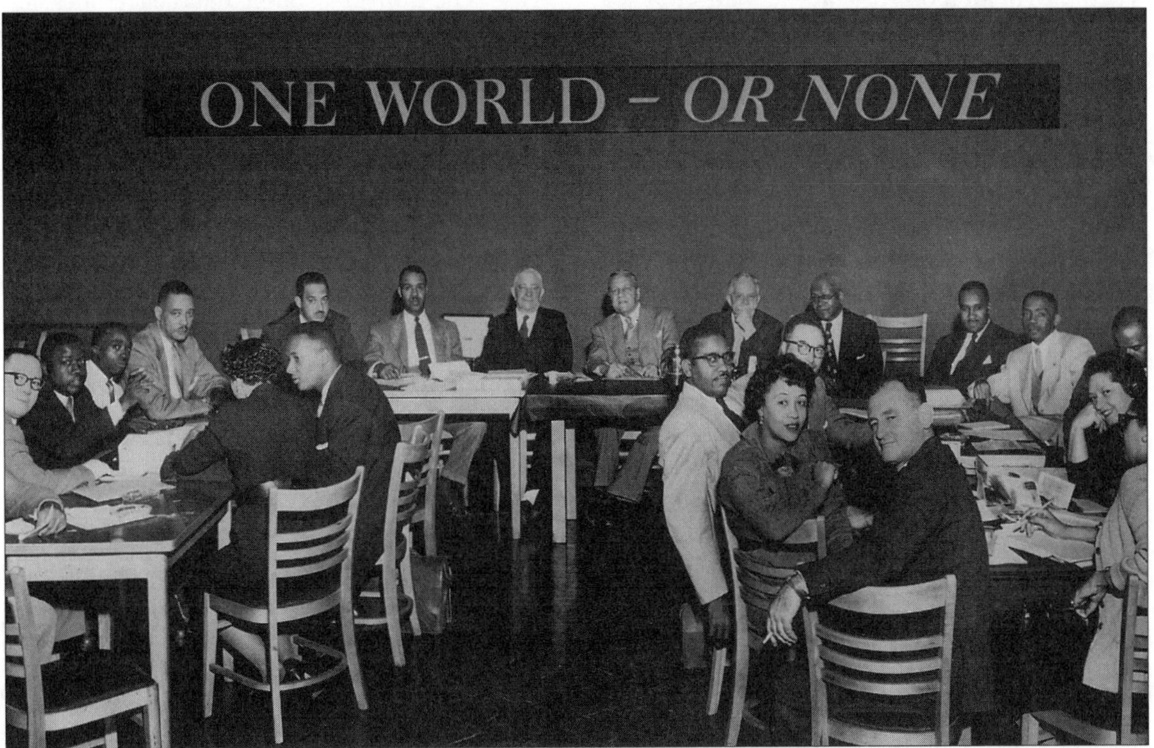

Thurgood Marshall (at left end of rear table) at an executive meeting of the NAACP in 1963; seated next to him is Roy Wilkins. *(Library of Congress)*

gation had become a fact of life. Nevertheless, the segregation law itself provided the NAACP with a basis for challenging the policy. Segregated facilities were never "equal," and in theory, facilities that failed to meet standards set forth in the *Plessy* decision violated the equal protection clause of the FOURTEENTH AMENDMENT. The NAACP recognized this area of vulnerability and launched a campaign against segregation.

Law School Admissions Cases

Marshall participated in his first major case in 1935. The case had special meaning for him because it involved the law school at the University of Maryland, which had denied him admission a few years earlier. Donald Murray, a Baltimore resident, had also been turned away by the university. Murray, a graduate of Amherst College, had met all the requirements for admission—except race. The university provided out-of-state scholarships for African Americans interested in legal studies. Murray refused its offer and appealed to the NAACP for advice. Marshall, joined by Houston and William I. Gosnell, argued that the university had violated the equal protection clause of the Fourteenth Amendment. The Maryland trial court agreed and issued a writ compelling the university to admit Murray. The state court of appeals upheld the ruling, and Murray enrolled at the law school in 1935.

The NAACP elevated Marshall to special counsel in 1938, and he went on to participate in a series of cases aimed at desegregating professional schools. Lloyd Lionel Gaines presented the NAACP lawyers an opportunity to test the racial policy of the University of Missouri. Gaines wanted to attend law school at the University of Missouri, but the university did not admit black students. The NAACP sued on his behalf in 1936. The Supreme Court upheld its ruling in the Murray case and ordered the school to admit Gaines or, at least, to provide him the same opportunity to study law as the state extended to whites. Instead of admitting Gaines, the state appropriated money to construct an all-black law school. Marshall and the NAACP staff recognized the opportunity to challenge the "equal" nature of school, which was hurriedly established in order to evade desegregation. Before they could try this issue in court, though, Gaines disappeared.

More than ten years elapsed before the NAACP could test the action of Missouri in the Gaines case. The case of SWEATT V. PAINTER (1950) provided such an opportunity. The University of Texas Law School refused to admit a black applicant solely on the basis of race. Once litigation began, the state established a law school, hoping to satisfy the Supreme Court. In previous opinions, the Court had seemed willing to uphold the *Plessy* rule, so long as a state satisfied the equal protection clause, but the Court rejected this notion in the *Sweatt* case. The Court reasoned that the facilities, faculty, and standing of a law school specifically established to educate African Americans would not provide the students with an education equal to the training available to whites.

Landmark Ruling

Although Marshall had successfully litigated landmark cases before 1950, his most famous was the 1954 *Brown v. Board of Education* case. The NAACP had deliberately pursued desegregation in professional schools rather than in public schools, believing that southern whites would more willingly accept the casual mixing of a relatively few adults than that of many children. In the fall of 1952, a class-action suit came before the Supreme Court. Marshall, aided by a battery of lawyers and scholars, asked the Court to void the separate-but-equal doctrine. The Court, under Chief Justice Earl Warren's leadership, announced in a unanimous decision that segregation was inherently unequal. The Court ordered desegregation with "all deliberate speed."

Judicial Appointments

In 1961 President John Kennedy appointed Marshall to the U.S. Court of Appeals, Second Circuit, where he served until 1965. President Lyndon Johnson then appointed him U.S. solicitor general. One year later, Johnson invited Marshall to the White House to give a talk on civil rights. Marshall expressed his strong faith in the United States and insisted that law could be used to further social reform. The president agreed, and in 1967 Johnson nominated Marshall to fill a vacancy on the Supreme Court.

Thurgood Marshall (left) conferring with staff attorneys during his tenure as solicitor general in 1965. *(AP/Wide World Photos)*

Marshall had impeccable credentials. He had a superior knowledge of constitutional law; out of the thirty-two cases he had argued before the Supreme Court, he had won twenty-nine. Few Americans could deny his preparation. A few senators from the South opposed his nomination nonetheless. Senators Strom Thurmond and Robert Byrd argued that Marshall would be an activist justice, and they attempted to abort his nomination. During the confirmation hearings, Republican senators spent hours on trivial questions. They questioned Marshall about historic figures such as Congressman John Bingham, who had supported constitutional reform after the Civil War, made him explain the basis for the Civil Rights Act of 1866, and asked him about the author of the Thirteenth Amendment. After Marshall's ordeal, a few members of the Judiciary Committee admitted that his had been the most searching examination ever conducted by the committee. On August 30, the Senate confirmed his nomination by a vote of sixty-nine to eleven.

In his years on the Court, Marshall wrote many significant decisions as well as a number of important dissenting opinions. He wrote decisions regarding federal jurisdiction, antitrust law, Native American rights, and, most important, constitutional law. His majority opinions included *Bounds v. Smith* (1977); *Stanley v. Georgia* (1969), a First Amendment case that upheld one's right to possess pornography in one's own home; and *Police Department of Chicago v. Mosley* (1972), which held that it was unconstitutional for government to favor some types of speech over others.

Noteworthy dissents included *Dandridge v. Williams* (1970) and a lengthy dissent in *San Antonio School District v. Rodriguez* (1973) in which he argued against allowing unequal school funding for urban and suburban schools. One of Marshall's crusades was his consistent opposition to capital punishment, beginning with his dissent in *Gregg v. Georgia*

Justice Thurgood Marshall. *(Collection of the Supreme Court of the United States)*

(1976). Marshall's propensity for writing powerful dissenting opinions eventually earned him the nickname "great dissenter."

As the Court's lone black justice during his tenure, Marshall served with distinction, earning a reputation as a skillful jurist with a particular concern for the rights of the poor and the disadvantaged. Marshall retired from the Court in 1991 at the age of eighty-three.

—Stephen Middleton

See also: Constitution, U.S.; Judges.

Suggested Readings:

Ball, Howard. *A Defiant Life: Thurgood Marshall and the Persistence of Racism in America.* New York: Crown, 1998.

Bass, Jack, and Walter Deveries. *The Transformation of Southern Politics: Social Change and Political Consequences Since 1945.* New York: Basic Books, 1976.

Davis, Michael D., and Hunter R. Clark. *Thurgood Marshall: Warrior at the Bar, Rebel on the Bench.* New York: Carol, 1992.

Friedman, Leon, and Fred L. Israel, eds. *The Justices of the United States Supreme Court, 1789-1969.* New York: Chelsea House, 1969.

Goldman, Roger. *Thurgood Marshall: Justice for All.* New York: Carrol & Graf, 1992.

Harley, Sharon, Stephen Middleton, and Charlotte M. Stokes. *The African American Experience: A History.* Englewood Cliffs, N.J.: Globe Book Company, 1992.

Tushnet, Mark V. *Making Civil Rights Law: 1936-1961.* New York: Oxford University Thurgood Marshall and the Supreme Court, Press, 1994.

_______. *Making Constitutional Law: Thurgood Marshall and the Supreme Court, 1961-1991.* New York: Oxford University Press, 1997.

Williams, Juan. *Thurgood Marshall: American Revolutionary.* New York: Times Books, 1998.

Martha and the Vandellas: Female vocal trio. Martha and the Vandellas drew on African American gospel music and blues traditions to make some of the most popular dance records of the 1960's. Utilizing the Motown formula of simple songs with constant refrains, an emphatic bass beat, and the call-and-response mode of gospel music, they popularized hits that helped make the Motown corporation one of the most successful independent recording ventures in history.

Martha Reeves, Annette Sterling, and Rosalind Ashford sang as the Del-Phis in high school and cut one early single on Check-Mate Records. In the 1960's, when Reeves was a secretary at Motown Records in Detroit, the three friends served as backup vocalists in a Motown recording session for singer Marvin Gaye. As a result, they landed their own Motown contract and released "Heat Wave" (1963) as Martha and the Vandellas. The song, with its brassy sound and nonstop percussion, earned the number four spot on the pop charts and sold more than a million copies.

The name "Vandellas" may be a composite of Detroit's Van Dyke Street and the name of Reeves's favorite singer, Della Reese. Some rock-and-roll historians claim that it derives from "vandal," since Martha and the Vandellas easily stole the spotlight from other musical artists. In any case, membership in the two-person Vandellas changed over time. Betty Kelly, Sandra Tilley, and Lois Reeves (Martha's younger sister) sang as Vandellas, complementing Reeves's earthy, flamboyant singing style.

Conceived as an antidote to summer violence in America's inner cities, Martha and the Vandellas' greatest hit was a million seller entitled "Dancing in the Streets" (1964). Their other popular tunes include "Nowhere to Run" (1965), "I'm Ready for Love" (1966), "Jimmy Mack" (1967), and "Honey Chile" (1967). Martha and the Vandellas gave their farewell performance on December 21, 1972, in Detroit. For a while, Reeves performed solo and then worked as an actor, but she never again achieved the commercial success she had enjoyed with the Vandellas.

Martin, Sallie (November 20, 1896, Pittfield, Georgia—June 18, 1988, Chicago, Illinois): Gospel music singer. Martin's father died when she was very young, and she was raised by her mother and grandparents. As a child, she traveled with her mother, who sang in various churches. When her mother died, Martin left school, in the eighth grade. She moved to Atlanta and joined the Fire Baptized Holiness Church in 1916, singing in the choir. She was married and had a son. The family moved first to Cleveland, Ohio, and later to Chicago.

On February 7, 1932, Martin joined Thomas A. Dorsey's choir at the Ebenezer Baptist Church in Atlanta, Georgia. In that year, she helped Dorsey organize the National Convention of Gospel Choirs and Choruses. A year later, Dorsey assigned solos to her. Their association developed into a professional relationship that lasted for more than thirty years, as Martin traveled throughout the South and Midwest performing Dorsey's compositions. They both set up choruses in various major cities and sponsored performances of young singers such as Mahalia Jackson and Roberta Martin (no relation). Martin visited Philadelphia in 1937 and engaged the Clara Ward Singers in performances of Dorsey's works. She also traveled to Los Angeles, where she organized choral groups and performed at the Angelus Temple of famed evangelist Aimee Semple McPherson.

In 1940 Martin left Dorsey's group and toured for a while as a soloist, with Ruth Jones (later known as Dinah Washington) as her accompanist. Later, she collaborated with Roberta Martin in establishing the short-lived Martin and Martin Gospel Singers. After that, she formed the Sallie Martin Singers. Following the suggestion of the Reverend Clarence Cobb of the First Church of Deliverance in Chicago, Martin entered a business venture with Kenneth Morris, a pianist and a member of Cobb's church, to form the Martin and Morris Publishing Company, in 1940. In this partnership, Martin took advantage of the contacts she had made during her extensive travels. She ran the business while Morris wrote music. The Sallie Martin Singers limited their performances to the works and publications of Martin and Morris songs. They toured widely and made several recordings, including the well-known "Just for a Closer Walk with Thee" and "Dig a Little Deeper." The group visited Los Angeles in 1944 and appeared in radio and television performances with the choir of J. Earle Hines of the St. Paul Baptist Church.

Martin retired her group in the mid-1950's, after touring the United States and Europe. She was a guest at the independence ceremonies in Nigeria in 1960. Following this, she actively provided financial support and paid personal visits to a mission in midwestern Nigeria. Although she retired in 1970, she gave occasional performances. In 1979 she performed with Marion Williams in a program, "Gospel Caravan," in Paris.

On January 14, 1989, local skinheads marched through Pulaski, Tennessee, to protest the celebration of King's birthday as bystanders mocked their Nazi salute. *(AP/Wide World Photos)*

Martin, Tony (b. February 21, 1942, Port-of- Spain, Trinidad and Tobago): Educator. Born in TRINIDAD, Martin received his higher education in Great Britain and the United States, where he earned master's and doctoral degrees from Michigan State University. He also qualified as a barrister in Britain and Trinidad. After teaching in Trinidad and several American universities, he became a full professor at Wellesley College in 1977. He also served as the chair of the college's African studies department (1979-).

Martin's research and writings have focused on PAN-AFRICANISM, and he has been especially prolific in publishing about Marcus GARVEY and the UNIVERSAL NEGRO IMPROVEMENT ASSOCIATION. His books include *Race First: The Ideological and Organizational Struggles of Marcus Garvey and the Universal Negro Improvement Association* (1976), *Literary Garveyism: Garvey, Black Arts, and the Harlem Renaissance* (1983), and *Amy Ashwood Garvey: Pan-Africanist, Feminist and Wife Number One* (1996). His edited works include *The Poetical Works of Marcus Garvey* (1983) and *African Fundamentalism: A Literary Anthology of the Garvey Movement* (1989). He has also contributed to many scholarly journals.

Martin Luther King, Jr., Day: Legal holiday celebrated in most states on the third Monday of each January. President Ronald Reagan, on November 2, 1985, signed the bill creating this national holiday. Observance of it has not been universal, and many nongovernmental employers have failed to recognize it. The holiday in honor of the slain civil rights leader thus remained controversial even after its creation by law.

See also: Juneteenth; Kwanzaa.

Martinsville Seven: Group of seven African American men from VIRGINIA who were convicted and later executed for the rape of a white woman. This incident graphically demonstrated racial inequities in the implementation of justice that existed in the South in the early half of the twentieth century.

On the night of January 8, 1949, thirty-two-year-old Ruby Stroud Floyd, wife of a local store manager, left the black section of East

Martinsville, Virginia, and reported that she had been attacked and raped. Seven young black men were arrested and charged with attacking and raping Floyd: twenty-year-old Joe Henry Hampton; nineteen-year-old Howard Lee Hairston; twenty-year-old Booker T. Milner; nineteen-year-old Frank Hairston, Jr.; twenty-two-year-old James Clabon Taylor; twenty-one-year-old James Luther Hairston; and thirty-eight-year-old Francis Desales Grayson. The group was dubbed the "Martinsville Seven" by local journalists.

When the case came to trial, defense attorneys requested a change of venue to try the case in another jurisdiction, but their request was denied. The all-white jury convicted each of the men, and the judge gave each one the death penalty. The prisoners appealed their sentence. After hearing about the case, the National Association for the Advancement of Colored People (NAACP) provided legal counsel for these appeals.

NAACP defense attorneys did not seriously question the guilt of the defendants, choosing instead to argue that the accused men had been denied equal treatment under the law as guaranteed by the Fourteenth Amendment. As evidence that the seven defendants did not receive a fair and impartial trial, the attorneys pointed to the severity of the prisoners' sentences and to the lower court judge's failure to change the trial venue. The attorneys also pointed out that since 1908, the state of Virginia had executed forty-five African American men convicted on charges of rape, while white men with similar convictions received only jail time. Despite these challenges, the Virginia Court of Appeals upheld the convictions and sentences imposed by the lower court. Although the seven defendants appealed their case to the state supreme court, that court twice refused to hear the matter.

More than ten thousand demonstrators marched in front of the White House and the Virginia governor's mansion to protest the severity of the sentences imposed on the Martinsville Seven and demand their release. Governor John S. Battle responded "These people were not convicted because they were Negroes. Neither should they be released because they are Negroes." The attorneys lodged an appeal with the U.S. Supreme Court in early 1951, but Chief Justice Fred M. Vinson and Associate Justice Harold H. Burton refused to grant any further stays of execution. When Governor Battle refused to grant clemency, the seven convicted prisoners were executed in Richmond, Virginia, on February 2 and February 5.

In an interesting coincidence, a twenty-seven-year-old white man named George Thomas Hailey was also executed on February 2 for the rape of a fourteen-year-old white girl. Although whites had been executed for rape previously, Hailey was the first white man in the twentieth century to suffer capital punishment for rape in the state of Virginia.

See also: Crime and the criminal justice system; Jury selection; Scottsboro cases.

Marxism: The Communist Party of the United States (CPUS) is the oldest of America's explicitly Marxist political parties. Founded by former members of the Socialist Party, the CPUS came into existence in 1922, as an affiliate of the Moscow-headquartered and Soviet Communist Party-directed Third Communist International (Comintern), which was itself a consortium of communist parties from nations all over the world.

Communist Party Appeals to Blacks

Shortly after its formation, the CPUS began to make direct and specific appeals to American blacks. In the view of Bolshevik leader Vladimir Lenin, blacks, as the most exploited group in America, had a greater revolutionary potential than members of the white working class and were therefore destined to play a central role in the expected American socialist revolution. As a result, during the 1920's, the CPUS began vigorous efforts not only to increase its rank-and-file black membership but also to increase the number of blacks who held formal positions of leadership within the party.

During the 1920's, Comintern leaders also put forth the contention that American blacks, being more politically, economically, and educationally advanced than blacks in other parts of the world, could and should be trained to assume leadership positions in the struggles for national liberation in AFRICA and the Caribbean. As a result, the Comintern created organizations such as the International Labor Defense, which was charged with fighting for and expanding the rights of blacks throughout the world and which came to be headed by William L. Patterson, an African American who, along with other African Americans, had received special training at communist schools in Moscow.

All in all, however, black membership in the CPUS during the 1920's was small, never exceeding two hundred persons. In part, the paucity of blacks in the CPUS could be attributed to the party's sometimes virulent criticisms of black church leaders and the leaders of non-Marxist black civil rights groups such as the NATIONAL ASSOCIATION FOR THE ADVANCEMENT OF COLORED PEOPLE (NAACP) and the NATIONAL URBAN LEAGUE. Such organizations, in the eyes of the party, were leading blacks astray, hindering the development of a truly revolutionary black consciousness by holding out false hopes of attaining full social and economic equality within the confines of an inherently exploitive capitalist economic system that would never give full equality to blacks or to any other working-class group. A great many urban blacks also resisted approaches by communist organizers because they saw themselves as having little to gain by becoming, as such organizers urged, part of a united labor movement consisting largely of organizations that refused to accept blacks as members.

Influenced by the HARLEM RENAISSANCE, by the large number of followers of the 1920's BLACK NATIONALIST leader Marcus GARVEY, and by the fact that the Soviet Union consisted of theoretically autonomous, territorially based political entities each with its own ethnic identity, leaders at the Sixth World Congress of the Comintern in 1928 put forth the goal of political self-determination for American blacks. The Comintern leaders called for creation of a politically independent, black-ruled "black belt republic" stretching from VIRGINIA westward all the way into TEXAS.

The republic proposal did not win the CPUS many new black members. Instead, it opened the party to charges of having suddenly placed itself in alliance with those seeking to perpetuate racial segregation. Thus, despite the fact that the CPUS could count Langston HUGHES, Richard WRIGHT, and Paul ROBESON among its black sympathizers, and despite the fact that the party had nominated a black man, James Ford, as its 1932 candidate for vice president of the United States, from 1928 to 1938 fewer than twenty-five hundred blacks formally joined the party's ranks. A few other blacks, however, joined other Marxist parties, the most notable of which was the Communist League of America, the members of which eventually merged with other Trotskyites to form the Socialist Workers' Party. The CPUS, however, was to remain the largest and most influential of the American Marxist parties.

United Front Period

In 1935 the CPUS dropped its advocacy of the creation of a separate black republic. Fearful of attacks on the Soviet Union by fascist Germany and Italy, Comintern leaders in Moscow placed the CPUS and other Comintern-affiliated communist parties under new orders.

They were to abandon temporarily their efforts to bring about a swift end to capitalism in their home countries. Instead, they were to help form a "United Front" against the spread of fascism by working with labor unions, CIVIL RIGHTS groups, political organizations, and all other groups of nonfascist political persuasion—overtly if possible, covertly if necessary. The CPUS carried out its new orders with great vigor, and during the United Front period (1935-1941), its membership grew significantly. The number of Party members grew from twenty-five thousand in 1934 to seventy-five thousand in 1938; from 10 to 15 percent of those members were black. Also during the United Front period, black member Benjamin J. Davis was elected to serve as a member of the NEW YORK CITY Council.

Benjamin J. Davis (center right), a member of the Communist Party who was elected to the New York City council in 1943, at a demonstration in 1949. *(Library of Congress)*

The CPUS began to lose black members after the 1939 signing of the German-Soviet nonaggression pact at the beginning of WORLD WAR II. communists of all nations were suddenly ordered to cease their United Front activities. CPUS members were exhorted to convince American blacks that the war against fascist Germany was not their war, and they resumed their attacks on the moderate black leaders within whose organizations they had worked during the United Front period. From 1939 to 1941, black membership in the CPUS declined by approximately one half, even though the party continued to oppose racial segregation and the continued denial of basic civil rights to blacks in the South.

In June of 1941, Germany launched an all-out military invasion of the Soviet union, causing the Soviets to enter World War II on the side of the Allies. Placing the survival of the Soviet Union above all other goals, the CPUS suddenly began urging American military involvement in the war against Nazi Germany. During the war, CPUS members adopted postures befitting the most patriotic Americans, sometimes seeing fit to criticize black leaders of non-Marxist civil rights groups for not being supportive enough of the war effort.

In turn, CPUS members came under attack for having greatly reduced their activities oriented toward improving the lot of black workers. In fact, so intent was the CPUS on disassociating itself from its past criticism of American society that in 1944 it became the CPA (Communist Political Association); its leaders began claiming that it was indeed possible for blacks to attain full equality within a capitalist United States. As the war came to a close, however, the CPA once again became the CPUS and quite abruptly renounced its contention that blacks could attain equality under capitalism.

After the war, the CPUS played a leading role in getting the 1948 platform of the Progressive Party to include strong statements of commitment to the extension of full legal, economic, and political rights to all blacks in all areas of the country. The party, though, was still unable to shake off accusations that it had forsaken blacks during WORLD WAR II. Moreover, the Soviet Union and the United States were entering into the Cold War; rather than being regarded as a U.S. ally, the Soviet Union was now seen as America's number-one enemy. Soviet Communism had spread into Eastern Europe, and communists had taken power in China; anticommunists in the United States feared that American communists in sympathy with the aims of the leaders in Moscow occupied influential positions at all levels of government and in many other American institutions.

The McCarthy Years

During the 1950's, the number of CPUS members, black and otherwise, declined more drastically than ever before. As a result of fears that CPUS members were part of a Moscow-directed plot to destroy the United States and its institutions from within, there occurred extensive purges of communists and suspected communists from positions in government agencies, labor unions, civil rights organizations, academia, the information and entertainment industries, and many other institutions. Many of those who were purged and subsequently placed on employment blacklists also spent time in jail as a result of the passage of various laws defining the CPUS and other Marxist groups as threats to national security. In effect, these laws made membership in such groups illegal. Between 1955 and 1957, overall CPUS membership dropped from near twenty-two thousand to less than four thousand.

The number of black members of the CPUS and other Marxist groups remained small for both practical and ideological reasons. During the years immediately preceding the 1954 U.S. SUPREME COURT decision in BROWN V. BOARD OF EDUCATION, the energies of most politically active, socially conscious blacks were directed toward breaking down barriers to racial integration. To that end, blacks needed the support of staunchly anticommunist presidents, senators, congressmen, and other whites who would under no circumstances have given support to any group suspected of communist affiliations.

The 1960's and Beyond

During the 1960's and 1970's, as black efforts at integration met with white resistance, increasing numbers of blacks came to hold the view that full integration into American society was neither a realizable nor a desirable goal. Black nationalism, cultural separatism, and the creation of a truly culturally pluralistic society became the professed goals of more and more blacks. Since the 1950's, many blacks have ascended to the lower and middle levels of political power (as MAYORS, state legislators, city councilmembers, JUDGES, congressional representatives, and heads of state and federal government agencies. Even more have risen to middle and upper-middle levels of economic affluence, thus causing Karl Marx's contention that "you have nothing to lose but your chains" to have less validity to many black Americans.

By the end of the twentieth century, black membership in the CPUS, Socialist Workers' Party, Progressive Party, and other Marxist groups was no greater than it was at the end of the 1950's. Marxist political parties still exist, however, and their members still seek to involve themselves in efforts to eradicate racial prejudice and to end racially discriminatory practices against blacks and other members of minority groups.

—*Phillip T. Gay*

Suggested Readings:

Altschuler, Glenn C. *Race, Class, and Ethnicity in American Social Thought, 1865-1919.* Arlington Heights, Ill.: Harlan Davidson, 1989.

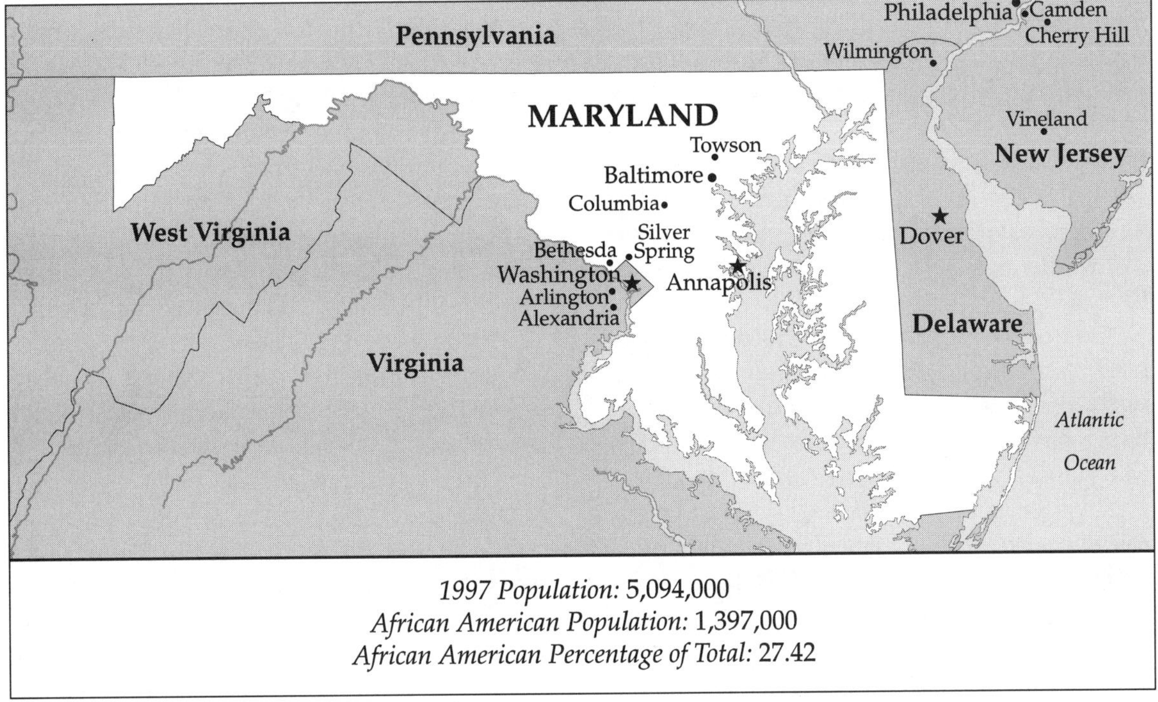

1997 Population: 5,094,000
African American Population: 1,397,000
African American Percentage of Total: 27.42

Gay, Phillip T. *Perspectives on Minority-Majority Group Conflict: The Theoretical Foundations*. Washington, D.C.: American Political Science Association, 1980.

Heale, M. J. *American Anti-Communism: Combating the Enemy Within, 1830-1970*. Baltimore: Johns Hopkins University Press, 1990.

Marable, Manning. *Race, Reform, and Rebellion: The Second Reconstruction in Black America, 1945-1982*. Jackson: University Press of Mississippi, 1991.

Record, Wilson. *The Negro and the Communist Party*. Westport, Conn.: Greenwood Press, 1980.

Robinson, Cedric J. *Black Marxism: The Making of the Black Radical Tradition*. Totowa, N.J.: Biblio Distribution Center, 1983.

Maryland: In 1997 there were approximately 1.4 million African Americans living in Maryland. This number represented about one-third of the total population of the state. In 1997, of the counties in the United States with the largest number of African Americans, BALTIMORE County, Maryland, ranked tenth, with 400,000. Also in 1997, Maryland's African American citizens owned 11 percent of the businesses in the state, putting Maryland second only to WASHINGTON, D.C., in the percentage of businesses owned by blacks.

The first African to arrive in Maryland was Matthias De Sousa (also rendered Matt Das Sousa). After serving a seven-year term as an indentured servant, De Sousa was elected to the Maryland Colonial General Assembly. After 1634, however, all Africans who came to Maryland had to be considered slaves. Maryland and VIRGINIA both instituted restrictive SLAVE CODES in the 1660's and were the first colonies to outlaw MISCEGENATION; Maryland's law was passed in 1664.

A number of African Americans born in Maryland before the CIVIL WAR made significant contributions to American history. One of these was Benjamin BANNEKER, born of free parents in Ellicott in 1731. Banneker studied mathematics and astronomy, constructed the first striking clock built totally in the colonies, published an almanac, and worked on the survey for establishing the District of Columbia. A Maryland slave named Prince WHIPPLE served in the revolutionary army and is believed to have been with George Washington during his famous crossing of the Delaware River.

One of the original thirteen states, Maryland ratified the U.S. Constitution in 1788. It was a slave state with large PLANTATIONS, and tobacco was a primary crop. In the late 1700's Maryland had an active ABOLITIONIST MOVEMENT, spearheaded by the Maryland Society for the Abolition of Slavery. Banneker was among its prominent members. In 1810 Maryland prohibited black suffrage. The COLONIZATION MOVEMENT was also active in Maryland, and a group of African Americans from the state were among those who first emigrated to LIBERIA in 1821.

One of early Maryland's most accomplished citizens, Benjamin Banneker helped lay out Washington, D.C. *(Associated Publishers, Inc.)*

American educator, journalist, and government official Frederick DOUGLASS was born into SLAVERY in Tuckahoe in 1817. Douglass eventually became America's most famous runaway slave and spent some time in England in exile. After returning from England, he began publishing his own newspaper, *The North Star*, in 1847. Two years after Douglass began publishing his newspaper, Harriet TUBMAN escaped from slavery in Maryland to freedom in PENNSYLVANIA. During the years before the Civil War Tubman served as a conductor on the UNDERGROUND RAILROAD.

At the beginning of the Civil War in 1861, Maryland hovered on the brink of secession but decided to remain part of the union (as did two other slaveholding states, KENTUCKY and MISSOURI). Many Marylanders' sympathies were with the South nonetheless, and in 1861 there was some destruction of bridges and telegraph lines by troops who favored the South. Maryland was invaded by the South during the war, and a bloody battle occurred at Antietam. Maryland's government finally abolished slavery in the state in 1864, the year before the Civil War ended. By the beginning of the twentieth century, Maryland had instituted segregation in many aspects of life.

In April, 1907, Matthew HENSON from Baltimore became the first man to reach the North Pole, where he planted an American flag. During the 1940's, Billie HOLIDAY, originally from Baltimore, became a famous and influential blues and jazz singer. In 1954 Thurgood MARSHALL, also a native of Baltimore, served as Linda Brown's lawyer in the U.S. SUPREME COURT case that would eventually desegregate the American public schools, BROWN V. BOARD OF EDUCATION. (Marshall later served as solicitor general of the United States, and in 1967 he became the first African American justice on the U.S. Supreme Court.) Baltimore was one of the early cities to begin desegregation efforts, which started the same year as the *Brown* decision.

Maryland did not escape the racial unrest of the 1960's, with a significant occurrence happening in July, 1967, in Cambridge. Activist H. Rap BROWN delivered speeches that, later the same day, inspired crowds to riot and burn buildings.

During the 1980's and 1990's African Americans gained much political power in Maryland. In 1984 Bishop Robinson became Baltimore's first African American police chief, and in 1987 Baltimore elected its first African American mayor, Kurt SCHMOKE. In 1991 Vera Hall was chosen the first African American woman chair of Maryland's DEMOCRATIC PARTY.

Many middle-class black families moved from Washington, D.C., to suburbs in Maryland and Virginia in the 1980's and 1990's, in large part to escape worsening conditions in the capital. By the 1990's Maryland and Virginia combined had the largest suburban population of African Americans in the country (around 600,000, according to the 1990 census), many living in Prince George's County, Maryland.

—Annita Marie Ward

See also: Baltimore Afro-American; Cambridge, Maryland, race riot.

Mason, Biddy (August 15, 1818, Hancock County, Georgia[?]—January 15, 1891, Los Angeles, California): Community leader and entrepreneur. Biddy Mason, who was originally known only as Bridget, was born into SLAVERY and was sold as a young girl to MISSISSIPPI planters Robert and Rebecca Smith. Bridget performed various duties and was valued for her services as a midwife and nurse for everyone—black and white—on the plantation. In her twenties, she bore three daughters who were considered the Smiths' property under the law.

After converting to the CHURCH OF JESUS CHRIST OF LATTER-DAY SAINTS, the Smiths decided to move to the new Mormon settlement in the territory of UTAH. They joined with other Mississippi Mormons in making the eight-month trek to Utah in 1848. Although she had three small children to care for, Bridget was responsible for herding her owners' twenty-odd cows, mules, and other livestock during the arduous journey. In 1851 the Smiths and several other Mormon families left Utah for San Bernardino, CALIFORNIA, where they intended to found another settlement. The Smiths took Bridget and their other slaves with them.

Unlike Mississippi and Utah, California did not allow slavery under the provisions of its state constitution. Most whites ignored the law, however, and slaveholders continued to bring their black slaves into California for years after the territory had entered the Union as a "free" state in 1850. Some people began questioning the legal status of blacks residing in California. Fearing the loss of their property, the Smiths decided to move to TEXAS, where the status of their fourteen slaves would not be in doubt.

With help from some friends of both races, Bridget sued Robert Smith for her freedom and that of her three daughters. She also sued on behalf of the Smiths' other slaves before the group could leave California. In January of 1856, a judge ruled in the slaves' favor and set them free. This groundbreaking case established a precedent that allowed other African Americans who were held illegally in bondage in California to gain their freedom.

Once she was free, Bridget moved with her daughters to LOS ANGELES and adopted the last name of Mason. She soon began working for a doctor, putting to use the skills of midwifery and nursing she had learned as a slave. During the last thirty-five years of her life, Biddy Mason helped deliver hundreds of babies born to both black and white mothers in Southern California. She wisely saved some of the money she earned for her services.

In 1866 Mason spent $250 for two unimproved lots on the edge of town; later, she bought other lots. As the city of Los Angeles grew in the late nineteenth century, its business district expanded to include Mason's property, which had increased greatly in value. Although Mason eventually became a wealthy woman, she continued to live in a modest and unpretentious manner. She also became an important leader in the city's African American community. In 1872 Mason helped found the first African Methodist Episcopal Church in Los Angeles and provided funds for the building of the church edifice. Moreover, she put her faith into action by giving money to the poor, visiting prisoners frequently, and generally doing whatever she could to help those in need.

Although Mason's house on Spring Street was torn down to make way for new municipal buildings, her achievements are commemorated on a long concrete wall that stands on Los Angeles's Third Street between Spring Street and Broadway. Photographs and documents, including her manumission papers and the deed to the Spring Street property, illustrate Mason's life narrative as displayed on this striking and unusual memorial.

Suggested Readings:

Hardaway, Roger D. "African-American Women on the Western Frontier." *Negro History Bulletin* 60 (January-March 1997): 8-13.

Hayden, Dolores. "Biddy Mason's Los Angeles, 1856-1891." *California History* 68 (Fall, 1989): 86-99, 147-149.

Mason-Dixon line: Boundary between Pennsylvania to the north and Maryland and West Virginia to the south. Prior to the Civil War, it was designated as the boundary between the slave states and the free states.

Between 1763 and 1767, the eastern portion of the Mason-Dixon line was surveyed by British astronomers Charles Mason and Jeremiah Dixon to settle a boundary dispute between Pennsylvania and Maryland. The western portion of the line was completed in 1784. The line was marked with granite shafts bearing the coats of arms of William Penn and Lord Baltimore.

During the debates in Congress over the Missouri Compromise of 1820, the line was used to distinguish the boundary between the so-called slave and free states. As a result, during and after the Civil War, it came to be seen as the boundary between the North and the South. Most of the original granite markers are still visible.

—*Alvin K. Benson*

Massachusetts: Fourth largest of the six New England states and forty-fifth largest state in the nation. Massachusetts is the most populous of the New England states, however, and thirteenth largest in the nation in population. It had about 6.1 million residents in 1997, according to estimates of the Census of the United States. The state's approximately 384,000 black residents made up 6.3 percent of the total population. Twenty-five percent of the population of the state's capital and largest city, Boston, is African American.

One of the original thirteen colonies of the United States, Massachusetts was the first colony to legalize slavery. In 1641 the capture of slaves using "unjust violence" was prohibited. Massachusetts attained statehood in 1788. Slavery gradually became rare in Massachusetts after the mid-1700's, and by the 1790 U.S. Census there were no slaves listed in the state.

In the first half of the nineteenth century, Massachusetts was the home of much activity of the abolitionist movement. Among the radical abolitionists in the state was William Lloyd Garrison. John Brown, who led a raid on the federal armory at Harpers Ferry, Vir-

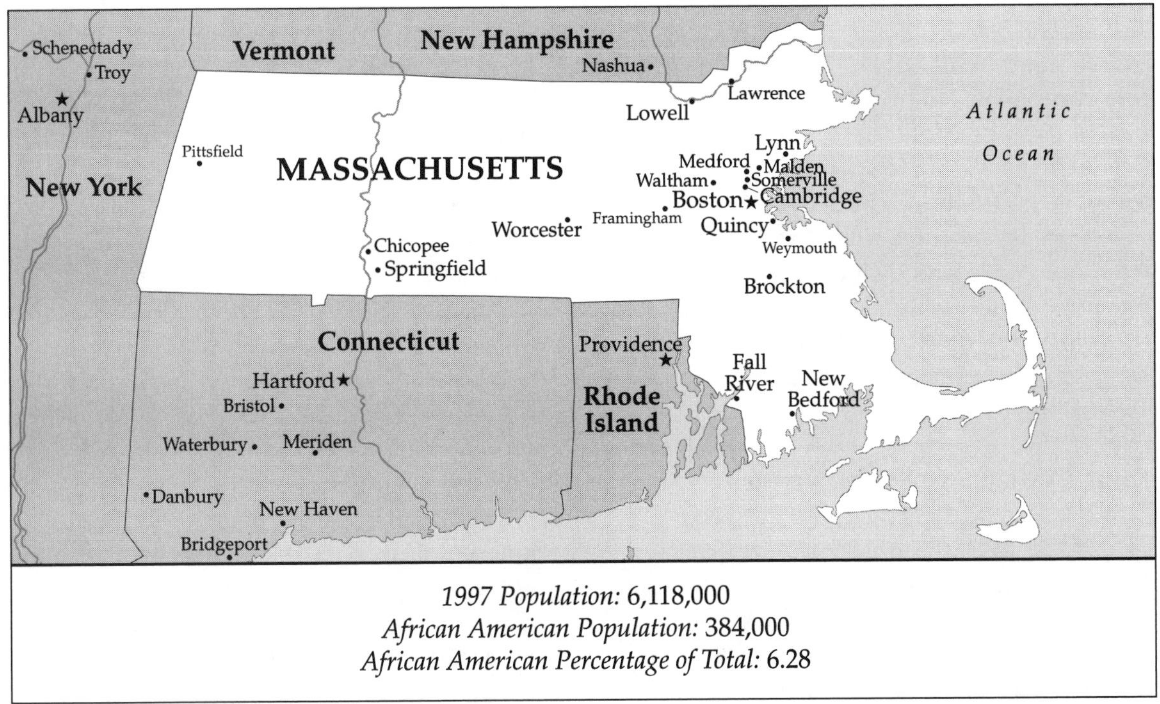

1997 Population: 6,118,000
African American Population: 384,000
African American Percentage of Total: 6.28

ginia, in 1859, got financial support and advice from a group of Massachusetts abolitionists. Two African American regiments, the FIFTY-FOURTH MASSACHUSETTS COLORED INFANTRY (formed in 1863) and the Fifty-fifth Massachusetts Colored Infantry, fought in the CIVIL WAR.

Throughout the 1800's, many immigrants came to Massachusetts from Europe to find work in industry. The largest group, about 26 percent, was the Irish. African Americans were always a part of the population of Massachusetts, but there was not a significant number of blacks until after WORLD WAR II, when there was an influx of southern blacks.

In the 1970's, Boston was the site of extreme racial tension. Boston public school administrators developed a plan to integrate the city schools via BUSING. The plan was to bring together black and white children to foster better education and to promote peace. However, demonstrations and riots ensued, particularly among white parents from South Boston. The end result of the busing program was a 35- to 50-percent increase of blacks in previously white schools; however, the non-Hispanic white population fell from 57 to 26 percent. Some public schools in Boston remained segregated.

Two particularly significant individuals in black history hail from Massachusetts. Phillis WHEATLEY was born on the West Coast of Africa. When she was seven or eight, a Bostonian, John Wheatley, purchased her and brought her to America. Once in Boston, she learned to read and write. She excelled in this endeavor and published a book of poetry, *Poems on Various Subjects, Religious and Moral*, in 1773. She was the first black person in America to achieve this distinction and the second woman to do so.

W. E. B. DU BOIS is considered one of the most important black leaders in the history of the United States. He was the first black person to receive a Ph.D. degree in the United States; he earned his degree from Harvard University in 1895. Du Bois was an acclaimed writer and published a collection of essays,

The Souls of Black Folk, in 1903. In the company of five other (white) men, Du Bois was also a founder of the NATIONAL ASSOCIATION FOR THE ADVANCEMENT OF COLORED PEOPLE (NAACP) in 1909. He spent his life working for civil rights for African Americans.

Other significant African American figures from Massachusetts include William Monroe TROTTER, a civil rights activist and journalist in the early twentieth century, and Edward BROOKE, a Republican U.S. senator from Massachusetts from 1967 to 1979.

—*Betsy L. Nichols*

See also: Oak Bluffs, Massachusetts.

Massey, Walter Eugene (b. April 5, 1938, Hattiesburg, Mississippi): Theoretical PHYSICIST, educator, and university administrator. Massey was the son of Almar Massey and Essie Nelson Massey. Massey received a B.S. degree in physics from Morehouse University in 1958 and an M.A. degree and a Ph.D. degree in physics from Washington University in 1966. He was married to Shirley Anne Streeter on October 29, 1969, and together they had two children, Keith and Eric.

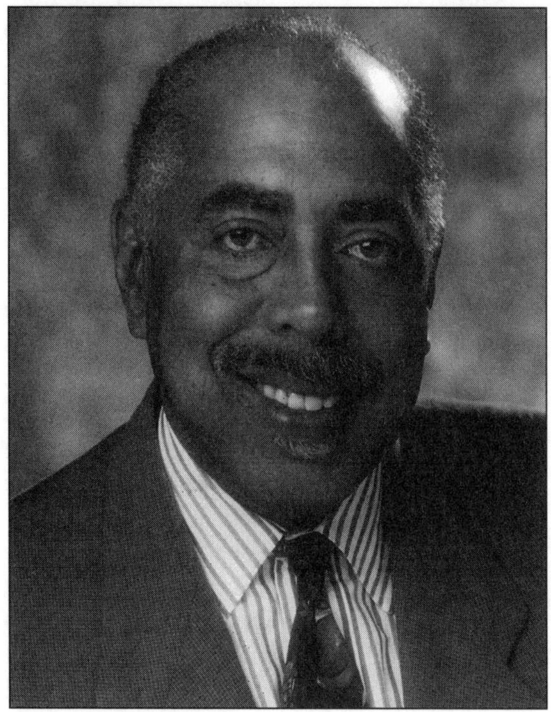

Physicist Walter Eugene Massey. *(AIP Emilio Segrè Visual Archives)*

At the Argonne National Laboratory at the University of Chicago, Massey served as staff physicist (1966-1968), consultant (1968-1975), and director (1979-1984) before being named vice president for research in 1984. In the classroom, Massey served as an assistant professor at the University of Illinois from 1968 to 1970, before going on to serve as associate professor (1970-1975) and later full professor and dean (1975-1979) at Brown University. In 1979 he became a professor at the University of Chicago.

Massey was interested in mathematics as a boy. When he enrolled at Morehouse University at age sixteen, however, he was not well prepared for advanced studies at the college level. With the assistance of excellent teachers and an especially committed physics teacher, Massey was given a firm foundation for the study of physics. These teachers inspired him to see physics as an exciting way to use mathematics as a means to better comprehend the physical world.

Building on the knowledge he gained at Morehouse, Massey went on to become a man of many achievements. He authored numerous scientific works and was the recipient of a National Defense Education Act fellowship (1959-1960), a National Science Foundation fellowship (1961), the Distinguished Service Citation from the American Association of Physics Teachers (1975), and at least ten honorary doctor of science degrees.

An outstanding physicist, Massey became an active member of numerous professional societies and organizations. In 1971 he was selected as a member of the review committee of the National Science Association; he later served as a member of the review committee of the National Academy of Science in 1973. From 1978 to 1984, he served as a member of the National Science Board. Active with the American Association for the Advancement of Science, Massey was a fellow of the board of directors from 1981 to 1985, before serving as president elect and as president in 1987 and 1988, respectively. He also became a member of Sigma Xi, the American Nuclear Society, the American Physical Society, the New York Academy of Sciences, the Illinois Governor's Commission on Science and Technology, and the Illinois Governor's Science Advisory Committee.

In addition to his professional memberships, Massey was appointed to serve on the boards of several major corporations and private institutions, including Amoco, Argonne-Chicago Development Corporation, Motorola, Chicago Tribune Company, Continental Materials Corporation, First Bank of Chicago, and the Chicago Orchestral Association. He was named a member of the board of fellows of Brown University and a member of the board of trustees of RAND.

Massey also contributed vital time and energy to the African American community. For him, such duties and responsibilities are defined alongside obligations and rights. Massey once said that he felt he had a moral obligation to support activities that would enhance the lives of other African Americans.

Mathis, Johnny (b. September 30, 1935, San Francisco, California): Singer whose ballads were among the most popular songs of the 1950's and 1960's. The fourth of seven children, Mathis was reared in a basement apartment in the Filmore District of San Francisco, CALIFORNIA. After becoming a star, he credited his parents and his music teacher, Connie Cox, for his success. Although poor, his mother and father, Clem and Mildred Mathis, bought a used piano at which his father taught him to sing. Cox gave him free voice lessons whenever she could.

Crooner Johnny Mathis in a studio portrait taken early in his singing career. *(Archive Photos)*

Although shy, Johnny was the first black president of his junior high school student body and treasurer of his high school class. Beginning at age fourteen, he won several talent shows and sang for weddings. Besides being a talented musician, he was an excellent athlete. At San Francisco College, he ran hurdles, played basketball, and set a record of 6 feet 5½ inches in the high jump.

Mathis performed in a JAZZ sextet until 1955, when Helen Noga and her husband heard him "jamming" in their nightclub in San Francisco. Noga became his manager and arranged an audition that led to a recording contract with Columbia records and engagements in several NEW YORK CITY nightclubs. He was successful from his first album, *Wonderful, Wonderful* (1956), which sold in the millions. It was followed by *Chances Are* (1957), *The Twelfth of Never* (1957), and *Misty* (1959). His specialty was romantic ballads, and his rich tenor voice and unconventional phrasing became very popular. In his first big year in show business, when he was twenty-one, he earned $100,000; by age twenty-nine, he was earning $1 million per year.

Mathis lived with the Nogas for the first six years of his phenomenal career. Although Noga was an excellent businessperson and Mathis credited her with being indispensable to the development of his career, she was overbearing and domineering. Johnny finally reached a point at which he wanted to manage his own legal and personal life, and he moved out on his own. In the mid-1970's, he moved into a home in the Hollywood Hills of California.

Despite the popularity of competing forms of music, such as jazz and rock and roll, Mathis's sentimental love songs secured for him a large and faithful following. In his later years, he recorded several popular duet albums, including a Christmas album with Gladys Knight, *Too Much, Too Little, Too Late* (1978) with Deniece Williams, and *Friends in Love* (1982) with Dionne WARWICK.

See also: Music.

Matthews, Victoria Earle (May 27, 1861, Fort Valley, Georgia—March 10, 1907, Brooklyn Heights, New York): Journalist. Ann Victoria Earle Matthews was born a slave. Her mother escaped to New York when Matthews was a child, then came back to claim the four of her nine children that she could locate, moving the family to NEW YORK CITY in 1873. Matthews wrote for numerous secular and religious papers and was one of the most popular black female writers of her time. She occasionally contributed short articles about dialect to the Associated Press. Matthews founded the White Rose Mission in 1897 as a training center and school for children from kindergarten age up. She also founded the Home for Colored Women, a shelter and training facility, and collected works of black LITERATURE, which she used to teach a course on race history.

Matzeliger, Jan Earnst (September 15, 1852, Paramaribo, Dutch Guiana—August 24, 1889, Lynn, Massachusetts): INVENTOR noted for his advances in the shoemaking industry. Matzeliger was the son of a Holland-born engineer and a black mother. At the age of ten, he began an apprenticeship in government machine shops superintended by his father. In 1871 he left Dutch Guiana (later Suriname) on

A victim of tuberculosis, Jan Matzeliger died before he was able to profit from his revolutionary shoe lasting machine. *(Arkent Archive)*

an East Indian ship, intending to train as a sailor. He disembarked from that vessel two years later, in PHILADELPHIA, PENNSYLVANIA. He left Philadelphia for the New England area in 1876. He lived in BOSTON, MASSACHUSETTS, briefly and eventually settled in Lynn, Massachusetts.

Matzeliger found work in a shoe factory in Lynn and began taking evening classes to improve his proficiency in English. At the time he was working in that factory, various machines could cut, sew, or tack shoes, but none could perform the final task, called lasting, which involved adjusting the shoe, arranging leather over the sole, and driving in nails. Artisans called lasters performed that last set of steps. They were paid highly and, in effect, controlled the shoe industry. Matzeliger believed that a machine could perform the lasting process, and in his spare time he began developing such a machine, undaunted by the fact that he had no formal education. His first models were made of wood, and later models were made of scrap iron. He was ready to present a working model in 1880.

Matzeliger needed financing to finish the final model, arrange demonstrations, and secure a patent, so he sold two-thirds of the rights to his invention. When he finally sent patent diagrams to WASHINGTON, D.C., they were so complicated that a patent office employee had to travel to Lynn to see the machine in operation. The original patent was granted in 1883. Matzeliger received further patents later, including those for an improved lasting machine and a nailing machine. Matzeliger sold his share of the original patent for stock in the Consolidated Lasting Machine Company, which manufactured and marketed the invention, but he did not live long enough to see the full effect of his invention.

By 1897 Sidney Winslow, who had put up some of the original money to develop the lasting machine, had formed the United Shoe Machinery Corporation from the Consolidated Lasting Machine Company and several other firms. The corporation earned more than $50 million in the next twelve years. The lasting machine cut shoe prices by about half, and a machine could last between 150 and 700 pairs a day, compared with about 50 pairs a day from a human laster. The invention made Lynn, Massachusetts, the shoe capital of the world.

Mayfield, Curtis (June 3, 1942, Chicago, Illinois—December 26, 1999, Roswell, Georgia): Singer, guitarist, songwriter, and record company executive. Mayfield's early musical influence was a local GOSPEL MUSIC group, the Northern Jubilee Gospel Singers, which included three of his cousins and Jerry Butler. The gospel influence could be heard in his music throughout his career.

Mayfield began writing music at the age of eleven, and he left high school in the tenth grade to begin performing with the Impressions at the encouragement of Butler, the group's leader. The group was composed of Butler, Mayfield, Fred Cash, Sam Gooden, Emanuel Thomas, and brothers Richard and Arthur Brooks. After a few singles for Vee Jay Records, including "For Your Precious Love," Butler left the group for a solo career (that proved very successful), and Mayfield took over the leading role. Vee Jay dropped the group in 1959, and it temporarily split up.

Mayfield did other work, and by 1961 he had saved enough money to regroup the Impressions and record a song for ABC-Paramount Records. The Brooks brothers left the group in 1962, and the Impressions continued as a trio comprising Mayfield, Gooden, and Cash. In 1963 "It's All Right" was a hit on the pop and rhythm-and-blues charts.

They became a major act in 1964 with a series of strong singles inspired by the CIVIL RIGHTS movement: "I'm So Proud," "Keep on Pushing," and "Amen." Martin Luther KING,

Singer-guitarist Curtis Mayfield. *(AP/Wide World Photos)*

Jr., and Jesse JACKSON chose "Keep on Pushing" as an unofficial theme song for the movement. "People Get Ready" and "We're a Winner" were hits in 1965 and 1968 respectively.

Mayfield left the Impressions in 1970 to pursue a solo career. His first solo effort, *Curtis* (1970), was marked by biting social commentary and songs of up to ten minutes in length. His most popular music in the 1970's was his sound track for the 1972 film *Superfly*, which spawned two top-ten singles, "Freddie's Dead" and "Superfly." The Impressions regrouped in 1983 for a reunion tour, reestablishing their place in history as one of the top groups of the 1960's and reminding current listeners of the continued relevance of Mayfield's message, especially his antidrug stance.

Mayfield's first album in five years, *Take It to the Streets*, was released in 1990. He was preparing to tour in support of the album when tragedy struck. While preparing for an outdoor concert in Brooklyn, New York, Mayfield was struck by a stage lighting tower that was toppled by a gust of wind. He broke three vertebrae and was paralyzed from the neck down. He made his first postaccident public appearance in 1991 to set up the Curtis Mayfield Research Fund at the Miami Project to Cure Paralysis. The accident slowed Mayfield's pace, but he continued to release albums. *New World Order* (1996) was his last album of new material to be released before his death.

In 1994 and 1995, respectively, Mayfield was awarded the Grammy Legend and Grammy Lifetime Achievement Awards. He was inducted into the Rock and Roll Hall of Fame in 1999—eight years after the Impressions had been inducted.

Mayfield, Julian (June 6, 1928, Greer, South Carolina—October 20, 1984, Tacoma Park, Maryland): Writer, editor, and educator. Although he described African American life in various media, including plays, screenplays, and literary and political essays, and served as adviser to the leaders of two Third World governments, Mayfield's reputation rests on the novels he wrote during the 1950's and 1960's.

Reared in WASHINGTON, D.C., Mayfield began his career as an actor. He made his Broadway debut in the 1949 production of *Lost in the Stars*, an adaptation of a novel about South African apartheid. He subsequently co-wrote (with director Jules Dassin and actor Ruby Dee) and starred in *Up Tight*, a 1968 film about black militants.

Mayfield's novels deal with the American dream in general and with the lost dreams and aspirations of African Americans in particular. *The Hit* (1957) centers on the father of a Harlem family whose dreams for a better future rest on a "hit," or lucky break, in the numbers game. *The Long Night* (1958) is the story of a Harlem boy searching for his father. *The Grand Parade* (1961), a political novel that raises racial and human rights issues, describes how characters in a fictional southern town vie for power. These novels have been translated into French, Japanese, Czech, and German.

Mayfield also wrote articles, editorials, academic papers, and reviews for the *Puerto Rico World Journal*, *Commentary*, *The New Republic*, *The Nation*, *Negro Digest*, and *Freedomways*. He was editor of *Ten Times Black* (1972), a collection of short stories about the African American experience.

Mayfield spent many years in Africa, Europe, and the Caribbean. From 1962 to 1966, he served as communications aide and speech writer for Ghanian president Kwame Nkrumah. During that time, he became founding editor of *African Review*. From 1971 to 1974, he was senior political adviser to Prime Minister Forbes Burnham in Guyana.

In the late 1960's, Mayfield entered university teaching. He taught at Cornell University and New York University before becoming a Fulbright lecturer in West Germany, visiting professor at the University of Maryland, and writer-in-residence at HOWARD UNIVERSITY.

Maynard, Robert Clyve (June 17, 1937, Brooklyn, New York—August 17, 1993, Oakland, California): Journalist and newspaper publisher. Maynard was the first person to orchestrate the purchase of a major daily American newspaper by the management staff of the newspaper (the *Oakland Tribune*). As a result of the deal, Maynard also became the first African American to own a major daily American newspaper in general circulation. Ownership of the *Oakland Tribune* was the capstone of many major achievements in journalism for Maynard, whose career spanned roles as a distinguished reporter, national correspondent, syndicated COLUMNIST, ombudsman, editor, and journalism educator; much of his journalistic career was spent with *The Washington Post*.

As a high school student in Brooklyn, Maynard wrote for the black weeklies, the *New York Age-Defender*, and, later, the BALTIMORE AFRO-AMERICAN. Wanting to write full-time, Maynard, the son of Barbadian immigrants, dropped out of high school at age sixteen. Later, he spent a year at Harvard University as a Nieman fellow.

Maynard's first job on a general circulation daily was with the *York Gazette and Daily* in PENNSYLVANIA from 1961 to 1967. In 1967 he was hired by *The Washington Post* as a national correspondent, rising to positions as assistant managing editor and ombudsman for the paper. Between 1972 and 1974, while still with the *Post*, Maynard codirected a summer training program for journalists at Columbia University in New York.

He left the *Post* in 1977 to start the Institute for Journalism Education at the University of California at Berkeley, a national program to

Robert Maynard, the first African American owner of a major metropolitan daily, in 1991. *(AP/Wide World Photos)*

help train minority students to become journalists. During this time, Maynard also began working for the Gannett newspaper chain as a consultant on AFFIRMATIVE ACTION before joining Gannett's *Oakland Tribune* as its editor. Maynard "took pride in hiring what he often claimed was the most ethnically diverse staff on any paper," said journalist and author Ellis COSE.

In 1983, after serving as editor of the *Oakland Tribune* for four years, Maynard bought the paper from the Gannett Company for $22 million. Notably, Maynard managed to buy the paper without spending any of his own money for the down payment. In carrying out the purchase, Maynard put together a "leveraged buyout," using money borrowed from banks and long-term special financing arrangements and backing from the Gannett Company.

Conditions for the sale of the *Oakland Tribune* to Maynard originally came about because the Gannett Company began negotiations to purchase a television station in Oakland. The Federal Communications Commission (FCC), which regulates television and radio stations in the United States, said Gannett could own either a newspaper or a television station in Oakland, but could not own both in the same city. Gannett decided to sell the *Tribune*, thus prompting Maynard to make a bid for the paper's ownership.

Maynard owned the *Oakland Tribune* for nine years. Rising costs, a deepening recession, and declining circulation led Maynard to sell the paper in 1992.

Maynard died of cancer in his OAKLAND, CALIFORNIA, home on August 17, 1993, at the age of fifty-six. His founding of the Institute for Journalism Education helped train hundreds of journalists of color. At the same time, through his many journalistic roles and extraordinary persona, Maynard left a lasting influence on journalists of all races and colors.
See also: Black press.

Opera singer Dorothy Maynor in 1947. *(AP/Wide World Photos)*

Maynor, Dorothy (Dorothy Leigh Mainor; b. September 3, 1910, Norfolk, Virginia): Opera singer. Maynor came to prominence after auditioning for conductor Serge Koussevitzky at the Berkshire Music Festival in 1939. Her subsequent well-received performance with the festival's orchestra led to her Town Hall debut on November 19, 1939. By the 1950's, she had forged an international reputation with performances in Central and South America, Australia, and Europe. After twenty-five years of performing, she decided to retire and devote her time to community outreach, especially to African American children. She founded the Harlem School for the Arts in 1964 and served as its director until 1979. She was appointed to the Metropolitan Opera Board of Directors in 1975.
See also: Classical and operatic music.

Mayors: The growth of the number of black elected officials in the United States in the late

African American Mayors of Major Cities, January, 1999

Mayor	*City*	*Total Population*	*Black Percentage of Total Population*
Lee Brown	Houston, TX	1,660,533	26.9
Ron Kirk	Dallas, TX	1,053,292	28.2
Dennis Archer	Detroit, MI	1,027,974	63.1
Kurt Schmoke	Baltimore, MD	736,014	54.8
Willie Brown	San Francisco, CA	723,959	10.9
W. W. Herenton	Memphis, TN	610,337	54.8
Anthony Williams	Washington, D.C.	606,909	70.3
Michael R. White	Cleveland, OH	505,616	43.8
Marc Morial	New Orleans, LA	496,938	55.3
Wellington E. Webb	Denver, CO	467,610	12.8
Emanuel Cleaver II	Kansas City, MO	435,146	29.6
Clarence Harmon	St Louis, MO	396,685	47.5
Bill Campbell	Atlanta, GA	394,017	66.6
Sharon Belton	Minneapolis, MN	368,383	13.0
Sharpe James	Newark, NJ	275,221	58.2
Richard Arrington	Birmingham, AL	265,968	55.6
Elzie Odom	Arlington, TX	261,721	8.4
W. Johnson	Rochester, NY	231,636	31.5
Harvey Johnson	Jackson, MS	196,637	55.7
Martin G. Barnes	Paterson, NJ	148,394	36.0
Woodrow Stanley	Flint, MI	140,761	47.9
Floyd Adams	Savannah, GA	137,560	51.3
Chris Holden	Pasadena, CA	131,591	19.0
David Moore	Beaumont, TX	114,323	41.0
Roosevelt F. Dorn	Inglewood, CA	109,602	51.9

Source: National Conference of Black Mayors - Primary source, U.S. Census Bureau.

twentieth century, notably black mayors, was significant. This increase can be partly attributed to demographic shifts, legal changes that broadened electoral access, and the proactive efforts of the black population.

In particular, there was a dramatic increase in the number of black elected officials after passage of the VOTING RIGHTS ACT OF 1965. In 1964 there were a total of 103 black elected officials in the United States; ten years later, the figure had mushroomed to 3,503 (135 of whom were black mayors). By January of 1987, there were 6,646 black elected officeholders, including 289 mayors. Of the 289 black mayors, 28 presided over municipalities with populations exceeding fifty thousand people. In 1999 there were 36 African American mayors representing U.S. cities with populations of fifty thousand or more. While the majority of elected mayors were men, African American women had attained office in some larger cities, including Minneapolis, MINNESOTA (with mayor Sharon Belton), and Evanston, Illinois (Lorraine Morton).

Many observers believed that this increase signaled the integration of blacks into U.S. politics. Historically, the status of blacks in the United States has largely been characterized by exclusion, deprivation, and subordination. Blacks assumed that electoral power would result in an equitable distribution of goods and services. Symbolically, black officials were seen as an affirmation of black political maturity, capability, and power.

Electing Black Mayors
Securing leadership of local government was thought by many blacks to be pivotal and attainable. Cities are the most immediate, visible, and accessible level of government, and cities provide a wide array of tangible services (police, fire, roads, parks, libraries, sewage treatment, and more) that significantly affect quality of life. Demographic shifts (the culmination of black migration from the South to the cities of the North and West, accompanied by white migration from cities to the suburbs) had created significant concentrations of blacks in urban areas, which thus possessed the potential to become bases for local black electoral victories. Moreover, the maturation of local black political organizations provided a leadership nucleus that could organize black populations. The combination of these factors in the politically vibrant atmosphere fostered by the CIVIL RIGHTS and black liberation movements made expanded electoral efforts possible.

Mayoral campaigns mounted in cities throughout the United States, although sharing the objective of replacing white political hegemony with black executive power, differed with the specific political conditions prevailing in the various localities. Increased numbers of blacks in close proximity did not automatically translate into political representation or power, and in some cities, support of nonblack voters was critical to the success of black candidates.

Such was the case in Cleveland's mayoral election of 1967, when African American candidate Carl STOKES defeated Seth Taft by less than one percentage point. Stokes won with solid black support and with his ability to attract 19 percent of the white vote. The dependence on nonblack voters was even more pronounced in the LOS ANGELES mayoral election of 1973. At its peak in 1970, the black population in Los Angeles did not reach 18 percent of the city's total population. Even with core black support, therefore, Tom BRADLEY was dependent on a nonblack coalition in order to defeat incumbent mayor Sam Yorty.

In cities where black population majorities provide a higher degree of confidence for black mayoral candidates, other factors may dissuade potential candidates. Lack of political party support, the intrusive influence of state politicians, organized militant white opposition, and levels of voter turnout have been points of concern for black mayoral aspirants. The Gary, Indiana, mayoral election of 1967 featured opposition by the white leadership of the political party of black mayoral hopeful Richard HATCHER. In addition, there was voter fraud perpetrated by the local board of elections; nevertheless, Hatcher was victorious.

Early mayoral contests with black candidates were characterized by deep racial antipathy, often accompanied by disputes focused on police practices, hiring policies, and the distribution of city services. In spite of initial fears on the part of many white residents and businesses, most black mayors have gained enough public confidence to retain their posts beyond the first term. It is now not at all unusual to find black mayors in alliance with the corporate community engaging in urban redevelopment efforts. Overtly hostile mayoral contests have generally given way to more subtle forms of contention and to a resignation by whites that blacks will have a substantive role in local governance. Subsequent elections have been characterized by whites voting for black candidates in increasing numbers.

Mayoral Power
It has been noted that black urban dwellers support black mayoral candidates because they seek substantive changes in the way

(continued on page 1625)

African American Mayors

Archer, Dennis. Mayor of Cleveland, OHIO. *See main text entry.*

Arrington, Richard. Mayor of BIRMINGHAM, ALABAMA. *See main text entry.*

Barnes, Thomas (b. July 23, 1936, Marked Tree, Ala.). Mayor of Gary, INDIANA. In 1987 Barnes was elected mayor of Gary, defeating longtime mayor Richard Hatcher. He ran for reelection in 1991 and defeated Hatcher for a second time.

AP/Wide World Photos

Barry, Marion. Mayor of WASHINGTON, D.C. *See main text entry.*

Barthelemy, Sidney John (b. Mar. 17, 1942, New Orleans, La.). Mayor of NEW ORLEANS, LOUISIANA. From 1974 to 1978, Barthelemy, who had once studied for the priesthood, served as the first African American elected to the Louisiana state senate since RECONSTRUCTION. He was a member of the New Orleans city council until his successful run for mayor in 1986, in which he became only the second African American mayor in the city's history.

Berry, Theodore M. (b. Nov. 8, 1905, Maysville, Ky.). Mayor of Cincinnati, OHIO. In addition to maintaining a legal practice, Berry was a civil rights activist who served on the board of directors for the Cincinnati chapter of the NATIONAL ASSOCIATION FOR THE ADVANCEMENT OF COLORED PEOPLE (NAACP) between 1946 and 1968 and later became chairman of the Ohio Commission on Civil Rights Legislation. In 1972 he was elected Cincinnati's first African American mayor, a position he held until retiring from politics in 1975.

AP/Wide World Photos

Blackwood, Ronald A. (b. Jan. 19, 1926, Kingston, Jamaica). Mayor of Mount Vernon, NEW YORK. Born and reared in JAMAICA, Blackwood moved to New York while attending college. He served on the city council of Mount Vernon, a suburb of New York City, for fifteen years and in 1988 was elected mayor. He was involved in urban renewal and industrial development agencies, and was recognized for his achievements in promoting minority business enterprise.

Box, Charles E. Mayor of Rockford, ILLINOIS. Box began his political career in 1981 as the legal director of the city of Rockford and later served as city administrator. In 1981 he was elected mayor, winning in all fourteen wards even though Rockford's black population was only 15 percent of the city's total.

Bradley, Tom. Mayor of LOS ANGELES, CALIFORNIA. *See main text entry.*

Brown, Willie L., Jr. Mayor of San Francisco, CALIFORNIA. *See main text entry.*

Burney, William D., Jr. (b. Apr. 23, 1951, Augusta, Maine). Mayor of Augusta, MAINE. Burney worked with the housing authority before becoming the first African American to serve on the Augusta city council as representative from the city's third ward. He was elected mayor in 1988, becoming the first African American mayor in Maine's history.

Busby, Jim (b. July 16, 1944, Houston, Tex.). Mayor of Victorville, California. Busby, a native of Texas and a VIETNAM WAR veteran, worked at TRW Space and Defense in California for twenty-two years before being elected to the Victorville city council in 1988. Shortly after, he was appointed mayor pro tem by his fellow council members—filling the office formerly held by the elected mayor, who had been killed in a traffic accident.

Campbell, Bill. Mayor of ATLANTA, GEORGIA. *See main text entry.*

Chase, James E. (b. 1914?, Ballinger, Tex.—May 19, 1987, Spokane, Wash.). Mayor of Spokane, WASH-

(continued)

INGTON. Chase moved to Spokane during the GREAT DEPRESSION and worked as the manager of an auto body shop for forty years. He was a member of the chamber of commerce and head of the local chapter of the National Association for the Advancement of Colored People (NAACP), and he served on the city council. With his election as mayor in 1981, he became Spokane's first African American mayor and one of the few African Americans to serve as mayor of a predominantly white city. He completed his term in December, 1985.

Cleaver, Emanuel, II. Mayor of Kansas City, MISSOURI. *See main text entry.*

Cooper, Algernon J. (b. May 30, 1944, Mobile, Ala.). Mayor of Prichard, ALABAMA. Cooper's first brush with politics came when he served as a staff aide to Senator Robert Kennedy in the 1968 presidential campaign. He was also the national director of the Black American Law Students Association and participated in a special investigation of the treatment of Alabama state prison inmates. He was elected Prichard's mayor in 1972, defeating the white incumbent.

AP/Wide World Photos

Dinkins, David. Mayor of NEW YORK CITY. *See main text entry.*

Dixon, Richard Clay (b. Dayton, Ohio). Mayor of Dayton, Ohio. Dixon was appointed Dayton's city commissioner in 1979 and was elected mayor in 1987. He served as director of the city's Adult Basic Education Program and was involved in a variety of organizations including the National Advisory Council on Advanced Education, the U.S. Olympic Committee, and the human development committee of the U.S. Conference of Mayors.

Dixon, Sharon Pratt. Mayor of Washington, D.C. *See main text entry for* Sharon Pratt KELLY.

Evers, Charles. Mayor of Fayette, MISSISSIPPI. *See main text entry.*

Foley, Lelia Kasenia Smith (b. 1941, Taft, Okla.). Mayor of Taft, OKLAHOMA. In 1973 Foley, a former welfare recipient, became the first black woman to serve as mayor in the continental United States. With her children's help, she waged a door-to-door campaign in the all-black township for election to Taft's city council. She was selected mayor by her fellow council members.

Gaines, Paul L., Sr. (b. Apr. 20, 1932, Newport, R.I.). Mayor of Newport, RHODE ISLAND. Gaines's career in public office began when he was elected as committeeman for the Newport school district in 1969, becoming the first African American to serve in this position. His election to the Newport city council in 1977 was another first. From 1981 to 1983 he served as the city's first African American mayor.

Gantt, Harvey Bernard (b. Jan. 14, 1943, Charleston, S.C.). Mayor of Charlotte, NORTH CAROLINA. In 1963, by order of the U.S. SUPREME COURT, Gantt was admitted as Clemson University's first African American student. An architect by profession, he later entered local politics and in 1974 was elected to the city council of Charlotte. From 1981 to 1983, he served as the city's first African American mayor pro tem, winning the mayoral election in 1983 and serving until 1987. As the first African American in North Carolina's history to receive the DEMOCRATIC PARTY nomination to the U.S. Senate, he was later defeated by veteran Republican incumbent Jesse Helms.

Garner, James N. Mayor of Hempstead, Long Island, New York. Garner, the owner of an extermination business in the village of Hempstead, was elected as a member of the board of trustees in 1984 and as a trustee in 1987. Running as a Republican, he became Long Island's first African American mayor in 1989.

Gibson, Kenneth A. (b. May 15, 1932, Enterprise, Ala.). Mayor of NEWARK, NEW JERSEY. A former chief engineer with the Newark Housing Authority, Gibson became chief structural engineer for the city. He was elected as Newark's first African American mayor in 1970 and went on to serve four consecutive terms before losing a 1986 reelection bid to Sharpe James.

Goode, W. Wilson (b. Aug. 19, 1938, Seaboard, N.C.). Mayor of PHILADELPHIA, PENNSYLVANIA. Goode, executive director of the Philadelphia Council for

AP/Wide World Photos

Community Advancement, was appointed by Pennsylvania's governor in 1978 to the state's Public Utility Commission. This commission was involved in the investigation of the 1979 accident at the Three Mile Island nuclear reactor. In 1983 Goode won the mayoral election. A major challenge in his first term came during the police confrontation with the radical MOVE ORGANIZATION on May 13, 1985. He authorized the police plan to drop gel explosive on the group's row-house headquarters; the resulting fire quickly spread out of control, causing an estimated $8 million in property damage. Despite lingering disapproval of his handling of this incident, he was elected to a second term in 1988. The city's charter prevented Goode from being able to run for a third consecutive term.

Hatcher, John C., Jr. Mayor of East Orange, New Jersey. Hatcher was elected to serve as a member of the city council for East Orange before serving a four-year term as mayor beginning in 1985. He was succeeded in office by two other African American mayors, Cardell Cooper and Robert L. Bowser.

Inman, Dorothy J. "Lee" (b. Birmingham, Ala.). Mayor of Tallahassee, FLORIDA. Inman worked in the San Antonio Independent School District in Texas and served as an administrator for the TORCH project at Florida State University's Center for Policy Studies. She was elected a Tallahassee city commissioner in 1986 and served in that post until becoming mayor in 1988.

Jackson, Maynard, Jr. Mayor of Atlanta, Georgia. *See main text entry.*

James, Sharpe (b. Feb. 20, 1936, Jacksonville, Fla.). Mayor of Newark, New Jersey. For sixteen years, James served on the Newark city council as a representative from the city's second ward, and in 1980 he worked on Senator Edward Kennedy's presidential campaign. In 1986 he defeated Newark's first African American mayor, Kenneth A. Gibson, who was seeking reelection to a fifth term.

Kelly, Sharon Pratt. Mayor of Washington, D.C. *See main text entry.*

Larkins, E. Pat. Mayor of Pompano Beach, Florida. Larkins was first elected to serve as a commissioner for Pompano Beach before becoming mayor of the city in 1985. She held office through December of 1988.

Lee, Howard N., Jr. (b. July 28, 1934, Lithonia, Georgia). Mayor of Chapel Hill, North Carolina. Lee worked as a director of youth and employee programs at Duke University from 1966 to 1969. With his election as mayor of Chapel Hill in 1969, he became the first African American man to hold the position in that predominantly white city. He remained in office until 1975.

AP/Wide World Photos

Livingston, George. Mayor of Richmond, California. Livingston was first elected to serve on the Richmond city council as a member-at-large. In June of 1987, he was elected to his first term as mayor; he was subsequently reelected to serve through November of 1993.

McGee, James Howell (b. Nov. 8, 1918, Berryburg, W.Va.). Mayor of Dayton, Ohio. A former attorney, McGee began his political career when he served as city commissioner of Dayton from 1967 to 1970. He was elected mayor in 1980.

Milner, Thirman L. (b. Oct. 29, 1933, Hartford, Conn.). Mayor of Hartford, CONNECTICUT. Milner was elected to the Connecticut State House of Representatives and served as assistant majority leader during the 1981-1982 legislative session. He left to campaign for mayor of Hartford, and in 1981 he was the first African American to be popularly elected mayor of a New England city. In 1985 he served as first vice president of the NATIONAL CONFERENCE OF BLACK MAYORS.

Moore, Walter Louis (b. Mar. 14, 1946, Pontiac, Mich.). Mayor of Pontiac, MICHIGAN. Moore, a former firefighter and county commissioner, was

(continued)

elected mayor of Pontiac in 1989 and took office in 1990. He helped found the I-75 Mayor's Conference and was a member of the U.S. Conference of Mayors and the National Conference of Black Mayors.

Morial, Ernest Nathan "Dutch" (Oct. 9, 1929, New Orleans, La.—Dec. 24, 1989, New Orleans, La.). Mayor of New Orleans, Louisiana. Morial, who grew up in a large middle-class Catholic Creole family, achieved a number of professional firsts: He was the first African American to be graduated from the law school at Louisiana State University (1954), the first black to be appointed assistant U.S. district attorney in Louisiana (1965), the first black elected to serve as a Louisiana state legislator since Reconstruction (1968), and the first elected black JUDGE on the Fourth Circuit Court of Appeals for Louisiana (1973-1977). In 1977 he was elected mayor of New Orleans, serving until 1986.

Morial, Marc H. (b. Jan. 3, 1958, New Orleans, La.). Mayor of New Orleans, Louisiana. When Morial was twenty years old, his father "Dutch," who was then serving as a judge, was elected as the first African American mayor of New Orleans. The elder Morial held this office from 1978 until 1986, providing his son with extensive exposure to politics. In 1992 Marc Morial won his first elective office as a state senator from Louisiana's Fourth District. While serving in the state legislature, Morial became a candidate for the office of mayor. By February of 1994, Morial and Donald Mintz, a white man with a strong civil rights background and close ties to many African American political leaders, had emerged as the two leading candidates. Morial won the bitter race in 1994.

Officer, Carl E. (b. Apr. 3, 1952, St. Louis, Mo.). Mayor of EAST ST. LOUIS, ILLINOIS. Officer was a mortician who began serving as vice president of his family's funeral home business in 1970. He also served as deputy county coroner for St. Clair County between 1975 and 1977. In 1979 he defeated incumbent black mayor William E. Mason in a landslide victory that made him the youngest mayor of a major metropolitan city at that time.

Perry, Carrie Saxon (b. Aug. 10, 1931, Hartford, Conn.). Mayor of Hartford, Connecticut. Perry, an administrator of community renewal projects and the executive director of Amistad House, Inc., was first elected to political office in 1978, when she campaigned for a seat as representative from Hartford to the Connecticut General Assembly. She held office for eight years and was elected mayor of Hartford in 1986.

Primas, Melvin Randolph "Randy," Jr. (b. Aug. 31, 1949, Camden, N.J.). Mayor of Camden, New Jersey. In 1971 Primas began working for the Black People's Unity Movement, an economic development agency devoted to promoting self-help initiatives in minority neighborhoods. In 1973 he became the Camden city council's youngest elected member at the age of twenty-three. In 1978 he became the city's first African American mayor. That same year, Primas received an award for outstanding achievement in politics from the Congressional Black Caucus. He was reelected in 1985 and served as mayor until 1990.

AP/Wide World Photos

Rice, Norman Blann (b. May 4, 1943, Denver, Colo.). Mayor of Seattle, Washington. Rice became involved in local government in 1974 when he took a position as executive assistant director of government service for the Puget Sound Council of Governments. He was elected to Seattle's city council in 1978 and served for eleven years. In November of 1989, he became Seattle's first African American mayor, winning a majority of votes in a city whose population was approximately 75 percent white and only 9.5 percent African American at that time.

Sawyer, Eugene (b. Sept. 4, 1934, Greensboro, Ala.). Mayor of CHICAGO, ILLINOIS. Before his election as mayor, Sawyer served as alderman from Chicago's sixth ward, until April of 1987. In 1987 he was elected mayor of Chicago, succeeding Harold Washington, who died in office on November 25, 1987. Sawyer was the second African American mayor of Chicago and held the office through April of 1991.

Schmoke, Kurt Liddell (b. Dec. 1, 1949, Baltimore, Md.). Mayor of BALTIMORE, MARYLAND. A Baltimore native, Schmoke was a Rhodes scholar and a 1976 graduate of the Harvard Law School. In 1977 he was selected by President Jimmy Carter to serve on the White House Domestic Policy Staff and later was appointed as assistant director of the Department of Transportation. Eager to pursue local politics, in 1982 he ran for the office of Baltimore state's attorney, beating the incumbent by a landslide. He was elected mayor in 1987 and served until 1999.

Shackelford, Lottie Holt (b. Apr. 30, 1941, Little Rock, Ark.). Mayor of Little Rock, ARKANSAS. Shackelford became a member of Little Rock's city council in 1978 and served until 1986. She was mayor of Little Rock from 1987 to 1989. In 1991 she served as vice chair of the Democratic National Committee.

Stokes, Carl. Mayor of Cleveland, Ohio. *See main text entry.*

Taylor, Noel C. (b. July 15, 1924, Bedford City, Va.). Mayor of Roanoke, VIRGINIA. Taylor, an ordained BAPTIST minister, was first elected to the Roanoke city council in 1970. He served as vice mayor from 1974 to 1975 and was elected mayor in 1975.

Tucker, Walter, III. Mayor of Compton, California. *See main text entry.*

Vincent, Edward. Mayor of Inglewood, California. *See main text entry.*

Washington, Harold. Mayor of Chicago, Illinois. *See main text entry.*

Washington, Walter E. (b. Apr. 15, 1915, Dawson, Ga.). First black mayor of Washington, D.C. Washington was appointed commissioner of the District of Columbia by President Lyndon Johnson in 1967. The post, in effect, was that of mayor of Washington, D.C., the nation's largest predominantly black city. He had also been a member of the NATIONAL ADVISORY COMMISSION ON CIVIL DISORDERS, which was formed to investigate the causes of rioting during the 1960's. He served as appointed mayor until 1975, when he won an election for the post and then served until 1979.

Webb, Wellington Edward (b. Feb. 17, 1941, Chicago, Ill.). Mayor of Denver, COLORADO. Webb served as a representative in the Colorado state legislature from 1973 to 1977 and as the principal regulation official of the U.S. Department of Health and Human Services (1977). He was elected Denver mayor in 1991 and served until 1999.

West, Roy A. Mayor of Richmond, Virginia. West was elected to serve as a member of the city council from Richmond's Third District. He was elected by his fellow council members as the city's mayor and served from 1985 through June of 1986.

White, Michael Reed (b. Aug. 13, 1951, Cleveland, Ohio). Mayor of Cleveland, Ohio. White served on the Cleveland city council from 1977 to 1984 and was a member of the Ohio state senate from 1984 to 1989. He took office as the mayor of Cleveland in 1990.

Wilson, Lionel J. (Mar. 14, 1915, New Orleans, La.—Jan. 23, 1998, Oakland, Calif.). Mayor of OAKLAND, CALIFORNIA. Wilson began working as an attorney in Oakland in 1950. In 1960 Governor Edmund "Pat" Brown appointed him to the Oakland Piedmont Municipal Court as the first African American judge to preside in Alameda County. He became presiding judge of the Alameda County Superior Court in 1973 and was elected as the first African American mayor of Oakland in 1977. Wilson was reelected in 1981 and served until 1990.

Young, Andrew. Mayor of Atlanta, Georgia. *See main text entry.*

Young, Coleman. Mayor of DETROIT, MICHIGAN. *See main text entry.*

collective goods are distributed. Yet there are inherent limits on mayoral prerogatives. Federalism—the national/state division of governmental responsibilities—local fiscal capacity, differences in local government type, and individual capabilities all affect a mayor's ability to produce substantive change.

Federalism has a significant impact on black mayoral power. Cities are not mentioned in the U.S. CONSTITUTION; they therefore do not have explicit or implicit institutional powers, as do states. Rather, their powers are subject to the limitations imposed by their state legislatures.

Mayoral power is also limited by the fiscal capacity of a city. Municipalities cannot raise revenue to the same extent as state and federal governments. Even when taxing local constituents maximally, cities are limited by their local resource base. Heavy taxation can lead to the loss of businesses and affluent citizens. Cities with black mayors generally shoulder an additional burden of servicing poorer citizens who are less capable of providing the resources needed to improve physical surroundings and provide needed social services. Black mayors often inherit cities dependent on state and federal aid for much-needed funds, which further limits mayoral discretion and engenders subordination to outside authority. The need to retain and attract income-producing and job-creating enterprises creates further difficult financial considerations. Black mayors must often determine whether scarce resources should be used to attract new business or should be directed to meet the immediate needs of constituents.

The types of local government structures in which black mayors operate also can limit their powers. The term "mayor" is not indicative of a uniform level of executive power; a mayor's power and influence vary from city to city. A mayor may be a largely ceremonial figure if functioning in a council-manager form of government, in which departmental supervision is vested in a professional manager appointed by a city council. In such a situation, a mayor may be merely another council member who has the responsibility of chairing council meetings. Such an office provides little if any appointive power and no legal veto capability over council actions.

If functioning in a mayor-council form of government, a mayor is afforded more decision-making latitude (the city of Detroit is a good example), but such power is never uncontested. City councils, the legislative arms of municipal governments, are structural restraints that limit executive power. Between these polar positions are varying manifestations of mayoral power. It is quite possible to have a mayor-council form of government in which the mayor's appointive powers are severely restricted by city statutes, as is the case in Los Angeles. Black mayors, therefore, differ in their grants of power, a fact that necessarily affects their ability to meet the needs of their citizenry.

Black Mayoral Performance

The tasks facing black mayors are formidable. Assessments of black mayoral performance reflect frustrations that the high expectations of many black communities have not been entirely met. Such assessments also indicate that white fears that black administrations would result in sweeping local government changes were unconfirmed. Black mayoral administrations have been characterized by attempts to rebuild urban cores, ensure equal employment opportunity, and increase police accountability while curbing abuses. They have simultaneously come under criticism for inattentiveness to neighborhood needs for housing and rehabilitation, as many black mayors have pursued agendas consistent with the desires of the corporate community.

Decisions made by black mayors in favor of economic development have often been interpreted as signs of bias in favor of the corporate elite. Increasingly, the black working classes and poor sectors of the population have expressed disenchantment with such decisions, and this displeasure has become manifest in shifting electoral support. The presence of a black mayor does appear to engender policy change in the areas of employment opportunities and appointive posts, as well as in police-community relations. Black mayors are more likely to be rigorous in ensuring fairness and

As the leader of the nation's third-largest city during the mid-1980's, Chicago mayor Harold Washington was one of the most powerful city politicians in America. *(AP/Wide World Photos)*

in attempting to impose independent civilian supervision of law enforcement. Their ability fundamentally to alter prevailing social and economic relationships, however, appears to be limited at best.

Fears associated with black ascension to executive offices in local governments have dissipated, and whites are less inclined to oppose black candidates categorically, largely as a result of the knowledge that wholesale change in local government is unlikely. Black expectations for policy redirection remain unrealized. Although black mayors continue to grapple with the problems of urban life, the power of the offices and the resource bases afforded them are not sufficient to reverse a legacy of inequity.

—*Adewole A. Umoja*

See also: Electoral politics; Politics and government; Urbanization; Voters.

Suggested Readings:

Bennett, Larry. "Harold Washington and the Black Urban Regime." *Urban Affairs Quarterly* 28 (March, 1993): 423-440.

Biles, Roger. "Black Mayors: A Historical Assessment." *Journal of Negro History* 77 (Summer, 1992): 109-125.

Frady, Marshall. "An American Political Fable: How San Francisco's Mayor Willie Brown Became One Consummate Example of Democracy in Action." *The New Yorker* (October 21, 1996): 200-219.

Hornsby, Alton, Jr. "Andrew Jackson Young: Mayor of Atlanta, 1982-1990." *Journal of Negro History* 77 (Summer, 1992): 159-182.

Joint Center for Political Studies. *Profiles of Black Mayors in America*. Washington, D.C.: Joint Center for Political Studies, 1977.

Karnig, Albert K., and Susan Welch. *Black Representation and Urban Policy*. Chicago: University of Chicago Press, 1980.

Nelson, William E., Jr., and Philip J. Meranto. *Electing Black Mayors: Political Action in the Black Community*. Columbus: Ohio State University Press, 1977.

"New Wave of Black Mayors." *Ebony* (February, 1994): 92-96.

Rich, Wilbur C. *Coleman Young and Detroit Politics : From Social Activist to Power Broker*. Detroit: Wayne State University Press, 1999.

Swain, Johnnie D., Jr. "Black Mayors: Urban Decline and the Underclass." *Journal of Black Studies* 24 (September, 1993): 16-28.

Mays, Benjamin Elijah (August 1, 1895, Epworth, South Carolina—March 28, 1984, Atlanta, Georgia): Educator and author. Mays was the youngest of eight children. His parents had been slaves. He received his B.A. from Bates College in MAINE in 1920, then went on to teach higher math at Morehouse College in ATLANTA, GEORGIA, from 1921 to 1924. He continued his higher education at the University of Chicago, receiving an M.A. in

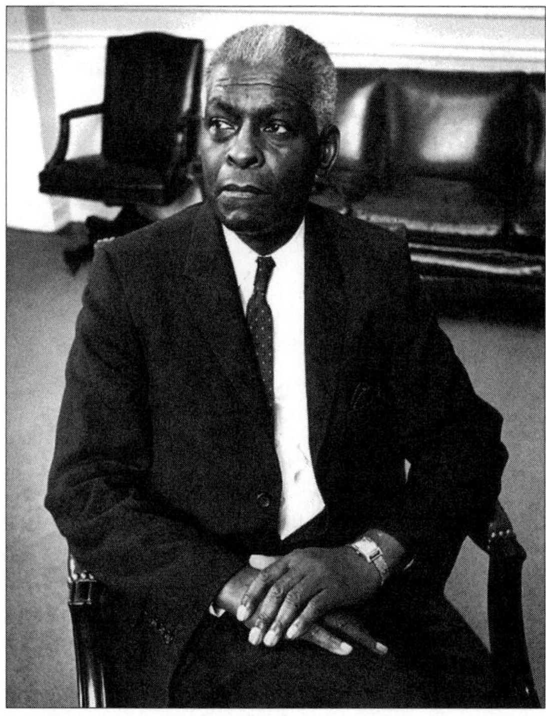

Morehouse College president Benjamin E. Mays in 1963. *(AP/Wide World Photos)*

1925 and a Ph.D. in 1935. While undertaking graduate study, he taught English for several years at South Carolina State College and worked in various positions for the state government. He was an activist and organizer for the NATIONAL URBAN LEAGUE. In 1934 he became dean of the school of religion at HOWARD UNIVERSITY. It was at this time that he had the opportunity to travel to India and talk with Mahatma Gandhi. He continued his work at Howard University until 1940, when he was offered the presidency of Morehouse College. He directed Morehouse until his retirement in 1967, when he was named president emeritus.

Mays achieved some notoriety for his early scholarly work. In 1933 he published, in collaboration with Joseph Nicholson, *The Negro's Church*, an assessment of the religious participation and life of the African American community and a pioneering study of African American sociology. Of greater importance was his 1938 work, *The Negro's God as Reflected in His Literature*, which was both a theological study and one of the first extended works of criticism of African American LITERATURE by an African American.

It was his invigoration of Morehouse College, however, that is Mays's greatest legacy. At Morehouse, he exerted a strong personal influence on many students, the most notable of whom was Martin Luther KING, Jr., to whom he sintroduced the thought of Mohandas Gandhi. He was effective at attracting philanthropic support to the college and ensured that Morehouse would be an outstanding African American institution for decades to come.

As his status as president was assured and expanded, he became outspoken on various CIVIL RIGHTS issues. He coauthored, in 1941, an early civil rights manifesto, *The Durham Statement*. Mays also became a central figure in the NATIONAL ASSOCIATION FOR THE ADVANCEMENT OF COLORED PEOPLE (NAACP), the World Council of Churches, the International Young Men's Christian Association, and the United Nations Children's Fund. In 1977 Mays became an adviser to President Jimmy Carter. He received numerous awards and honorary degrees for his work. In 1971 Mays published his autobiography, *Born to Rebel*.

Mays, Willie (b. May 6, 1931, Westfield, Alabama): BASEBALL player. William Howard "Willie" Mays, Jr., was born in Westfield, ALABAMA, a suburb of Birmingham. His parents were divorced before he started elementary school, and Willie was reared by his mother. His father, Willie, Sr., was a semiprofessional baseball player and was a factor in his son's early interest in playing the sport. Willie, Sr., worked in a steel mill, and in his early teens, Willie, Jr., began playing for his father's factory team alongside men twice his age.

Mays attended Fairfax Industrial High School in BIRMINGHAM, where he was a star athlete in baseball, basketball, and football. He was the leading scorer on the basketball team, but baseball was the sport he loved. In 1948, when he was barely seventeen years old, Mays left school to play baseball with the Birmingham Black Barons in the Negro American League. The year before, Jackie ROBINSON had become the first African American to play in the major leagues in the twentieth century, and prospects looked bright for talented black ballplayers.

Early Career

In 1948 the Birmingham Black Barons had an excellent team, and they won the Negro American League title. As one of the Black Barons, Mays played with Negro League All-Stars Piper Davis, Art Wilson, Bill Powell, and Alonzo Perry. Eddie Montague, a scout for the major league New York Giants, came to Birmingham in 1950 to sign Alonzo Perry to a contract, but he was impressed more by Mays, the flashy center fielder. Montague gave the team ten thousand dollars for Mays. Mays received a five-thousand-dollar bonus for signing and was sent to Trenton, NEW JERSEY, to play the remainder of the 1950 season in the Interstate League. In 1951 he was promoted to the Triple-A Minneapolis Millers. After thirty-five games, Mays was hitting .477 and was again promoted, this time to the New York Giants.

The first few games in the majors were a blow to the self-esteem of the twenty-year-old rookie. Mays had no hits in his first twelve at bats. At one point, the shy, reserved Mays broke down and cried and told his manager, Durocher, to send him back to Minneapolis. To help him adjust to New York, Durocher arranged for Mays to live with a black couple, David and Anna Goosby, who had a home near the Polo Grounds, where the Giants played. Mays was often seen playing stickball with the neighborhood kids.

His first hit in the major leagues was a home run against the future hall of famer Warren Spahn. By the end of the season, Mays was making a major contribution to one of the most thrilling come-from-behind pennant races in the history of baseball. The Giants caught the Brooklyn Dodgers on the last game of the season. In the ninth inning of the deciding playoff game, with the Dodgers leading by two runs, the Giants had runners on second and third. The Giants' third baseman, Bobby Thomson, then hit the "shot heard 'round the world," a home run to win the game. When asked why he did not walk Thomson with first base open, Dodgers manager Charlie Dressen said it was because Willie Mays was the next batter. For the young rookie who had started so miserably, this was the ultimate compliment and demonstrated the respect he had earned.

Willie Mays hits a single in the 1968 major league all-star game that his running skills eventually turned into a score. *(AP/Wide World Photos)*

National League All-Star
In 1952 and 1953, Mays served in the U.S. Army, putting his major-league career on hold. In 1954 he picked up where he left off, hitting forty-one home runs and leading the National League in hitting and slugging average. He helped the Giants win a league championship, and after his memorable opening-game catch, Mays and the Giants defeated Cleveland in four straight games in the World Series. Mays was elected to the National League all-star team in 1954 as well, his first of a record twenty consecutive appearances in the all-star game. At the end of the 1954 season, he was voted the league's most valuable player.

Mays quickly became a favorite of the fans in New York. He was already a favorite of the neighborhood kids. With his speed and ability, both on defense and at bat, he was an exciting player to watch. He had an infectious smile, and his spirited "Say Hey" greeting prompted the sports media of New York to call him the "Say Hey Kid." His "basket" catches, an underhand waist-level catch of fly balls, became a trademark. New York loved him.

He shared the New York spotlight, however, with the other two major-league center fielders in the city. Mays, Mickey Mantle of the New York Yankees, and Duke Snider of the Brooklyn Dodgers were the premier center fielders in the major leagues. Debates raged between the various team loyalists as to who was the best; regardless, the rivalry made baseball in New York exciting, and each of the three were esteemed by their respective fans.

Career in San Francisco
When the Giants moved to San Francisco in 1958, conditions changed for Mays. He had been the darling of New York, but in San Francisco, Giants fans attached themselves to the large crop of new players who had no history in New York. Orlando Cepeda and Willie McCovey reaped the affection of the CALIFORNIA fans the way Mays had in New York. Mays, however, continued to be among the league's leading ballplayers in his fourteen years in San Francisco. After twenty-two years with the Giants, he was traded to the New York Mets in 1972 and there played his last two seasons of major-league ball. He was back in New York, and although he was no longer the flashy rookie they saw in the 1950's, the fans remembered and loved him.

His career statistics place Mays among the premier ballplayers of all time. He ranks in the top ten in several categories: at bats, slugging average, hits, runs, runs batted in, and home runs. His total of 660 home runs has been exceeded only by Hank AARON and Babe Ruth. Mays received numerous awards and recognition for his accomplishments. In 1951 he was named National League rookie of the year. He won the league's most valuable player award in 1954 and 1965. Mays led the league in batting once and in home runs four times. He played in twenty-four all-star games and won the Gold Glove award for defensive play twelve times.

The Catch

In baseball lore it is merely called "The Catch." In the eighth inning of the first game of the 1954 World Series, the New York Giants and Cleveland Indians were tied, 2 to 2. The Indians had two runners on base, and Indian slugger Vic Wertz hit a long drive to center field. Willie Mays turned his back to the plate and sprinted toward the wall. On a dead run, he looked up and caught the ball over his shoulder 440 feet from home plate. Mays spun around and fired the ball back to the infield, thus preventing at least two runs from scoring and ending the Cleveland threat in the inning. The photograph of that catch is familiar to legions of baseball fans and epitomizes Willie Mays as a ballplayer.

Later Years
Willie Mays ended his playing career after helping the New York Mets to the World Series

in 1973. It was his fourth appearance in the fall classic. Afterward, he continued as a goodwill ambassador and part-time coach for the Mets. His greatest honor was his election to the Hall of Fame in 1979.

In the same year that Mays was elected to the Hall of Fame, baseball commissioner Bowie Kuhn made him choose between his job with the Mets and his employment as a greeter for a hotel casino. When Mays chose his job at the casino, he was barred from having anything to do with baseball. The ban was lifted by a new commissioner, Peter Ueberroth, in 1985. Mays then began serving as a part-time hitting coach with the Giants.

Whether Willie Mays was the greatest baseball player of all time is a subjective judgment. Even in a sport in which statistics are kept on virtually every nuance of the game, there is no good way to determine the overall best. Mays's first manager, Leo Durocher, once said that only a few players can do all five things that make a great player—hit for average, hit for power, run, throw, and catch the ball—and he declared Willie Mays to be one of those players. In fact, many people consider Willie Mays to be the greatest ballplayer of all time.

—*Jerry E. Clark*

See also: Negro League baseball.

Suggested Readings:

Einstein, Charles. *Willie's Time: A Memoir.* 2d ed. New York: Viking Press, 1992.

Honig, Donald. *Mays, Mantle, and Snider: A Celebration*. New York: Macmillan, 1986.

Kiernan, Thomas. *The Miracle at Coogan's Bluff.* New York: Thomas Y. Crowell, 1975.

Mays, Willie, and Lou Sahadi. *Say Hey: The Autobiography of Willie Mays*. New York: Simon & Schuster, 1988.

Mays, Willie, as told to Charles Einstein. *Born to Play Ball*. New York: G. P. Putnam's Sons, 1955.

"Willie Mays." *New York* (December 21, 1998): 60-61.

McCoy, Elijah (May 2, 1844, Colchester, Ontario, Canada—October 10, 1929, Eloise, Michigan): Inventor. Elijah McCoy ranks alongside George Westinghouse, J. F. Appleby, Thomas Alva Edison, and George Selden as one of the geniuses who made the great American industrial revolution of the late nineteenth century possible. He was a prolific inventor whose more than fifty patents relate primarily to the automatic lubrication of moving parts in machinery. His method of providing oil to machinery from a drip cup earned him the title "father of lubrication."

Early Life

McCoy was the son of runaway slaves who had escaped from KENTUCKY via the UNDERGROUND RAILROAD to Canada in 1840. After the CIVIL WAR, his family returned to the United States and settled near Ypsilanti, MICHIGAN.

McCoy first became interested in mechanical engineering at home, where he was constantly tinkering with household machines. He decided on engineering as a career while he was still in grammar school. Convinced that he could not receive adequate training in the United States, McCoy went to Edinburgh, Scotland, where he apprenticed in mechanical engineering.

Early Career

When he returned to the United States, McCoy found that his dream of becoming a mechanical engineer conflicted with the widely held notion that mechanical engineering was a white man's profession. Even though he had a certificate and letters of recommendation as a top-flight mechanical engineer, he was unable to find a company that would hire him. McCoy finally found work as a fireman on the Michigan Central Railroad. Because one of his duties involved oiling the moving parts of the engine at periodic intervals, McCoy soon came to realize that the frequent shutting down of machinery for lubrication was an inefficient and wasteful process.

First Patent

McCoy then set about to find a solution to this problem in a makeshift machine shop that he had set up in a shed. He wanted to find a way to lubricate machines while they worked. On July 2, 1872, he received a patent for his first lubricating system, which he called a "lubricating cup." The device consisted of a hollow stem that projected from the bottom of a cup into a cylinder. Inside the stem was a rod that had a valve at the upper end and a piston at the lower end. The valve rose when steam pressed on the cylinder, thereby permitting oil in the cup to lubricate the cylinder automatically. His invention, which was designed for stationary machines, was ideally suited for the steam engine and the steam cylinder. Like the locomotive engine that had inspired McCoy, heavy machinery in factories also had to be turned off for lubrication prior to McCoy's invention.

After McCoy completed work on his lubricating cup, he began a pattern that he continued to follow with each of his subsequent inventions. McCoy often made a partial or total assignment of the rights to his inventions to obtain sufficient money to continue his work. Thus, his first patent was assigned outright to William and S. C. Hamlin of Ypsilanti, but he retained the second for himself. His third and fourth patents, which were granted May 27, 1873, and January 20, 1874, were also assigned to Ypsilanti investors.

McCoy began working on an improved version of his lubricating system even before the patent was granted. On May 27, 1873, McCoy was granted a patent for an improved version of his original device. McCoy's new lubricating cup, which was fitted directly into the cylinder, supplied oil when the steam was exhausted. This process occurred at the time when lubrication was most needed. His lubricating cups found a ready market in factories across the United States. McCoy continued to patent improvements on his invention through the next several years.

Lubricating Steam Locomotives

After satisfying himself that he had perfected the lubricating systems for stationary machinery, McCoy set about to find a method for lubricating locomotives. Unlike stationary machinery, locomotives built up steam at great pressure, making continuous lubrication extremely difficult. McCoy solved this problem by using an independent steam pipe and an independent overflow pipe to equalize the pressure at the points where the oil would enter the engine. This device illustrated a basic principle of invention: The less complicated a device is, the more reliable it tends to be.

McCoy's invention was viewed as a time-saving device by railroads, which adopted it readily. Before long, McCoy's lubricating system was being used by Canadian and northwestern railroads and by shipping lines in the West and on the Great Lakes. By speeding up the railroads, McCoy's ingeniously simple system helped to spur the economic growth of the entire nation.

McCoy had no sooner obtained a patent for his device than hoards of imitators began to flood the market with cheap copies, most of which did not work nearly as well as McCoy's. The expression "the real McCoy" may have originated with purchasers of machinery who wanted to make sure that it had McCoy's lubricating system. Ironically, most of these factory owners or railroad owners, many of whom discriminated against blacks in employment, did not know that the inventor of this device was a black man.

McCoy obtained six patents for lubricators and one for an ironing table between 1872 and 1876. His creative activity apparently stopped altogether for the next six years. Then, in 1882, McCoy moved to DETROIT, where he began work on a steam dome for locomotives, which he finished in 1885.

Final Years

McCoy sustained his productivity well into the twentieth century. On June 4, 1907, he secured a patent for a scaffold support. He also patented a valve-and-plug-cock assembly on June 30, 1914, and a lawn sprinkler on May 20, 1916.

In 1920 McCoy organized the Elijah McCoy Manufacturing Company. That same year, McCoy adapted his lubrication system for use on the air brakes on locomotives and other vehicles. His device lubricated the pistons of the cylinders of air brakes by furnishing oil and graphite to the steam cylinders and dry graphite to the air cylinders. This invention made the operation of air brakes much more efficient.

Even though he was in poor health for the last eight years of his life, McCoy continued to invent. On October 2, 1923, he patented a vehicle tire, and on November 10, 1925, a rubber heel. McCoy was forced to retire from inventing altogether in 1926 when his health took a turn for the worse. After his wife died, McCoy was left alone with no one to care for him. Consequently, he was put in the Eloise Infirmary in Eloise, Michigan, in 1928.

Influence

By the time McCoy died in 1929, he had obtained fifty-seven patents, the largest number of inventions ever assigned to a black inventor. All but eight of his devices were designed to streamline his lubrication systems. McCoy's influence, though, was extended by countless other inventors who applied his principles to other moving parts of locomotives and other machines. Today, navy vessels, oil rigs, mining and construction machinery, and even space-exploration vehicles are lubricated by refinements of McCoy's inventions.

McCoy is generally regarded as a pioneer in the science of lubrication. Although he died in relative obscurity, his inventions rank in importance with those of the other great inventors of the nineteenth century. McCoy's greatest accomplishment, though, was the evidence that he and other black inventors provided to counteract the racist belief that genius was a characteristic possessed only by the white people.

—*Alan Brown*

See also: Inventors.

Suggested Readings:

Aaseng, Nathan. *Black Inventors*. New York: Facts on File, 1997.

Chappell, Kevin. "How Black Inventors Changed America." *Ebony* (February, 1997): 40-45.

Haber, Louis. *Black Pioneers of Science and Invention*. New York: Harcourt, Brace and World, 1970.

Haskins, James. *Outward Dreams: Black Inventors and Their Inventions*. New York: Walker, 1991.

"His Name Is Part of Our Language, His Inventions Are Part of Our Lives." *Ebony* (December, 1966): 27.

James, Portia P. *The Real McCoy: African American Invention and Innovation, 1619-1930*. Washington, D.C.: Smithsonian Institution Press, 1989.

Jenkins, Edward S. *To Fathom More: African American Scientists and Inventors*. Lanham, Md.: University Press of America, 1996.

Klein, Aaron E. *The Hidden Contributors*. Garden City, N.Y.: Doubleday, 1971.

Odom, Retha. "Pioneers in Technology." *Black Enterprise* (June, 1981): 182-186.

McCree, Wade Hampton, Jr. (b. July 3, 1920, Des Moines, Iowa): Political appointee. After his graduation from Fisk University in 1941, McCree received his LL.B. degree from Harvard Law School in 1944. He was admitted to the Michigan State Bar in 1948 and went into

Wade McCree in 1977. *(AP/Wide World Photos)*

private practice in Detroit. In 1954 McCree became a JUDGE on the Michigan Circuit Court in Wayne County and was later named judge of the U.S. District Court for the Eastern Michigan District. He was appointed by President Jimmy Carter to fill the post of solicitor general in 1977.

McDaniel, Hattie (June 10, 1895, Wichita, Kansas—October 26, 1952, Hollywood, California): First African American FILM actor to win an Academy Award. She was the thirteenth child of a Baptist minister. She began her career at age sixteen, as a singer in tent shows. By 1924 she was playing VAUDEVILLE circuits as a headliner billed as "The Colored Sophie Tucker" or "The Female Bert Williams." In the early 1930's, she moved to Los Angeles to work in radio on such programs as *Amos 'n' Andy, The Eddie Cantor Show,* and *Hit Hat Hattie*, as the title character.

McDaniel quickly became a favorite character actor in the movie industry. She most frequently played the "mammy" role, fitting the characteristics of the large, bossy, dark-skinned servant woman quick to belittle any black man who earned her contempt. McDaniel also seemed to transcend the restrictions of this stereotype. Unlike her counterparts, she tended to take more liberties with her white employers by being assertive and openly critical of their actions when necessary.

During the 1930's, McDaniel worked with most of Hollywood's leading actors, including Shirley Temple, Katharine Hepburn, Clark Gable, Marlene Dietrich, Jean Harlow, and Barbara Stanwyck. She often dominated her

Hattie McDaniel (right) with Vivian Leigh in *Gone With the Wind. (Arkent Archive)*

scenes with her strong visual presence and comic timing. By the end of her film career, she had appeared in more than seventy films, including *Blonde Venus* (1932), *Judge Priest* (1934), *Alice Adams* (1935), *The Mad Miss Manton* (1935), *Show Boat* (1936), and *Saratoga* (1937). McDaniel is best remembered for her portrayal of the faithful "Mammy" of the O'Hara household in the classic film *Gone With the Wind* (1939). This performance earned McDaniel an Academy Award for best supporting actor. This was the first Oscar awarded to an African American. She and her fellow African American cast members were not, however, permitted to attend the film's premiere performance in a segregated ATLANTA, GEORGIA, theater.

At the end of her career, McDaniel returned to radio to play another maid, in the popular *Beulah* series (1947-1951). She was scheduled to perform the role in the television series of the same name but died before acting in any episode.

McDonald, Gabrielle Kirk (b. April 12, 1942, St. Paul, Minnesota): Federal JUDGE. McDonald was educated at Boston University and Hunter College of the City University of New York. She graduated first in her class in 1966 from Howard University Law School. At law school, McDonald was an editor of the *Howard Law Journal* and received an award for academic excellence from the Kappa Beta Pi legal sorority. Upon graduation, she served as a staff attorney for the National Association for the Advancement of Colored People Legal Defense and Educational Fund until 1969. She and her husband founded their own law firm in HOUSTON, TEXAS, in 1969.

McDonald taught law at Texas Southern University from 1970 to 1977 and lectured at the University of Texas at Houston from 1977 to 1978. McDonald was appointed judge of the U.S. District Court, Southern District, in Houston on May 11, 1979. In recognition of her achievements in the fields of law and education, she was made a member of the board of visitors for Thurgood MARSHALL School of Law and was selected as a trustee of HOWARD UNIVERSITY in 1983.

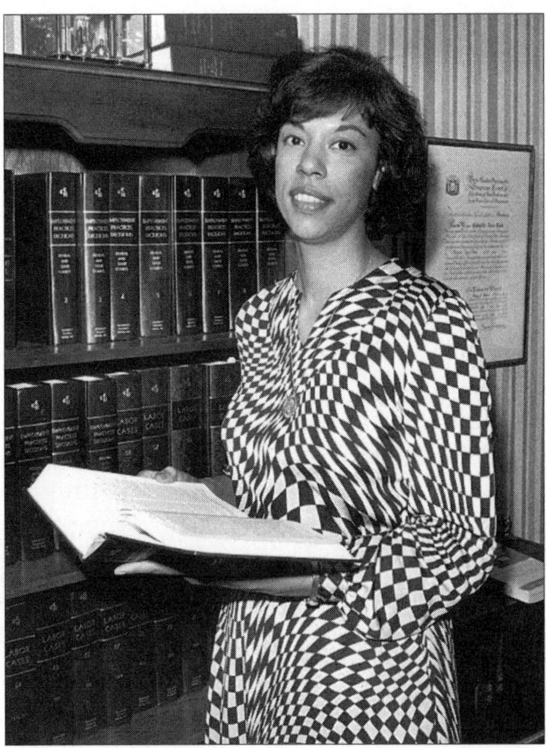
Gabrielle McDonald in 1978. *(AP/Wide World Photos)*

McEwen, Mark (b. September 16, 1954, San Antonio, Texas): RADIO BROADCASTING personality. As one of six children born to a U.S. Air Force colonel and his wife, McEwen grew up in Germany and at various American bases. After attending the University of Maryland from 1972 to 1977, McEwen took a job as a sports director and late-night disc jockey at an FM radio station in BALTIMORE, MARYLAND. After working at a rock radio station in DETROIT, MICHIGAN, from 1978 to 1980, he took a post as a disc jockey and research director at a popular CHICAGO, ILLINOIS, station and launched a second career as a stand-up COMIC.

McEwen continued his dual careers in New York City, where he became one of the few African American disc jockeys to achieve prominence in the competitive New York market. A CBS television industry producer hired McEwen as a weather reporter for the network's morning show in 1986, and McEwen was the only anchor retained on the revamped *CBS This Morning* show in 1987. McEwen began to share interviewing responsibilities with cohosts Harry Smith and Paula Zahn, serving as music editor and later as entertainment editor on the show. Eventually, McEwen was invited to serve as an official announcer providing voice-overs to promote CBS prime-time programs. In 1996 CBS announced that McEwen would take over in August as one of the new cohosts of *CBS This Morning*. McEwen was still hosting the program in early 2000.

McGuire, George Alexander (March 26, 1866, Sweets, Antigua—November 10, 1934, New York, New York): Founder and bishop of the African Orthodox Church. After emigrating to the United States, McGuire joined the Episcopalian Church. Racist conflict within the church prompted him to leave to start his own church and to work as the chaplain-general of Marcus Garvey's Universal Negro Improvement Association (UNIA). He lectured and formed churches not only in the United States but also in Australia, Canada, Cuba, the Dominican Republic, Antigua, Venezuela, and Uganda. He is remembered for his work among the sick and the poor, and for combating racism and instilling a sense of global pride in black heritage.

McHenry, Donald F. (b. October 13, 1936, St. Louis, Missouri): Educator and political appointee. McHenry grew up in East St. Louis, Illinois, and attended Illinois State University, where he received his bachelor of science degree in 1957. He then pursued graduate studies in public speaking and international affairs at Southern Illinois University and received his M.S. degree in 1959. McHenry held a position as an instructor of English at Howard University between 1959 and 1962 and undertook graduate studies in international relations at Georgetown University before joining the U.S. Department of State in 1963.

While working at the State Department, McHenry served in the Office of United Nations Political Affairs from 1963 to 1966. After working as assistant to the secretary of state from 1968 to 1969, McHenry became special assistant to the counselor of the State Department. He served as an alternate representative to a United Nations (U.N.) seminar on apartheid, as an alternate representative to the U.N. Trusteeship Council, and as a delegate to the U.N. Conference on Human Rights.

McHenry received the department's Superior Service Award in 1966. He took leave from the department in 1971 to do research as a guest scholar at the Brookings Institution, to take a fellowship in international affairs on the Council on Foreign Relations, and to lecture at Georgetown University's School of Foreign Service. In 1973 McHenry became director of humanitarian policy studies with the Carnegie Endowment for International Peace in Washington, D.C. He wrote a 1975 book, *Micronesia, Trust Betrayed: Altruism Versus Self-Interest in American Foreign Policy.* The topic had been of special interest to him while serving at the State Department.

President Jimmy Carter appointed McHenry to serve on the transition staff at the State Department in 1976. McHenry served as U.S. deputy representative to the United Nations Security Council in 1977. While serving on the U.N. Security Council, McHenry negotiated a compromise between South Africa and the representatives of the South West Africa People's Organization (SWAPO), calling for a cease-fire between the warring factions in Namibia (also known as South West Africa) and arranging for elections to be supervised by the United Nations. Although South Africa reneged on its promises, the agreement was an important diplomatic achievement in the region. President Carter appointed McHenry as the U.S. permanent representative to the United Nations on August 31, 1979, following Ambassador Andrew YOUNG's resignation earlier that month.

During his ambassadorship, McHenry was faced with two diplomatic crises that had far-reaching political consequences. He had to deal with the seizure of fifty-two American citizens and embassy staff members as hostages in Tehran, Iran, in 1979. McHenry skillfully won support in the General Assembly and on the Security Council for a declaration demanding the immediate release of the hostages. He also won support for a proposal that security council members impose an economic boycott on Iran, but a Soviet veto prevented implementation of a complete embargo. McHenry also had to cope with the diplomatic problems triggered by the Soviet Union's invasion of Afghanistan in December of 1979.

Upon leaving his United Nations post, McHenry became research professor of diplomacy and international affairs at Georgetown University in 1981 and became president of International Relations Consultants, Inc., a private consulting firm. He also served as a member of the editorial board for *Foreign Policy* magazine.

See also: Diplomats.

McKay, Claude (September 15, 1889, Sunny Ville, Jamaica—May 22, 1948, Chicago, Illinois): Poet, novelist, and essayist. McKay usually is considered both a forerunner of and a key figure in the HARLEM RENAISSANCE. He lived in Sunny Ville, JAMAICA, until 1912. He wrote his first two books of poetry, *Constab Ballads* (1912) and *Songs of Jamaica* (1912), mostly in Jamaican dialect. The poems in *Constab Ballads* draw on his experience as a constable in Kingston, Jamaica, while *Songs of Jamaica* celebrates Jamaican peasant life.

McKay moved to the United States in 1912, to study first at TUSKEGEE INSTITUTE and then at Kansas State University. He soon gave up his studies, moving to NEW YORK CITY to pursue a writing career while supporting himself in a variety of menial jobs.

In this early New York phase (1914-1919), McKay wrote short lyrics, mostly sonnets, in the style of the English Renaissance and

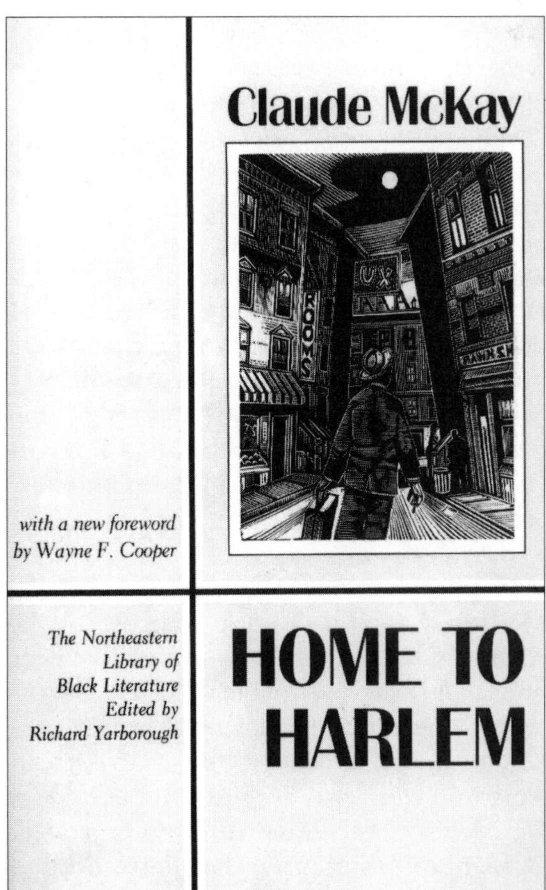

Claude McKay's 1928 novel *Home to Harlem* captured the spirit of the Harlem Renaissance and portrayed the struggles of young African Americans finding their way in a racist society. *(Arkent Archive)*

Romantic writers whom he had read before leaving Jamaica. The subject matter of these poems, however, is his own experience, especially of American racism. McKay voiced a sentiment to which many African Americans, tired of discrimination and violence against them, responded. "If We Must Die," reprinted in his 1922 collection *Harlem Shadows*, helped secure his reputation as a major figure of the Harlem Renaissance and was quoted by Winston Churchill in an address to a joint session of the American Congress when he sought to secure American support for the Allies in World War II.

McKay traveled extensively—to England in 1919, to Russia in 1922, and then to France and Morocco in 1923. During this time, he wrote fiction that never achieved the acclaim of his poetry: the short stories of *Gingertown* (1932) and the novels *Home to Harlem* (1928), *Banjo: A Story Without a Plot* (1929), and *Banana Bottom* (1933). The last is generally considered artistically to be the most successful of these, with its Jamaican setting and resolution in a marriage that reconciles the educated and the peasant. McKay returned to the United States in 1934. He published his autobiography, *A Long Way from Home*, in 1937 and the nonfiction *Harlem: Negro Metropolis* in 1940. Eight years later he died of heart failure in Chicago. *See also:* Literature.

McKinney, Cynthia Ann (b. March 17, 1955, Atlanta, Georgia): Educator and government official. A Democrat from the Georgia's Eleventh Congressional District, Cynthia McKinney in 1992 became the first African American elected to Congress from Georgia. During her 1988-1992 term in the Georgia state legislature, McKinney also had the distinction of being part of the country's only father-daughter team to serve in the same legislature.

McKinney received her undergraduate degree in international relations from the University of Southern California in 1978. After graduation, she continued to pursue her education at Georgia State University and at the University of Wisconsin. In 1993 McKinney completed her Ph.D. degree from Tufts University's Fletcher School of Law and Diplomacy.

McKinney's career included a mix of educational and political appointments. In 1984 she accepted a position as diplomatic fellow at Spelman College. She later served as a political science instructor at Atlanta University before accepting a similar post at Agnes Scott College. McKinney launched her political career in 1986, when she ran unsuccessfully for a seat in the Georgia state legislature. (Her father, J. E. "Billy" McKinney, had been serving in the state house since 1973.) Running again in 1988, she joined her father in the Georgia House of Representatives.

During McKinney's career in the Georgia state legislature, she made a name for herself as tough challenger to the establishment. She questioned the state's lack of contracts with minority-owned businesses and was later rewarded when Governor Zell Miller issued an executive order emphasizing an increased number of minority contracts. Greater black representation in the Congress, as well as in state and local affairs, became an issue which McKinney helped promote. She led the fight for reapportionment which would create a third black-majority district in southwest Georgia. She refused to accept two different maps that maintained a white majority in the area. Eventually these maps were rejected because they did not protect the rights of the minority according to the Voting Rights Act. Eventually the state's second congressional district was fairly reapportioned as a result of McKinney's persistence.

After a surprising win in the 1992 Democratic Party primary, McKinney was able to take 73 percent of the vote, beating Republican Woodrow Lovett. McKinney's father served as her campaign manager and treasurer, helping her to become the first black female congressional representative from Georgia.

After taking her seat in January of 1993, McKinney was appointed to serve on the House Agricultural Committee and the House Foreign Affairs Committee. In addition to her work as a member of the CONGRESSIONAL BLACK CAUCUS and the Congressional Caucus for Women's Issues, McKinney served as a member of the Arms Control and Foreign Policy Caucus, the Congressional Children's Working Group, the Congressional Hunger Caucus, and the Reinventing Government Caucus. The 103rd Congress chose her to head the Women's Caucus Task Force on Children, Youth, and Families. A single parent herself, McKinney was the first freshman ever chosen for this position. She was reelected in 1994, 1996, and 1998.

Among her many community activities, McKinney served as a member of the Metro Atlanta HIV Health Services Planning Council (on which she served as a board member), the NATIONAL COUNCIL OF NEGRO WOMEN, the NATIONAL ASSOCIATION FOR THE ADVANCEMENT OF COLORED PEOPLE (NAACP), and the Sierra Club.

See also: Congress members; Politics and government; Redistricting.

McKinney, Nina Mae (1913, Lancaster, South Carolina—May 3, 1967, New York, New York): Stage and FILM actor. Sometimes billed as the "Black Greta Garbo," McKinney emerged as Hollywood's first African American sex symbol. At the age of fifteen, she appeared in the chorus line of Lew Leslie's Broadway revue *Blackbirds of 1928*. She was almost immediately propelled to fame when she starred as Chick in King Vidor's all-black musical *Hallelujah!* (1929). Hollywood, however, provided few follow-up roles. With the exception of an appearance in the musical short *Pie Pie Blackbird* (1932), Hollywood had little to offer her.

With little reason to stay in CALIFORNIA, McKinney went on a European tour, performing in cabarets and clubs. While in England, she costarred with Paul ROBESON in *Sanders of the River* (1939). Following her return to the United States, McKinney was featured in such black independently produced films as *St. Louis Gal* (1938), *Gang Smashers* (1938), *Straight to Heaven* (1939), *The Devil's Daughter* (1939), *Dark Waters* (1944), *Night Train to Memphis* (1946), and *Mantan Messes Up* (1946), with Mantan Moreland and Lena HORNE. Her last screen performance came in a supporting role in the miscegenation drama *Pinky* (1949).

Periodically, McKinney returned to the stage. She appeared in an all-black revue at the APOLLO THEATER in 1939, and in the drama *Good Neighbor* (1941). McKinney's final important performance was in 1951, as Sadie Thompson in a Brooklyn production of the drama *Rain*. McKinney was honored posthumously by being inducted into the Black Filmmakers Hall of Fame in 1978.

McKissack, Patricia, and Fredrick Lemuel McKissack (Patricia: b. L'Ann Carwell, August 9, 1944, Nashville, Tennessee) (Frederick: b. August 12, 1939, Nashville, Tennessee): Children's book authors. The McKissacks received their undergraduate education at Tennessee State University: Patricia received her bachelor's degree in English, and Fredrick received his degree in civil engineering. Patricia later went on to earn a master's degree from Webster University in St. Louis, MISSOURI. Patricia worked as a schoolteacher and as a book editor, and Fredrick served as an engineering contractor for city and federal governments before the pair began their joint career as authors.

The McKissacks' books fall into several subject groups: historical biographies and fictional stories that re-create moments in African American history; stories about family relationships and conflicts; religious stories; and adaptations of traditional European folktales. Although their books are designed to appeal to all audiences, the McKissacks have selected topics that specifically appeal to African American children and young adults. There are colorful picture books for young toddlers, reading readiness books for beginning readers, and young adult texts for older adolescent readers. As authors, the McKissacks aim to educate and enlighten young readers, instilling them with a sense of pride and self-worth.

Patricia and Fredrick McKissack have profiled many African American historical figures, including abolitionists such as Frederick Douglass and Sojourner Truth, authors such as Langston Hughes and Zora Neale Hurston, musicians such as Marian Anderson and Louis Armstrong, and social activists such as Paul Robeson and Ida B. Wells-Barnett. Other notable biographies have covered educator Mary McLeod Bethune, military leader General Benjamin O. Davis, and sports hero Satchel Paige. Some of their historical works have dealt with specific social issues, such as racial discrimination. In 1986 the McKissacks published *A History of the Civil Rights Movement* in order to provide young readers with an introduction to the key figures and events of this important social movement.

Although the McKissacks have published most of their works as joint authors, they have also produced several books as solo authors. Patricia's 1986 book *Flossie and the Fox*, based on a folktale she collected from her grandfather, was named one of the best children's books by *School Library Journal* and by *Time* magazine. The pair won the 1985 C. S. Lewis Silver Medal Award and the Christian Education Association Award for *Abram, Abram, Where Are We Going?*; the 1990 Coretta Scott King Award from the American Library Association; and the Jane Addams Peace Award for *A Long Hard Journey: The Story of the Pullman Porters*; the Carter G. Woodson Book Award for *Madam C. J. Walker*; and the 1995 Coretta Scott King Award for *Christmas in the Big House, Christmas in the Quarters*. As sole author, Patricia McKissack won the 1993 Coretta Scott King Award for *The Dark Thirty: Southern Tales of the Supernatural*, which was also named a 1993 Newbery Honor Book.

See also: Children's literature; Folklore; Juvenile and young adult fiction.

McKissick, Floyd Bixler, Sr. (March 9, 1922, Asheville, North Carolina—April 28, 1991, Durham, North Carolina): Civil rights activist and founder of Soul City, North Carolina. Soul City, the first modern-era African American community, was designed as an industrial and residential township in Warren County. It was the only free-standing community financed by the U.S. Department of Housing and Urban Development. McKissick's work with Soul City was a small part of a life dedicated to community service.

McKissick served in the U.S. Army from 1941 through 1945, receiving a Purple Heart. He was a graduate of Morehouse College and the law school at North Carolina College for Negroes at Durham. He received national recognition from the civil rights community when he successfully sued for admission to the all-white University of North Carolina Law School. After receiving his law degree in 1952, he began his law practice. Durham and Oxford, North Carolina, were the locations of his law practice for many years.

As a prominent attorney, he represented the National Association for the Advancement of Colored People (NAACP) in several civil rights cases. When the Civil Rights movement stepped up its activity in the Durham and Chapel Hill area, activists from the Congress of Racial Equality (CORE) played a major role. It was McKissick's reputation as an NAACP attorney who was an outspoken and articulate spokesman for equal rights that led to his selection as the North Carolina CORE leader and later the director of the national CORE office. McKissick made invaluable contributions as the national chairman (1963-1966) and national director (1966-1968) of CORE. His predecessor, James FARMER, noted that McKissick played an important role in developing CORE's "Freedom Highways" campaign in North Carolina. As CORE director, McKissick helped organize James MEREDITH's march in MISSISSIPPI in 1966 and was an interpreter of the BLACK POWER MOVEMENT. Although the Black Power movement placed considerable strain on McKissick's leadership of CORE as an interracial body, he did not expel whites from the group.

McKissick was an ordained BAPTIST minister who served as the pastor of the First Baptist Church of Soul City. He was also the author of *Three-Fifths of a Man* (1968). In 1989 he was appointed to a North Carolina state judgeship.

McLaurin v. Oklahoma State Regents: U.S. SUPREME COURT decision on segregation in HIGHER EDUCATION decided in 1950. In 1948 George W. McLaurin, a sixty-eight-year-old African American educator, applied to graduate school at the University of Oklahoma and was turned down. A special three-judge district court forced the university to accept McLaurin because the state did not have separate graduate programs available for African Americans. McLaurin attended the University of Oklahoma but was forced to sit in segregated sections in the classroom, library, and dining facilities. When the district court upheld this internal segregation, Thurgood MARSHALL of the NATIONAL ASSOCIATION FOR THE ADVANCEMENT OF COLORED PEOPLE (NAACP) Legal Defense Fund appealed to the Supreme Court.

In 1950 the Court handed down its decision on *McLaurin v. Oklahoma* at the same time it ruled on SWEATT V. PAINTER and *Henderson v. United States*. While not addressing the issue of "SEPARATE BUT EQUAL" segregated facilities (that would come four years later), in a unanimous decision the Court held that if separate educational facilities did not exist, then restrictions, or any form of harassment, could not be placed on individuals at the University of Oklahoma.

—*Craig S. Pascoe*

M.C. Lyte (b. 1970?): RAP vocalist. Lyte and her brother, Audio Two, had a combined act in the early days of rap music. Their father, Nat Robinson, founded the First Priority record label for their rap recordings, and the label was distributed by Atlantic records. Lyte was one of the first female rappers to go solo. She was one of the performers involved in recording the single and video "Self-Destruction" to raise money for the NATIONAL URBAN LEAGUE and to increase teens' awareness of the tragedies of black-on-black crime. Lyte was also featured in public service ads about WOMEN, birth control, and ACQUIRED IMMUNODEFICIENCY SYNDROME (AIDS). Her third album, *Act Like You Know* (1992), included the single "When in Love." She is known for her blunt and direct lyrics touching on serious social issues such as TEENAGE PREGNANCY and drug abuse.
See also: Black-on-black violence.

McMillan, Terry (b. October 18, 1951, Port Huron, Michigan): Novelist. McMillan grew up in a factory town about 60 miles northeast of DETROIT, MICHIGAN. Her mother was divorced when she was fourteen. As a teenager, McMillan discovered the writing of James BALDWIN, which eventually made her decide to try writing. She earned her bachelor's degree in journalism from the University of California at Berkeley in 1979. Thereafter she moved to New York, where she joined the Harlem Writers Guild.

Taye Diggs and Angela Bassett (Stella) in the 1998 film adaptation of McMillan's *How Stella Got Her Groove Back*. *(Museum of Modern Art, Film Stills Archive)*

McMillan wrote her first novel, *Mama* (1987), while working as a word processor and rearing her infant son alone. Her second novel, *Disappearing Acts* (1989), was written from a black man's point of view. McMillan achieved startling success with her third novel, *Waiting to Exhale* (1992), which quickly became a best-seller. Her conversational writing style and her sympathetic depictions of four black women's struggles with romance, families, and careers struck a chord with a wide readership.

Her work (and *Waiting to Exhale* in particular) has sometimes been criticized for containing negative portrayals of black men, but McMillan does not present caricatures. Her characters are generally middle-class African Americans with real-life problems. It has been noted that McMillan was among the writers who first proved to major publishing houses that there was indeed a large black reading audience for fiction that was of interest them.

The success of her writing attracted film producers, and the successful 1995 film version of *Waiting to Exhale* brought her further acclaim. Her 1996 novel, the somewhat autobiographical *How Stella Got Her Groove Back*, was also adapted into a successful film, released in 1998.
See also: Literature.

McMillian, Theodore (b. January 28, 1919, St. Louis, Missouri): Federal JUDGE. McMillian received his B.S. degree in 1941 from LINCOLN UNIVERSITY. In 1942 McMillian joined the U.S. Army Signal Corps, attaining the rank of lieutenant before he was discharged in 1946. After the war, he enrolled in law school at St. Louis University and graduated with his LL.B. degree in 1949. After graduation, McMillian worked as a lecturer at St. Louis University Law School and served on the faculty of Webster College.

McMillian's public legal career began when he worked as assistant circuit attorney for the city of St. Louis from 1953 to 1956. His first judicial posting came in 1972, when he was selected to serve as a judge on the MISSOURI Court of Appeals. McMillian held this post until 1978, when President Jimmy Carter appointed him to serve on the federal bench as U.S. circuit judge for the Eighth Circuit of the U.S. Court of Appeals. McMillian's judicial district covered Arkansas, Iowa, Minnesota, Missouri, Nebraska, North Dakota, and South Dakota.

McNair, Ronald E. (October 12, 1950, Lake City, South Carolina—January 28, 1986, Cape Canaveral, Florida): Astronaut. McNair was one of the seven crew members aboard the space shuttle *Challenger* when it exploded, soon after takeoff. McNair earned his Ph.D. at the Massachusetts Institute of Technology in 1976, in physics. He was a physicist at Hughes Research Laboratories before becoming a mission specialist astronaut with the National Aeronautics and Space Administration in

Ronald E. McNair (lower right) with fellow crew members of the ill-fated *Challenger* mission, including schoolteacher Christa McAuliffe (standing, second from left). *(AP/Wide World Photos)*

1978. The Massachusetts Institute of Technology named a building for him.
See also: Aviators and astronauts.

McPherson, James Alan (b. September 16, 1943, Savannah, Georgia): Author. A 1981 MacArthur fellow, McPherson achieved distinction as a fiction writer and a teacher. McPherson's fiction draws on his own childhood and later experiences during the Civil Rights movement. He never connected himself with the Black Arts movement or with any other literary movement.

McPherson received his baccalaureate degree from Morris Brown College, Atlanta, in 1965 and a law degree from Harvard Law School in 1968. A 1962 summer job with the Great Northern Railroad Company yielded material for the book *Railroad: Trains and Train People in American Culture*, which he and Miller Williams published in 1972.

"Gold Coast" and other stories that appeared in the *Atlantic Monthly* between 1965 and 1969 led to his first published collection, *Hue and Cry*, and to a Rockefeller and National Institute of Arts grant in 1970 and to a Guggenheim Fellowship for 1972-1973. In 1995 McPherson was elected to the American Academy of Arts and Sciences.

Acknowledging Ralph Ellison as a major influence, McPherson once said that he writes about "people, all kinds of people." In addition to *Elbow Room*, for which he won a Pulitzer Prize in 1978, McPherson published *A World Unsuspecting* (1987), *The Prevailing South* (1988), *Confronting Racial Differences* (1990), *Lure and Loathing* (1993), and *Crossing* (1993). He also served as editor of *Double Take* magazine. In 1981 McPherson began teaching at the Iowa's Writers' Workshop, where he earlier had earned his master of fine arts degree.

—*Bes Stark Spangler*

See also: Literature.

McQueen, Butterfly (b. January 8, 1911, Tampa, Florida): Stage and FILM actor. The daughter of a stevedore and a domestic, Thelma "Butterfly" McQueen moved north to Harlem to pursue a stage career in 1935. Almost immediately, she joined Venezuela Jones's Negro Youth Group. While part of the troupe, she performed the "Butterfly Ballet" in a production of *A Midsummer Night's Dream*. Following that performance, McQueen was nicknamed "Butterfly."

McQueen made her Broadway debut in George Abbott's musical *Brown Sugar* (1937). Abbott, who had been impressed by McQueen's talents, wrote a part specifically for her in *What a Life* (1938). The play became a smash hit, and McQueen won acclaim for her performance. Her other theater credits include *Swingin' the Dream* (1939), an all-black touring production of *Harvey* (1946), and the pre-Broadway company of *The Wiz* (1975).

Butterfly McQueen is best remembered for her role in *Gone With the Wind. (Archive Photos)*

McQueen's screen debut came when she was chosen to portray the maid Prissy in David Selznick's CIVIL WAR epic, *Gone With the Wind* (1939). She was originally deemed unsuitable for the role because she was twice the age of the fourteen-year-old character. McQueen's performance made both positive and negative impressions on audiences. Her FILM career never seemed to capitalize on her newfound notoriety. Her other film appearances, usually as a domestic, include roles in *The Women* (1939), *Cabin in the Sky* (1943), *Mildred Pierce* (1945), and *Duel in the Sun* (1947). Although she was included in the filming of *Since You Went Away* (1944), all her scenes were deleted from the final edited version. By the late 1940's, her film career temporarily had ended.

McQueen produced a one-woman concert at Carnegie Hall in 1951. It was a financial disaster. Afterward, she drifted from job to job. Having moved to Augusta, GEORGIA, in 1957, McQueen returned to HARLEM in 1967. There, she waited tables. In 1968 McQueen was hired to perform in *Curly McDimples*, an Off-Broadway spoof of Hollywood of the 1930's. She had parts in the films *The Phynx* (1970), *Amazing Grace* (1974), and *Mosquito Coast* (1986).

In 1975, after a period of thirty years and attendance at five different colleges, McQueen received her B.A. degree from City College of New York. Her honors include induction into the Black Filmmakers Hall of Fame (1975).

McRae, Carmen (April 8, 1922, New York, New York—November 10, 1994, Beverly Hills, California): JAZZ singer. McRae's legitimately can be identified as one of the most original jazz voices. McRae studied piano as a child. A child of immigrants from the West Indies, she won the prestigious amateur talent contest at the APOLLO THEATER when she was only seventeen. She began her professional singing career with Benny CARTER's orchestra, in 1946.

Eventually, still in the mid-1940's, McRae worked with both the Count BASIE and the Mercer Ellington bands. During a stint at MINTON'S PLAYHOUSE in HARLEM, as an intermission singer and pianist, she was attracted to the new jazz called BEBOP. She also learned from and was influenced by the great jazz-bop singer Sarah VAUGHAN.

McRae's importance as a jazz vocalist heavily influenced by bebop should never be underestimated. Her rich voice, often accompanied by her own piano playing, delighted jazz audiences. Frequently, she employed scat techniques reminiscent of Sarah Vaughan and Ella FITZGERALD, and she used a variety of other techniques in her renditions of ballads or other kinds of standards. McRae brought to each song she performed an impressive and comprehensive range of knowledge and insight. She brought to every performance, whether in a concert hall, a jazz club, or a recording studio, an artistry of style coupled with a sheer rhythmic exuberance.

McRae's 1990 album, *Carmen Sings Monk*, was judged by many critics to be her best. Highlighting her pure, uncompromising approach to jazz, the album features tunes by pianist and composer Thelonious MONK, an originator of the bebop style that heavily influenced McRae. McRae selected the tunes herself and had lyrics written for them. An accomplished pianist, McRae held that one "should know an instrument to be a good jazz singer." For McRae, jazz was "all about improvising"; she explained that "you have to have something of your own" to bring to a song. Throughout her recording career, McRae toured constantly, performing live for audiences in the United States, Europe, and Japan. During most of the 1980's, she fulfilled two engagements a year at the famed Blue Note jazz club in New York.

McRae also accepted film roles. She appeared in the multicharacter drama *Hotel* (1962) and in comedian Richard PRYOR's semiautobiographical *Jo Jo Dancer, Your Life Is Calling* (1982).

Singer Carmen McRae. *(AP/Wide World Photos)*

In May of 1991, McRae retired from singing after suffering respiratory failure following a performance. In January of 1994, she was honored with a National Endowment for the Arts Fellowship Award for lifetime achievement. She died eleven months later, four days after falling into a semi-coma and a month after being hospitalized for a stroke. Her recording career had spanned nearly five decades.

—Updated by Amy Adelstein

McTell, Blind Willie (May 5, 1901, Thomson, Georgia—August 19, 1959, Milledgeville, Georgia): BLUES musician. McTell began playing blues guitar with traveling shows as a teenager. He stopped playing in his late teens. By the mid 1920's, when blues became popular, he began playing again. In 1927 and 1928, he had two recording sessions with Ralph Peer for Victor. These were his strongest sessions. He was in his early twenties, but his voice sounded much younger. His lyrics were typical country blues combined with an innocent sadness that accompanied his recurring themes of wandering. Among the songs recorded were "'Tain't Long fo' Day," "Mr. McTell Got the Blues," "Dark Night Blues," and "Statesboro Blues."

The rest of McTell's career was marked by occasional recordings on various labels, which released little of what they recorded. He had occasional masterpieces, such as "Dyin' Crapshooter Blues" and "Broke Down Engine Blues," but seemed to be searching for an identity, as were many of the Atlanta bluesmen. Blues had become popular, and musicians believed they had to imitate the more successful artists. McTell imitated Blind Willie Johnson.

Blind Willie McTell playing his twelve-string guitar. *(Frank Driggs/Archive Photos)*

Record companies recorded anyone they could, with little concern for the welfare of the musicians. McTell was recorded under the names Georgia Bill, Barrelhouse Sammy, Red Hot Willie, and Pig 'n' Whistle. Once, he was recorded in a hotel room and given ten dollars as payment.

McTell played his Stella twelve-string guitar with the same ease he played a six-string. His restless playing contrasted with his knowledge and use of standard blues patterns. His lyrics presented a direct and emotional statement that mirrored his life experience. McTell's individual voice did not fit the blues that became popular around the time of WORLD WAR II. He ended up playing in parking lots, in alleys, and at food stands. He drank heavily and suffered several strokes, for which he was hospitalized. His death records and gravestone mistakenly listed his name as Eddie McTier.

Medicine: In many respects, the position of blacks in medicine has been similar to the position of blacks in other areas of American life. As late as the middle 1940's, only two medical colleges in the southern states and the District of Columbia admitted African American students—HOWARD UNIVERSITY MEDICAL SCHOOL AND HOSPITAL in WASHINGTON, D.C., and MEHARRY MEDICAL SCHOOL in Nashville, TENNESSEE. As late as the mid-1960's, black medical college graduates were often denied equal access to internships and residencies, while black physicians were denied staff appointments in many southern hospitals and in a number of private hospitals in the North. At the same time, African American doctors were likely to be excluded from membership in some medical associations. Just as blacks were able to achieve despite the odds in the larger society, they were also able to make significant contributions in the field of medicine in spite of discrimination and unequal opportunities.

Early Black Physicians

The earliest known African American physician in the colonies was Lucas Santomee Peters, a Dutch-educated doctor. Little is known about him except that the colony of New York awarded him a special grant for his services in 1667. The best-known of the early black medical men was James Durham. Born a slave in Philadelphia in 1762, he belonged to several different owners, all of whom were physicians. At a tender age, Durham became the slave of John Kearsley, Jr., a physician who taught him to compound medicines and to perform other simple duties. In 1772, at the time of Kearsley's death, ten-year-old James became the property of Gregory West, an apothecary with the British forces in the colonies. At the close of the revolutionary war, Durham, who was still a slave, was sold to Robert Dow, a Scottish physician living in New Orleans who employed Durham as an assistant. On April 2, 1783, Dow granted Durham his freedom in exchange for the sum of five hundred pesos.

In 1788 Durham visited Philadelphia, where he met Benjamin Rush, America's foremost physician of his era. Soon after his return to New Orleans, he sent Rush a paper describing his method for treating putrid sore throat (diphtheria), as he believed that he had found the most efficient method for treating the malady. On August 4, 1789, Rush read Durham's paper, "An Account of the Putrid Sore Throat at New Orleans," before the distinguished College of Physicians of Philadelphia. Durham's medical practice, however, was not confined to treating throat ailments. In 1796, when a yellow-fever epidemic ravaged New Orleans, more that fifty people turned to him for medical treatment. Two years later, during another outbreak of the disease, Durham lost only eleven of his sixty-four patients. He believed that his success was attributable to "a decoction of garden sorrell and sugar" that he prescribed for his patients.

On August 14, 1801, Durham's medical practice was restricted by New Orleans's governing commissioners when they ruled that only licensed physicians—persons holding medical degrees—could practice in New Orleans; however, the commissioners agreed to allow Durham to continue to treat diseases of the throat.

Acquiring Medical Degrees

An inability to secure a formal medical education was a prime factor in limiting the number of blacks in the medical profession. It was true that apprenticed physicians were numerous throughout the eighteenth and nineteenth centuries, but many doctors were reluctant to apprentice blacks. Some blacks, however, did secure formal medical training. In 1847 David J. Peck became the first African American to earn a medical degree from an American medical college, Rush Medical College in Chicago.

In 1849 two blacks, John V. De Grasse and Thomas J. White, were awarded medical degrees from the medical school at Bowdoin College. Both were sponsored by the American Colonization Society, which had established the African country of Liberia as a future home for free African Americans. The society had hoped that De Grasse and White would become medical missionaries in the colony. There is also some evidence that even before 1847 the colonization society had financed the medical education of three blacks from Washington, D.C., with hopes that they too would work in Liberia.

By 1860 at least nine northern medical colleges had admitted one or more blacks to their programs. Yet opportunities for blacks remained limited, and some elected to pursue their medical educations outside the United States. The best-known of this group was James McCune Smith. Born in New York in 1811, he received his basic education at the Free African School. In 1837 he was awarded a medical degree from the University of Glasgow in Scotland. Upon completing his training, he returned to America and became a successful physician who ran two drugstores in New York.

Another well-known black physician of the antebellum era was Martin R. DELANY. Born in VIRGINIA in 1812, Delany moved to PENNSYLVANIA, where he secured a sound basic education. At age nineteen, he was living in Pittsburgh, where he became an apprentice with a prominent physician. Delany later served two additional apprenticeships, although only one was a prerequisite for medical school admission. Like other qualified blacks of the day, however, Delany had his application to medical school rejected. He applied to Harvard University's medical school and was accepted in 1850, but student resentment toward black admissions soon drove him away. Delany returned to Pittsburgh, where he practiced medicine without a formal degree. Delany, however, is best remembered for his activism rather than for his medical practice; he was a prominent abolitionist who gave serious thought to black colonization as an answer to America's race problem.

Achievements in Surgery

Toward the end of the nineteenth century, black physicians began to make some noteworthy contributions in the fields of medicine and surgery. One of the best-known of this group was Daniel Hale WILLIAMS, who in July of 1893 performed what many believe was the earliest heart surgery in the United States. Born in Pennsylvania in 1856, Williams later moved to WISCONSIN, where he graduated from Haire's Classical Academy in Janesville. He also served a two-year apprenticeship under Henry Palmer, a prominent Wisconsin surgeon. Williams later received his medical degree from the Chicago Medical College, an affiliate of Northwestern University.

Williams was the prime mover in organizing the Provident Hospital in Chicago, which afforded opportunities to black medical graduates as interns and also offered professional nurses' training to black women. He was also a founder of the NATIONAL MEDICAL ASSOCIATION and the only black charter member of the American College of Surgeons. By all accounts, he was one of the best-known and most respected physicians of his day.

Treatment of Syphilis

During the first half of the twentieth century, several talented African Americans contributed to medical science. Among them was William Augustus HINTON. Born in Chicago in 1883, he earned his bachelor's and medical degrees from Harvard University. At a time when many lay persons and physicians argued that blacks were at greater risk for syphilis than other Americans, allegedly because of racial characteristics, Hinton worked to dispel ignorance about the disease and to find a more accurate means of detecting syphilis. He discovered a flocculation method for detecting the disease. In 1934 the U.S. Public Health Service reported that, of the most widely used tests for syphilis, the Hinton test seemed most effective. In 1936, in his study *Syphilis and Its Treatment*, Hinton argued that race did not place one at greater risk for syphilis, but that such risk was produced by socioeconomic conditions. His study was well received in the United States and England.

Innovative Instruments

Another African American doctor who made a significant contribution to medical knowledge was William H. Barnes. Born in Philadelphia in 1887, he was awarded a medical degree from the University of Pennsylvania in 1912. Barnes became well known for his bloodless operative techniques. He also received recognition for his inventive genius when he developed an instrument that allowed easier access to the pituitary gland. Barnes also invented other surgical instruments and modified some of those that were already in use.

Blood Preservation

Perhaps the best-known black medical scientist of the twentieth century was Charles R. Drew. Born in Washington, D.C., in 1904, he earned an M.D. and master of surgery degree from McGill University in Montreal, Canada. There, Drew became interested in the study of blood groupings. After his graduation, he received a grant enabling him to study at the Columbia University Presbyterian Hospital. He sought to devise methods for preserving blood for transfusion purposes. In 1940 he published his findings in a treatise entitled *Banked Blood: A Study in Blood Preservation*. Essentially, he was able to prove that blood plasma could be more reliably preserved than could whole blood. The blood banks that Drew helped to develop were credited with saving many lives in England during the Blitz—the German bombing of England in World War II.

Despite his interest in the blood banks and his much-needed expertise in the field, Drew took a position at Howard Medical School as a professor. It was rumored that the blood bank position Drew had at one time occupied was considered too important to be entrusted to an African American.

—*Betty L. Plummer*

See also: Health; Health care professionals; Meharry Medical School; Morehouse School of Medicine.

Suggested Readings:

Crute, Sheree, ed. *Health and Healing for African-Americans: Straight Talk and Tips from More than 150 Black Doctors on Our Top Health Concerns*. Emmaus, Pa.: Rodale Press, 1997.

Curtis, James L. *Blacks, Medical Schools, and Society*. Ann Arbor: University of Michigan Press, 1971.

Gamble, Vanessa N. *Making a Place for Ourselves: The Black Hospital Movement, 1920-1945*. New York: Oxford University Press, 1995.

Hayden, Robert C., and Jacqueline Harris. *Nine Black American Doctors*. Reading, Mass.: Addison-Wesley, 1976.

Henderson, Algo D., and Natalie B. Gumas. *Admitting Black Students to Medical and Dental Schools*. Berkeley, Calif.: Center of Research and Development in Higher Education, 1971.

Jones, Woodrow, Jr., and Mitchell F. Rice, eds. *Health Care Issues in Black America: Policies, Problems, and Prospects*. New York: Greenwood Press, 1987.

McBride, David. *Integrating the City of Medicine: Blacks in Philadelphia Health Care, 1910-1965*. Philadelphia: Temple University Press, 1989.

Morais, Herbert M. *The History of the Negro in Medicine*. New York: Publishers Company, 1967.

Samson, Vivian O. *Blacks in Science and Medicine*. New York: Hemisphere, 1990.

Semmes, Clovis E. *Racism, Health, and Postindustrialism: A Theory of African American Health*. Westport, Conn.: Praeger, 1996.

Meharry Medical School (Nashville, Tennessee): As of the 1990's Meharry was the largest predominantly black medical school in the United States. It was founded in 1876 by businessman Samuel Meharry. The school, adjacent to Fisk University, was credited in the 1950's with graduating more than half the black doctors in the United States. After segregation of medical schools ended, more black students attended other schools and Meharry attracted a substantial minority of white students.

See also: Medicine.

Melanin theory: Belief that many cultural differences among "races" can be attributed to varying amounts of melanin in the skins of members of those races. More particularly, advocates of this theory hold that darker skin tones represent a biologically superior stage in human evolution. The word "melanin" refers to the biological substance or pigment that affects the color of human skin, hair, and eyes. Melanin ranges in color from golden-brown to black. It is manufactured in the human body from reactions between various chemical units, including dopamine, epinephrine (adrenalin), and melatonin. Most of these reactions have a common starting point in the amino acid known as tyrosine. Once melanin is formed, it is insoluble in most solvents; it is extremely difficult to dissolve even in strong acids and bases.

Scientific Background

The modern investigation of melanin is said to have begun around 1917 by a German scientist, B. Block, who is credited with suggesting the role of tyrosine, tryptophan, and adrenalin in the formation of melanin. The American researcher H. S. Raper introduced a more detailed concept of melanin formation in 1929 that has since been used as a base in melanin research.

In the 1990's, some melanin theorists identified support for their claims in scientific findings showing that melanin exists not only in the skin but also in the human brain. Some of the research these theorists cited indicated that melanin enhances both brain function and physical performance, neutralizes harmful free radicals (radiation), and rids the body of harmful organisms, chemicals, and invading bacteria. Research also showed that melanin exhibits certain toxic properties, since it reacts with harmful electromagnetic radiation, drugs, and chemicals and is believed to cause certain mental and physical disorders.

Many molecular biologists and geneticists were wary of endorsing melanist claims of black biological superiority. These scientists noted that scientific research has revealed a very complex genetic model of how skin pigment is produced—a model in which a collection of minute genetic differences contributed to color variation within the human population over the course of human evolution.

Afrocentric Educational Theory

Although they have faced challenges in proving their scientific claims, some advocates of melanin theory have proposed that the mental and physical disturbances caused by melanin chemical reactivity may be responsible for the social, cultural, and political conditions experienced in the everyday lives of Africans in "white America" and other Europeanized regions of the world. Leonard JEFFRIES, a professor of black studies at the City College of New York, became a leading proponent of melanin

City College of New York professor Leonard Jeffries is one of the leading advocates of melanin theory. *(AP/Wide World Photos)*

theory. In exploring various aspects of the theory, Jeffries and other proponents sought to provide what they believed to be a long overdue corrective to the prevalent Eurocentric worldview. They sought to overcome the legacy of racism in the United States by disproving arguments advanced to support white biological superiority.

Some melanin theorists have created a model that compares the attributes and behaviors of dark-skinned "sun people" (those living closer to the equator) with those of light-skinned "ice people" (those living closer to the polar regions). By developing more melanin, sun people are purported to be better attuned to the rhythms of life, to exhibit greater intelligence, and to possess warm and outgoing personality characteristics. Ice people are denied these advantages because of their melanin deficiency.

A number of researchers have pointed to widespread evidence that blacks do not show signs of aging as dramatically and as early as whites and that blacks have a low incidence of skin CANCER. According to these researchers, this low rate of skin cancer is primarily the result of melanin's ability to neutralize the effects of radiation.

Melanin theorists, and African American melanin theorists in particular, have called for further research on the social and psychological effects of melanin. They are convinced that a thorough understanding of the exact function of melanin in all systems in the black human must be gained by people of African descent to ensure their good mental and physical health.

—*Abdul Karim Bangura*

See also: Afrocentricity.

Suggested Readings:

Barnes, Carol. *Melanin: The Chemical Key to Black Greatness*. Houston, Tex.: Black Greatness Series, 1987.

Hughes, Michael G., and Bradley R. Hertel. "The Significance of Color Remains: A Study of Life Chances, Mate Selection, and Ethnic Consciousness Among Black Americans." *Social Forces* 68, no. 4 (1990): 1105-1120.

Kissinger, Katie. *All the Colors We Are: The Story of How We Get Our Skin Color*. St. Paul, Minn.: Redleaf Press, 1994.

Montagna, William, Giuseppe Prota, and John A. Kenney, Jr. *Black Skin: Structure and Function*. San Diego, Calif.: Academic Press, 1993.

Ortiz Montellano, Bernard R. "Melanin, Afrocentricity, and Pseudoscience." *Yearbook of Physical Anthropology* 36 (Annual, 1993): 33-58.

Prota, Giuseppe. *Melanins and Melanogenesis*. San Diego, Calif.: Academic Press, 1992.

Robins, Ashley H. *Biological Perspectives on Human Pigmentation*. New York: Cambridge University Press, 1991.

Russell, Kathy, Midge Wilson, and Ronald Hall. *The Color Complex: The Politics of Skin Color Among African Americans*. New York: Harcourt Brace Jovanovich, 1992.

Wills, Christopher. "The Skin We're In." *Discover* (November, 1994): 76-81.

Memphis Minnie (Minnie or Lizzie Douglas; June 3, 1896, Algiers, Louisiana—August 6, 1973, Memphis, Tennessee): BLUES musician. She moved to MISSISSIPPI at the age of seven, where she first became known as "Kid Douglas" among the Beale Street crowd. She was quick and eager to imitate the finger-picking guitar licks of the musicians around her, among them Will Weldon and the Memphis Jug Band. Eventually she moved in with Joe McCoy, who also became her musical partner.

She was recorded first by Columbia in NEW YORK CITY in 1929, playing as part of the duo Memphis Minnie and Kansas Joe. Both songs released from those sessions, however, were written by McCoy. The next year, Mayo Williams heard her and McCoy in MEMPHIS, TENNESSEE, and recorded them, this time with

Minnie in the forefront. "Bumble Bee," a sexual blues number, was released on the Vocalion label and became Memphis Minnie's first major hit.

After twenty years among the Beale Street musicians, Memphis Minnie moved to CHICAGO, where she released the bulk of her work. Her most productive recording period was between 1934 and 1941. She was able to maintain her popularity for as long as she did because she was a flexible musician, willing to change with the trends of popular music. Although her dominant theme of the mistreated woman was widespread among female blues musicians, her lyrics were often humorous and sexually curious. She is noted for the individuality of her voice, expressed through the clarity of the details in her lyrics. Her imagery and simple melodies allowed her voice to retain the flavor of her southern blues roots.

Among her most popular hits are "Bumble Bee," "Me and My Chauffeur Blues," and "Nothin' in Ramblin'." She is noted for a particularly long recording career, in which she was able to bring traditional blues closer to popular music. The last ten years of her life were spent in and out of a nursing home near Memphis, in obscurity and poverty.

Memphis Slim (Peter Chatman; September 3, 1915, Memphis, Tennessee—February 24, 1988, Paris, France): BLUES singer and pianist. Memphis Slim's father was a pianist and guitarist. As a child, he often fell asleep at night listening to the piano from the barrelhouse next door. He began playing by imitating the boogie-woogie style of Roosevelt Skykes. Around 1937, he moved to CHICAGO, ILLINOIS, where he became the piano player for the Big Bill BROONZY combo. Broonzy suggested that he stop imitating Skykes and develop his own style.

In 1944 Memphis Slim formed the House Rockers, a band consisting of saxophones, a bass, drums, and an electric guitar. The House Rockers were part of the postwar CHICAGO BLUES, in which guitars, harmonicas, and sometimes even pianos were amplified electrically. The Chicago blues sound was produced from the tension between what had been inherited from the African American churches of the South and the frustrations of life in the northern cities. The music was hypnotic and driving. Memphis Slim was a leading Chicago urban blues singer and was prominent in rhythm and blues in the 1940's and 1950's.

The 1960's brought the folk revival and a new interest in old blues styles. Memphis Slim began recording honky-tonk and boogie woogie blues. He moved to the East Coast in 1959 and played Carnegie Hall and the Newport Jazz Festival. Shortly after, he toured Europe and within a number of years moved to Paris, where blues musicians were receiving more acknowledgment. He regularly performed a show called "The Story of the Blues," in which he discussed the blues, told stories about growing up in Memphis, and played.

Among his most notable tunes, out of some three hundred songs, are "Every Day I Have the Blues," "Beer Drinking Woman," and "Feel Like Screamin' and Cryin'." His lyrics are preoccupied with the meaning of the blues. He believed in the blues as a state of mind, an attitude, or a feeling that influences music.

Memphis, Tennessee: Memphis is the largest city in TENNESSEE and is the home of the National Civil Rights Museum. In the 1990's, of the more than 650,000 inhabitants of Memphis, about 47 percent were African American. Decades earlier, Memphis had lost nearly half its black population to the GREAT MIGRATION of African Americans to the North, but it had regained most of its black community by the 1980's.

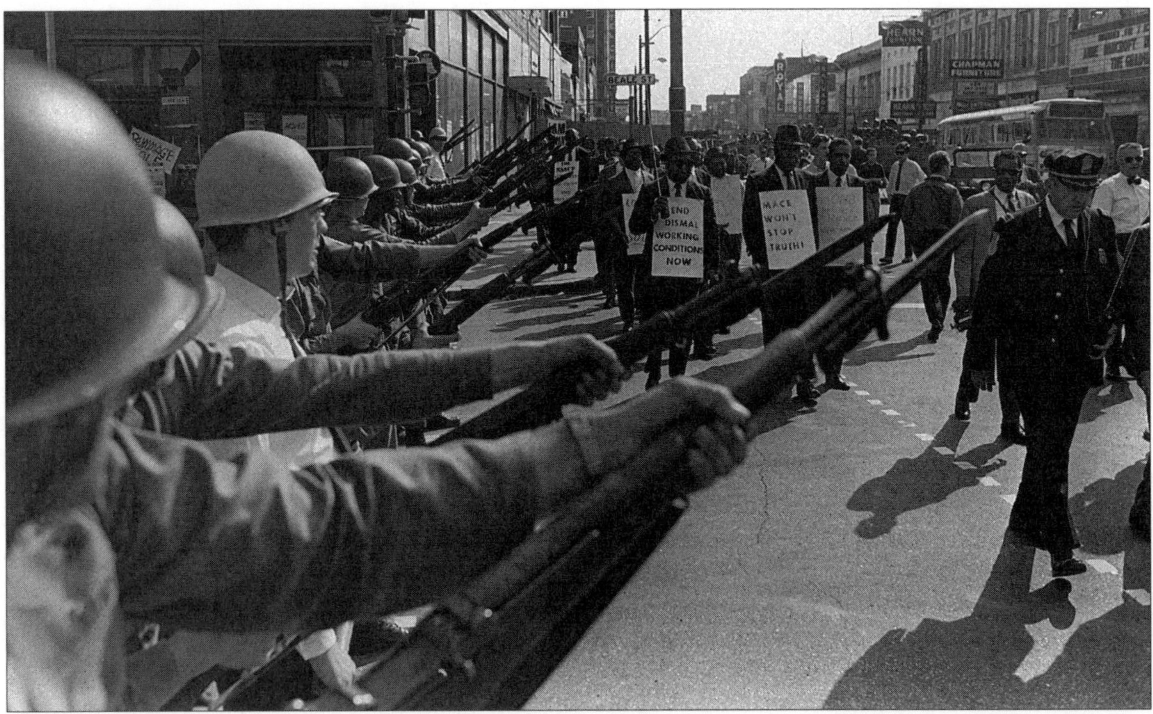

Striking sanitation workers march through Memphis under the observation of National Guard troops on March 29, 1968—shortly before Martin Luther King, Jr., arrived in the city to support the strikers. *(AP/Wide World Photos)*

In the early 1800's settlers and their slaves began to push west toward Memphis. Its location on the Mississippi River made Memphis an important slave market, resulting in a high African American population. The city soon became the largest slave market in Tennessee and was second only to Louisville, Kentucky, in the entire South.

Slavery may have ended after the Civil War, but deep-seated social and economic problems related to poverty and racism remained. Memphis was part of the segregated South. In the early 1900's, poverty and unemployment became major problems for African Americans in the city's overcrowded downtown area. Years after the 1954 U.S. Supreme Court case Brown v. Board of Education mandated an end to school segregation, school segregation remained in Memphis. It was a major problem until the 1970's. Most African American children were still attending all-black schools in the early 1970's, when a federal court ordered these students to be bused to previously white schools.

The assassination of civil rights leader Martin Luther King, Jr., was a defining event in the history of Memphis. In April, 1968, James Earl Ray shot King following a speech in which King voiced his support for striking Memphis sanitation workers, most of whom were African Americans. One immediate result of King's death was an increased strain in race relations in the city. However, with time and the combined efforts of black and white leaders, Memphis entered a period of rebuilding and improving race relations as well as improving the living conditions for the city's African American population. In 1991 Memphis opened the National Civil Rights Museum, the first such institution of its kind. Located in the former Lorraine Motel, where King was assassinated, the museum traces the Civil Rights movement from its earliest efforts.

Throughout its history, Memphis has been the home of influential African Americans. Robert Church, the South's first African American millionaire, helped Memphis reinstate its city charter, lost during a yellow fever epidemic in the 1880's. During the 1970's, social and political change in Memphis resulted in the election of Representative Harold FORD as Tennessee's first black representative in the U.S. Congress. Formerly a state representative, Ford was elected to Congress in 1974 and served for many years.

Among the cultural contributions of Memphis is the style of music that developed in the taverns and music halls along Beale Street. By the beginning of the twentieth century, Beale Street had become a center of civic, social, and cultural activities for the African American community of Memphis. MUSIC was a prominent part of these activities, and ultimately Memphis became known as the birthplace of the BLUES.

—*Kimberley H. Kidd*

Men: In AFRICA, before black Africans came into contact with Europeans, men enjoyed an array of roles in relation to their families, tribes, neighbors, and environment. They were fathers, husbands, patriarchs, warriors, farmers and hunters, artists and artisans, leaders, and slaves. Their standing was based on various strengths contributed to and wielded by their tribal communities. In order to survive and flourish, many of these diverse tribes and villages depended on the leadership and protection of men.

SLAVERY and the subsequent post-emancipation experience in the United States transformed the black male experience from one of inclusion to one of exclusion. On American soil, black men were denied the realization of traditional male roles. Although they could father children, often they could not protect and provide for their families. Although they could lead, leadership was asserted at their peril and only under the most narrowly circumscribed circumstances. Although they could work, black men after slavery were largely shunned from the American workplace and were typically given the most menial and ephemeral types of employment. Hence, the experience of black men in the United States following emancipation has been marked by efforts to recoup and re-create what was lost to enslavement and racism centuries ago.

The African Experience

Most of the black men who were traded into slavery between the sixteenth and mid-nineteenth centuries were captured along the western coast of Africa. They came from peoples called Ibo (or Igbo), Ewe, Biafada, Bakongo, Bambara, Serer, and Arada, and countless others. Very different in terms of language and affiliation, these peoples shared one important common factor: All were prolific farmers committed to raising families and developing communities in settled areas.

There are few accounts of African male life before enslavement, but one that has survived was written by Gustavus Vassa, also known as Olaudah EQUIANO, the son of an Ibo tribal elder. Born in 1745 in what is now eastern Nigeria, Equiano described an intensive agricultural life in which maize, tobacco, plantains, yams, beans, spices, and pineapples were produced and bullocks, goats, and poultry were raised. His family was strictly patriarchal and polygamous, with women serving subordinate but important roles alongside men in the fields, marketplaces, and homes. His narrative indicates that for West African men, positions of patriarch and chief farmer were of foremost importance and dictated much of the cultural lifestyle in precontact Africa.

The Black Male Experience During Slavery

Enslavement by white Europeans completely disrupted the black male experience. From the moment of capture, each male-defining role possessed by the black man was violently taken away. Documents show that on SLAVE SHIPS, during the Middle Passage, black men were viewed as a particular menace, automatically deserving closer scrutiny and more severe restrictions than black women. African men attempted resistance of various forms. Although many efforts failed, some succeeded. Even the deliberate act of self-destruction might be seen as a success.

Healthy African men were valued as slave labor in the United States because of their proven agricultural expertise. Their cost was high. Bought for as little as ten dollars in Africa, they were sold to white slaveholders for as much as six hundred dollars. The fact that these valued slaves were also men posed special problems to the slaveholder in terms of their potential to resist or run away. According to historian Nathan Huggins, research on a set of 134 runaway notices from eighteenth-century newspapers showed that 76 percent of the fugitives were under the age of thirty-five and 89 percent of them were men.

In the light of the risk of resistance, slaveholders devised various methods to keep black men under control. On some PLANTATIONS, male slaves were encouraged to "bond and breed," on the belief that they would be less likely to commit any transgression that would endanger their loved ones. Other slaveholders depended on brutal forms of punishment to set examples whenever slaves disobeyed. Others enlisted trusted black slaves to act as overseers empowered to steer rewards to acquiescent slaves and punishments toward defiant ones.

Despite the dehumanizing conditions slavery imposed, black men did manage to cultivate a few roles within the system that utilized their manhood in ways highly appreciated by their slave communities. Some were conjurers, whose knowledge of the medicinal value of roots and herbs to cure certain illnesses was respected by slaves and whites alike. Others were literate preachers, capable of providing spiritual comfort, hope, and guidance to a beleaguered flock. Although many eschewed the role of father and mate because of their powerlessness to protect their families, there were men who did so hopefully, sometimes doing additional work for slaveholders in order to get favors for their families, thereby gaining some esteem in the eyes of loved ones.

After Emancipation

Life after slavery posed unique challenges for the ordinary black man. Although free, the masses were without property, without EDUCATION, and without power in a region hostile to them. Long used to hard work, most attempted farming and building families on land purchased with money accumulated during slavery or by sharecropping. When the agricultural depression of the 1890's set in, many African Americans were forced off their land by whites who wanted it for themselves. Angry over the loss of slave labor and the devaluation of their properties, whites began to tyrannize blacks, particularly black men, in the form of lynching and torture. Thus, toward the end of the nineteenth century, thousands of black men migrated to southern cities in hopes of finding jobs in the newly industrializing South.

Black women usually were able to find work in the cities as domestics, but black men often were unable to obtain secure employment in the new commercial and industrial urban areas because of racist attitudes among employers. As a result, many young black men turned to a disorganized, itinerant way of life. Viewed by whites as dangerous degenerates, black men in the early twentieth century South frequently were "susceptible to lynchings, violence, and riots—easily swept into convict labor where they were leased to private entrepreneurs," according to historian

Joel Williamson. In an attempt to curb the violence against black men in the South, such leaders as Booker T. WASHINGTON urged accommodation and subservient self-help tactics as the route to racial harmony and survival.

In the twentieth century, black men on average made substantial gains in many areas of their lives through political and social leadership, though many still lived within a framework of violence and discrimination. More than 1.9 million African americans moved to northern cities between 1900 and 1940. Many adopted new militant attitudes toward American discrimination. Inspired by leaders such as W. E. B. DU BOIS, A. Philip RANDOLPH, and Marcus GARVEY, black men and women pushed during these years for equal rights in housing, education, and employment. Although the social attitudes of whites largely remained discriminatory, significant legal barriers to equal schooling and employment fell, enabling greater numbers of black men to provide a decent existence for their families.

The Final Barrier

The efforts black men have made to create a fulfilling male identity have been hampered by the power of distasteful stereotypes and images held by white America. During the last decades of slavery, black men were regarded as childlike, harmless creatures, unable to provide for themselves outside the civilizing controls of slavery. Whites typically disregarded signs that this stereotype was untrue. Many slaveholders were truly perplexed when their supposedly helpless slaves suddenly became successful fugitives.

After emancipation, the southern white image of black men turned from that of gentle caretakers to that of dangerous, violent, even beastly creatures. Some scholars have attributed this changing image to the anger that whites felt at losing control of African Americans and to their fear that black men would retaliate for the injustices committed against them as slaves. A Freudian view theorized that whites projected their own past rapes of black women onto black men, thereby invoking black men as potential rapists of white women. According to the TUSKEGEE INSTITUTE statistics kept on LYNCHING, 3,446 African Americans were tortured and then lynched between 1882 and 1968. More than 95 percent of the victims were men, and more than one-third of the lynchings were for the presumed crime of rape.

The image of the dangerous black man persisted through the twentieth century. It was notably illustrated by presidential candidate George Bush's use, in the 1988 campaign, of the image of criminal Willie Horton in Bush's television advertisements. Despite the significant strides made by black men in all areas of American life, black men of all socioeconomic classes continued to be viewed suspiciously by whites. A 1990 study conducted by the University of Chicago found that 56 percent of whites believed that African Americans were prone to violence. Crime statistics indeed show that about one-fourth of all African American men between the ages of twenty and twenty-nine were in jail, on parole, or on probation. These statistics, however, present a misleading picture. A large portion of these arrests are for nonviolent drug offenses. Moreover, black social and political activists and legal experts agree that poor, uneducated black men are too easily swept into the criminal justice system because they do not have the funds, community support, or expertise to defend themselves against racially formed presumptions of guilt.

By the year 2000, increasing numbers of black men had become leaders and participants in all areas of American life. Black politicians, educators, businessmen, entertainers, scientists, and astronauts were widely respected for their professional acumen in an array of roles. Even with such success, a large number of black men still faced the challenges posed by POVERTY, unemployment, and poor education.

—*Tana R. McDonald*

See also: Aviators and astronauts; Chemists; Employment and unemployment; Engineers; Intellectuals and scholars; Women.

Suggested Readings:

Akbar, Na'im. *Visions for Black Men.* Nashville, Tenn.: Winston-Derek, 1991.

Bolden, Tonya, and Herb Boyd. *Strong Men Keep Coming: The Book of African American Men.* New York: John Wiley & Sons, 1999.

Bush, Lawson V. "Am I a Man?: A Literature Review Engaging the Sociohistorical Dynamics of Black Manhood in the United States." *The Western Journal of Black Studies* 23 (Spring, 1999): 49-50.

Gates, Henry Louis, Jr. *Thirteen Ways of Looking at a Black Man.* New York: Random House, 1997.

Hare, Nathan, and Julia Hare. *Bringing the Black Boy to Manhood: The Passage.* San Francisco: Black Think Tank, 1985.

Madhubuti, Haki R. *Black Men: Obsolete, Single, Dangerous?* Chicago: Third World Press, 1990.

Majors, Richard, and Jacob U. Gordon, eds. *The American Black Male: His Present Status and His Future.* Chicago: Nelson-Hall, 1994.

McGhee, James D. *Running the Gauntlet: Black Men in America.* Washington, D.C.: National Urban League, 1984.

Staples, Robert. *Black Masculinity: The Black Male's Role in American Society.* San Francisco: Black Scholar Press, 1982.

Mercury Athletic Club: Early twentieth-century women's TRACK AND FIELD team. In NEW YORK CITY, the club boasted many record-setting athletes. Members set American records in the 880-yard relay and the 440-yard medley in the 1930's. Gertrude Johnson, a part of record-setting relay teams, won the Amateur Athletic Union (AAU) 200-meter championship in 1937 with an AAU record time.

Meredith, James (b. June 25, 1933, Kosciusko, Mississippi): CIVIL RIGHTS activist. James Howard Meredith received worldwide attention in 1962 when he became the first black to attend the University of Mississippi, the leading public university in MISSISSIPPI. In later years, he became a controversial figure, challenging not only racism but also the tactics and leadership of established African American rights groups.

Upbringing and Values

Born the seventh of thirteen children, James was impressed very early in life with a sense of pride and independence. His father, a farmer, was the first member of his family to own land. Partly as a result of his father's teachings and partly because he grew up in a relatively isolated area and had few dealings with white Mississippians, James never humbled himself before racists.

After serving nine years in the U.S. Air Force (1951-1960), Meredith returned to his home state of Mississippi "to fight a war." His autobiography, *Three Years in Mississippi* (1966), states that he felt a "divine responsibility" to direct civilization "toward a destiny of humaneness," to defeat the system of white supremacy in Mississippi, and to improve the lives of his people. Encouraged by the election of John F. Kennedy, who had insisted on a civil rights plank in the Democratic platform of 1960, Meredith decided to challenge the University of Mississippi's policy of excluding African Americans.

Challenging Segregation at the University

Four African Americans, including Medgar EVERS, a Mississippi civil rights leader, are known to have tried entering the University of

Mississippi prior to Meredith. All had been rejected on technicalities, and all had lacked the legal backing to challenge those rejections. Well aware of their experiences, Meredith sought the legal assistance of the National Association for the Advancement of Colored People (NAACP), first contacting Evers, then Thurgood Marshall, director of the organization's Legal Defense Fund. Attorney Constance Baker Motley was assigned to his case; for two and one-half years, she saw the litigation surrounding Meredith's effort through the courts.

On May 31, 1961, Meredith filed a class-action lawsuit in U.S. District Court alleging that the University of Mississippi's requirement that applicants submit recommendations from alumni was discriminatory and unconstitutional. Since no African Americans had ever been allowed to attend the university, and since the majority of whites in the state did not favor integration, it was virtually impossible for a black applicant to meet this requirement. The court, finding that the University of Mississippi was "not a racially segregated institution," ruled against Meredith.

The U.S. Fifth Circuit Court of Appeals, however, overturned the decision. Noting that segregation at the university was "a plain fact known to everyone," Judge John Minor Wisdom agreed with Meredith that the alumni recommendations were an unfair burden, and he noted that the school had adopted the requirement only a few months after the 1954 Brown v. Board of Education ruling, an obvious attempt to circumvent the U.S. Supreme Court decision outlawing segregation. Eventually, on June 25, 1962, the appeals court ruled that "James H. Meredith's application for transfer to the University of Mississippi was turned down solely because he was a Negro" and ordered that he be admitted as a student.

Word of Meredith's application and subsequent court case aroused the fear and anger of Mississippians opposed to desegregation. To persuade Meredith to abandon his lawsuit, they harassed those citizens who had recommended him and warned neighbors that he would be killed. The police jailed Meredith for false voter registration because when he was a student at Jackson State University he had registered as a citizen of Hinds County rather than as a citizen of his home county of Attala. The court of appeals issued an injunction to prevent his prosecution, calling the charge "frivolous" and designed to discriminate by harassment.

James Meredith receiving his degree at the University of Mississippi in 1963. *(Associated Publishers, Inc.)*

Attending Ole Miss

Meredith attempted to register at the university three times before he was finally admitted. Each time he was surrounded by

Meredith grimaces in pain after being shot during his "March Against Fear" in June, 1966. *(AP/Wide World Photos)*

mobs threatening violence, and each time the governor or the lieutenant governor of Mississippi literally blocked his way. Governor Ross Barnett had withdrawn all power from university officials and made himself registrar. Calling the court order to admit Meredith a federal usurpation of states' rights, Barnett signed a state law that overruled the federal law. At that point, the courts could do no more, but President Kennedy ordered the secretary of defense "to remove all obstructions of justice in the State of Mississippi" and to use military force if necessary. On the evening of September 30, 1962, after Meredith had been secretly installed in a dormitory room, a riot erupted on the Mississippi campus. Two people were killed and many more wounded. Meredith registered the next morning amid the rubble of bricks, burned automobiles, and empty tear-gas canisters.

Meredith's life as a student was far from normal. The university and the adjoining town of Oxford were occupied by some fifteen thousand troops, and Meredith was escorted to class by federal marshals. Harassment was common; students who tried to befriend him were ostracized. Yet he also had sources of support. Black cooks and janitors on campus quietly encouraged him, as did some residents of Oxford. Some students visited him in his room, and a few faculty members invited him to play golf and visit them in their homes. In addition, he received hundreds of supportive letters, many from schoolchildren. Nevertheless, despite this support, he noted that he felt himself to be "the most segregated Negro in the world."

Meredith did not view his enrollment as a triumph. He decided not to enroll for a second semester unless steps were taken to make his life as a student normal. He wrote that the "conditions tended to make me a superhuman or nonhuman individual." He feared that such a precedent would make it difficult for other African Americans after him. He was also disturbed because some of the letters of his black supporters indicated that they were too willing to regard him as a hero who would solve their problems for them. In "I Can't Fight Alone," an essay written for *Look* magazine, he argued that blacks could not expect others to win their freedom for them. His ardent wish was that his example would inspire others to take responsibility for and insist on their own rights. After much internal debate, Meredith eventually decided to stay at the university, and he graduated in the summer of 1963 with a degree in history and political science.

March Against Fear

Shortly before Meredith's graduation, Meredith's friend Medgar Evers was murdered in Jackson, Mississippi. This incident and Meredith's own experiences with intimidation convinced him that black Mississippians had to unite to overcome their fear of racist violence. In June of 1966, while a law student at Columbia University, Meredith organized a march that was to begin in MEMPHIS, TENNESSEE, and end in Jackson. As the caravan marched on Route 51 in northern Mississippi, a lone gunman shot Meredith three times with a shotgun. Wounded with nearly seventy shotgun pellets, he was hospitalized in Memphis. As a result of this experience, Meredith rejected nonviolence as a practical strategy and asserted that he would strike back if attacked again. In an essay published in the *Saturday Evening Post*, he wrote that "nonviolence is incompatible with American ideals. America is a tough country, and a man has to look out for his own, to be his own man."

Black Conservative

From his days at the University of Mississippi, James Meredith had had disputes with the black political establishment. For example, he objected to the NAACP's claim that the organization had chosen him to integrate the University of Mississippi when, in fact, he had approached the NAACP. He generated even more controversy in 1967—and was threatened with assassination by Harlemites—when he challenged HARLEM politician Adam Clayton POWELL, Jr., for his seat in the U.S. House of Representatives. Powell had been censured by Congress and found in contempt of court; many felt that Meredith was a pawn of a white establishment using him to rid itself of Powell. Meredith, however, said he felt that the people of Harlem "deserve something more" than Powell's controversial representation. He condemned the harassment of Powell but argued that "to reelect Powell just because he is a Negro, regardless of everything else, would be as wrong as what the Congress did." Powell, though, was reelected.

In 1989, again to the chagrin of the civil rights establishment, Meredith joined the staff of Senator Jesse Helms, an arch-conservative from NORTH CAROLINA who had opposed civil rights legislation and the creation of a national holiday commemorating Martin Luther KING, Jr. In a 1988 letter to the *Washington Times*, Meredith had urged African Americans to support Republican Party candidates in the national election "because the key to the American dream is citizenship, with all of its rights and privileges, and also with all of its responsibilities and obligations." Citing a series of social ills, from welfare and unemployment to abortion and promiscuity, he blamed white liberals and the black elite for encouraging black dependence and irresponsibility. In the mid-1990's Meredith began teaching in Mississippi with the goal of teaching African American men and boys to speak standard English rather than Black English.

Sometimes condemned as a maverick, Meredith also garnered high praise for his individualism. Senator Jacob Javits termed him "a symbol of the dignity and participation in our national life for which [blacks] have been working for decades." James BALDWIN called him "the most noble individual that I have ever known." A man with a mission, James Meredith permanently changed American life and the position of African Americans in it.

—*William L. Howard*

Suggested Readings:

Barrett, Russell H. *Integration at Ole Miss*. Chicago: Quadrangle, 1965.

Bradley, John E. "The Man Who Would Be King." *Esquire* (December, 1992): 101-106.

Lord, Walter. *The Past That Would Not Die*. New York: Harper & Row, 1965.

Meredith, James. "Big Changes Are Coming." *Saturday Evening Post* (August 13, 1966): 23-27.

_______. *Three Years in Mississippi*. Bloomington: Indiana University Press, 1966.

Silver, James. *Mississippi: The Closed Society*. New York: Harcourt, 1966.

"Whatever Happened to James Meredith?" *Ebony* (December, 1984): 38.

Meriwether, Louise (b. May 8, 1923, Haverstraw, New York): Novelist and biographer. Meriwether received a B.A. from New York University and an M.S. from the University of California at Los Angeles. Her novel *Daddy Was a Number Runner* (1970) depicts the collapse of a family in Depression-era HARLEM, New York. The novel was praised for showing the communal quality of black life. Meriwether is an example of African American writers who suffer in a critical limbo when black literature is read as sociology. Even critics of the 1960's and 1970's who took black fiction seriously as literature tended to use fiction to support sociological and psychological arguments.

One of Meriwether's short stories, "A Happening in Barbados," is included in Mary Helen Washington's anthology *Midnight Birds: Stories by Contemporary Black Women Writers* (1980). The story succinctly portrays the thirty-nine-year-old divorced narrator's realization of how racially motivated are her sexual choices. It ends with her alone on a beach, separating herself from all the other players in a game in which she will no longer participate. She asks herself, "how could I have been such a bitch?"

Meriwether turned her attention to making black history accessible to the youngest readers. *The Freedom Ship of Robert Smalls* (1971) presents the story of a slave who brought a Confederate ship into Union waters during the CIVIL WAR. *The Heart Man: Dr. Daniel Hale Williams* (1972) helps to give Williams his due as the first surgeon to perform successful open heart surgery. *Don't Ride the Bus on Monday: The Rosa Parks Story* (1973) presents this MONTGOMERY, ALABAMA, woman as a courageous example of standing up for one's own dignity.
See also: Children's literature; Literature.

Methodists: Other than the BAPTISTS, Methodists historically have been the largest religious grouping among African Americans in the United States. In addition to its evangelical tone, with an emphasis on personal conversion, the strong antislavery impulse of early American Methodism undoubtedly appealed strongly to African Americans. Many slaves and free blacks converted to Methodism at frontier camp meetings and as itinerant preachers made their rounds. Beginning with the Methodist general conference of 1784, however, Methodist rules against slavery underwent a steady process of erosion, and the Methodists emerged as leaders in the development of religious instruction among the slaves rather than as abolitionists. Schisms along sectional lines among Methodists in 1845 led to intensified efforts to establish plantation missions. In the north, African Americans found that they increasingly were relegated to the side aisles, rear, and balconies of Methodist congregations.

Black Methodists, although they were slower than black Baptists to establish independent congregations, were able to move toward denominational structures well before their Baptist counterparts. The growth of the AFRICAN METHODIST EPISCOPAL CHURCH, the AFRICAN METHODIST EPISCOPAL ZION CHURCH, and some smaller Methodist bodies was confined primarily to the North during the antebellum period.

Major Black Methodist Denominations

When a group of FREE BLACKS belonging to the FREE AFRICAN SOCIETY, a mutual-aid society affiliated with St. George's Methodist Episcopal Church in PHILADELPHIA, severed ties with their white brethren over discriminatory practices, a minority joined Richard ALLEN in the establishment of the Bethel African Methodist Episcopal Church. In 1816 Bethel joined four other congregations in establishing the African Methodist Episcopal (AME) Church. The AME Church found its most fertile fields in the Northeast and the Midwest during the antebellum period, although it established some congregations in the South, including one in Charleston, South Carolina.

The racially mixed St. John's Street Church in New York City served as the focal point for the development of what eventually became the second major black Methodist denomination. Segregation in church facilities and lack of access to influential positions convinced several black members of St. John's Methodist Episcopal Church in New York in the late 1780's to obtain permission to conduct occasional prayer meetings by themselves, a move that ultimately resulted in the establishment of Zion Church in 1801. In 1816 Zion members, along with other congregations from New York, Long Island, New Haven, Connecticut, Philadelphia, and Easton, Pennsylvania, established the African Methodist Episcopal Zion Church. James Varick, then pastor of Zion Church, was elected the first bishop of the new denomination in 1822. When the 1824 general conference of the Methodist Episcopal Church failed to grant the Zionites official recognition as a separate African American conference, they finally announced their independence from the parent body.

Although the two African Methodist denominations appealed to many southern black worshipers after the Civil War, most black preachers affiliated with the Methodist Episcopal Church, South opposed their efforts, often because the literacy requirements demanded of ministers by the African Methodists barred them from the ministry in the northern-based churches. In order to counter the missionary activities among the freed people of the African Methodists as well as the Methodist Episcopal Church, North, the Methodist Episcopal Church, South created the structure for what became the third major black Methodist denomination. In December, 1870, the first general conference of the Colored Methodist Episcopal Church convened in Jackson, Tennessee, and two bishops, Henry Miles and Richard H. Vanderherst, were elected.

Like the parent United Methodist Church, the three major black Methodist denominations are organized into general, annual, and quarterly conferences. The general conferences, which meet quadrennially in different cities, act as the supreme governing bodies of their respective denominations. Like lower-order conferences, they consist of both clergy and laity. Women are eligible to hold any office at the local church, district, annual conference, and national levels. Annual conferences meet once a year and assign presiding elders, pastors, and other ministers to their respective jurisdictions and ordain ministers, deacons, and elders. In addition to the quarterly conference, presiding elders in the AME Zion Church hold district conferences each year.

The AME Church is organized into eighteen episcopal districts spread across the United States, Canada, Africa, and the Caribbean and by the 1990's claimed to have 2.2 million members in the United States. The AME Zion Church consists of twelve episcopal areas, all of which are headquartered in the United States, and claims a U.S. membership of 1.2 million. The Christian Methodist Episcopal Church (CME), which became the name of the Colored Methodist Episcopal Church in 1954, has ten annual conferences and claims 900,000 members in the United States. Out of 9.4 million members, the United Methodist Church has an estimated 360,000 African American members, most of whom belong to some 2,600 predominantly black congregations.

The black Methodist denominations operate universities, four-year colleges, junior colleges, seminaries, and other educational institutions. AME schools include Wilberforce University in southwestern Ohio, Allen University in South Carolina, and Morris Brown College in Atlanta. The AME Zion Church operates only one four-year college, Livingston College in North Carolina. The CME Church operates Lane College in Jackson, Tennessee, Texas College in Tyler, TEXAS, Miles College in ALABAMA, and the Phillips College of Theology at the Interdenominational Theological Center in Atlanta.

Periodically, the black Methodist denominations have discussed the possibility of merger, but all these efforts have failed. In 1908 the bishops of the AME, AME Zion, and CME Churches formed what eventually came to be called the Tri-Federation Council. The council developed a plan for tripartite union, which was approved by the general conferences of the AME and AME Zion Churches but was decisively defeated by the general conference of the CME Church. The Tri-Council was revived in 1965, but periodic negotiations have not produced a serious merger proposal. The AME Zion and CME Churches, however, discussed the possibility of merger during the 1980's.

Other Black Methodist Bodies

Several religious bodies, most of which emerged as schisms from the two African Methodist denominations, continue to function on the periphery of black Methodism. The Union Church of Africans was incorporated in Wilmington, DELAWARE, in 1805 after Peter Spencer and some forty other African Americans left the Asbury Methodist Episcopal Church to protest racial discrimination. The Union Church split into the African Union Methodist Protestant (AUMP) Church and the Union American Methodist Episcopal (UAME) Church in 1851. The AUMP merged with an AME splinter group, the First Colored Methodist Church, in 1906. Other black Methodist bodies include the Reformed Methodist Union Episcopal Church (established in 1885) and the Free Christian Zion Church of Christ.

Methodist Congregations

Like black Baptist churches, Methodist churches affiliated with the three major black Methodist denominations range from large, prestigious congregations to small storefronts. In contrast to Baptist congregations, which select their own pastors, the Methodist episcopal polity places the selection of pastors in the hands of the district bishop. Members of a particular congregation may petition the bishop for a different pastor, but he may disregard their request. Methodist ministers periodically receive new assignments, which means that they do not generally enjoy the long tenures that Baptist ministers typically do. As a result of the episcopal structure, Methodist ministers are not as autonomous in their actions as are Baptist ministers. For example, as a result of operating, between 1900 and 1904, the Institutional Church and Settlement House, which was based upon a philosophy of Social Gospel outreach, R. R. Wright and Reverdy Ransom were forced by the AME hierarchy to resign as coministers of this innovative CHICAGO congregation.

The pastor is assisted by a trustee board and a steward board. In theory, the trustees are responsible for temporal affairs and the stewards for spiritual ones, but in reality their respective roles overlap considerably. Although the black Methodist denominations ordain female ministers, the vast majority of black Methodist pastors are men. The AME Church has deaconesses, who are designated by the pastor and consecrated by the bishop but who are not regarded as ministers per se. Women, who generally outnumber men at religious services, play a supportive role, including in the area of fund-raising; serve on missionary, Sunday school, nurses', and mothers' boards; and constitute the bulk of the congregations' choirs. Services in black Methodist churches tend to be more liturgical and more subdued than those performed in Baptist churches.

Although the black Methodist denominations have been mass churches that have attracted African Americans from a range of social strata, their members have historically been somewhat more affluent than black Baptists. Undoubtedly this has been an important factor in black Methodists' strong emphasis on education, social uplift programs, and foreign mission programs. Although certain Methodist ministers and congregations played instrumental roles in the CIVIL RIGHTS movement, the episcopal structure of Methodism apparently precluded the emergence of as many charismatic and dynamic leaders from the ranks of black Methodists as emerged from the Afro-Baptist tradition.

—*Hans A. Baer*

See also: Religion.

Suggested Readings:

Beck, Carolyn S. *Our Own Vine and Fig Tree: The Persistence of the Mother Bethel Family*. New York: AMS Press, 1989.

Campbell, James T. *Songs of Zion: The African Methodist Episcopal Church in the United States and South Africa*. New York: Oxford University Press, 1995.

Dvorak, Katharine L. *An African-American Exodus: The Segregation of the Southern Churches*. Brooklyn, N.Y.: Carlson, 1991.

Gregg, Howard D. *History of the African Methodist Episcopal Church*. Nashville: AME Sunday School Union, 1980.

Walker, Clarence E. *A Rock in a Weary Land: The African Methodist Episcopal Church During the Civil War and Reconstruction*. Baton Rouge: Louisiana State University Press, 1982.

Walls, William. *The African Methodist Episcopal Zion Church*. Charlotte, N.C.: A.M.E. Zion Publishing House, 1974.

Metropolitan Spiritual Churches of Christ: The Metropolitan Spiritual Churches of Christ (MSCC) was established on September 22, 1925, in Kansas City, MISSOURI, by William F. Taylor and Leviticus L. Boswell. The MSCC grew into the largest African American Spiritual association, particularly under the dynamic presidency of the Reverend Clarence Cobbs, the flamboyant pastor of the First Church of Deliverance on the South Side of CHICAGO. Like other Spiritual groups, the MSCC blends elements of Spiritualism, Catholicism, black Protestantism, and VOODOO.

See also: Religion.

Mexican-American War: The Mexican-American War began as a series of skirmishes along the ill-defined borders between the two countries in 1846. The Republic of TEXAS, which had succeeded in establishing its independence from MEXICO ten years earlier, sought annexation by the United States in 1845. When the United States granted Texas statehood, the Mexican government considered the action a violation of existing treaties and tantamount to a declaration of war. Soon fighting broke out along the border, and the United States invaded Mexico.

Not all the country's political powers favored the annexation of Texas. Many of the original U.S. settlers in Texas had been from the southern states. Although SLAVERY was prohibited by Mexican law, the new arrivals brought the slaves that they owned prior to their immigration to Mexico. In the U.S., a previous compromise in Congress had designated certain states as either "free" or "slave" states, permitting the ownership of slaves in the latter. Southern congressmen sought to have Texas admitted to the union as a slave state. Northerners, seeing Texas as a valuable new market for their manufactured goods, agreed to a compromise. On October 13, 1846, the Texas legislature ratified the terms of the annexation.

War between Mexico and the United States swiftly followed. The Mexican army, ill-trained and inadequately equipped, was no match for its northern adversary. U.S. forces succeeded in conquering Mexico and taking its capital. They occupied NEW MEXICO and

CALIFORNIA as well. On January 2, 1848, at the California village of Guadelupe Hidalgo, representatives of the Mexican government sued for peace and agreed to sell to the United States the land it sought for fifteen million dollars.

The U.S. government had not intended to conquer Mexico and to hold it; it sought only to secure the Mexican territory situated between its borders at the time and the Pacific Ocean, roughly where the present states of New Mexico, ARIZONA, and California lie. This area, President James K. Polk and his supporters in Congress believed, should be part of the United States in order to fulfill what they termed the country's Manifest Destiny.

Friction continued between the proslavery and antislavery forces in Congress regarding the status under which the new state of California should be admitted to the union. The antislavery block in Congress won out, and the new territory became a free state. In addition to the purchase price of the land it won from Mexico, the Mexican-American War cost the United States more than thirteen thousand lives and an estimated one hundred million dollars for military payroll, equipment, and supplies.

—*Carl Henry Marcoux*

The climax of the Mexican-American War came when U.S. general Winfield Scott occupied Mexico City. *(Institute of Texas Cultures, San Antonio, Texas)*

Suggested Readings:

Crawford, Mark, David S. Heidler, and Jeanne T. Heidler, eds. *Encyclopedia of the Mexican-American War.* Santa Barbara, Calif.: ABC-Clio, 1999.

Dufour, Charles L. *The Mexican War: A Compact History, 1846-1848.* New York: Hawthorne Books, 1968.

Eisenhower, John S. D. *So Far from God: The U.S. War with Mexico, 1846-1848.* New York: Random House, 1989.

McCaffrey, James M. *Army of Manifest Destiny: The American Soldier in the Mexican War, 1846-1848.* New York: New York University Press, 1994.

Mexico: Black immigrants played a major role in the Spanish exploration and colonization of Mexico beginning in the sixteenth century. At that time Mexico was a colony called New Spain. Between the years 1519 and 1650, the Spaniards imported an estimated 100,000 slaves into the colony. Without this involuntary influx of black labor and skills, the Spanish task of developing New Spain could not have taken place.

It is virtually impossible to trace the racial effects of that early migration in today's Mexican population because of centuries of mixing of the Spanish, black, and Indian populations. Because of that mixing, there is no significant distinct group of black Mexicans today. José

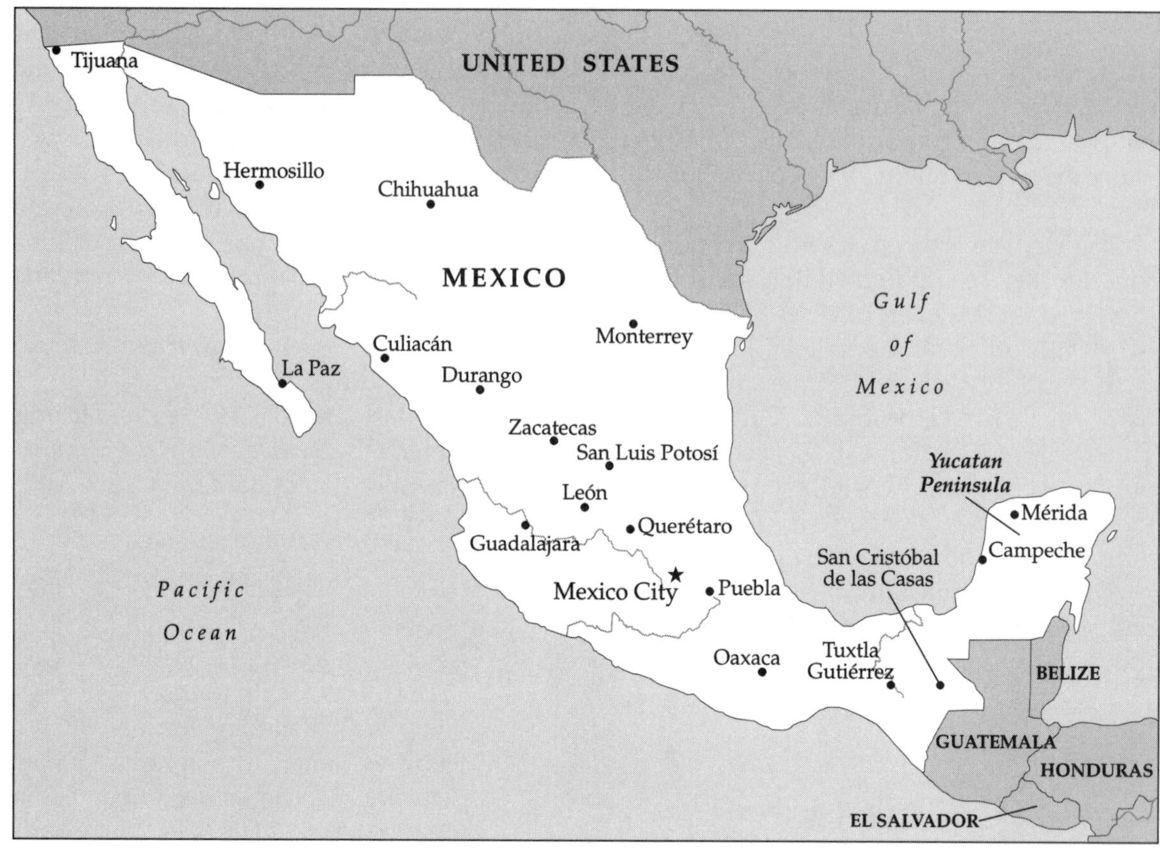

Vasconcelos, one of Mexico's noted educators, describes its people as belonging to a "cosmic race"—a medley of different racial and cultural backgrounds, including European, Indian, black, and Asian strains.

Early Colonial Era

Hernán Cortés, New Spain's conquistador, introduced black slaves to the colony shortly after he completed his subjugation of the Aztec empire. The Spaniards called this initial group of blacks *ladinos*, for they had been born or raised either in Spain or in the Spanish Caribbean possessions prior to their arrival in New Spain. Cortés put them to work in various capacities on the large estates granted him by the Spanish crown.

Unlike the British to the north, the Spanish colonizers did not try to populate their American colonies with working families. Instead, they sought to exploit the indigenous peoples that they found when they landed. They attempted to persuade or force the Indians to labor on sugar plantations, in mines or textile factories (*obrajes*), or at whatever other types of economic endeavor they undertook.

As had previously proved to be the case on the Spanish-held Caribbean islands, attempts to drive the Indians to work in New Spain proved to be impractical. The constant backbreaking labor on sugar plantations, for example, conflicted with the cultural mores of the indigenous peoples. The Indians rejected Spanish attempts to utilize them to produce a profit from sugar cultivation. Additionally, and more devastating, the natives proved to be extremely susceptible to European communicable diseases.

The mortality rate among the Indians, both in the Caribbean and in New Spain, took on disastrous proportions as time went on. Historians estimate that as much as 90 percent of the local populations died from such European-introduced diseases as smallpox, typhoid, yellow fever, dysentery, and bubonic plague. Even milder sicknesses such as influenza, measles, mumps, and chickenpox proved to be deadly.

Major Importation of Slaves

Since the Spaniards had no intention of performing necessary manual labor themselves, they began to import black slaves to replace Indian labor. Both the Spaniards and Portuguese had already employed African slaves successfully in continental Iberia and on the islands lying off AFRICA's west coast, and Spain had brought slaves to its Caribbean possessions. The alarming death rate among the native workers on the island of Hispaniola led to the first shipment of black slaves to that location as early as 1503.

When disease began to destroy the Indian population in New Spain as well, the Spaniards began the mass importation of blacks to replace the rapidly diminishing workforce. Between the years of 1580 and 1620 the colonists in New Spain acquired more slaves for their various enterprises there than they had for all the other Spanish colonies in America combined. The numerous sugar plantations—sugar cane had become Spanish America's leading cash crop—required a constant supply of laborers, both skilled and unskilled. Cattle ranches, cotton mills, silver mines, and the construction industry also called for continuous infusions of new workers. The heavy physical demands placed on the slaves in the sugar industry resulted in a very high death rate among them. The average life of a sugar plantation worker from the time of assignment seldom exceeded six years. The mines also took a heavy toll.

Initially the Spaniards relied on their existing supply of Europeanized slaves to fill the high demand for workers in New Spain. This source proved inadequate as the colony's economy continued to expand. Spanish entrepreneurs began to arrange for shipment of bondsmen directly from Africa. At first they drew from the Congo, on the continent's west coast. Ultimately they had to import slaves from sources further inland. European slave traders encouraged wars among the African kingdoms, because a primary source for their commodity lay in purchasing prisoners of war. African kings found the traders to be willing to furnish them with a wealth of consumer goods in exchange for their prisoners.

The Spaniards called the slaves shipped to the Americas directly from Africa *bozales*, to distinguish them from those who had been Hispanicized to some degree by previous experience in Spain or the Caribbean. The much higher cost of the transportation of this new group of workers from Africa caused the price of slaves at the points of final destination to be very high. (When the wind failed them, the captains of slave ships could lose their whole cargo because of a lack of sufficient food and water for their unwilling passengers.) Spanish landowners therefore preferred to use the local Indians for labor if any were available. They purchased blacks at the slave marts only as a last resort.

The Growth of the Casta Population

Because both the Spanish slaveowner and his black charges were predominantly men, sexual relations between both these groups and indigenous women soon began to occur. Two new groups emerged as a result: mestizos (Indian/Europeans) and zambos (Indian/black). Since there also were some African women, a group of MULATTOES (black/European) also emerged. Although Spanish law forbade sexual relations among the races, the demands of nature prevailed. Soon the population of New Spain included a large segment of castas (persons of a mixed racial ancestry).

Not all slaves accepted their role in colonial society with equanimity. Despite harsh penalties imposed on those who tried to escape, many took the risk and fled to New Spain's hinterland. Some of the escapees formed colonies in secluded areas to better resist a return to captivity. One such group, called Yanga—after the name of their leader—successfully resisted the continued attempts by the Spanish to recapture them. Yanga and his followers operated independently outside Spanish authority for some thirty years. Initially they lived by stealing and raiding Spanish settlements. They also sometimes kidnapped colonial women to add to their group.

The offspring of this system of cohabitation ultimately changed the demographics of the area. The practice also resulted in an alteration of the lifestyles of the Yanga group and other similar groups, which came to be called *cimarrónes*. The former slaves became settled, turned to agriculture instead of raiding the Spaniards, and ultimately concluded a treaty with their former owners. The Yanga colony received a charter from the Spanish authorities as well as recognition of their MANUMISSION. The community became known as San Lorenzo de los Negros. As the decades passed and the descendants of the *cimarrónes* intermingled with the populations of surrounding towns, the African strain melded into the society as a whole.

Decline of Slavery

Ultimately New Spain's Indian population began to recover and to become a viable part of the colony's economy. The survivors of the previous epidemics had developed a greater resistance to communicable European diseases. In many cases, because they had been deprived of their land and possessions, the surviving natives had no choice but to work for the Spanish colonists. Since the majority of the laboring class could not read or write, quite often its members were persuaded or coerced into signing long-term labor contracts at marginal wage rates. Free mulattoes and mestizos also entered the labor market. As the supply of workers from these three groups increased, the importation of expensive black slaves diminished.

The high tide of black slavery in New Spain ran from 1560 to 1630. By 1700 the institution had experienced a marked decline. In 1777 a population census in Veracruz, which had been one of the areas of heaviest slave use, revealed that more than 90 percent of workers were free men. Slavery had lost its economic rationale.

However, although they were nominally free, nonwhites held a social, political, and economic status that was totally subordinated to the white upper class. The colonial authorities established strict rules to control the lifestyle and activities of the castas. Often the nonwhites could not vote, carry weapons, or own horses. Some jurisdictions required them to register by name, place of residence, and occupation. Local priests kept careful records of their parishioners' racial antecedents. Some wealthy nonwhites made substantial contributions to the local clerical authorities in order to "whiten" their baptismal and marriage records.

Wars of Independence

When Mexico's wars of independence commenced at the beginning of the nineteenth century, the ranks of the rebel forces were filled with castas dissatisfied with their position in colonial society. In 1810 a parish priest, Miguel Hidalgo, one of the first of a series of revolutionary leaders, led an army of Indians, mestizos, and mulattoes on a campaign to destroy Spanish control of the country. His ragged army swept through the center of the country destroying cities, haciendas, and mines as well as robbing and killing any Spaniards they encountered in the course of their depredations.

Although Hidalgo was captured and executed the following year, another priest, José María Morelos, continued to oppose the Spaniards. Part mestizo and part black, Morelos proved to be a much more effective military leader than Hidalgo. He attempted to legitimize his rebellion by creating an assembly of civilians to formalize his authority. Five years later, better-equipped and well-disciplined royalist forces under Spanish general Felix Calleja defeated Morelos. In 1815 the Spaniards executed him.

Nevertheless, New Spain continued as a colony for only another six years. Colonel Augustín Iturbide, a leader born in New Spain, rallied the liberals, the clergy, and the army under his banner and declared the independence of a new nation—Mexico. In his 1821 Plan of Iguala, Iturbide held out promises to all the local groups. The plan called for equal rights for all nonwhites under the law and even offered the opportunity for those among them who so desired to join the new national army.

After Independence

At the time of independence, a government survey revealed that the new nation contained only three thousand slaves, less than 0.02 percent of the population. In 1830 President Vicente Guerrero, part black himself, declared slavery at an end in Mexico. For nearly a century prior to the act itself, slavery as an economic institution had been in decline.

Slaveowners were not replacing their bondsmen who could no longer perform adequately because of age or infirmities; additionally, they had begun the lengthy process of disengaging themselves from the responsibility of maintaining their slave operations. Releasing older slaves from bondage made good economic sense if they could no longer perform. Some slaves who had access to funds from one source or another were offered by their owners the opportunity to buy their freedom. The offspring of female slaves who were sired by their masters were quite often given their freedom.

By the end of the twentieth century, blacks did not represent a significant distinct racial group within the Mexican population. The virtual termination of the importation of black slaves into New Spain as far back as the early eighteenth century cut off the supply of African additions to the gene pool from that time forward. Additionally, the extensive pattern of MISCEGENATION among blacks, whites, and Indians, which developed almost from the time that blacks first arrived in the colony, made the preservation of Africans as a distinct social and racial entity in Mexico impossible.

—*Carl Henry Marcoux*

Suggested Readings:

Carroll, Patrick J. *Blacks in Colonial Veracruz: Race, Ethnicity, and Regional Development*. Austin: University of Texas Press, 1991.

Gibson, Charles. *The Aztecs Under Spanish Rule*. Palo Alto, Calif.: Stanford University Press, 1964.

Lockhart, James, and Stuart B. Schwartz. *Early Latin America*. Cambridge, England: Cambridge University Press, 1983.

MacLachlan, Colin M., and Jaime E. Rodriguez. *The Forging of the Cosmic Race: A Reinterpretation of Colonial Mexico*. Berkeley: University of California Press, 1980.

McAlister, Lyle N. *Spain and Portugal in the New World, 1492-1700*. Minneapolis: University of Minnesota Press, 1984.

Palmer, Colin P. *Negro Slavery in Mexico, 1570-1650*. Ann Arbor, Mich.: Xerox University Microfilm, 1974.

Mfume, Kweisi (b. Frizell Gray, October 24, 1948, Baltimore, Maryland): Politician and civil rights leader. Mfume's family life was disrupted by the death of his mother, and he dropped out of school. He became something of a street hustler and ran numbers for racke-

Kweisi Mfume during an appearance on NBC's *Meet the Press* in July, 1994. *(AP/Wide World Photos)*

teers. Mfume eventually completed high school and entered Morgan State University, where he graduated magna cum laude with a bachelor's degree in urban planning in 1976. He later completed graduate studies at Johns Hopkins University, earning a master's degree in 1984. Mfume then returned to Morgan State University, where he joined the faculty of the political science and communications departments and served as the campus radio station's program director.

In 1979 Mfume was elected to the BALTIMORE city council. He served on the council's health subcommittee as chairman. During his term as councilman, Mfume sponsored legislation to make Baltimore divest itself of its investments in companies doing business in South Africa. He was active in MARYLAND's Democratic state central committee and served as a delegate to the Democratic National Conventions in 1980, 1984, and 1988. During that time, he helped coordinate the local party's activities in support of Edward M. Kennedy's 1980 presidential campaign and the state party's support for Jesse JACKSON's 1984 and 1988 presidential campaigns.

Mfume entered the congressional race to replace retiring Representative Parren J. Mitchell and won the general election held in November of 1986. Mfume took his seat the following January and served as a member of the House Committee on Banking, Finance, and Urban Affairs, the House Committee on Small Business, and the House Select Committee on Hunger. He was reelected in 1988, 1990, and 1992. In the 102d Congress, Mfume was also a member of the House Select Committee on Narcotics Abuse and Control and the Joint Economic Committee.

Mfume became chair of the CONGRESSIONAL BLACK CAUCUS in 1993. He struggled to make the group more independent of a specifically Democratic agenda; he also upset some people by inviting the controversial Louis FARRAKHAN to attend a leadership summit. In 1994 President Bill Clinton appealed to the caucus to help him pass a major crime bill, and Mfume successfully lobbied other caucus members to support it; the bill passed.

After the 1994 elections, however, Democrats were in a minority in the House of Repesentatives. The Republican majority attacked programs that aided the poor and minorities; in addition, beginning in January, 1995, they eliminated funding for twenty-eight legislative service organizations (LSOs), including the Congressional Black Caucus. Increasingly frustrated by the situation, Mfume surprised many when he resigned his congressional seat in February, 1996. He became president and chief executive officer of the NATIONAL ASSOCIATION FOR THE ADVANCEMENT OF COLORED PEOPLE (NAACP), at the time a deeply troubled organization.

He announced that there would be swift and constructive changes. In little more than a year Mfume managed to rid the NAACP of its nearly $4-million debt. He sought to attract new, younger members to the organization, realizing that its continuation depended upon this, and he reoriented the group toward its original focus on civil rights and antidiscrimination work and away from the more service-oriented approach it had taken more recently. Mfume's autobiography, *No Free Ride,* was published in 1996.

Miami riots: In 1980 the black community of Dade County, FLORIDA, was shocked and angry when an all-white jury found four white policemen not guilty of the beating death of Arthur McDuffie, a black man. Three days of racial violence followed the announcement of the jury's decision. The Miami riots caused eighteen deaths and $100 million in property damage, making them among the most severe racial disturbances in U.S. history.

Background

Before the Miami riots, many Americans believed that the racial and social problems associated with the urban violence of the 1960's had been alleviated. Despite such complacency, American urban areas were continuing to experience severe levels of social distress. Dade County and the metropolis of Miami, for example, had seen extensive population growth and white flight, developments that triggered segregation and residential decline. In the 1960's, Miami's population was less than one million, but the city's population nearly doubled in the 1970's and reached 1.8 million in 1979. The settlement of more than 200,000 Cuban refugees in Dade County created a major Latin community in the Miami area. As Cubans moved into the city, many non-Latin whites fled to the suburbs.

During the period of Cuban resettlement, the black community of Overtown in the downtown Miami area was undergoing urban renewal. Black residents who needed to relocate were blocked from moving into nearby areas by Cuban refugees, who created the ethnic community of "Little Havana." Blacks moved to "model cities" in the northern areas of Dade County, where they had to compete with Cubans and other southern black migrants for housing. At the same time, many whites moved from the Model Cities zones, creating high levels of residential black segregation. Extensive urban growth outpaced Miami's capacity to provide for new residents, and blacks had to compete for jobs and housing with Cubans. Blacks who moved into the Model Cities area and blacks remaining in Overtown alike experienced social and economic problems. Between 1960 and 1970, black income declined, and the black unemployment rate in Dade County was higher than those of the area's white and Cuban populations.

In the 1970's, the economic problems of Dade County blacks worsened as a result of two recessions. Although Miami developed into a center of international trade, its status as a major Hispanic community resulted in a demand for bilingual employees, further limiting employment opportunities for many blacks.

Police Brutality Charges

In the period leading up to the riots, Miami racial tensions were heightened by a series of incidents in which local police were perceived by many blacks as having acted inappropriately without receiving just punishment. In one instance, a substantiated charge of sexual abuse of a black woman was made against a highway patrolman; the officer resigned and was placed on probation. Extensive publicity also resulted after the Dade County Department of Public Safety searched the home of Nathan LaFleur, a black schoolteacher, for narcotics. LaFleur resisted the search attempt and was seriously injured; an investigation established that the warrant authorizing the search had been issued for a different address, and that the search of LaFleur's residence was illegal.

No criminal prosecution resulted, however, and the officers involved were put on temporary leave. Moreover, an off-duty policeman working as a security guard shot and killed twenty-two-year-old Randy Heath. The officer claimed that he had observed Heath in the act of breaking and entering, but a witness stated that Heath had merely been in the act of urinating against a building. A state attorney's investigation found the death to be the result of negligence but did not order a criminal prosecution.

Racial tensions were further heightened in the months prior to the riot by a state attorney's investigation of Johnny Jones, the popular black superintendent of the Dade County school system. Jones was indicted for using school funds to purchase plumbing for a vacation house; he was dismissed by the school board one day after he was found guilty. Immediately prior to the riot, Jones was awaiting sentencing. As a result of such incidents, much of the Dade County black community came to the conclusion that police violence against blacks was not punished, whereas blacks were prosecuted for any offenses.

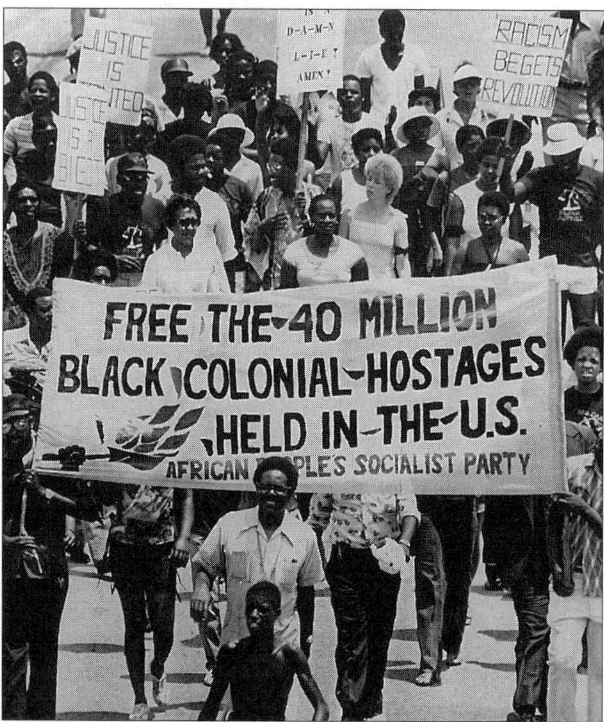

After the rioting that disrupted Miami died down, many African Americans peacefully marched on the city's justice building to protest the city's "double standard" of justice. *(AP/Wide World Photos)*

The McDuffie Beating

The spark that set off the rioting was the acquittal of four white officers charged with the beating death of Arthur McDuffie. On December 17, 1979, McDuffie ran a red light while riding a motorcycle and was pursued by Miami and Dade County officers. McDuffie was apprehended after a long chase, and he later died of severe head injuries allegedly caused when his motorcycle crashed. A medical examiner, however, found that McDuffie's injuries were inconsistent with the circumstances of the case as reported by police, and the testimony of one officer led to an investigation of charges of evidence tampering. Five Dade County Department of Public Safety officers were dismissed, and four were indicted on criminal charges for their roles in the incident; four others were placed on leave. Extensive pretrial publicity resulted in the removal of the trial to Tampa, where, on Saturday afternoon, May 17, 1980, an all-white jury acquitted the police officers.

The news of the acquittal was broadcast during an anticrime rally at Africa Park in the Model Cities area. Within an hour, violence was reported in the Africa Park neighborhood. The rioting soon spread to Overtown and other black communities. By 10 P.M., the National Guard had been called in, and a curfew was established. Model Cities and Overtown experienced the brunt of the rioting. Whites were pulled from cars and beaten, businesses were looted, buildings were vandalized, police cars were set on fire, and sniping and other violence occurred.

Riot Participants

In the wake of the riots, the *Miami Herald* commissioned a survey of riot-area residents. Twelve percent of those surveyed admitted to having participated in the riots. A majority of the area's black residents reported having taken countermeasures to protect their property and children. The *Herald* survey also indicated that, relative to the nonrioters polled, riot participants were slightly better educated, were twice as likely to have had police encounters, and were more likely to be underemployed or unemployed. A substantial majority of riot participants and nonparticipants alike believed that their community suffered from police brutality, poor housing, drug use, poverty, a lack of jobs, inadequate political representation, and other serious social problems.

Causes and Conclusions

While the strongest riot precipitant may have been a black perception of police brutality and a sense that the justice system was biased, Miami blacks also felt angry about other problems. A survey taken before the riots showed that Dade County blacks believed that they were losing out economically to Cuban competitors. In essence, Miami in 1980 suffered many of the same problems that had prompted large-scale rioting in DETROIT, WATTS, and other black communities in the 1960's. Blacks were not well represented politically, many police actions were considered to be biased, and economic problems had intensified interethnic competition. Blacks were experiencing a decline in economic opportunities and living conditions, while Cubans were perceived to be moving ahead. Months of police incidents had created tensions, and the disappointment caused by the McDuffie verdict provoked extensive anger. Rioters and nonrioters alike felt that the riot was justified.

The Miami riots of 1980 demonstrated that urban problems that had led to the riots of the 1960's had not been solved. More than a decade later, the LOS ANGELES RIOTS of 1992 offered further violent evidence of the persistence of serious urban ills in the United States.

—*Judith Warner*

See also: Jury selection; King, Rodney, arrest and beating; Race riots; Racial violence and hatred.

Suggested Readings:

Campbell, Ernest Q., ed. *Racial Tensions and National Identity*. Nashville, Tenn.: Vanderbilt University Press, 1972.

Feagin, Joe R., and Harlan Hahn. *Ghetto Revolts: The Politics of Violence in American Cities*. New York: Macmillan, 1973.

Frye, Charles A., ed. *Values in Conflict: Blacks and the American Ambivalence Toward Violence*. Washington, D.C.: University Press of America, 1980.

Harris, Daryl B. *The Logic of Black Urban Rebellions: Challenging the Dynamics of White Domination in Miami*. Westport, Conn.: Praeger, 1999.

Ladner, R. A., et al. "The Miami Riots of 1980: Antecedent Conditions, Community Responses, and Participant Characteristics." In vol. 4 of *Research in Social Movements, Conflicts, and Change*, edited by Louis Kreisberg. Greenwich, Conn.: JAI Press, 1981.

Massoti, Louis H., and Don R. Bowen, eds. *Riots and Rebellion: Civil Violence in the Urban Community*. Beverly Hills, Calif.: Sage Publications, 1968.

Micheaux, Oscar (January 2, 1884—1951): Novelist and FILM producer. As one of the first African American filmmakers, Micheaux wrote, produced, and distributed some forty-eight silent and sound features between 1918 and 1948. He also founded one of the earliest all-black film companies.

Micheaux earned a reputation as a resourceful and driven filmmaker. He saved film by shooting scenes only once, enhanced natural illumination with mirrors, and convinced some actors to work for free. He raised money by selling stock in his film company to the same farmers who had bought his novels and distributed his works by motoring from town to town. Although critics complained about the craftsmanship of Micheaux's films (directorial promptings remain on the sound track of one film, and an actor's exit reveals offstage technicians in another), the self-taught director provided entertainment for millions of African Americans who patronized the segregated inner-city theaters of his time.

Micheaux's early life provided the material for most of his novels and films. The fifth of thirteen children, Micheaux was raised in Metropolis, Illinois. After moving to CHICAGO in 1901, he worked as a stockyard hand, coal hauler, and Pullman porter until he resettled in SOUTH DAKOTA to homestead in 1904. Micheaux fell in love with the daughter of a white homesteader, but he married an African American woman whose preacher father reportedly cheated Micheaux out of property and ruined his marriage.

Micheaux's films provided a unique black context for Westerns, melodramas, and gangster stories, and they included trademark cabaret scenes with singing and dancing. Micheaux's melodramas, like his novels, were based on key events in his own life. The theme of interracial love is explored in such films as *The Homesteader* (1919), *The Exile* (1932), and *The Betrayal* (1948), as well as in the novels *The Wind from Nowhere* (1941) and *The Case of Mrs. Wingate* (1944). Micheaux's other films, such as *Within Our Gates* (1920) and *Lem Hawkins' Confession* (1935), deal with the themes of wrongful accusation and racial prejudice.

Micheaux died on the road as he was promoting his last film. He was admitted to the Screen Directors' Guild posthumously. His *Birthright* (1918) is considered to be the first full-length black film.

See also: Film directors.

Michigan: According to 1997 estimates of the CENSUS OF THE UNITED STATES, Michigan had an African American population of just under 1.4 million, giving the state the tenth largest black population in the country. The African American population made up about 14 percent of the state's total population of 9.8 million. In the consolidated metropolitan statistical area comprising DETROIT, Ann Arbor, and Flint, African Americans made up 21 percent of the population in 1996. Michigan in the twentieth century was significant in the areas of labor relations, race relations, politics, and social and religious movements.

Michigan was admitted to the union as a free state in 1837. By the middle of the nineteenth century, a number of small black farming communities had been established in Cass County, in the southwest of the state. Writer and poet James D. CORROTHERS was born in Cass County in 1869.

Until the twentieth century, Michigan, like most northern states, had a relatively small black population. Then Michigan's cities became a destination for blacks leaving the South during the era of the GREAT MIGRATION. The state's African American population grew steadily through the first half of the twentieth century, boosted in particular by a need for factory workers during WORLD WAR I and WORLD WAR II. Michigan was the home of the automobile industry, and plants manufacturing automobiles, trucks, and related commodities operated in many of the state's cities, such as Detroit ("Motor City," by far Michigan's largest city), Pontiac, Battle Creek, Flint, Lansing, and Dearborn.

In the twentieth century, Michigan has been important in black politics—both tradi-

1997 Population: 9,774,000
African American Population: 1,392,000
African American Percentage of Total: 14.24

tional electoral politics and radical movements. Among Michigan's representatives in the U.S. Congress have been thirteen-term Congressman Charles DIGGS, John CONYERS, and George William CROCKETT, Jr. Many black local officials have been elected in the state as well. Detroit, with its majority black population, had two consecutive black mayors—Coleman YOUNG and Dennis ARCHER—and a black police chief.

The FREEDOM NOW PARTY, formed in 1963 during the MARCH ON WASHINGTON, focused on electing candidates in Michigan's 1994 elections. The party, based in New York, sought to build a national black political party committed to racial equality but never achieved broad black support. It suffered from internal dissension, and the Michigan branch began operating independently under black nationalist Albert CLEAGE, who ran for governor. After a very poor showing in the nearly forty Michigan state and local races the party entered in 1964, the organization crumbled.

In a more radical vein, both the revolutionary nationalist group Republic of New Africa and the militant Revolutionary Action Movement, whose stated goal was overthrowing the U.S. government in favor of a socialist state, were formed in Detroit in the 1960's.

Michigan has also had an active labor history. Nelson Jack Edwards was one of the first African Americans to become prominent in the labor movement. He moved to Detroit in 1937 and found work in the automobile industry. The United Auto Workers (UAW) union was struggling to organize the automobile industry. Edwards became an active unionist and was the first African American to head a UAW local. In 1962 he became the first African American to sit on the union's executive board.

Future judge and congressman George Crockett, Jr., moved to Detroit in 1944 to work for the UAW as founder and director of its fair employment practices department. After returning to private practice in 1946, Crockett remained active in labor law and provided legal advice and representation for civil rights organizers and labor unions.

At the end of the 1960's, the Black Power movement influenced labor movements in Michigan, and workers formed their own black labor organizations. The Dodge Revolutionary Union Movement (DRUM) was formed at the Dodge automobile plant in Detroit. DRUM argued that the UAW was a racist union. Other auto plant caucuses such as CADRUM (at the General Motors Cadillac plant) and FRUM (the Ford Revolutionary Union Movement) grew out of DRUM's influence. DRUM and other organizations joined together to form the League of Revolutionary Black Workers. Internal dissension caused the league to split into small factions during the early 1970's, and most had merged into the union mainstream by the 1980's.

Michigan, primarily Detroit, has been the home of religious as well as political movements. The Spiritual Israel Church and Its Army was founded in Detroit by Derks Field and W. D. Dickson between the mid-1920's and the late 1930's. Wallace D. Fard founded the First Temple of Islam in Detroit in the 1930's, and Elijah Muhammad subsequently built on Fard's teachings to found the Nation of Islam there. Later, in the 1960's, Albert Cleage founded his Black Messiah movement, the Shrine of the Black Madonna church, there. In traditional black Christianity, C. L. Franklin founded the New Bethel Baptist Church in Detroit and was its pastor for thirty-eight years. Franklin became a central figure in the Detroit civil rights movement. He and Martin Luther King, Jr., led a march of more than 125,000 people along Detroit's Woodward Avenue in June of 1963.

—*McCrea Adams*

See also: Detroit, Michigan; Detroit riots; *Milliken v. Bradley*; Motown.

Mighty Clouds of Joy: Generally considered to be the foremost traditional gospel music group. The five-member group formed in Los Angeles in 1961 and recorded more than twenty-five albums, earning a number of Grammy Awards. The Clouds are noted for being the first gospel group to incorporate guitars and drums into their performances and are especially well known for their spirited, stirring recordings.

Military: Blacks have participated in the American military since the prerevolutionary colonial period. Black Americans had few opportunities in the colonial era, but through colonial militias, they could become defenders of the English colonies. English settlers initially formed militias to protect themselves against hostile Native Americans. Whenever the colonies ran low on troops or faced a desperate military situation, they impressed black men into service. Colonial militias, therefore, became the first American institutions joined by African Americans.

Colonial Wars

People of African descent served in colonial wars before SLAVERY had become a reality in the colonies. In 1643, for example, the name of Abraham Pearse, who probably was a free black, made the roster with other men eligible for militia service. In 1660 a MASSACHUSETTS law recognized Africans as eligible for military training. Africans soon fought alongside English soldiers in King William's War (1689-1697) and the Tuscarora War in NORTH CAROLINA (1711). More than four hundred Africans saw action in the Yamasee War (1715-1716) in South Carolina.

By the mid-eighteenth century, French merchants in America had also become menacing to English settlers. The final French and Indian War (1754-1763) was the most serious conflict to involve the colonies. Soon after the conflict arose, the colonies turned to their black veterans, who swelled the ranks of colonial militias. Not all black soldiers carried muskets or served in combat or scouting positions. Some were cooks and wagon masters. Black fighting men helped rout the French at Fort Duquesne and Fort Cumberland. Ultimately, black soldiers played a key role in defeating the French in North America.

The British were never comfortable with arming black people, however. As soon as the threat from the Indians and French had passed, the English dismissed black militiamen. RACIAL PREJUDICE and fear of insurrections were obvious reasons for this action.

The Revolutionary Era

Tension in Anglo-American affairs surfaced soon after the French and Indian Wars. African Americans joined in protests against royal taxes. As consumers, free African Americans were affected by the stamp duty and other internal taxes levied by Parliament. Furthermore, the growing cries for natural rights provided a basis for African Americans to press for greater liberty for free blacks and emancipation for those enslaved.

These considerations undoubtedly influenced Crispus ATTUCKS, the first African American to die from British fire during the revolutionary movement. Attucks was not confused about his status in the colonies. He was a runaway slave from Framingham, Massachusetts, whose master had advertised for his capture. By the time tension surfaced with the British, he had become a well-recognized seaman in BOSTON. When British soldiers confronted Americans on March 5, 1770, white colonists followed Attucks when he admonished them not to be afraid. His courage cost him his life. Attucks most likely anticipated greater liberty for himself and freedom for enslaved blacks should the revolution succeed.

Attucks was not the only African American to hold this belief. Blacks filed freedom suits declaring that slavery deprived them of their natural right to liberty. They also filed petitions in Massachusetts and CONNECTICUT complaining that they had not voluntarily surrendered their natural right to freedom. The belief in natural rights also influenced black veterans of previous wars to join whites when British regulars marched to Lexington and Concord in April, 1775. Peter SALEM, Prince Estabrook, Lemuel HAYNES, and other black Americans fought alongside white Americans during the first skirmishes of the AMERICAN REVOLUTION.

Two months later, the British and Americans met again. On June 17, 1775, the settlers dug in their heels at Breed's Hill. They repelled several assaults by the redcoats. They might have won the Battle of Bunker Hill had they not run out of gunpowder. In addition to black veterans of previous skirmishes, Salem

Poor, Cuffe Whitmore, Jordan Freeman, and other black Americans stood by their white countrymen at Breed's Hill. The American Revolution had begun in earnest, although the Americans did not issue the Declaration of Independence until 1776.

In the early months of the war, the Continental Army and the states could not agree on the enlistment of black soldiers. The Army debated the question until October, 1775, when it decided to bar all blacks from military service. Led by South Carolina, the southern states played a crucial role in this decision. Some northern states were indecisive. Massachusetts, for example, initially enrolled free blacks. It bowed to complaints by southern states.

The policy of exclusion adopted by the Continental Army was typical. Throughout the colonial period, only manpower shortages made whites set aside their fears and prejudices to arm blacks. The revolution brought up another question that troubled whites. They were fighting for liberty. To allow blacks to defend that principle might instill in them the false hope that they too would benefit from the war. This concern came too late. African Americans had already adopted the belief that natural rights applied equally to them. The British took advantage of their hope for freedom in November, 1775.

Lord Dunmore, the royal governor of Virginia, issued a proclamation offering to free enslaved blacks who joined the Royal Army. Dunmore's proclamation was a wartime measure designed to incite enslaved blacks to run away. Without enslaved blacks to work their farms, slaveholding troops in the Continental Army would be forced to return home to harvest their crops. In addition, escaping African Americans would surely threaten the peace in slaveholding communities. Lord Dunmore's plan had some success. Hundreds of enslaved African Americans joined him, and thousands more fled slavery to seek refuge behind British lines.

African Americans probably joined the British army for the same reason they volunteered for service in the Continental Army—a thirst for freedom. Scorned by the Americans, they answered the call when Dunmore promised them freedom. Dunmore, for all his promises of freedom, nevertheless segregated black troops into what he called the Ethiopian Regiment. Black soldiers, some with the inscription "Liberty to Slaves" written across their breasts, put up a good fight for their own liberation.

For African Americans, however, the best chance for liberty was with the United States. When the Continental Army finally called for their enlistment, they came forward to defend the principles of liberty. As the fighting became intense and white soldiers deserted to return to their farms, the Continental Army welcomed blacks, both slave and free. The states followed, with the exception of Georgia and South Carolina. By the time the war was over, more than five thousand African Americans had served on the side of the Continental Army.

The Revolution brought few changes for African Americans. A few southern states liberated black veterans for meritorious service. Northern states abolished slavery, in part because of the principle of natural rights but also because of the economic basis of their region. Geography in the North had made extensive use of slave labor unprofitable. The British had promised to evacuate enslaved African Americans who supported their cause, and they removed nearly twenty thousand blacks from the states to settle them in Canada, England, and Jamaica. To paraphrase one British official, justice demanded that Great Britain not abandon its black supporters.

America did recognize black heroes from the war. A Colonel Middleton commanded a company of black volunteers from Massachusetts called the Bucks of America. John Hancock honored the Bucks with an inscribed banner after the war. James Armistead served as a spy and provided valuable intelligence for the Continental Army. Armistead served with French General Marquis de Lafayette, who recommended to the Virginia legislature that it free Armistead. Saul Matthews spied for the Virginia militia.

Soon after the American victory in 1781, however, whites forgot the contributions of African Americans and failed to reward them. Blacks had fought for liberty; their status, however, remained unchanged. Slavery remained a fact of life in many of the states. Where slavery was abolished, virulent racial prejudice replaced it. Some states adopted laws that severely restricted the CIVIL RIGHTS of black residents. Nevertheless, when future crises arose, African Americans came forward to defend the United States.

The War of 1812

Following the Revolutionary war, the armed forces of the young nation returned to peacetime status and saw little need to keep African Americans enlisted. In 1792 Congress passed a statute restricting military service to white men. The Navy officially barred blacks but did enlist some. Secretary of War Henry Knox admonished recruiters not to enroll African Americans. When the Navy formed the Marine Corps, Knox again advised its commander not to enroll blacks. The secretary of the Navy repeated the dictum in 1798, when the United States was engaged in hostilities with France. White Americans considered service aboard ship unattractive, however, so the Navy continued to enlist African Americans.

By the early nineteenth century, most Americans anticipated a war with Britain or France, because both nations interfered with American neutrality. President George Washington had declared this policy in 1793, when he vowed to keep the nation out of foreign wars. The United States succeeded in this until 1812, when it found itself embroiled in another war with Great Britain.

The WAR OF 1812 was primarily a naval war, and African Americans, already enrolled in the Navy, played a significant role in the conflict. Early in the war, John Johnson and John Davis gave their lives when a British ship attacked an American vessel. Although the war was fought primarily at sea, there were land battles. African American leaders in PHILADELPHIA advised blacks to set aside their grievances to defend their city when the British threatened an invasion.

The Battle of New Orleans was the most decisive land battle to involve blacks. Andrew Jackson, commander of the troops there, promised African Americans equal pay, rations, and clothing, along with the land allotment promised to white soldiers. In an attempt to avoid unfair treatment, he kept whites and blacks segregated. The existence of black units created opportunities for black officers. Major Vincent Populus led a 350-man battalion of black soldiers. Major Joseph Savoy led a unit of about 250 African Americans. In a battle beginning on January 8, 1815, African Americans helped Jackson defeat the British. Neither side knew that the war had been officially ended two weeks earlier.

Although black soldiers made a significant contribution to the American victory in the War of 1812, the armed forces reverted to their policy of exclusion following the war. The Navy remained an exception. LOUISIANA had maintained a black militia called the New Orleans Free Negro Battalion ever since the colony was under French rule. For the rest of the states, however, only white men were eligible for militia service.

During the intervening years before the CIVIL WAR, which began in 1861, the United States turned its back on black veterans. Unrest over slavery continued to haunt the nation. Fugitive slave legislation did little to dampen the quest of enslaved blacks for free-

(continued on page 1688)

Notable Military Officers

U.S. Army Officers

Adams-Ender, Clara Leach (b. Wake County, N.C.). A surgical nurse who attained the rank of brigadier general, Adams-Ender held a variety of assignments in the Army, including chief of nursing at Walter Reed Army Medical Center and then chief of the Army Nurse Corps (1987-1991), before retiring from active duty in 1993.

Arnold, Wallace Cornelius (b. July 27, 1938, Washington, D.C.). Arnold reached the rank of major general in his more than thirty years of military service.

Becton, Julius Wesley, Jr. (b. June 29, 1926, Bryn Mawr, Pa.). One of the highest ranking African Americans ever in the U.S. Army, Becton had a distinguished military career and served in Vietnam. As a lieutenant general, he also commanded the Army's Seventh Corps in Germany. After his retirement in 1985, Becton headed the Federal Emergency Management Agency from 1985 to 1988.

Brailsford, Marvin Delano (b. Jan. 31, 1939, Burkeville, Tex.). Brailsford retired in 1992 as a lieutenant general after completing more than thirty-two years of active service. Following his retirement, Brailsford became president of Metters Industries, Inc., located in McLean, Virginia.

Brooks, Harry William, Jr. (b. May 17, 1928, Indianapolis, Ind.). Brooks was made a major general in 1974 and retired from military service in 1976. After his retirement, Brooks served in several corporate executive positions, culminating in his post as chairman of Brasher, International, in Burlingame, California.

U.S. Army

Brooks, Leo Austin (b. Aug. 9, 1932, Washington, D.C.). Before retiring in 1984, Brooks attained the rank of major general.

Brown, Dallas C., Jr. (b. Aug. 21, 1932, New Orleans, La.). Brown retired as a brigadier general in 1984, after completing thirty years of active service duty. Upon leaving the Army, Brown became an associate professor of history at West Virginia State College.

U.S. Army

Brown, John Mitchell, Sr. (b. Dec. 11, 1929, Vicksburg, Miss.). A graduate of the U.S. Military Academy at West Point, Brown saw combat duty in the Korean and Vietnam Wars. During his Army career, spanning from 1955 until his retirement in 1988, he achieved the rank of major general and was known for his expertise as a military history specialist.

Bryant, Cunningham Campbell (b. Aug. 8, 1921, Clifton, Va.). Army National Guard officer. Bryant served with the U.S. Army from 1943 to 1949 and from 1969 to 1971, but he achieved his greatest career distinctions with the National Guard.

Bussey, Charles David (b. Dec. 8, 1933, Edgefield, S.C.). Bussey retired in 1989, as a major general, with more than thirty-three years of commissioned service.

Byrd, Melvin Leon (b. Nov. 1, 1935, Suffolk, Va.). Byrd retired as a brigadier general on Aug. 31, 1991, with more than thirty-two years of active commissioned service. Byrd's command positions involved logistics, division support, and electronics material readiness.

Cadoria, Sherian Grace (b. Jan. 26, 1940, Marksville, La.). Cadoria had attained the rank of brigadier general by the time she retired from the U.S. Army on November 30, 1990. Much of her service was devoted to personnel and human development work as well as law enforcement.

Cartwright, Roscoe Conklin (May 27, 1919, Kansas City, Kans.—Dec. 1, 1974, Virginia). Cartwright retired as a brigadier general in 1974, having earned promotion to that rank in 1971. In 1972, he was named as assistant division commander of U.S. military headquarters and the Seventh Army, Third Infantry Division. He was only the second African American to hold this position, which involved administering, housing, and training several thousand troops and officers. He died in an air crash.

Chambers, Andrew Phillip (b. June 30, 1931, Bedford, Va.). Chambers retired in 1989 with the rank of lieutenant general after completing more than thirty-four years of active commissioned service.

Cromartie, Eugene Rufus (b. Oct. 3, 1936, Wabasso, Fla.). Cromartie commanded the 503d Military Police Battalion, was provost marshal of the 82d Airborne Division, at Fort Bragg, N.C., and later served as deputy provost marshal of the U.S. Army in Europe. In 1990, after his retirement, Cromartie was named executive director and chief of staff of the International Association of Chiefs of Police, located in Alexandria, Virginia.

Curry, Jerry Ralph (b. Sept. 7, 1932, McKeesport, Pa.). Curry began military service in 1950, and by the time of his retirement in 1984, he had attained the rank of major general. Upon his retirement, Curry became active in publishing, serving as president of the National Perspectives Institute. In 1989, he became an administrator with the National Highway Traffic Safety Administration under President George Bush. He also served as a deputy assistant secretary of defense for public relations.

U.S. Army

Davis, Benjamin O., Sr. *See main text entry.*

Davison, Frederic Ellis (b. Sept. 28, 1917, Washington, D.C.). Davison was the first African American Army combat general and retired from the Army in 1974 after attaining the rank of major general.

Delandro, Donald Joseph (b. New Orleans, La.). Delandro reached the rank of brigadier general during a military career that spanned more than twenty years.

Doctor, Henry, Jr. (b. Aug. 23, 1932, Oakley, S.C.). Doctor retired with the rank of lieutenant general in 1989, after more than thirty-four years of commissioned service.

Forte, Johnnie, Jr. (b. Dec. 20, 1936, New Boston, Tex.). Forte was promoted to brigadier general in 1979. After retiring, he served as assistant superintendent of the Fairfax County Public Schools in Virginia.

Gaskill, Robert Clarence (b. Yonkers, N.Y.). Gaskill retired from active duty in 1981 with the rank of major general, which he earned in 1979.

Gorden, Fred Augustus (b. Feb. 22, 1940, Anniston, Ala.). A graduate of the U.S. Military Academy at West Point, Gorden attained the rank of major general on July 1, 1989.

Gray, Robert E. (b. Oct. 18, 1941, Algoma, W.Va.). Gray achieved the rank of brigadier general after serving on active duty since receiving his initial commission in 1966.

Greer, Edward (b. Mar. 8, 1924, Gary, W.Va.). Commissioned as a second lieutenant in 1948, Greer was promoted to major general in 1972.

Gregg, Arthur James (b. May 11, 1928, Florence, S.C.). Gregg was commissioned as a second lieutenant in the Army in 1950 and advanced to lieutenant general.

Hall, James Reginald, Jr. (b. July 15, 1936, Anniston, Ala.). During the course of his career, Hall attained the rank of brigadier general.

Hamlet, James Frank (b. Dec. 13, 1921, Alliance, Ohio). Hamlet attained the rank of major general in 1973 and retired from active duty in 1981.

Harleston, Robert Alonzo (b. Jan. 28, 1936, Hempstead, N.Y.). Harleston became a brigadier general before retiring in 1989 after some thirty years of active service. Having earned his J.D. degree from George-

(continued)

town Law Center in 1984, Harleston became director of the criminal justice program at the University of Maryland, Eastern Shore, after leaving the Army.

Hines, Charles Alfonso (b. Sept. 4, 1935, Washington, D.C.). Hines achieved the rank of major general in 1988, after some thirty-four years of active service. He retired at that rank in 1992. After his retirement, Hines became director of protection and health services at the Smithsonian Institution. He later accepted the position of president of Prairie View A&M College in Texas.

Holmes, Arthur, Jr. (b. May 12, 1931, Decatur, Ala.). Holmes received his commission as a second lieutenant in 1952 through the Army ROTC and advanced to major general in 1981. He served in various maintenance, materiel, and personnel positions before retiring from active duty in 1987. After his retirement, Holmes took an executive position with Automated Sciences Group, in Silver Springs, Maryland, where he was promoted to president and chief executive officer in 1990.

Honor, Edward (b. Mar. 17, 1933, Melville, La.). Honor retired in 1989 with the rank of lieutenant general after completing more than thirty-four years of commissioned service. His later command postings involved transportation and military traffic management in Europe.

Honore, Charles Edward (b. Apr. 20, 1934, Baton Rouge, La.). Honore retired in 1990 with the rank of major general, having received his initial commission through the Army ROTC in 1956. His thirty-three years of commissioned service included two combat stints in Vietnam. From 1964 to 1967, Honore was an assistant professor of military science at Southern University and A&M College.

Hunton, Benjamin Lacy (b. 1919, Hyattsville, Md.). As reservist in the Army, Hunton was elevated to brigadier general, having been released from active duty in 1949 after serving in various command posts. Hunton worked as a teacher and administrator in Washington, D.C., for more than twenty years. He entered government service in 1966 and worked in the Department of Interior at the Bureau of Mines and at the Department of Health, Education, and Welfare. He also served on the White House Committee on Civil Rights and Minority Affairs.

Johnson, Hazel Winifred (b. Oct. 10, 1927, West Chester, Pa.). Johnson holds the distinction of being the first female African American general in the U.S. armed forces. Johnson's military career spanned more than twenty years before her retirement from military service in 1983. After her retirement, Johnson taught nursing at Georgetown University and at George Mason University.

U.S. Army

Johnson, Julius Frank (b. Feb. 8, 1940, Fort Leavenworth, Kans.). Johnson achieved the rank of brigadier general, having embarked on his military career in 1964. In addition to serving in Korea and Vietnam, he held command positions overseas in Europe.

Klugh, James Richard (b. June 22, 1931, Greenwood, S.C.). Klugh retired in 1990 as a major general, having received his initial commission through the Army ROTC in 1953. His duty included service in Europe and later in Vietnam, where he earned the Air Medal on July 23, 1970, by volunteering to fly into the target area of an emergency extraction to provide weather data.

Leigh, Frederic H. (b. Mar. 29, 1940, Columbus, Ohio). Leigh retired as a major general in 1994, after serving some thirty-one years. His assignments included postings as deputy director in the Army's Office of Chief of Staff (1983-1985), commander of the 101st Airborne Division (1989-1990), deputy director of the National Military Command Center (1991-1993), and director of management in the Army's Office of Chief of Staff (1993-1994).

Lenhardt, Alfonso Emanuel (b. Oct. 29, 1943, New York, N.Y.). Lenhardt attained the rank of brigadier general, having embarked on his military career in 1966. Most of his career was spent with the U.S. Army military police, and his overseas postings included service in Vietnam. For several years, he served as deputy commanding general of USAREC at Fort Sheridan, Illinois.

McCall, James Franklin (b. June 25, 1934, Philadelphia, Pa.). McCall retired in 1991 as a lieutenant general. His thirty-three years of active commissioned service included a posting with the U.S. Army Europe in Berlin, a year in Vietnam as an adviser with the U.S. Military Assistance Command, and a command position with an infantry battalion in Korea. His later postings included staff positions with the Army Materiel Command.

Monroe, James W. (b. Mar. 12, 1942, Laurinburg, N.C.). Monroe attained the rank of major general, having received his initial commission through the Army ROTC in 1963. His overseas postings included service in Vietnam. For several years, he served as commanding general of the U.S. Army Ordinance Centers at Aberdeen Proving Ground, Maryland.

Paige, Emmett, Jr. (b. Feb. 20, 1931, Jacksonville, Fla.). Paige retired as a lieutenant general in 1988, after completing thirty-five years of active commissioned service. Much of his service involved positions supporting telephone and telegraph communications for the Army, including overseas postings in Europe and Korea. He saw combat duty in Vietnam. At one time, he was the Army's senior ranking African American officer.

U.S. Army

Parker, Julius, Jr. (b. Apr. 14, 1935, New Braunfels, Tex.). Parker retired in 1989, having achieved the rank of major general. He received his initial commission through the Army ROTC in 1955, and his military service included postings in Korea, Europe, and Vietnam.

Powell, Colin Luther. *See main text entry.*

Robinson, Hugh Granville (b. Aug. 4, 1932, Washington, D.C.). A graduate of the U.S. Military Academy at West Point, Robinson reached the rank of major general in 1981. He was the son of Army officer James Robinson, the first African American to serve as a U.S. presidential military aide. Hugh Robinson began service as a second lieutenant in June, 1954, and retired from active duty in 1983. After his retirement, Robinson became chairman and chief executive officer of Tetra Group, located in Texas.

Robinson, Roscoe, Jr. (Oct. 11, 1928, St. Louis, Mo.—July 22, 1993, Washington, D.C.). Robinson holds the distinction of being the first African American to attain the rank of four-star general. After graduating from the U.S. Military Academy at West Point, Robinson distinguished himself in the Korean and Vietnam wars. He was also a member of the North American Treaty Organization Military Committee.

Rogers, Charles Calvin (b. Sept. 6, 1929, Claremont, W.Va.). Rogers earned the Congressional Medal of Honor for his service as a lieutenant colonel in the Vietnam War with the First Infantry Division. In a brave action, he held his fire support base during an assault by numerically superior forces. Upon earning this distinction, Rogers was the highest-ranking African American officer to receive the Congressional Medal of Honor during the Vietnam War. He reached the rank of major general in 1975.

Rozier, Jackson Evander, Jr. (b. Mar. 21, 1936, Richmond, Va.). Rozier retired in 1990, as major general, having received his initial commission through the Army ROTC in 1960. He served overseas in Korea and Europe and had more than a year of combat experience in Vietnam.

U.S. Army

Sheffey, Fred Clifton, Jr. (b. Aug. 27, 1928, McKeesport, Pa.). Sheffey was commissioned through the Army ROTC as a second lieutenant in 1950 and rose to major general in 1976 before retiring from active duty in 1980. He served as the director of research and engineering at Vought Corporation in Dallas, Texas, and later became an aerospace executive at Lockheed-Martin. His military experience included posts in Europe and Vietnam.

Short, Alonzo Earl, Jr. (b. Greenville, N.C.). Short received his initial commission through the Army ROTC in 1962, and eventually attained the rank of major general. Short's military duty included service in Vietnam and appointments at the Armed

(continued)

Forces Staff College and the Defense Communications Agency.

Smith, Isaac Dixon (b. May 2, 1932, Wakefield, La.). During his thirty years of military service, Smith attained the rank of major general. Commissioned through the Army ROTC in 1954, Smith served as a commander in Vietnam. Most of his military assignments centered on commanding artillery divisions, and he was also active in ROTC and worked in the office of the assistant secretary of the Army.

Stanford, John Henry (b. Sept. 14, 1938, Darby, Pa.). As a member of the Army ROTC, Stanford was commissioned as a second lieutenant after his college graduation and achieved the rank of major general before his retirement in 1991. As an Army officer, Stanford was a platoon leader, fixed wing aviator, chief of the electrical section of the Army Transportation School, and executive assistant to the secretary of defense.

Waller, Calvin Augustine Hoffman (Dec. 17, 1937, Baton Rouge, La.—May 9, 1996, Washington, D.C.). Waller retired in 1991 as a lieutenant general. His combat experience included a year in Vietnam and service as a deputy commander in chief during Operation Desert Storm (1989-1991). He was criticized for expressing his opinion that U.S. forces would not be ready by January 15, 1991, the date given as a deadline by the United Nations for Iraq to withdraw from Kuwait. After his retirement, Waller served in executive positions with two companies from 1991 to 1992 and from 1995 to 1996.

U.S. Army

Watkins, John M., Jr. (b. July 2, 1942, Evergreen, Ala.). Watkins achieved the rank of brigadier general, having served on active duty since receiving his initial commission through the Army ROTC in 1966. He served in Vietnam, and his later command postings included service at the Pentagon and as staff commander of the Eleventh U.S. Army at Fort Huachuca, Arizona.

Williams, Charles Edward (b. Aug. 8, 1938, Wedgeworth, Ala.). Williams retired in 1989, as a major general, having served on active duty since receiving his initial commission through the Army ROTC in 1960. His combat experience included two stints in Vietnam, during which he earned a Distinguished Flying Cross and an Army Commendation Medal with V device.

Wilson, Johnnie Edward (b. Feb. 4, 1944, Baton Rouge, La.). Wilson attained the rank of four-star general before his retirement in April, 1996. During his thirty-eight-year career, Wilson served in a variety of command and staff positions in the Army, including command postings in Vietnam and Europe, deputy chief of staff for logistics at the Pentagon, commanding general of the ordnance center at Aberdeen Proving Ground in Maryland, and his final assignment as chief of staff of the U.S. Army Materiel Command in Alexandria, Virginia.

Young, Charles (Mar. 12, 1864, Mayslick, Ky.—Jan. 18, 1922, Lagos, Nigeria). One of three African Americans who graduated from the U.S. Military Academy in the late 1880's, Young served in the all-black Tenth Cavalry and fought in the SPANISH-AMERICAN WAR and in the Mexican military campaign in 1915. The War Department declared him medically unfit as an excuse to keep him from serving in WORLD WAR I. He is buried in Arlington National Cemetery, and his home in Wilberforce, Ohio, was declared a national historical landmark.

National Archives

U.S. Air Force Officers

Boddie, James Timothy, Jr. (b. Oct. 18, 1931, Baltimore, Md.). Boddie attained the rank of brigadier general before retiring on July 1, 1983. He was promoted to that position in 1980. A veteran pilot who completed 201 combat missions in Southeast Asia (1966-1967), Boddie logged more than four thousand hours in jet fighter aircraft before his retirement.

Brooks, Elmer T. (b. Dec. 30, 1932, Washington, D.C.). Brooks attained the rank of brigadier general in 1981 and retired in 1985. After entering the Air Force in April, 1955, Brooks served with the Organization of the Joint Chiefs of Staff and was appointed by President Ronald Reagan as deputy commissioner of the U.S.-U.S.S.R. Standing Consultative Commission.

U.S. Air Force

Brown, William E., Jr. (b. New York, N.Y.). A command pilot with more than forty-nine hundred hours of flying time who attained the rank of major general, Brown flew various jets with fighter- interceptor squadrons and with the New York Air Defense Sector.

Clifford, Thomas E. (b. Mar. 9, 1929, Washington, D.C.). Clifford attained the rank of major general before his retirement in 1979. As wing vice commander, while in Vietnam, he flew more than ninety combat missions.

Davis, Benjamin O., Jr. *See main text entry.*

Durham, Archer L. (b. June 9, 1932, Pasadena, Calif.). A command pilot with more than six thousand flying hours, Durham was promoted to major general in 1984. Among his overseas postings, Durham served in Japan, the Philippines, France, and Korea.

Ferguson, Alonzo L. (b. Jan. 10, 1931, Washington, D.C.). Ferguson retired in 1982, as a brigadier general, after some thirty years of active duty service. He was commissioned as a second lieutenant through the ROTC and became a brigadier general in 1977. He served overseas in Korea, Libya, Germany, Thailand, and Vietnam.

Hall, David McKenzie (b. June 21, 1928, Gary, Ind.). Before his retirement from active duty, Hall attained the rank of brigadier general. His military career included assignments related to accounting, finance, and computer operations. In the private sector, Hall became director of data processing at the Delco-Remy division of General Motors in 1983. He was hired by Electronic Data Systems, in Saginaw, Michigan, in 1985, and rose to the level of regional manager before leaving the company in 1993. Hall later became a professor at Northwood University in Midland, Michigan.

U.S. Air Force

Hall, Titus C. (b. Pflugerville, Tex.). A graduate of Tuskegee Institute in 1942, Hall attended navigator school in the Army and quickly gained recognition as a master navigator. He eventually became chief avionics engineer for the B-1 strategic manned bomber.

Harris, Marcelite J. (b. Jan. 16, 1943, Houston, Tex.). Harris reached the rank of major general in 1995 and was the first African American woman to achieve this distinction within the U.S. Armed services. Commissioned as an officer in 1965, Harris was one of the first women officers to hold a command position at the U.S. Air Force Academy. She was the first African American woman to achieve the rank of brigadier general within the U.S. Air Force when she was promoted to this rank in 1990. She retired from the Air Force in February of 1997.

James, Avon C., Jr. (b. Hampton, Va.). During the course of his career, James reached the rank of brigadier general. His Air Force duties included working as computer systems staff officer with the automatic data processing equipment selection directorate, serving as chief of staff in the electronic systems division, and acting as first duty commander for data automation.

James, Daniel "Chappie." *See main text entry.*

Jiggetts, Charles B. (b. 1926, Henderson, N.C.). Before retiring as a brigadier general, Jiggetts held various assignments in communications and data pro-

(continued)

cessing work. He served as assistant to the director of the Office of Telecommunications Policy and in the executive office of the president of the United States.

Lyles, Lester Lawrence (b. Apr. 20, 1946, Washington, D.C.). Lyles attained the rank of brigadier general, having begun his military career in 1968. Most of his postings involved research and development in the areas of science and engineering.

Marchbanks, Vance Hunter. *See main text entry.*

Newton, Lloyd W. "Fig" (b. Ridgeland, S.C.). Newton achieved the rank of four-star general in 1997. Commissioned through the ROTC in 1966, Newton flew 269 combat missions while stationed in Vietnam. A veteran command pilot with more than 4,000 flight hours, he holds the distinction of being the first African American pilot to fly with the Thunderbirds (1974-1978).

Powers, Winston D. (b. Dec. 19, 1930, Manhattan, N.Y). Powers advanced to the rank of lieutenant general in 1983, after some thirty-three years of distinguished service. Among his overseas postings, Powers served in Korea, England, and Vietnam (where he flew seventy-five combat missions in EC-47 aircraft). Powers has more than four thousand flying hours.

Randolph, Bernard P. (b. July 10, 1933, New Orleans, La.). Randolph was promoted to general in 1987. He was the third African American to achieve the rank of four-star general in the U.S. armed forces and the second one to achieve that rank within the Air Force. During much of his career, Randolph was assigned to Los Angeles Air Force Station, where he was involved with the Space Systems Division.

Theus, Lucius (b. Oct. 11, 1922, near Bells, Tenn.). Theus joined the Air Force in 1942 and was commissioned as a second lieutenant in 1946. He advanced to major general in 1975. Theus retired from military service in 1979 to become assistant corporate controller and corporate director of civic affairs for the Bendix Corporation of Southfield, Michigan.

U.S. Air Force

Trowell-Harris, Irene. Trowell-Harris attained the rank of brigadier general serving as a nurse with the Air National Guard at Andrews Air Force Base in Washington, D.C. She was the first African American woman to achieve that rank in the National Guard.

U.S. Marine Corps Officers

Fields, Arnold (b. Early Branch, S.C.). Fields attained the rank of major general in 1998, having received his initial commission as a second lieutenant in 1969. Among his overseas assignments, Fields served in Japan and North Africa, and he saw combat duty in Vietnam and in Kuwait during the Persian Gulf War.

Petersen, Frank Emmanuel, Jr. (b. Mar. 2, 1932, Topeka, Kans.). Petersen retired in 1988, as a lieutenant general, having completed more than four thousand flying hours in various fighter and attack aircraft during his military career. Petersen had become the first black general in the Marine Corps when he was promoted in 1979. He flew sixty combat missions in Korea. In Vietnam, he served as commanding officer of Marine Fighter Attack Squadron 314, becoming the first black officer to command a squadron in the U.S. Navy or Marine Corps. While in Vietnam, he flew three hundred missions. After retirement, Petersen accepted an executive position with the Delaware-based chemical firm DuPont, where he was promoted to vice president before leaving the company in 1997.

U.S. Marine Corps

Stanley, Clifford L. Stanley attained the rank of major general within the U.S. Marine Corps in 1998. During the course of his career, Stanley served in a number of command and staff positions, including special assistant and Marine Corps Aide to the assistant secretary of the Navy, desk officer in the office of the assistant secretary of defense, and fleet marine officer on the USS *Mt. Whitney*.

Walls, George Hilton, Jr. (b. Nov. 30, 1942, Coatesville, Pa.). Walls retired from the Marine Corps in 1993 as a brigadier general after nearly thirty years of active duty service. Upon retiring, Walls accepted the position of special assistant to the chancellor of North Carolina Central University.

Williams, Leo V., III. Williams attained the rank of major general in the Marine Corps Reserve in 1998. He served on active duty from 1970 through 1978, when he transferred to the Marine Corps Reserve. Williams served as commanding general of the 4th Force Service Support Group in New Orleans, Louisiana, before assuming command of the Marine Corps Reserve Support Command in Kansas City, Missouri. Williams is a division manager for sport utility vehicles with Ford Motor Company in Kansas City.

U.S. Naval Officers

Brewer, David L., III (b. May 19, 1946, Farmville, Va.). Brewer attained the rank of rear admiral, having received his initial commission through the Naval ROTC in 1970. He served as executive officer on various ships before accepting command of the U.S. Naval Forces in the Marianas Islands.

Cochran, Donnie L. (b. July 6, 1954, Pelham, Ga.). Cochran attained the rank of lieutenant commander in the U.S. Navy and holds the distinction of being the first African American naval aviator to fly with the Blue Angels (1985-1989). He served as an aviator in various postings after joining the Navy in 1976 and became an instructor pilot in 1985. He was called to serve as commander of the Blue Angels from 1994 to 1996 as a replacement for the previous commander, who had been grounded in the wake of the Tailhook scandal.

Combs, Osie V. Combs attained the rank of rear admiral, having received his initial commission through the Naval ROTC in 1971. He served on the USS *Coral Sea* in Vietnam (1971-1974) and later had sea assignments on the USS *Woodrow Wilson* (1980) and USS *Proteus* (1983-1985). Combs put his engineering skills to use in various managerial postings during the 1980's and 1990's, most notably on the SEAWOLF Attack Submarine Program.

Fishburne, Lillian (b. Mar. 25, 1949, Patuxent River, Md.). Fishburne holds the distinction of being the first African American woman to attain the rank of rear admiral in the Navy. She received her initial commission as an ensign after completing her training at the Women Officer School in Newport, Rhode Island. During her career, Fishburne served in a number of positions related to naval communications and control systems. She was promoted to rear admiral in 1998 during her service as a director under the chief of naval operations in Washington, D.C.

Gaston, Mack Charles (b. July 17, 1940, Dalton, Ga.). Gaston became a rear admiral after serving on active duty for some twenty-eight years. He began his career in the Naval Reserve in 1964, and his later command postings included assignments as commander of field command at the Defense Nuclear Agency from 1990 to 1992 and commander of the Naval Training Center at Great Lakes, Illinois, in 1993.

U.S. Navy

Gravely, Samuel Lee, Jr. (b. June 4, 1922, Richmond, Va.). In 1971 Gravely was promoted to rear admiral, becoming the first African American admiral in the U.S. Navy. He began his naval career in the Naval Reserve, saw active duty during World War II and the Korean War, and transferred to the regular Navy in 1955. Gravely retired as a vice admiral in 1980. In 1991 he served as aide-de-camp to Governor L. Douglas Wilder of Virginia.

Hacker, Benjamin Thurman (b. Sept. 19, 1935, Washington, D.C.). Hacker became a rear admiral in

(continued)

1980, having begun his military career in 1958. He was one of the first African Americans to serve as a naval base commander.

Moore, Edward, Jr. Moore attained the rank of vice admiral, having begun his career in the Naval Reserve in 1963. Moore completed a number of sea duty tours and held shore assignments on the staff of the commander in chief of the U.S. Pacific Command and in the Bureau of Naval Personnel. He led missile strikes against Iraq in 1993 and again in 1996 (Operation Desert Strike). On August 7, 1998, Moore assumed duties as commander of the Naval Surface Force, U.S. Pacific Fleet, in San Diego, California.

Reason, Paul (b. Washington, D.C.). Reason holds the distinction of being the first African American to advance to the rank of four-star admiral in the Navy. A 1965 graduate of the U.S. Naval Academy, Reason served in Vietnam and Southeast Asia aboard a missile cruiser. From 1976 to 1979, he was Naval Aide to President Jimmy Carter. He served as commander of the Naval Surface Force for the U.S. Atlantic Fleet before becoming deputy chief of naval operations in 1994. After attaining the rank of four-star admiral, Reason was made commander in chief of the U.S. Atlantic Fleet in 1996.

Thomas, Gerald Eustis (b. June 23, 1929, Natick, Mass.). Thomas joined the Naval ROTC while a student at Harvard University. He studied Russian while serving with the cruiser USS *Worcester* and earned a certificate as an interpreter from the Defense Language Institute. In 1974, he was designated as a rear admiral, only the second African American in U.S. Navy history to reach that rank. Thomas became commander of the training command of the U.S. Pacific Fleet at San Diego, California, in December, 1978, and retired in August, 1981. He then embarked on a diplomatic career, serving as U.S. Ambassador to Guyana from 1981 to 1983 and U.S. Ambassador to Kenya from 1983 to 1986.

U.S. Navy

Watson, Anthony J. (b. May 18, 1949, Chicago, Ill.). A graduate of the U.S. Naval Academy in 1970, Watson attained the rank of rear admiral after many years of distinguished service. He holds the distinction of being the first African American submariner to achieve flag rank within the U.S. Navy.

dom. Runaway slaves sought refuge in the North and the West. By the 1840's, most of these states had adopted judicial policies that favored emancipation of slaves brought into their jurisdictions. In *Commonwealth v. Aves* (1836), the Massachusetts supreme court declared a slave free because she had been brought into the state by her mistress. In *Jackson v. Bulloch* (1837), the Connecticut supreme court agreed. Supreme courts in Ohio and other northern states established similar precedents. The slaveholding states disapproved of this legal theory. This dispute helped to set the stage for the Civil War.

A White Man's War

South Carolina seceded from the United States on December 20, 1860, soon after the election of Abraham Lincoln as president. Lincoln had tried to assure the South that his administration would not threaten slavery in the states where it existed. He and the Republican Party opposed only the expansion of slavery. This sort of compromise no longer interested most slaveholding states. By February, 1861, six more southern states had joined South Carolina to form the Confederate States of America, or the Confederacy. President Lincoln disagreed that a state could lawfully leave the Union. By March, the Union and the rebel states were engaged in civil war.

African American leaders considered the war an opportunity to free blacks still in bondage. Abolitionist Frederick Douglass urged Lincoln to enlist free blacks into the armed forces to fight for the liberation of slaves. President Lincoln did not see liberation as a primary objective of the war; he wanted most to reunite the nation. Most whites considered the conflict a white man's war.

Some of Lincoln's field generals did not agree with the decision to uphold the 1792 law that excluded blacks from the military. General John C. Frémont, a well-known abolitionist, began to free enslaved blacks early in the war. He also advised the War Department to enlist as soldiers the slaves he had freed. Lincoln objected to Frémont's emancipation plan and removed the general from his command. General Thomas W. Sherman intended to follow Frémont's lead, but Lincoln aborted his plan. Other generals followed the field emancipation of Frémont in GEORGIA, KANSAS, and Ohio. Lincoln did not succeed in blocking their efforts.

As in previous wars, when manpower needs became serious, military commanders became more willing to enlist African Americans. In July, 1862, for example, Lincoln's call for 300,000 white volunteers produced few results. The situation forced the president to consider arming African Americans, but he did not want to appear desperate or to lose the support of the border states, the southern states that had remained loyal to the Union.

The Emancipation Proclamation

By the summer of 1862, Lincoln recognized that emancipation was inevitable, and he began to take steps toward freeing the slaves and holding the border states. He supported emancipation in the nation's capital and in federal territories. In January, 1863, Lincoln announced the EMANCIPATION PROCLAMATION, which freed all slaves in the rebel states. These states could join the border states in

African American troops led the Union assault on South Carolina's heavily defended Fort Wagner during the Civil War. *(Mollus, Mass. Collection, USAMHI)*

maintaining slavery if they would cease the war and return to the Union. The states in the Confederacy ignored the proclamation, so it did not immediately free any slaves.

The United States began to recruit African Americans in March, 1863. With the help of African Americans such as Frederick Douglass, the plan was an immediate success. To speed recruitment, the government established the Bureau of Colored Troops. The Army organized several black regiments, including the Fourth U.S. Colored Infantry and the Fifty-fourth Massachusetts Colored Infantry. Whites did not welcome black fighting men into the Army. Many whites believed that blacks were cowards, in spite of their military service since the colonial period. Whites taunted black soldiers, and the Army as a whole mistreated them. They were provided with inadequate equipment, clothing, and medical care. The Army also initially paid black troops less than it did white troops. Most African American soldiers declared that they were fighting for the liberation of enslaved blacks rather than for the money. In the last months of the war, facing a crippling manpower shortage, the Confederacy began to enlist slaves as soldiers.

African American soldiers performed gallantly in battle. They played significant roles at the battles of Fort Pillow and Fort Wagner, among many others. By the end of the war, more than two hundred thousand African Americans had served in the armed forces. After the war, Congress cited many African American veterans for their valor. William H. Carney, Powhatan Beaty, Milton M. Holland, Decatur Dorsey, and several others received medals of honor.

Reconstruction and the West

African Americans soon found new challenges in the Army after the Civil War. In 1866 Congress created six black regiments. Four of these were infantry, and two were cavalry, the Ninth Cavalry and Tenth Cavalry. Congress did not provide for artillery, even though African Americans had served in this capacity during the Civil War. In 1869 the Army combined the four infantry units into two, the Twenty-fourth Infantry and the Twenty-fifth Infantry.

New tales surfaced among whites that black soldiers were lazy and undisciplined. Whites looked upon them as misfits, and African American soldiers again had to prove their worth. They did so in the Reconstruction South and the West. During Reconstruction the U.S. Army had responsibilities including setting up a temporary government, protecting the freedmen, and supervising elections. The Army assigned approximately eighty thousand black troops to the South. Their presence in uniform caused tension.

Most African American soldiers were assigned to the West to protect settlers from hostile Indians and to attempt to keep Indians on the reservations to which they had been ordered to move. The Indians called African American troops "buffalo soldiers" because of the texture of black hair. These troops continued to distinguish themselves, and black soldiers won seventeen medals of honor during the Indian wars. In 1889 Sergeant Benjamin Brown and Corporal Isaiah Mays of the Twenty-fourth Infantry earned special commendation during a fracas with bandits attempting to rob a regimental payroll. The bandits wounded both men, who fought gallantly to protect the payroll. The white paymaster who accompanied them praised the outnumbered Brown and Mays for their courage, even though the payroll was lost.

The Spanish-American War

The United States called upon African American troops again in 1898, when it decided to aid Cuban rebels in their struggle for liberation from Spanish rule. For black troops, the Spanish-American War was different from previous wars. It was the first time they fought an enemy outside the continental United States. Black soldiers represented some of the most experienced of all American fighting men. Consequently, the Army mobilized them first to see action in Cuba. The government called upon the black Twenty-fourth and Twenty-fifth Infantry units and the Ninth and Tenth Cavalry units. These units had been tested for battle in the Indian wars. Congress also raised several volunteer regiments, but the war ended before they left the states. Major Charles Young, among the first African American West Point graduates, commanded the Ohio volunteers.

Members of the all-black Ninth Volunteer Infantry around the time of the Spanish-American War. *(Library of Congress)*

The U.S. government had other motivations for calling black troops into action in Cuba. American prejudice was part of the decision. Cuba has a hot climate, and at the time it was infested with tropical diseases. Whites believed that blacks were better suited to live under these hostile conditions. Government officials also believed that blacks had some immunity against infections; they called black troops "immune regiments."

The Spanish-American War began on February 15, 1898, when a U.S. warship, the *Maine*, was sunk in Havana's harbor. Spanish responsibility for the sinking was never proved, but the U.S. government seized upon it as a justification for war. Several Americans went down with the vessel, including a few African Americans. The sinking of the *Maine* became the rallying cry for military action against Spain.

There were mixed feelings about the war among African Americans. They recognized the oppression of black people that existed in the United States even as the nation embarked on a campaign for liberty beyond its borders. Bishop Henry H. Turner, presiding over the African Methodist Episcopal Church in the United States, condemned the action of the United States as hypocrisy. He argued that the United States oppressed blacks more grievously than Spain had oppressed Cuba. He urged the United States to stop the lynching of blacks and end its policy of legalized segregation.

Many African Americans supported the war effort, however. Some merely wanted revenge for the deaths aboard the *Maine*. Others had political motivations. Booker T. Washington, a prominent spokesman for blacks, for example, believed the war was another opportunity for African Americans to demonstrate their loyalty to the United States. E. E. Cooper, editor of The Colored American, shared this view. He believed that if blacks could prove their worth, they would gain the respect of whites. Both Washington and Cooper saw the war as an opportunity to advance civil rights in the United States.

African American troops performed well in Cuba, as they had in wars since the colonial wars of the seventeenth century. Whites, however, were unwilling to believe that the people they had enslaved could ever be their equals. Black soldiers were part of many of the war's major battles. They helped to take San Juan Hill and actually saved Theodore Roosevelt and his Rough Riders, who had been pinned down. Roosevelt recognized the black soldiers' contribution to the battle in articles he wrote for *Scribner's Magazine*, praising their courage.

Yet Roosevelt did not overcome his prejudices. He considered black troops to be dependent on white officers to lead them. He also believed that black soldiers tended to panic under fire. Roosevelt drew these conclusions while in Cuba, when he saw black soldiers at the rear during a battle. He forgot about the ones at the front and concluded that the black troopers in the rear must have been retreating. Roosevelt was wrong: Those African American soldiers, along with a few Rough Riders, had been ordered to the rear to help with supplies.

World War I

Even by the time of WORLD WAR I, African Americans could not have considered themselves true American citizens. They had toiled as agricultural workers during slavery, and black soldiers had fought for the United States after emancipation. African Americans, however, still were not truly free. They could not vote in most states in the union. They were forced to attend segregated and inferior schools, and they were lynched frequently by white mobs and secret societies. In spite of black achievements in business, journalism, the arts, politics, and other social enterprises, most white Americans considered blacks unworthy of citizenship rights.

World War I began in 1914, but the United States escaped involvement in the war until 1917, when Germany submarines began attacking neutral ships. Even many radical African American leaders supported the American war effort; many believed that black participation would ultimately help the position of blacks at home. Civil rights leader W. E. B. DU BOIS advised African Americans first to defend their country, then to worry about their rights. Du Bois believed that a war to make the world safe for democracy would extend freedom in the United States. History proved otherwise, and Du Bois later left the country, disillusioned with the continuing racism in American society.

Soon after the United States declared war on Germany, it began a drive to recruit additional black Americans into the military. The Army called on prominent black leaders to help enlist recruits. President William SCARBOROUGH of Wilberforce University, Du Bois, and others encouraged enlistment, but they faced opposition. Labor leader A. Philip RANDOLPH articulated a popular sentiment when he said that black Americans should not die for liberty in Europe when the United States daily denied them liberty. Many black Americans undoubtedly agreed but believed that to stay out of the war would only hurt their case for civil rights. Consequently, African American troops swelled the ranks of the armed forces. Almost 400,000 black Americans answered the call.

The United States' entry into the war turned the tide in the Allies' favor. The military placed more than 350,000 black troops in service roles, and almost 100,000 black troops saw action in Europe. Only three black soldiers attained officer rank: Colonel Charles Young and first lieutenants Benjamin O. DAVIS, Sr., and John E. Green. Black troops who saw action served with distinction, but the United States largely ignored them. The French, on the other hand, awarded them several medals of honor. The European war did little to foster equality within the American armed forces or at home.

After a history of 167 years of rigid racial exclusion, the U.S. Marines allowed the first African American, Howard Perry, to enlist in June, 1942. *(National Archives)*

Colonel Young, a West Point graduate whom even white officers recognized as an experienced officer, might have been promoted to general had it not been for racism. Although Young's abilities and seniority would have qualified him for promotion to general, whites could not accept that prospect. The Army forced Young to retire, at least temporarily. He was later reinstated but was never promoted to general. Young was not the only uniformed black victim of racism. The very sight of an African American in uniform was sometimes enough to spark a racial confrontation.

African Americans made some progress during the decades following World War I. Blacks registered and voted in a few northern states, especially in cities such as New York, Philadelphia, and Chicago. A small middle class emerged to influence the political system with its votes. Civil rights organizations such as the Brotherhood of Sleeping Car Porters, the Congress of Racial Equality (CORE), and the National Association for the Advancement of Colored People (NAACP) began to win victories in civil rights. As these organizations were mounting their attack on segregation in the United States, Europe exploded in another world war.

World War II

In December, 1941, after Japanese planes attacked the U.S. naval base at Pearl Harbor, Hawaii, the United States entered the war on the side of the Allies. The United States fought on two fronts: U.S. troops fought against Germany in Europe and against Japan in the Pacific.

African American soldiers played important roles in World War II from the beginning. Dorie Miller, who worked in the mess hall on the USS *West Virginia*, was below deck when the attack on Pearl Harbor began. When he heard bombings, Miller ran on deck, dragged his wounded captain to safety, and manned a nearby machine gun. After hitting four planes, he continued to shoot until an officer ordered him to leave the sinking ship. For his act of courage, the Navy awarded him the Navy Cross. Miller was not alone. Approximately one million African American men and women served in the armed forces during World War II.

As in previous wars, African American troops recognized that they were fighting to make the world safe for democracy while they enjoyed few civil rights at home. They continued to hope that their patriotism would yield full citizenship rights for blacks. Many went into battle thinking of a Double V—victory abroad and at home. They did not achieve this goal, but the war did help to transform American politics. More than in any previous wars, black soldiers entered positions of leadership, with approximately six thousand black soldiers promoted to officer ranks. Black women also served, in the Women's Auxiliary Army Corps (WAACS) and as Women Accepted for Voluntary Emergency Services (WAVES) in the Navy. Civil rights leaders successfully pressured President Franklin D. Roosevelt to take action against hiring discrimination in industries doing war production for the government. Roosevelt signed EXECUTIVE ORDER 8802 banning this discrimination in 1941.

The decade after the end of World War II in 1945 saw transformations in the United States. The Supreme Court decision in BROWN V. BOARD OF EDUCATION (1954), which outlawed school discrimination, increasing protests by black Americans, and a growing sense among whites that discrimination was wrong produced a civil rights revolution. The Double V was not achieved immediately; nevertheless, the stage had been set for the racial integration of American society.

Benjamin O. Davis, Sr., was the only African American who saw service as a general during World War II. *(National Archives)*

The Korean War

The United States fought another foreign war, the KOREAN WAR, during the 1950's. By this time it appeared that the armed forces might finally integrate the races. President Harry S Truman had begun military integration in 1946, when he established the President's Committee on Civil Rights to consider desegregation in the federal government. In 1948 he issued EXECUTIVE ORDER 9981, calling for equal treatment in the military. He also formed a special commission headed by former U.S. solicitor Charles Fahey. The Fahey Committee recommended integration of the armed forces in January, 1950. The war in Korea delayed any further official action in this area.

The needs of the war itself, however, sped the process of integration in the military. A segregated Army arrived in Korea, but a number of field commanders, when threatened by manpower shortages, integrated their units. By the end of the decade, the armed forces were beginning to desegregate as official policy.

Vietnam War

The VIETNAM WAR was the first war fought by the United States that was widely and openly opposed by American citizens. American involvement in the conflict began slowly. First, the United States sent advisers to aid democratic South Vietnam. By the mid-1960's, the government was sending combat troops. A large number of these troops were African American. Because middle-class college students (most of whom were white) benefited from student deferments (until the early 1970's), and because some other white youths even fled the country to avoid service, a disproportionate number of blacks and poor whites swelled the ranks of the American military.

The 1980's and 1990's

In the years following Vietnam, African Americans developed a new impression of the mili-

African Americans in the U.S. Armed Forces, 1997		
	African American Personnel	*Percentage of Total Personnel*
Army Total	127,732	26.8
Officers	9,061	11.6
Enlisted	118,671	29.8
Air Force Total	56,741	15.0
Officers	4,327	5.8
Enlisted	52,414	17.3
Navy Total	68,967	17.4
Officers	3,313	5.9
Enlisted	65,654	19.3
Marines Total	27,024	15.7
Officers	1,161	6.5
Enlisted	25,863	16.8
Armed Forces Total	280,464	19.7

Sources: U.S. Department of Defense.

tary. Widely lacking career opportunities as civilians, urban African Americans turned to the military for jobs and training. By the 1990's, a large number of African Americans provided vital services and expertise for the military. General Colin Powell, a career soldier, became the first African American to head the Joint Chiefs of Staff. Other African Americans also rose to the highest ranks in the armed forces. During the Persian Gulf War, one of the briefest formal wars in American history, black American men and women were represented in virtually every specialty. They flew bombing missions into Iraq, led field combat raids, and worked in intelligence, special forces, and medical teams.

In 1997 seven African American World War II veterans had been awarded the Congressional Medal of Honor. Six of the awards were posthumous, but surviving veteran Vernon Baker was given the medal by President Bill Clinton at a White House ceremony. Previously, because of prejudice and segregation in the World War II military, black soldiers in World War II had been completely overlooked for Medals of Honor.

Another milestone was noted in 1998 in a speech by Secretary of Defense William Cohen. For the first time in history, he stated, African Americans were serving at the four-star rank in three of the armed services at the same time: Admiral Paul Reason (Navy, the first four-star admiral in U.S. Navy history), General Lloyd "Fig" Newton (Air Force), and General Johnnie E. Wilson (Army). Wilson retired in 1999.

—*Stephen Middleton*

See also: Golden Thirteen of the U.S. Navy; Tuskegee Airmen.

Suggested Readings:

Buchanan, Albert R. *Black Americans in World War II*. Santa Barbara, Calif.: Clio Books, 1977.

Eppinga, Jane. *Henry Ossian Flipper: West Point's First Black Graduate*. Plano, Tex.: Republic of Texas Press, 1996.

Hawkins, Walter L. *African American Generals and Flag Officers: Biographies of Over 120 Blacks in the United States Military*. Jefferson, N.C.: McFarland, 1992.

Hine, Darlene C. "Mabel K. Staupers and the Integration of Black Nurses into the Armed Forces." In *Black Leaders of the Twentieth Century*, edited by John Hope Franklin and August Meier. Urbana: University of Illinois Press, 1982.

Lanning, Michael L. *The African American Soldier from Crispus Attucks to Colin Powell*. Seacaucus, N.J.: Birch Lane Press, 1997.

Merchon, Sherie, and Steven Schlossman. *Foxholes and Color Lines: Desegregating the U.S. Armed Forces*. Baltimore: Johns Hopkins University Press, 1998.

Moebs, Thomas T. *Black Soldiers, Black Sailors, Black Ink: Research Guide on African-Americans in U.S. Military History, 1526-1900*. Williamsburg, Va.: Moebs, 1994.

Moskos, Charles C., and John S. Butler. *All*

That We Can Be: Black Leadership and Racial Integration the Army Way. New York: Basic Books, 1996.

Mullen, Robert W. *Blacks and Vietnam*. Washington, D.C.: University Press of America, 1987.

Rose, Robert A. *The Story of America's Black Air Force in World War II: The Lonely Eagles*. Los Angeles: Tuskegee Airmen, Western Region, 1976.

Wright, Roosevelt, Jr. "A Historical Perspective: Opportunities for African Americans in the Armed Forces." *The Black Collegian* 27 (February, 1997): 122-127.

Miller, Dorie (October 12, 1919, Waco, Texas—1943, the Pacific): WORLD WAR II hero. Doris "Dorie" Miller received the Navy Cross for heroism during the attack on Pearl Harbor on December 7, 1941. Miller braved enemy fire to pull his wounded comrades to safety, then manned a machine gun, even though he was not trained on it, and shot down at least two Japanese planes. Two years later, Miller was listed as missing in action and presumed dead.

"above and beyond the call of duty"
DORIE MILLER

Wartime poster celebrating Dorie Miller's heroism. *(National Archives)*

Miller, Kelly (July 18, 1863, Winnsboro, North Carolina—December 29, 1939, Washington, D.C.): Sociologist and educator. Miller's mother was a slave, and his father, to the best of his knowledge, was a Confederate soldier. Miller grew up during the period of RECONSTRUCTION and was influenced greatly by the spirit of racial uplift of that period. His entire life surrounded EDUCATION. He received his B.A. (1886), M.A. (1901), and LL.B. (1903) from HOWARD UNIVERSITY. He also did postgraduate work in mathematics at the Johns Hopkins University in BALTIMORE, MARYLAND. His teaching career began in 1889, in a WASHINGTON, D.C., high school, where he taught mathematics. By 1890 he was teaching at Howard University, where his prime responsibility was again mathematics. He also helped the struggling institution by teaching courses in other departments. In 1907 he was named the dean of the college of arts and sciences, in which position he remained until 1918. After serving in a number of other administrative offices, he retired from Howard in 1935.

Although his academic specialty was mathematics, Miller's historical and scholarly importance lies in his pioneering sociological work and in his political commentary. His work includes *Race Adjustment: Essays on the Negro in America* (1906), *Out of the House of Bondage* (1914), and *An Appeal to Conscience: America's Code of Caste a Disgrace to Democracy* (1918). As a product of the Reconstruction period, he was, early in his career, a supporter of the type of reform supported by Booker T.

Bust of Kelly Miller by sculptor May Howard Jackson. *(National Archives)*

WASHINGTON. As he observed how slowly change came and how often regression occurred, he became increasingly radicalized over his lifetime. He also differed from Washington on the question of higher education. Centrally involved in the struggle to keep Howard University open, Miller was always a supporter of a range of educational options for African Americans.

Miller was one of the outstanding African American essayists at the beginning of the twentieth century. He was a major contributor to the development of Howard University and was one of the founders of the AMERICAN NEGRO ACADEMY (1897), a society of intellectuals.
See also: Intellectuals and scholars.

Miller, Thomas Ezekiel (June 17, 1849, Ferrebeeville, South Carolina—April 8, 1938, Charleston, South Carolina): U.S. representative from SOUTH CAROLINA. The son of free black parents, Miller moved with his family to Charleston in 1851 and eventually was educated in black schools there. At the end of the CIVIL WAR, he traveled to New York, where he worked as a railroad newsboy. Miller received a scholarship to attend LINCOLN UNIVERSITY in PENNSYLVANIA and graduated in 1872.

Upon graduation, Miller returned to South Carolina to attend law school at the newly integrated University of South Carolina. He was admitted to the South Carolina Bar in December of 1875. Miller served as a member of the state general assembly from 1874 until 1880, when he became a state senator. He was state chairman of South Carolina's REPUBLICAN PARTY in 1884. In 1888 Miller was the Republican candidate for South Carolina's Seventh Congressional District. Although his Democratic opponent initially was declared the victor, the House Committee on Elections eventually ruled in Miller's favor. He took his seat in Congress on September 24, 1890.

Miller was appointed to serve on the House Committee on the Library of Congress. In a rematch against the Democratic opponent he had ousted, Miller ran for reelection later in 1890 and was the apparent winner. His victory was overturned when the state supreme court declared in favor of his opponent and the House Committee on Elections ruled against Miller in February of 1893. After losing the Republican nomination for the same seat in 1893, Miller returned to state politics, serving as a state representative from 1894 to 1896. He helped establish the State Negro College (later South Carolina State College) in Orangeburg and became its president in 1896. After being forced to resign the presidency of the college in 1911, Miller retired from public affairs and lived quietly in Charleston until 1923. He lived in PHILADELPHIA, PENNSYLVANIA, from 1923 to 1934, when he returned to Charleston.
See also: Congress members; Politics and government.

Milliken v. Bradley: U.S. SUPREME COURT ruling on BUSING. *Milliken v. Bradley* (1974) arose from a lower court effort to fix a school SEGREGATION problem in DETROIT, MICHIGAN, by busing children across neighboring school district lines. Since there was no evidence that the neighboring districts were unlawfully segregated or that any of the boundaries had been drawn to segregate their schools, the Supreme Court ruled that the lower court's remedy to Detroit's problem had to be worked out entirely within Detroit. The Court ruled that in designing a desegregation plan incorporating districts not found to be illegally segregated, the district court had exceeded its authority. *Milliken* was the first case in which the Supreme Court overruled a lower court order plan to achieve greater integration.

—*Christopher E. Kent*

Million Man March: Also billed as a Rights and Responsibilities Rally, this demonstration was held in WASHINGTON, D.C., on October 16, 1995. It was organized by Louis FARRAKHAN of the NATION OF ISLAM and Benjamin F. CHAVIS (who served as national march director). After the march, there was debate concerning the number of people who actually took part, with estimates ranging from the National Park Service's low estimate of 400,000 to estimates of more than a million; a later count by an independent Boston University group placed the number at about 870,000.

Regardless of discrepancies over the number of participants, the Million Man March will be remembered as a significant event. Promoted by organizers as a religious day of atonement, reconciliation, and empowerment, the march drew men and women from a

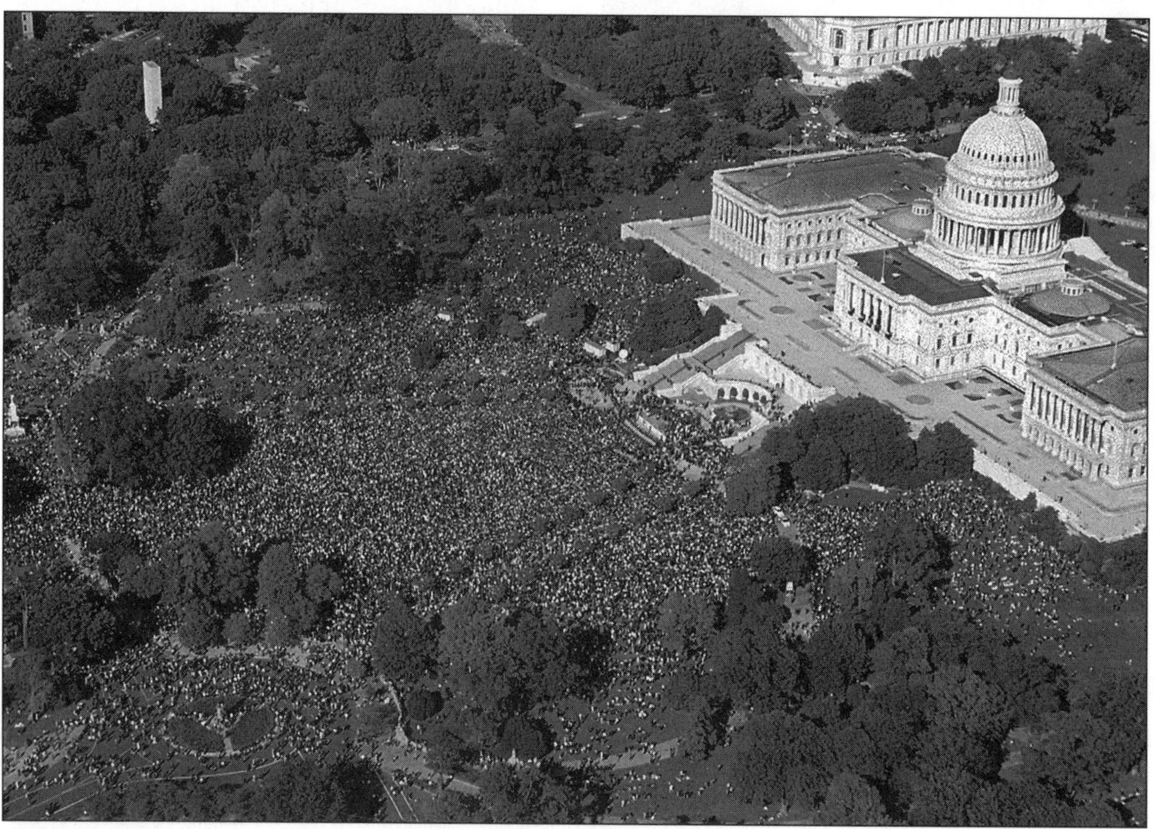

Aerial view of the marchers gathered in the Washington Mall to hear speakers on October 16, 1995. *(AP/Wide World Photos)*

variety of religious persuasions. Male members of the African American community gave their pledge to assume more responsibility for the social, political, economic, and familial problems within the community.

National of Islam leader Louis Farrakhan addresses marchers from Capitol Hill. *(AP/Wide World Photos)*

Farrakhan issued the initial call for the rally and was its principal spokesperson. As the keynote speaker, Farrakhan addressed a wide array of concerns, using "toward a more perfect union" as his general topic. Quoting liberally from both the Bible and the Koran, Farrakhan appealed to his audience's sense of spirituality and encouraged them to take a greater role in the moral and educational leadership of their families and communities.

Other notable speakers included Benjamin Chavis; Jesse JACKSON, founder and president of the National RAINBOW COALITION; Al SHARPTON of NEW YORK CITY; Bishop H. H. Brookins of the AFRICAN METHODIST EPISCOPAL CHURCH; Joseph LOWERY, president of the SOUTHERN CHRISTIAN LEADERSHIP CONFERENCE (SCLC); and twelve-year-old Ayinde Jean-Baptiste, a child evangelist who urged African American fathers to continue or to resume rearing their children.

Unlike the 1963 MARCH ON WASHINGTON, many prominent women speakers were invited to address the Million Man March. Among them were Rosa PARKS, "mother" of the CIVIL RIGHTS movement; Maya ANGELOU, noted poet, memoirist, and educator; Betty SHABAZZ, widow of MALCOLM X; Dorothy HEIGHT of the NATIONAL COUNCIL OF NEGRO WOMEN (NCNW); and Tynetta Muhammad, the widow of Elijah MUHAMMAD.

Several African American mayors also addressed the marchers, including Marion BARRY of Washington, D.C.; Kurt Schmoke of BALTIMORE, MARYLAND; and Dennis ARCHER of DETROIT, MICHIGAN. Even leaders of street gangs joined the mayors in a call for an end to inner-city violence. All the speakers embraced the common theme of putting aside religious, economic, and political differences in favor of unifying and rebuilding the African American community, using all its resources and strength.

Mills, Florence (January 25, 1895, Washington, D.C.—November 1, 1927, New York, New York): Dancer, singer, and comedian. This leading stage entertainer of the 1920's starred in revues in New York City, London, and Paris. Her greatest song hit was "I'm a Little Blackbird Looking for a Bluebird," from the musical revue *Dixie to Broadway* (1924). She did not record her music. Her early death followed a delayed operation for appendicitis.

Mingus, Charles (April 22, 1922, Nogales, Arizona—January 5, 1979, Cuernavaca, Mexico): JAZZ bassist, composer, and writer. A brilliant instrumentalist and composer, Charles Mingus was one of the finest bass players of his time. As a composer, his work is widely considered to be on a par with that of greats such as Duke ELLINGTON and Billy STRAYHORN.

Mingus was a man of many temperaments and moods. His music could range from the sweetness of a slow ballad to the intensity of his faster pieces to the sheer difficulty of some of his larger-scale works. He drew his inspiration from countless sources: Church and gospel music, the BLUES, Latin music, and twentieth-century classical compositions all figure into his music.

Born to a Swedish/African American father and a Chinese American/African American mother, Mingus was aware from an early age of not fitting into any particular racial group. Many of his song titles speak to his sense of the racial problems of his times: "Meditations for Integration," "Fables of Faubus," and "Free Cell Block F, 'Tis Nazi U.S.A." are all Mingus tunes that give a musical voice to his social concerns.

Jazz musician Charles Mingus in 1974. *(AP/Wide World Photos)*

Mingus's first instrument was the trombone, which he began playing at about the age of eight. Cello lessons followed shortly thereafter, and he spent some time playing in a classical setting with the Los Angeles Junior Philharmonic. He made the transition from classical cello to jazz bass with the help of some of the finest teachers in Los ANGELES: Lloyd Reese (a jazz composition and improvisation teacher), Red Callender (jazz bassist), and Howard Rheinschagen (classical bassist).

Mingus's professional career developed rapidly. He played with early jazz giants Kid ORY and Louis ARMSTRONG in the early 1940's and became a fixture on the thriving Los Angeles jazz scene, playing with the stars of modern jazz when they came to town. Before long, he had moved to New York City, where BEBOP, the most modern jazz of the day, was being played. His talent was quickly acknowledged by the bebop community, and his bass playing can be found on one of the seminal recordings of the bebop era, the Massey Hall Concert in Toronto, where he played with bebop pioneers Charlie PARKER, Dizzy GILLESPIE, Max ROACH, and Bud Powell.

The period of late 1950's and early 1960's was one of his most prolific in terms of recording. His group, the Jazz Workshop, released albums such as *Pithecanthropus Erectus*, *East Coasting*, *Blues and Roots*, *Oh Yeah*, and *The Black Saint and the Sinner Lady*.

The latter half of the 1960's was a difficult period for Mingus. Psychological troubles and an eviction from his apartment in New York City contributed to his near-invisibility in the jazz world. His career rebounded shortly after the publication of his autobiography, *Beneath the Underdog*, in 1971. He began recording again, producing a number of albums before he was diagnosed with amyotrophic lateral sclerosis (Lou Gehrig's disease) at the end of 1977.

Before Charles Mingus died in 1979, he and a group of his jazz peers were honored at the White House by President Jimmy Carter. Also, one of his pieces, *Revelations*, was performed by the New York Philharmonic in April, 1978, on his fifty-sixth birthday.

—*Alexander DuBois Jordan*

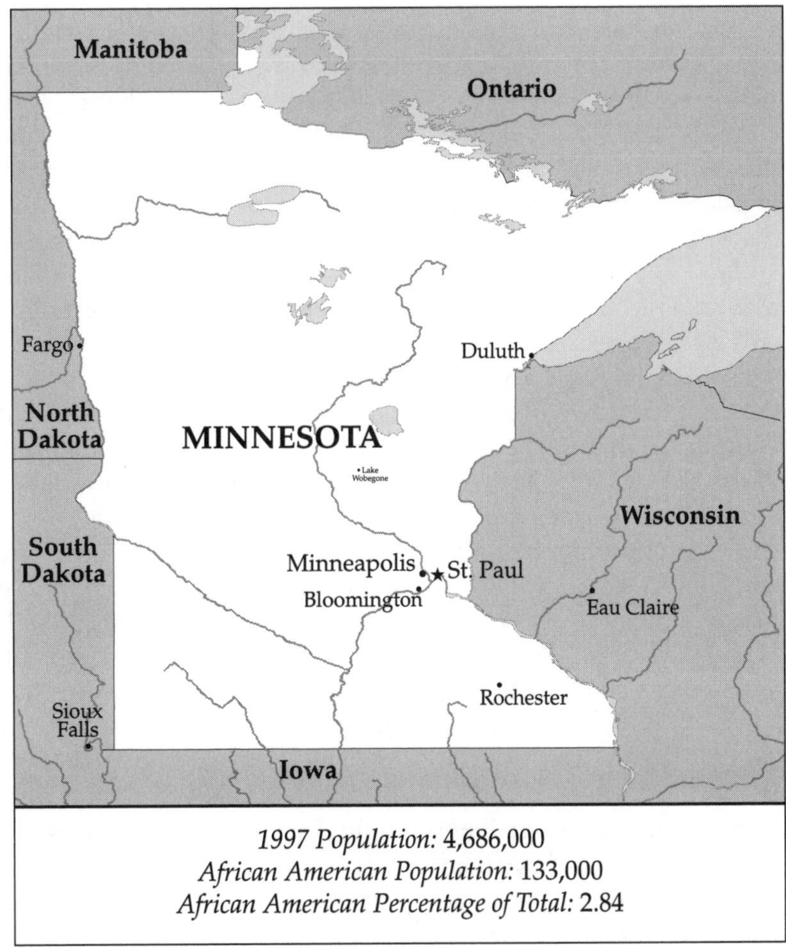

1997 Population: 4,686,000
African American Population: 133,000
African American Percentage of Total: 2.84

Minnesota: African Americans were present in Minnesota before it even became a federal territory. George BONGA, a baby of African American heritage, was horn near Duluth in 1802. Thirty-five blacks were residing in Minnesota when it became a territory in 1849. The state's African American population represented less than 1 percent of its total population from 1858 to the late 1970's, by which point the percentage had increased to 1.3 (53,342 people). In 1997 the state's total population was just under 4.7 million, according to CENSUS OF THE UNITED STATES, and its African American population was about 133,000, or 2.8 percent of the total.

After the CIVIL WAR and during the twentieth century, African Americans settled throughout the state, although most chose to live in the Twin Cities of St. Paul and Minneapolis because of more numerous employment opportunities. During the late 1970's, EBONY magazine listed the Twin Cities among the top ten recommended metropolitan locations for blacks in the United States.

Yet racism was also present, as is evidenced by the LYNCHING of three African American men at Duluth in 1920. The Minnesota state legislature reacted quickly by passing one of the first antilynching laws in the United States. African Americans also suffered from discrimination in housing, employment, and education. Through AFFIRMATIVE ACTION, equal employment opportunity programs, and federal, state, and local statutes, improvements were made during the latter decades of the twentieth century. The impact of African Americans on Minnesota gradually increased after the mid-1940's. A significant U.S. Supreme Court case, *R.A.V. v. City of St. Paul* (1992), came from a 1990 incident in St. Paul. A group of youths burned a cross in the yard of an African American family in their neighborhood and were charged under St. Paul's ordinance against "bias-motivated" disorderly conduct. The U.S. SUPREME COURT held that this particular ordinance, a type of HATE CRIME legislation, was unconstitutional because of the way it was written.

In 1993 Sharon Sayles Belton was elected mayor of Minneapolis, Minnesota's largest city. Alan Page, a lawyer and former Minnesota Viking football player from 1967 to 1981, was appointed to the Minnesota supreme court in 1993. Earlier he had served as a regent of the University of Minnesota. Other prominent black Minnesotans include Gordon PARKS, a photographer, film director, writer, and composer; August WILSON, an acclaimed playwright; and Roy WILKINS, former leader of the NATIONAL ASSOCIATION FOR THE ADVANCEMENT OF COLORED PEOPLE (NAACP).

—*John Quinn Imholte*

Minority group: Group that is racially, culturally, or otherwise identifiably different from a society's majority. The minority group often has values, goals, and needs that are different from those of the majority group. The values, goals, and needs of majorities and minorities may differ so much as to be mutually exclusive, a situation that leads to group conflicts. The minority group is usually at a disadvantage because of its smaller size. Because the minority group is different (physically, culturally, or both), the majority group often perceives it as inferior. As a result, minority groups are often the victims of prejudice and bias.

Originally, "minority group" referred to Europeans who, as a result of shifts in national boundaries, were suddenly without political power because of their small number and cultural differences. Later, "minority" was used to refer to any group that was different from the established population. Some scholars prefer a definition that addresses the power component, which they perceive as essential to the majority-minority relationship. A "minority," by this definition, could be a numerical majority that for some reason holds little power.

Anglo-Saxons became the dominant immigrant group in America. Native Americans, as a minority group, almost were exterminated and were relegated to reservations. African Americans were put legally into a subordinate caste. Restrictions limited the number of new immigrants allowed in the United States, and discrimination against them became the custom.

In the United States, various groups have occupied the position of minority group, including people of Irish, Jewish, Italian, and Polish descent. Most of these groups gradually became assimilated into the majority. Native Americans, Latinos, Asian Americans, and African Americans, however, continued to maintain minority-group status. African Americans composed about 10 percent of the U.S. population from 1790 to 1980, so they clearly were a numerical minority. Some areas, however, began to attract significant African American populations. By 1980, for example, African Americans composed a majority in the populations of DETROIT, MICHIGAN; WASHINGTON, D.C.; ATLANTA, GEORGIA; BALTIMORE, MARYLAND; and NEW ORLEANS, LOUISIANA. Local numerical majorities, however, did not necessarily remove minority-group status in society.

See also: Accommodation; Assimilation; Racial discrimination; Racial prejudice.

Minstrels: Performers of a comical form of music that mimicked African Americans. Minstrelsy was a popular part of the theatrical entertainment business during the nineteenth century, especially during the decades before the CIVIL WAR. Minstrel shows presented singers and dancers who were usually, but not always, white, wearing blackface and singing, dancing, telling jokes, and otherwise mimicking exaggerated stereotypes of African Americans.

Forerunners of minstrel songs, the so-called Negro songs, were in circulation at least as early as the mid-eighteenth century. New Orleans, Louisiana, hosted the first commercial performances of this entertainment when Louis Tabary, a white slaveowner, put together a public show using black slaves in 1791. By 1800 some white performers were using black makeup on their faces to look like slaves. They danced, however, like Englishmen and Irishmen.

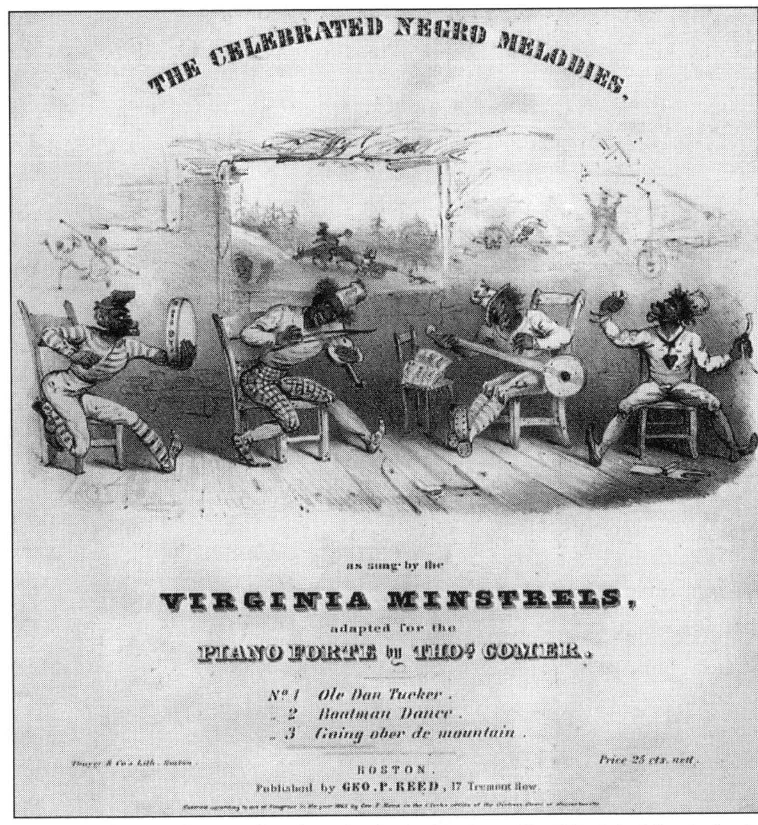

Program for the first professional minstrel troupe, the Virginia Minstrels, in 1847. *(Library of Congress)*

By the early nineteenth century, songs mimicking and ridiculing slaves were gaining popularity among white audiences. "Three-Fingered Jack" (1812), "The Negro and the Buckra Man" (1816), and "The Guinea Boy" (1816) are examples of early songs that featured exaggerated southern slave dialects. The instruments that most often accompanied minstrel music—banjo, tambourine, bone castanets, and fiddle—were known as "Ethiopian" instruments.

By the mid-1820's, individual white performers such as George Nichols, George Washington Dixon, and Thomas Rice had established themselves as popular entertainers in northern cities. The birth of true minstrelsy, which used only African American appearance and performance materials as its creative inspiration and focus, was in 1830. That year, Rice, a hitherto obscure white performer, claimed to have learned the "Jim Crow" song and its accompanying dance from an old, deformed African American, whom he called Daddy Jim Crow. Fascinated by what he saw and learned, Rice said, he decided to wear clothes similar to the old slave's, make himself up to look like the old man, and even took the old man's name as his stage name. Rice then took to the stage and became known professionally as the successful and famous Daddy "Jim Crow" Rice. He toured all over the United States and performed in London in 1836.

During the 1840's, Zip Coon (sometimes known as Dandy Jim) appeared as an urbanized counterpart to Jim Crow. A dandy and a buffoon, this caricature appeared overdressed in top hat, tails, and a cane. He grossly mispronounced words and boasted of his sexual prowess. Other caricatures, such as Rastus (the civilized African who, on a moment's notice, could revert to his "primary" past and turn violent), had the cumulative effect of stereotyping African American men and perpetuating negative myths. Popular melodies from the period included "Coal Black Rose," "Dandy Jim from Caroline," "Zip Coon," "Jim Along Josey" and "Dearest May."

The first professional troupe of minstrels, the Virginia Minstrels, performed in New York in 1843. Soon, more troupes sprang up in other American cities. These included the Christy Minstrels, the Ethiopian Serenaders (who entertained President John Tyler at the White House in 1844), the Georgia Minstrels, for which Master Juba (William Henry Lane) performed, Callender's Original Georgia Minstrels, Callender's Consolidated Spectacular Colored Minstrels, and Haverly's European Minstrels.

Contemporary rendering of the "Zip Coon" character. *(Arkent Archive)*

The Christy Minstrels gave minstrelsy a standard form that was later adopted by most minstrel shows. The first act put the performers in a half circle. Tambo (the "end man" who played the tambourine) stayed at one end of the half circle, and Bones (the end man who played the bone clappers) stayed at the other end. An interlocutor (master of ceremonies) stayed in the center to direct humorous exchanges between Tambo and Bones. The second act was a variety show, and the closing act was lively entertainment by the entire company.

After the Civil War, many African Americans themselves became minstrels. They had to follow the standard form and perform in blackface makeup even if they had naturally dark skins, because that was what audiences expected and wanted. These performers were, however, able to introduce fresh jokes as well as new African American music that eventually formed one of the bases of ragtime music.

Popular black minstrel groups included the Original Georgia Minstrels, Callender's Georgia Minstrels (later known as Haverly Colored Minstrels), and Hicks and Sawyer Minstrels. James A. Bland (1854-1911) was the foremost and most prolific African American minstrel song composer. Several of his songs, including "Carry Me Back to Ole Virginny," "Oh, Dem Golden Slippers," and "In the Evening by the Moonlight," were widely sung throughout the United States and in Europe. By the 1890's, several African American minstrels, such as Orpheus McAdoo, had gone to Southern Africa to establish the tradition there.

The most successful of the white minstrel song composers was Stephen Foster, whose songs "Camptown Races," "Oh Susanna," and "Old Folks at Home" were very popular. *See also:* Comedy and humor; Vaudeville.

Minton's Playhouse: Nightclub in HARLEM. It was opened by saxophonist Henry Minton in 1938 and taken over by Teddy Hill, a former bandleader, in 1940. It was most important in the early 1940's, when such young musicians as trumpeter Dizzy GILLESPIE, guitarist Charlie CHRISTIAN, pianist Thelonious MONK, and drummer Kenny Clarke performed there. The music that developed into BEBOP was developed mostly at MINTON'S PLAYHOUSE.

Miscegenation: Derived from a Latin word, *miscere*, for "mixing," miscegenation refers to mixing of the races, and particularly marriage or cohabitation between a white person and a person of another race.

Experts have estimated that fully 80 percent of African Americans have at least one white ancestor and that at least 20 percent of white Americans have at least one black ancestor; historically, moreover, whites, blacks, and Native Americans have engaged in racial mixing. Thus, miscegenation in the United States has a long history that stretches back to the early colonial era.

The Colonial Era

In the seventeenth century, miscegenation was a relatively common occurrence from MASSACHUSETTS to GEORGIA. For example, as early as 1630, VIRGINIA'S authorities sentenced a man named Hugh Davis to a public whipping because he would not end his liaison with an African American woman. Prevalent socioeconomic conditions encouraged such trends. For one thing, in the early colonial era, white men and women were on the market as indentured servants in the same markets where blacks were bought and sold as slaves. (Indentured servants signed agreements to work for another for a certain number of years and were treated much like slaves.) Once on plantations and farms, these groups might work—and live—in close proximity. Although relationships between white men and black women were the most common, black men and white women consorted as well. When MARYLAND enacted the first colonial antimiscegenation statute in 1664, the law was aimed at keeping white women from having relations with black men. The statute decreed that if a white woman married a slave, she herself would serve the slave's master during her husband's lifetime, while any children born of the union would become slaves for life.

The statute quickly led to exploitation. Some planters forced or coerced white women into marrying slaves in order not only to gain one more slave (at no cost) but also to gain more slaves if the couple had children. The most celebrated case was that of Irish Nell, one of Lord BALTIMORE'S indentured servants. When Baltimore returned to England, he sold Nell's contract to a planter, who in turn forced her to wed a slave named Butler. When Baltimore learned of what had occurred, he arranged in 1681 to amend the 1664 statute to read that if women were entrapped by procurement of a master, such women and their children would be free.

Prohibition of Intermarriage

No amount of persuasion—scorn, whippings, ridicule—could stem the tide of miscegenation in colonial America. Forbidding interracial marriage only drove the practice underground and led to illicit relationships and the birth of illegitimate mulatto children. Nevertheless, the colonies passed laws prohibiting intermarriage; Virginia passed such legislation in 1691, Massachusetts in 1705, NORTH CAROLINA in 1715, SOUTH CAROLINA in 1717, DELAWARE in 1721, and PENNSYLVANIA in 1725. Punishments for violating such laws varied; generally, however, free African Americans who broke the sexual color bar were enslaved; those already enslaved were sold out of the colony. White men and women

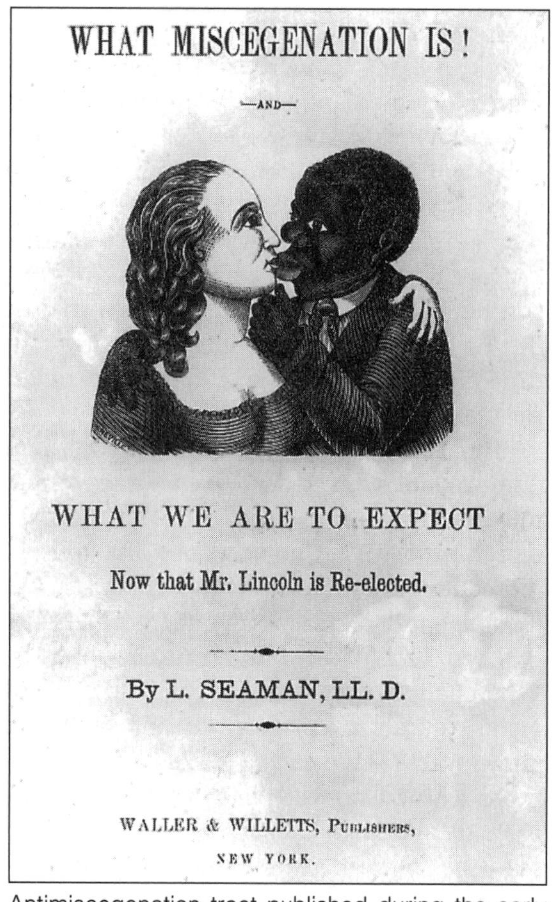
WHAT MISCEGENATION IS!
—AND—
WHAT WE ARE TO EXPECT
Now that Mr. Lincoln is Re-elected.
By L. SEAMAN, LL. D.
WALLER & WILLETTS, Publishers,
NEW YORK.

Antimiscegenation tract published during the early 1860's. *(Library of Congress)*

who married slaves were either fired, jailed, or reduced to slavery. In one famous case, a white woman, Ann Wall, violated Virginia's law and was indentured for five years; her two mulatto children were sold into involuntary labor for a term of thirty-one years. Further, the court ruled that when Ann Wall's indenture had expired, she was to be banished to Barbados.

Often, well-to-do white men in the colonial era stopped short of marriage and kept black women in a state of concubinage. White women, too, continued to mate illicitly with African American men. Such unions continued to produce mulatto offspring, some of whom became prominent. Lemuel HAYNES, the famous minister, was born to a black man and a white woman; later, he married Bessie Babbitt, a white woman. Benjamin BANNEKER was the grandson of an enslaved African prince and Molly Welsh, a white indentured servant who eventually acquired her own farm. Indeed, the African prince, Banneka, whom Welsh married had originally been one of her slaves.

The Nineteenth Century

Miscegenation continued into the early national and antebellum eras. In the expanding cotton economy of the South in the nineteenth century, the practice thrived. Although he no doubt exaggerated, the traveler Frederick Law Olmsted maintained that as of 1859, when he was touring the South, all the area's attractive African American girls and women served as concubines for white men. Olmsted also reported that every day he saw overseers whip the slave children or grandchildren of plantation owners. Indeed, the South seemed to abound in amalgamation coming as a result of casual rapes, concubinage, prostitution, and interracial incest. Regarding the last, a notorious case occurred in 1830 in Virginia when a slave, Peggy, and her black mate, Patrick, killed their master and burned his house. The reason they gave for their action was that Peggy's master had repeatedly tried to get her to consent to a sexual liaison; failing in that effort, he had locked her in a meat house, chained to a block. At her later trial, Peggy said that she had refused to consent to her master's sexual demands because he was her father.

Some very well-known white southerners kept black mistresses. There is evidence to suggest that such leaders as Thomas Jefferson, Patrick Henry, Daniel Boone, and Richard Johnson kept slave mistresses. So common was white male-black female coupling that one planter's wife lamented that she was only the "chief slave" in her husband's "harem." Moreover, in most cities, northern as well as southern, black prostitutes worked in brothels frequented by white men.

Miscegenation in the Modern Era

Interracial mixing probably reached its peak in the 1850's. During the RECONSTRUCTION era, miscegenation became less common as both freedmen and freedwomen asserted more control over their personal lives, and the decline continued into the twentieth century. In addition, after Reconstruction, white state governments in the South instituted strict segregation laws. Thus died a dream of some reformers who had hoped that interracial mixing would continue and that, as Americans became racially one people, racial issues would simply fade away.

In studies of BOSTON, PHILADELPHIA, and New York State in the twentieth century, researchers concluded that black-white marriages were insignificant statistically. When interracial marriages did occur, African American men married whites more frequently than African American women.

During the CIVIL RIGHTS era of the 1950's and 1960's, the decline in interracial unions was halted briefly as an upsurge of interracial dating, mating, and marrying occurred. Yet even in 1965, for example, experts estimated that fewer than two out of every one thousand new marriages were interracial. Indeed, both black and white society generally seem to discourage racial mixing. One modern study found that African American women seldom crossed the social barrier and reacted negatively to black men who did; black women often charged such men with engaging in material opportunism. Thus, despite the brief upsurge, experts have predicted that the rate of interracial black and white marriage in coming generations will barely exceed 1 percent of all marriages.

Historian Joel Williamson discovered that African Americans with light complexions believe that they are not white enough to join white society but are too white fully to join the African American world. Williamson found that some even experience "white guilt" and that, in a startling reversal of custom, some college-aged single MULATTOES wish to marry "dark" so that their children will not be rejected by the black world.

—*James Smallwood*

Suggested Readings:

Crester, Gary A., and Joseph J. Leon, eds. *Intermarriage in the United States*. New York: Haworth Press, 1982.

Johnston, James H. *Race Relations in Virginia and Miscegenation in the South, 1776-1860*. Amherst: University of Massachusetts, 1970.

Mathabane, Mark, and Gail Mathabane. *Love in Black and White: The Triumph of Love over Prejudice and Taboo*. New York: HarperCollins, 1992.

Russell, Kathy, Midge Wilson, and Ron Hall. *The Color Complex: The Last Taboo Among African Americans*. New York: Harcourt Brace Jovanovich, 1992.

Smith, John D., ed. *Racial Determinism and the Fear of Miscegenation, Pre-1900*. New York: Garland, 1993.

Stuart, Irving R., and Lawrence E. Abt, eds. *Interracial Marriage: Expectations and Realities*. New York: Grossman, 1973.

Williamson, Joel. *New People: Miscegenation and Mulattoes in the United States*. New York: Free Press, 1980.

Mississippi: Mississippi has the largest proportion of African American residents of any state in the union. In 1997 the CENSUS OF THE UNITED STATES estimated that there were about 993,000 African Americans in Mississippi, slightly more than 36 percent of the state's population. Mississippi's large African American population may be traced to the slave economy of the state in the years before the CIVIL WAR. Through the early nineteenth century, the slave population grew rapidly as the cotton economy boomed. By the beginning of the Civil War, there were more slaves than

1997 Population: 2,731,000
African American Population: 993,000
African American Percentage of Total: 36.36

whites in the state. Because so many people were held in bondage, Mississippi's slave laws were among the harshest in the South.

During Reconstruction, the freed slaves entered political life. Few had sufficient education or experience to hold more than minor offices. Three exceptions were Blanche K. Bruce and Hiram Revels, who were elected to the U.S. Senate, and John R. Lynch, elected to the House of Representatives. By 1875, however, the whites of Mississippi had begun to retake power. They instituted segregation and, by the early twentieth century, had excluded African Americans from public life by laws and terrorism.

The greatest concentration of African Americans in the state was in the Mississippi Delta, the region where the Mississippi and Yazoo Rivers join. In some Delta counties, 80 to 90 percent of the people were African American. Most worked as sharecroppers—farmers working the land for a share of the crop—on land owned by whites. Blues music developed as an expression of black culture in the Delta and spread to other parts of the country. One style of blues is still known as Delta blues.

After World War I, many African Americans left Mississippi to find work in northern cities. By 1940 slightly more than half of the state's people were white. Many whites still saw African Americans as a threat, and the state gained a reputation as the most racially oppressive place in the nation. In 1955 Mississippi received national attention when white men beat to death fourteen-year-old Emmett Till, who was visiting from Chicago and was accused of whistling at a white woman.

Mississippi leaders whose political careers were made possible by Reconstruction. *(Library of Congress)*

Mississippi became a central battleground of the CIVIL RIGHTS movement. In 1964 black and white college students working with civil rights organizations traveled to the state for Freedom Summer. They sought to provide expanded educational opportunities to local African Americans and to encourage minority voter registration. Three civil rights workers—Michael Schwerner and Andrew Goodman, both white, and James Chaney, an African American—became martyrs to the movement when they were murdered in Mississippi that summer.

After the passage of the Civil Rights Act of 1964 and the VOTING RIGHTS ACT OF 1965, segregation and discrimination in voting became illegal in the United States. Black Mississippians began to enter public life. By the 1990's, the Mississippi legislature had the highest percentage of African American members of any state legislature in the nation. Nevertheless, racial prejudice continued to be a problem. Mississippi was also by most measures the poorest state in the union, and black Mississippians showed substantially lower average incomes and educations than whites.

—*Carl L. Bankston III*

Mississippi Freedom Democratic Party: Political party organized on April 26, 1964. The Mississippi Freedom Democratic Party (MFDP) was developed as a means of addressing and combating the systematic exclusion of African American citizens from equal participation in the MISSISSIPPI state political process. Members hoped to demonstrate the white Mississippi Democratic Party's disloyalty to the national DEMOCRATIC PARTY and to challenge the segregationist leaders of Mississippi. The main goals of the MFDP were to establish a political organization that would become the official affiliate of the Democratic Party from the state of Mississippi and to unseat Mississippi's Democratic Party delegates at the 1964 Democratic National Convention.

The MFDP's organizational meeting was composed of two hundred delegates. During the interracial organizational meeting, a twelve-member temporary executive committee was chosen to design and implement policies for the MFDP. After the organization of the MFDP was established, its members attempted to participate in regular Democratic

Party precinct and county meetings. The MFDP members were denied participatory privileges in all but a few of these meetings. Subsequently, the MFDP held its own precinct and county meetings to establish its legitimacy as a party. As a result of being denied an opportunity to participate in the official state convention, the MFDP held its own state convention in Jackson on August 6, 1964. During the MFDP state convention, forty-four delegates and twenty-two alternates were chosen for the 1964 Democratic National Convention.

At the Democratic National Convention in Atlantic City, New Jersey, the small interracial band of political radicals from Mississippi captured the attention of the American public by challenging the all-white Mississippi delegation. The MFDP received support from civil rights activists from around the country. The Lyndon B. Johnson administration, however, used its power and influence to prevent the MFDP delegation from being accepted as the official delegation. The MFDP was offered a series of compromises which it rejected after a series of private meetings. The compromises included two votes for MFDP delegates and a resolution outlawing segregated delegations in the future.

In addition to the convention challenge, the MFDP's activities included sponsoring political candidates, voter registration and education, challenging the Mississippi congressional delegation, and organizing demonstrations. The MFDP continued to exist until 1968, when it was absorbed by a coalition of civil rights activists and southern white liberals known as the Mississippi Loyal Democrats.

ENUMERATION

OF THE INHABITANTS

OF THE

STATE OF MISSOURI.

COUNTIES	Free white males	Free white Females	Free persons of color	Slaves	Persons bound to service for a term of years	Total	Representatives
Boone,	1679	1456	1	576		3692	3
Cooper,	1612	1419	12	440		3483	3
Callaway	712	642		443		1797	1
Cole	532	444		53		1028	1
Chariton,	883	541	7	290	5	1446	1
Cape Girardeau	3526	3200	44	1082		7852	6
Franklin	880	853	9	186		1928	2
Gasconade	650	463	1	60		1174	1
Howard	3219	2690	2	1409	3	7321	5
Jefferson	875	749	4	209	1	1838	2
Lincoln	823	636	2	211	2	1674	1
Lillard	695	515		130		1340	1
Montgomery	928	802		302		2032	2
Madison	858	715	7	344	3	1907	1
New madrid	1155	972	7	310		2444	2
Pike	1256	1014	2	495		2677	2
Perry	740	623	1	229	6	1599	1
Ralls	742	581	1	358	2	1684	1
Ray	912	782	2	141	2	1739	2*
St. Louis	3564	2858	141	1603	24	8190	5
St. Charles	1856	1453	11	733	5	4058	3
St. Genevieve	1317	1081	62	717	4	3181	3
Saline	519	476	2	178	1	1176	1
Washington	1816	1562	2	560		3741	3
Wayne	720	645	1	246	2	1614	1
	32129	26903	321	11254	60	70647	54
*County divided.			County of St. Francois				1
							55

Results of a census of Missouri that appears to have been taken in 1830, when free and enslaved African Americans accounted for about 16 percent of the young state's population. *(Library of Congress)*

Missouri: The population of Missouri in 1997 was about 5.4 million, according to estimates of the Census of the United States. The state's African American population stood at about 607,000, or 11.2 percent of the total. African Americans and racial politics have always played a pivotal role in Missouri history.

Missouri gained statehood as a slave state in 1820 when the Missouri Compromise of 1820 temporarily halted slavery's expansion in the North. From 1830 to 1860, the state's black population increased from 25,091 to 114,931. Its economy was less dependent upon slavery than those of other southern states. Nonetheless, the state passed strict laws that prohibited free blacks from relocating to Missouri, subjected blacks to capture, and outlawed all African American schools.

Regardless of such intimidation, a prosperous middle-class aristocracy flourished in St. Louis. Approximately 60 percent of the state's three to four thousand free African Americans resided in the St. Louis city and county area. Many worked on the riverfront; some became successful barbers, property owners, and ministers.

In 1857 a Missouri slave named Dred Scott sued for his freedom, but in a landmark case (usually simply called the DRED SCOTT DECISION) that further divided the nation, the U.S. SUPREME COURT ruled that as a slave Dred Scott was not a U.S. citizen but property. Missouri refused to join the CONFEDERACY during the CIVIL WAR, but many residents with strong southern sympathies joined guerrilla bands and fought for the South. Since the state was not in open rebellion against the United

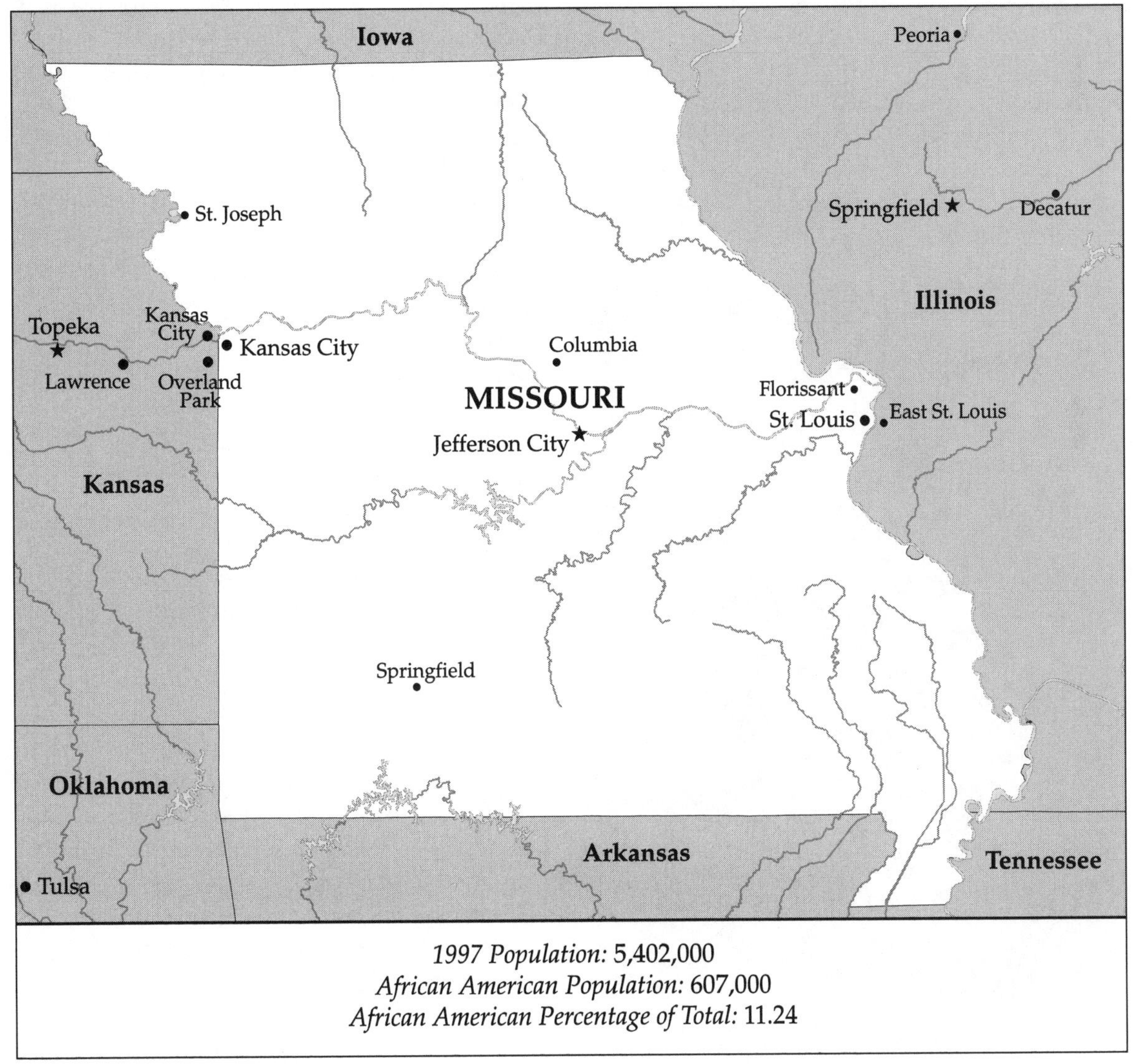

1997 Population: 5,402,000
African American Population: 607,000
African American Percentage of Total: 11.24

States, the EMANCIPATION PROCLAMATION did not apply there. Missouri's slaves therefore were not officially freed until after the war's end.

The post-Civil War RECONSTRUCTION era did not represent a revolutionary turning point for African Americans in the state. The black population steadily increased from 118,503 in 1860 to 161,234 in 1900, but this growth did not generate an increase in economic opportunity or socioeconomic mobility. Most whites accepted southern views on race and JIM CROW segregation laws.

Blacks were never disfranchised, but laws established segregation in housing, public accommodations, and education. Most blacks continued to reside in the urban centers of St. Louis and Kansas City and worked as laborers, seamstresses, deliverymen, and boatmen; others worked as sharecroppers in the cotton growing Bootheel region.

William Clay became Missouri's first African American congressman in 1968. *(Library of Congress)*

Since the majority resided in concentrated urban centers, African Americans eventually gained control of key political districts. In 1920 Walthall Moore was the first black to be elected to the state legislature. In 1928 Joseph McLemore became the first African American to run for Congress as a Democrat. Although he was unsuccessful, his effort and affiliation with the DEMOCRATIC PARTY convinced many African Americans to support Franklin D. Roosevelt's New Deal coalition. Militancy also increased. Some African Americans boycotted chain stores in St. Louis that refused to hire blacks, and sharecroppers in the Bootheel organized to secure New Deal aid.

Political activism escalated after WORLD WAR II. Black representatives from St. Louis and Kansas City entered the state legislature, and in 1968 St. Louis native William Clay became the first black U.S. congressmen from Missouri. Troubles persisted, however; the 1968 assassination of Martin Luther KING, Jr., fueled a series of riots in Kansas City, and school desegregation occurred only after a lengthy court battle.

The 1970's produced a monumental shift in power for both St. Louis and Kansas City in the state's General Assembly. In 1991 Emanuel CLEAVER was elected the first black mayor of Kansas City, followed by Freeman Bosley's victory in St. Louis two years later. Yet racial tensions could still divide the state. In 1999, for example, local blacks shut down an interstate highway to protest the lack of minority contracts in St. Louis construction.

African Americans in Missouri have helped shape the cultural and intellectual landscape of the United States. Former slave George Washington CARVER transformed American agriculture with his scientific discoveries. The Kansas City Monarchs were one of the dominant baseball teams in NEGRO LEAGUE BASEBALL. In the arts, both Pulitzer Prize-winning author Maya ANGELOU and rock-and-roll icon Chuck BERRY are from St. Louis. Lesser-known but influen-

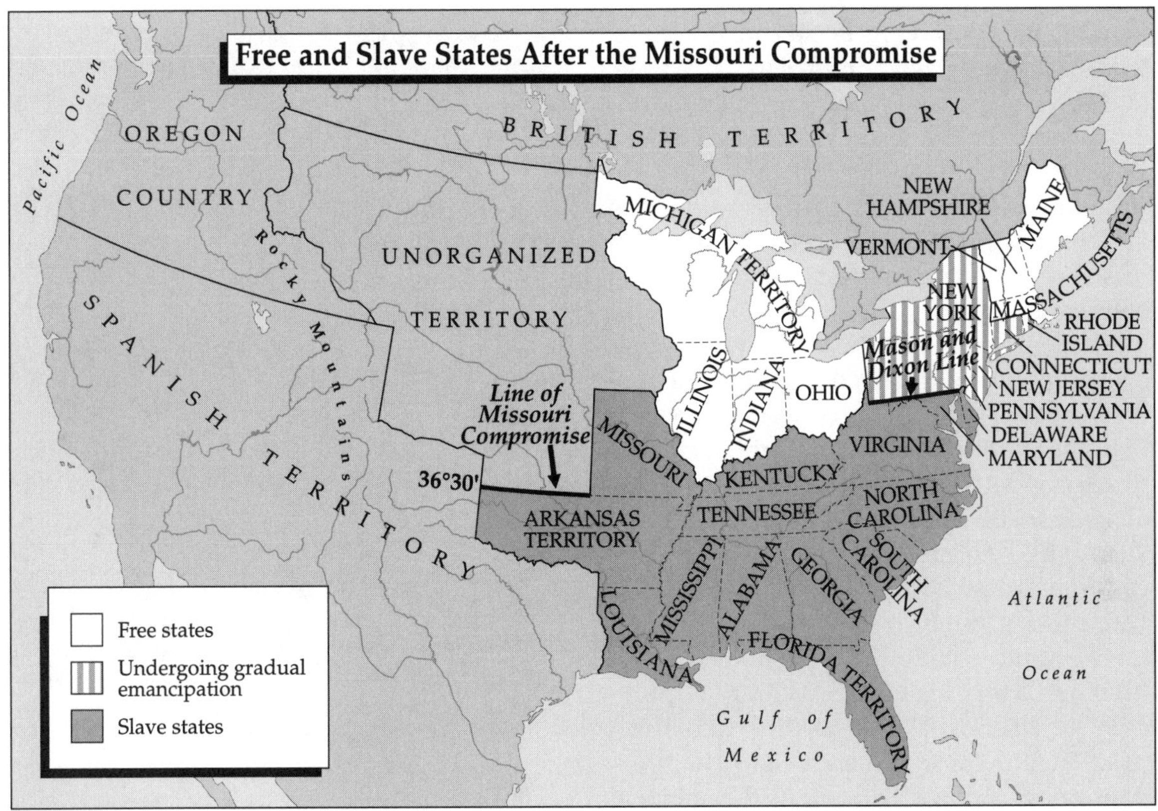

tial is Margaret Wilson, a public official and civil rights activist who chaired the national board of the National Association for the Advancement of Colored People (NAACP) from 1974 to 1983.

—*Robert D. Ubriaco, Jr.*

See also: East St. Louis, Illinois; *Jones v. Alfred H. Mayer Co.*; *Missouri ex rel Gaines*.

Missouri Compromise of 1820: Agreement that allowed Missouri to become a state, with no restrictions on slavery in its constitution. The compromise illustrates the highly political and highly contentious nature of nineteenth century debate over the issue of slavery. At issue was the expansion of slavery into newly acquired U.S. territories. Integral to the debate were concerns about constitutional limits on federal authority and concerns about the rights of individual states and territories. Slavery as a moral issue was, at times, only a secondary issue among lawmakers.

In 1819 Missouri petitioned to be admitted into the United States. During discussion of the petition, it was proposed by one state representative (James Tallmudge of New York) that slavery be prohibited in Missouri. Moral objections to slavery were genuine among some in Congress, but purely political questions were of importance to others. Did Congress have the right to mandate local state or territorial policy on slavery? For purposes of determining political representation, what would be the census status of newly acquired states? According to the U.S. Constitution, slaves counted as only three-fifths a person for purposes of population counts. These were serious political concerns in an expanding nation.

In the Missouri Compromise of 1820, Missouri was accepted as a state, and slavery was allowed to continue there; this agreement appeasing the proslavery faction in Congress. MAINE, however, was admitted as a free state, and slavery also was prohibited in the northern regions of the territory acquired in the Louisiana Purchase. The Missouri Compromise thus set new boundaries between slave and free territories but allowed the expansion of slavery into large sections of the growing country.

Later, in 1854, the Missouri Compromise effectively was repealed by the KANSAS-NEBRASKA ACT, which introduced the concept of popular sovereignty, or the right of citizens to choose for themselves whether to allow slavery. In the landmark DRED SCOTT DECISION of 1857, not only was it declared that African Americans had no claim to legal status as U.S. citizens, but also it was ruled that Congress had no constitutional grounds for prohibiting slavery in any U.S. territory. As a result, territories where slavery had been prohibited became vulnerable to further expansion of slavery. Ultimately the national wrangling over slavery led the South to secede and to the beginning of the CIVIL WAR in 1861.

Missouri ex rel Gaines: U.S. SUPREME COURT ruling in 1938 that MISSOURI owed African American Lloyd Gaines a legal education within the state. The ruling rested on the "SEPARATE BUT EQUAL" clause in the case of PLESSY v. FERGUSON (1896). Because Missouri had no separate law school for African Americans, the Court ruled that the University of Missouri Law School must admit minority students. Although Gaines disappeared following the Court's decision, possibly a victim of foul play, his case placed a crack in the walls of segregation.

Mitchell, Arthur Wergs (December 22, 1883, near Lafayette, Alabama—May 9, 1968, Petersburg, Virginia): U.S. representative from Illinois. Mitchell attended TUSKEGEE INSTITUTE in the 1890's, earning his way through school as a farm worker and as an office assistant for school president Booker T. WASHINGTON. After completing his studies, Mitchell worked as a schoolteacher in rural GEORGIA and ALABAMA, eventually founding Armstrong Agricultural School in West Butler, Alabama, and serving as its president. Mitchell studied law and was admitted to the bar in 1927. He began his legal practice in WASHINGTON, D.C., then moved to CHICAGO in 1929. Although he began his political career as a registered Republican, Mitchell shifted his allegiance to the DEMOCRATIC PARTY as a result of his admiration for Franklin D. Roosevelt's New Deal policies. In 1934 he ran for the Democratic nomination as a candidate for Illinois's First Congressional District but lost to Harry Baker.

Arthur W. Mitchell (right), the first African American elected to the House of Representatives as a Democrat, with a campaign worker in 1934. *(AP/Wide World Photos)*

Upon Baker's death prior to the general election, local party leaders selected Mitchell as their nominee. He campaigned vigorously against the black republican incumbent, Oscar Depriest, and elicited support from constituents who favored Roosevelt's public relief efforts. Mitchell defeated Depriest and became the first black Democrat to be seated in Congress. He took his seat on January 3, 1935, and was chosen to serve on the House Committee on Post Offices and Post Roads. As a reward for his staunch support of the president, Mitchell was selected to give a seconding speech for Roosevelt's nomination in 1936, becoming the first African American to make an address at a Democratic National Convention. Mitchell also served as western director of minority affairs in Roosevelt's reelection campaign.

On a train journey to Arkansas in 1937, Mitchell was ejected from his first-class seat in a Pullman car. He sued the railroad. Mitchell also filed a complaint with the Interstate Commerce Commission (ICC). Although the ICC and a federal district court dismissed the case, Mitchell appealed to the U.S. Supreme Court and argued his case before the justices in April of 1941. The Court issued a unanimous decision upholding black passengers' right to receive the same accommodations and treatment as white passengers, but the ruling was never interpreted as a mandate to integrate interstate passenger trains. Mitchell declined to run for reelection in 1942, preferring instead to fight outside of Congress for improved race relations. He moved to Petersburg, Virginia, and was active as a public lecturer until his death.

See also: Congress members; Politics and government.

Mitchell, Clarence M., Jr. (March 8, 1911, Baltimore, Maryland—March 18, 1984, Baltimore, Maryland): Civil rights leader. Mitchell was the director of the Washington, D.C., bureau of the National Association for the Advancement of Colored People (NAACP) from 1950 to 1978. He earned accolades as the "101st United States Senator" because of the major impact he had on Congress as he lobbied relentlessly for the poor, hungry, disfranchised, and uneducated. He fought to get various civil rights bills passed.

Mitchell was reared in a closely knit, religious family with six siblings. His family always stressed the importance of cleanliness, hard work, and respect for others, self, the family, and the Church. Mitchell attended the Baltimore public schools and graduated from Douglass High School in 1928. In the fall of 1928, Mitchell entered Lincoln University in Pennsylvania. He received his bachelor's degree in 1932. After graduation, he returned to Baltimore to work as a newspaper reporter. He attended the Atlanta University School of Social Work for one year, beginning in 1936.

Afterward, Mitchell worked as an executive for the federal National Youth Administration. He was appointed later as the executive director of the St. Paul, Minnesota, Urban League. Robert Weaver, a former secretary of housing and urban development, was impressed by Mitchell's work and strongly recommended him for a position in the Department of Labor.

In 1941 Mitchell accepted an appointment in the Office of Production Management in the Department of Labor. When A. Philip Randolph and Walter White of the NAACP threatened a protest march on Washington, D.C., President Franklin Roosevelt immediately formed the Fair Employment Practices Commission in 1942. Mitchell became the associate director in 1944, serving under director John Davis. Shortly thereafter, he was appointed the director.

In 1945 Mitchell was appointed as labor secretary of the NAACP, assisting the executive secretary, Walter White. Mitchell eventually was named director of the Washington bureau in 1950. He served as a civil rights lobbyist until his retirement in 1978. In 1981 Governor Harry Hughes of MARYLAND appointed Mitchell to the board of regents of the University of Maryland.

Mitchell, Loften (b. April 15, 1919, Columbus, North Carolina): Dramatist. With his plays, screenplays, and novels, Mitchell helped chronicle the history of black THEATER in America, raised awareness about black culture and racial issues, and provided realistic dramas about African Americans. Mitchell's interest in the theater began when he attended vaudeville theaters in HARLEM. He developed scripts for backyard shows and, while still in high school, wrote sketches for the Pioneer Drama group. In the late 1930's, he was an actor with the Rose McClendon Players. Finding few opportunities for African American actors in New York, he moved to ALABAMA to attend Talladega College on a scholarship. Mitchell won an award for the best student play and graduated with honors in 1943.

After two years of military service during WORLD WAR II, Mitchell enrolled as a graduate student at Columbia University and began writing plays in earnest. *Blood in the Night* (pr. 1946) and *The Bancroft Dynasty* (pr. 1948) were presented on New York City stages before Mitchell earned his master's degree from Columbia in 1951. *The Cellar* (pr. 1952) was his first commercially successful play.

Mitchell's plays focus on the struggles of African Americans and conflicts between violence and nonviolence. For instance, *A Land Beyond the River*, which premiered Off-Broadway in 1957, tells the story of the Reverend Joseph A. DeLaine, a SOUTH CAROLINA pastor and schoolteacher who led a legal desegregation battle. *Tell Pharaoh*, televised in 1963 and produced on stage in 1967, is a pageant-style history with classic black songs. *Star of the Morning* (pr. 1965) dramatizes the life of black comedian Bert WILLIAMS. In 1976 Mitchell's *Bubbling Brown Sugar*, a tribute to Harlem's entertainers, was nominated for a Tony Award as best musical.

Mitchell's most widely read work is an informal history, *Black Drama: The Story of the American Negro in the Theatre* (1967). *Voices of the Black Theatre* (1975) is an inspirational oral history that recounts the firsthand experiences of African American dramatists. Mitchell also wrote articles on black theater for *Theatre Arts Monthly* and the *Oxford Companion to the Theatre*, in addition to a novel, *The Stubborn Old Lady Who Resisted Change* (1973).

Mitchell, Nellie E. Brown (1845, Dover, New Hampshire—January, 1924, Boston, Massachusetts): Concert soprano. The *Cleveland Gazette* hailed Mitchell as "America's greatest singer of African descent" in 1886. As a young girl in private school in Dover, she studied voice with Carol Bracket. She sang at school concerts and at local churches from the mid-1860's to the mid-1870's. Around 1874, she went to BOSTON, where she studied with Mrs. J. Rametti, and then to the New England Conservatory. Her principal voice instructor was Professor O'Neil. She also made formal debuts in Boston and New York during the 1870's.

In 1876 Mitchell was invited to participate in Boston's music celebration for the centennial. She also gave concerts in BALTIMORE, MARYLAND, WASHINGTON, D.C., Portland, MAINE, and St. John, NEBRASKA, as well as in Canada. From the early to the mid-1880's, Brown was the leading soprano with James Bergen's Star Concert Company. Bergen, a white concert manager, promoted the careers of several African American musicians, including Flora Batson, Harry T. Burleigh, Sidney Woodward, and Sissieretta JONES. In 1886 Mitchell established the Nellie Brown Mitchell Concert Company in Boston, but she retired from the stage in the mid-1890's and devoted her time to private teaching.
See also: Classical and operatic music.

Mitchell, Parren James (b. April 29, 1922, Baltimore, Maryland): U.S. representative from MARYLAND. Mitchell grew up in BALTIMORE and graduated from high school there in 1940. He entered the Army as a commissioned officer in 1942 and served with the NINETY-SECOND DIVISION as a company commander before being discharged in 1946. During his service, Mitchell was awarded the Purple Heart. Mitchell attended Morgan State College and received his bachelor of arts degree in 1950. He completed his graduate studies at the University of Maryland and received his master's degree in 1952 before returning to Morgan State as an instructor in sociology from 1953 to 1954.

Mitchell left the college to work for the Supreme Bench of BALTIMORE City as supervisor of probation work from 1954 to 1957. His interest in minority affairs led him to accept the position of executive secretary of the Maryland Human Relations Commission from 1963 to 1965. He became director of the Baltimore Community Action Agency in 1965 and was in charge of its antipoverty programs in Baltimore's inner city until 1968. Mitchell then returned to academic life at Morgan State College, becoming a professor of sociology and assistant director of the college's Urban Affairs Institute. In 1969 he took the post of president of Baltimore Neighborhoods, Inc.

Although he was unsuccessful in his 1968 bid for the DEMOCRATIC PARTY nomination in Maryland's Seventh Congressional District race, Mitchell won the Democratic primary in 1970. He won the election in November, becoming the first African American representative from the state of Maryland. He took office on January 3, 1971, and served as a member of the House Committee on the Budget and the House Committee on Banking, Finance, and Urban Affairs. Mitchell worked hard for the passage of legislation assisting minority-owned businesses in bidding for federal projects, including defense contracts. He also called for strong sanctions to be imposed against new investments in South Africa by U.S. corporations. In 1981 Mitchell became chairman of the House Committee on Small Business. He declined to seek reelection after eight terms in Congress and returned to Baltimore in 1986, at the end of his final term.

See also: Congress members; Politics and government.

Monk, Thelonious (October 10, 1917, Rocky Mount, North Carolina—February 17, 1982, Englewood, New Jersey): Pianist and composer. Thelonious Sphere Monk created some of the most challenging and ultimately indis-

Pianist Thelonious Monk performing at the Newport Jazz Festival in 1963. *(AP/Wide World Photos)*

pensable music of the twentieth century. Monk, as house pianist at MINTON'S PLAYHOUSE in New York, was present during the formative stages of modern JAZZ, known as bebop. Although he did not possess the stunning technique of Bud Powell, the other major bebop pianist, Monk created a highly individual style through careful note selection and musical conception. His unique musical style, together with such personal mannerisms as walking or dancing around the piano during another musician's solo, made his music inaccessible to many. In time, his music became valued for its own sake, so much so that in the 1960's he was the subject of a cover story in *Time* magazine.

Monk recorded with many of the major figures in modern jazz, including trumpeters Dizzy GILLESPIE and Miles DAVIS and saxophonists Charlie PARKER, Sonny ROLLINS, and John COLTRANE. Monk's 1957 association with Coltrane helped the saxophonist to become the most influential jazz musician of the 1960's. Monk's longest-lived quartet, which lasted for most of the 1960's, featured saxophonist Charlie Rouse.

"'Round Midnight," "Epistrophy," "Well, You Needn't," "Blue Monk," and "Rhythm-a-ning" are only a few of Monk's compositions that have become jazz standards. Symphony orchestras perform his compositions, the Kronos Quartet recorded an entire album of his creations, and saxophonist Steve Lacy devoted a substantial portion of his career to playing Monk's tunes.

After performing in Europe in 1972, Monk was musically inactive for the remainder of his life. In 1988 an acclaimed documentary film, *Thelonious Monk: Straight No Chaser*, was released.

Montana: In 1997, according to estimates of the CENSUS OF THE UNITED STATES, Montana

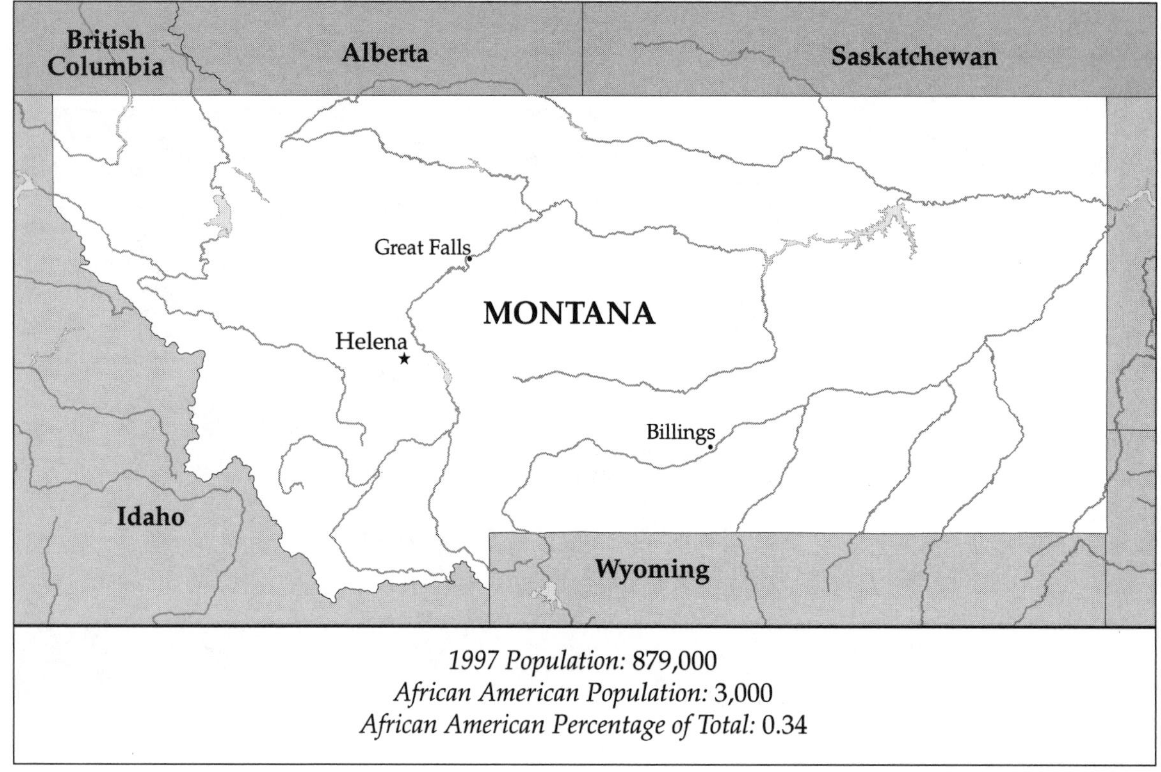

1997 Population: 879,000
African American Population: 3,000
African American Percentage of Total: 0.34

had a total population of about 879,000 people and an African American population of about 3,000, or only 0.34 percent of the total.

African Americans were more prominent in Montana in the nineteenth century than during most of the twentieth century. Montana's first permanent African American settlers came to the gold fields and mines in the 1860's. They staked claims or worked in the local businesses. According to the 1870 census, seventy-one blacks lived in Helena. Although there were few African American homesteaders, black COWBOYS and retired members of the TWENTY-FOURTH INFANTRY settled in Montana. Helena had a black community with stores that served black and white customers. In 1910 the state's 420 African American residents represented 3.4 percent of the population.

African Americans did not enjoy equal rights in Montana. In 1872 the territorial legislature required a separate school for Helena's blacks even though there were only twenty black students. However, both whites and blacks protested; eventually, for financial reasons, city voters eliminated Helena's segregated school in 1882. While there was prejudice, there were no recorded lynchings or other violent abuses toward blacks. African Americans lived throughout Helena and were accepted by the European Americans.

The African American population in Montana declined from 1910 to 1940 because of poor employment opportunities and segregation legislation. The Great Falls chapter of the NATIONAL ASSOCIATION FOR THE ADVANCEMENT OF COLORED PEOPLE (NAACP), for example, was organized in 1922 but was defunct by 1930. The small African American population, however, championed CIVIL RIGHTS legislation in the late 1940's and 1950's, eliminating discriminating practices. Following WORLD WAR II, the black population grew slowly, not reaching 2,000 until the 1980's. In the 1990's most of Montana's African Americans lived in Great Falls and Billings. The first black state legislator, Geraldine Travis, was elected in 1974.

—*Jessie L. Embry*

Montgomery, Alabama: Montgomery is the seat of Montgomery County and the capital of ALABAMA (it replaced Tuscaloosa as the capital in 1847). The city lies at the tip of the Appalachian Mountains and among the hills overlooking the Alabama River a hundred miles south of BIRMINGHAM. Once labeled the "cradle of the CONFEDERACY," the city, the third largest in the state in the 1990's, is spread over three counties. A river port and barge center, it is an important agricultural and trade center. Boosting local opportunities are the Maxwell and Gunter Air Force bases, Air Uni-

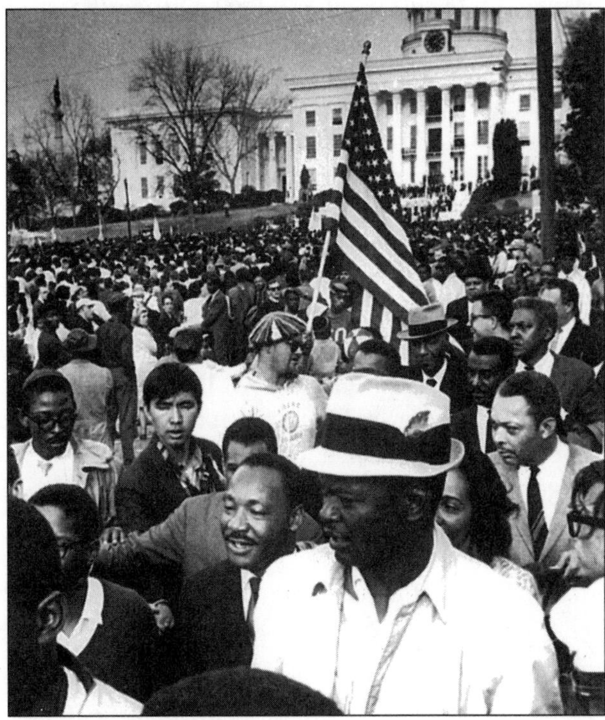

In March, 1965, Martin Luther King, Jr. (left of man in hat) made a triumphal return to Montgomery at the head of a five-day-march from Selma. *(AP/Wide World Photos)*

versity, Garrett Coliseum, Cramton Bowl, Alabama Shakespeare Festival Theater, Montgomery Museum of Art, Alabama University, Auburn University, Huntingdon College, and Alabama Christian College.

Before the coming of European settlers, the area around Montgomery was home to Creek, Chickasaw, Choctaw, and Cherokee tribes. The city developed from Fort Toulouse, a French installation founded in 1717. Montgomery is named for General Richard Montgomery, a Revolutionary War hero. It was incorporated as a town in 1819 and as a city in 1837. Montgomery served as Confederate president Jefferson Davis's headquarters for five months, until his move to Richmond, VIRGINIA.

Martin Luther KING, Jr., drew attention to the region in the late 1950's by organizing a nonviolent CIVIL RIGHTS movement, boycotting the city bus system in 1955, and climaxing his push for racial equality in 1965 with a four-day voters' rights march. The 1955 bus boycott is Montgomery's most famous moment in history. King helped organize African American residents to avoid using the city's bus system, which was segregated. He arranged for protests and for alternative means of transportation. The boycott was successful in gaining a court order to desegregate the bus system in 1956. From this turbulent era came Montgomery's designation as "birthplace of the Civil Rights movement." George Wallace's four terms as governor of Alabama, during which he opposed integration efforts, did not reverse the gains in civil rights. By 1980 Montgomery's population was 39 percent African American.

See also: Segregation and integration.

Montgomery bus boycott: Refusal of African Americans to ride buses in MONTGOMERY, ALABAMA, as a protest of segregation. The Montgomery bus boycott signaled the beginning of the CIVIL RIGHTS movement. It was launched after the founding of the Montgomery Improvement Association (MIA). Organized on December 5, 1955, the MIA selected as president a young minister at the Dexter Avenue Baptist Church, Martin Luther KING, Jr. Longtime Alabama NATIONAL ASSOCIATION FOR THE ADVANCEMENT OF COLORED PEOPLE (NAACP) leader E. D. Nixon and the Reverend Ralph David ABERNATHY spearheaded the first MIA organizational meeting. The MIA's objective was to challenge the Jim Crow system. An indication of the MIA's threat to segregation was shown when King's MIA leadership resulted in the bombing of his home.

The MIA initiated the bus boycott to protest RACIAL DISCRIMINATION experienced by African Americans on the Montgomery public buses. While paying the same fares as white passengers, African American passengers were forced to ride in the rear of the bus and relinquish their seats to white passengers. The MIA was prompted to stage the bus boycott by the arrest on December 1, 1955, of a prominent African American political activist, Rosa PARKS, who refused to give up her seat.

The MIA was assisted by the Women's Political Council (WPC), an organization composed of professional African American women, and the Citizens Steering Committee (CSC), an African American civic organization. The WPC was led skillfully by Jo Ann Gibson Robinson, an Alabama State College faculty member. The CSC was led by Rufus Lewis, a local African American businessman.

Through mass rallies and a systematic organizational approach to providing alternative transportation for African American bus riders in Montgomery, the MIA sponsored a year-long rider boycott that ended on December 21, 1956. The bus company was forced to end segregation on the buses through this public pressure and a U.S. SUPREME COURT ruling. The success of the Montgomery bus

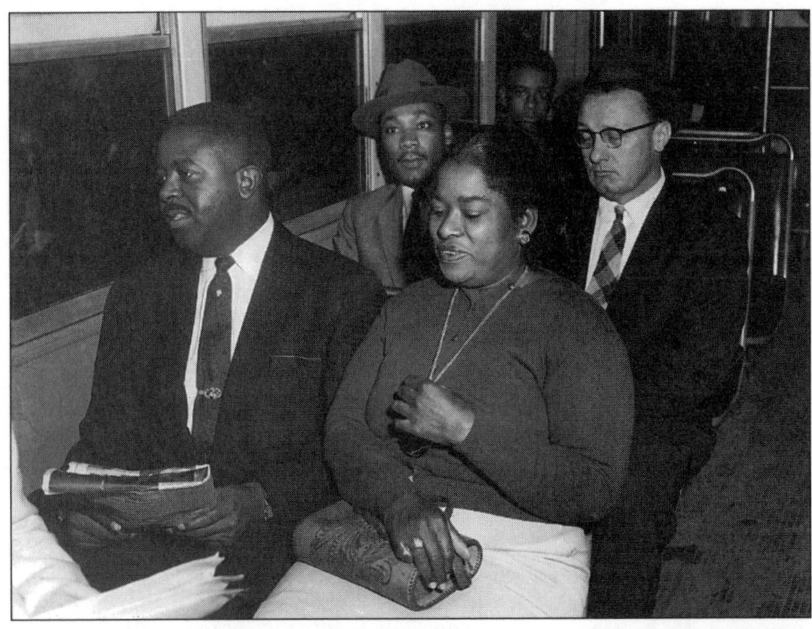

Ralph Abernathy (left) and Martin Luther King, Jr. (center) were among the first African Americans to ride a Montgomery bus after the Supreme Court's desegregation order went into effect in December, 1956. *(AP/Wide World Photos)*

boycott led to a realization of the possibilities of political mobilization and protest among African Americans. The boycott was the first of King's many successful mass protests.

Moore, Emerson (b. May 16, 1938, New York, New York): Religious figure. Ordained as a ROMAN CATHOLIC priest in 1964, Moore was named auxiliary bishop of New York in 1982. He became vicar for the northwest Bronx, responsible for all Catholic Church activities there. Moore earned a graduate degree in social work from Columbia University in addition to his degrees from Cathedral College and St. Joseph Seminary.
See also: National Office for Black Catholics.

Moore v. Dempsey: U.S. SUPREME COURT case involving the equal protection clause of the Constitution. The Court, in 1923, overturned the convictions of seventy-nine black defendants. At their original trial, a mob had threatened to lynch the defendants. In exchange for the safety of the defendants, the committee trying them had promised quick and full punishment. The fact that the trial had been dominated by the mob was held by the Supreme Court to violate provisions for due process of law. This case reversed *Frank v. Mangum* (1914), which held that the Court could not interfere as long as the form of a trial had been complied with.

Moorhead, Scipio (b. c. 1773): Painter. Scipio, a slave, took his last name from his owner, the Reverend John Moorhead of BOSTON, MASSACHUSETTS. Moorhead was probably the first African American artist in colonial America to receive formal training, studying with Mrs. Sarah Moorhead, an artist and art teacher. Phillis WHEATLEY dedicated a poem to Moorhead. No signed work by Moorhead has been found, but it is possible that the engraved portrait used as a frontispiece in some of Wheatley's published poetry was done by him.
See also: Painters and illustrators.

Moorland-Spingarn Research Center (Washington, D.C.): Repository for documentation of the history and culture of people of African descent. The center is one of Howard University's major research facilities. In 1914 Jesse Moorland, a black theologian, donated his private library to HOWARD UNIVERSITY. His col-

Howard University's Founders Library, which houses the Moorland Spingarn Research Center. *(Library of Congress)*

lection, along with other related materials, became known as the Moorland Foundation. Howard University acquired the library of Arthur B. Spingarn, an attorney and social activist, in 1946. The Spingarn Collection of Negro Authors, containing documents written by people of African descent, was for years maintained separately from the Moorland Foundation. The Moorland-Spingarn Research Center was created in 1973 from the Moorland and Spingarn collections, the Howard University Museum, the Howard University Archives, the Black Press Archives, and the Ralph J. Bunche Oral History Collection.

Morehouse School of Medicine (Atlanta, Georgia): Medical school associated with a historically African American institution. The school's first class entered in 1978, and the first class to graduate with M.D. degrees did so in May, 1985. Louis W. Sullivan, the founding president, left that position to serve as secretary of health and human services under President George Bush.

See also: Health care professionals; Medicine.

Morgan, Garrett Augustus (March 4, 1875, Paris, Kentucky—July 27, 1963, Cleveland, Ohio): Inventor famous for his contributions to public safety. These included a gas mask used by fire fighters, chemists, engineers, and World War I soldiers. Morgan is also known for inventing the first automatic traffic-signal system used to regulate vehicular traffic at intersections. These traffic signals alternately raised and lowered "Stop" and "Go" signs.

Early Life

Garrett Morgan was the seventh of the eleven children of Sydney Morgan and Elizabeth Reed Morgan. Garrett left school after the fifth grade and moved from Paris, Kentucky, a small town that offered few opportunities for education or advancement, to Cincinnati, Ohio. There, Morgan became a handyman in a sewing-machine shop. Opportunities for an African American did not seem to be much better in Cincinnati than in the small town of his birth, however, and Morgan moved to Cleveland, Ohio, in 1895.

Once situated in Cleveland, Morgan got a job as a sewing-machine mechanic. Working for several companies in the sewing-machine business, he lived frugally, saved his money, and in 1908 started a tailoring shop that soon employed thirty-two people who made dresses, suits, and other clothing items. After only one year in this business, Morgan was able to buy a home, where he and his wife, Mary Anne Hassek Morgan, lived happily and reared three sons.

Experiment Creates Hair Straightener

In 1913 Morgan invented a hair straightener that he marketed through the G. A. Morgan Hair Refining Company. The hair straightener became so popular that Morgan was able to concentrate much of his attention on a career as an inventor, beginning his life's work. Reportedly, the discovery of the straightener occurred accidentally when Morgan was experimenting with lubricating materials. Morgan was called to dinner while testing a lubricant, and he wiped his smeared hands on a piece of fur before leaving. On his return, Morgan observed that the hairs of the fur had become soft, straight, and pliable, and this discovery led him to invent the Morgan hair straightener.

Developing a Gas Mask

Garrett Morgan's fame rests on several inventions that contributed to the safety of the general public. His first business venture stemmed from the observation that fire fighters were often overcome by smoke and fumes when they entered burning buildings to fight fires. Morgan saw the need for a simple but dependable means of protection from smoke and other harmful fumes.

Morgan's efforts to protect fire fighters led to the gas mask that he developed in the early 1900's. His gas mask, patented in 1914, was much more dependable than any other in use at the time. Essentially, it was a canvas hood from which extended two tubes. These tubes merged into a single tube behind the wearer. The open end of the tube, which nearly reached the ground, was blocked with a sponge moistened with water. The moist sponge trapped smoke particles and cooled the air that entered the system. A metal tube inside the hood ran from the wearer's mouth to a ball valve atop the hood. Exhalation raised the valve ball from its seat and allowed spent air to escape. Inhalation caused the ball to drop back and prevent smoke or fumes from entering. Morgan's hood even provided covered ear holes so that the wearer could hear noises.

The operation of the gas mask depended upon the facts that hot, smoky air rises toward the ceiling of a room and that, in a smoky room, a layer of nearly smokeless air accumulates near the floor. Morgan's tube design allowed the wearer to take in this relatively clean air and both cleaned it further and cooled it.

As time went by, Morgan perfected his gas mask and changed it so that the device carried its own air supply. Because of its general safety utility, Morgan's gas mask saw wide additional use by engineers, chemists, World War I soldiers, and others who were exposed to toxic fumes and dusts. Morgan used his expertise to found the National Safety Device Company to sell the invention widely. The company was so successful that, within five years, the value of its stock rose from $10 per share to more than $250 per share.

Awards and Recognition

For the invention of his gas mask, Morgan was awarded a gold medal at the Second International Exposition of Safety and Sanitation in New York City in 1914. Another spontaneous testimonial to the use of these devices was their removal from the exposition booth for use by New York City fire fighters to rescue victims of a subway accident.

In 1916 Morgan used his gas mask to rescue several Cleveland workmen trapped by a tunnel explosion under Lake Erie. For this heroic act, during which he entered and reentered the tunnel numerous times, Morgan was awarded medals by the City of Cleveland and by the International Association of Fire Engineers. The latter organization also made Morgan an honorary member. One unexpected result of the publicity, which caused great increases in the demand for the Morgan gas mask in most states, was a decrease in orders from several southern cities after it was learned that the mask's inventor was an African American.

Creating a Traffic-Control Device

In 1923 Morgan patented his other major invention, a traffic signal used to regulate traffic at busy intersections. The signal was composed of "Stop" and "Go" signs that were automatically raised or lowered at regular intervals to improve traffic safety for both motor vehicles and pedestrians. The invention was essential because of the chaos that had become common in American cities, where ever-increasing numbers of automobiles and trucks were appearing. The semaphore-like arms of the signalwere often equipped with warning bells and lights for night use. Some years later, Morgan sold his patent to the General Electric Company, which replaced the signs with red, green, and yellow lights. Morgan's invention is generally regarded as the first automated traffic-control device in history.

Another major endeavor of Morgan's was the founding of the newspaper the *Cleveland Call and Post*. He and colleagues started the paper as the *Cleveland Call*. By the 1970's, the paper, which had become the *Call and Post*, had one of the largest circulations of any midwestern African American newspaper.

Philanthropic Endeavors

Morgan was always heavily involved in philanthropic activities involving African American affairs. One of his pet interests was fostering the education of African American students at American universities, especially Cleveland's Case Western Reserve University. There he provided financial assistance and organized the university's first fraternity for African American students. At the thirty-eighth anniversary of the founding of this fraternity, Morgan was honored alongside U.S. SUPREME COURT Justice Thurgood MARSHALL. Morgan was also heavily involved in the Cleveland Association of Colored Men, the predecessor of the NATIONAL ASSOCIATION FOR THE ADVANCEMENT OF COLORED PEOPLE (NAACP) in that city.

After suffering from glaucoma and a prolonged illness, Morgan died in 1963. He was widely respected for his many inventions, his business acumen, and his decency and character. Among the honors Morgan received was the erection of a stainless-steel plaque bearing his portrait and name mounted on a marble pillar in the Hall of Fame of the Cleveland Public Auditorium.

—*Sanford S. Singer*

See also: Inventors.

Suggested Readings:

Haber, Louis. *Black Pioneers of Science and Invention*. New York: Harcourt, Brace and World, 1970.

Hayden, Robert C. *Eight Black American Inventors*. Reading, Mass.: Addison-Wesley, 1972.

Jenkins, Edward S. *To Fathom More: African American Scientists and Inventors*. Lanham, Md.: University Press of America, 1996.

King, William M. "Guardian of Public Safety: Garrett A. Morgan and the Lake Erie Crib Disaster." *Journal of Negro History* 70 (Winter/Spring, 1985): 1-13.

Klein, Aaron E. *The Hidden Contributors: Black Scientists and Inventors in America*. Garden City, N.Y.: Doubleday, 1971.

Sammons, Vivian O. *Blacks in Science and Medicine*. New York: Hemisphere, 1990.

Morgan, Lee (July 10, 1938, Philadelphia, Pennsylvania—February 19, 1972, New York, New York): JAZZ trumpeter. Morgan grew up in PHILADELPHIA and began to play trumpet professionally in the city's clubs when he was fifteen years old. In 1956 Morgan moved to New York City and joined Dizzy Gillespie's orchestra. While still working with GILLESPIE, Morgan recorded with John COLTRANE on the 1957 album *Blue Train*. When the Gillespie orchestra broke up in 1958, Morgan became a member of Art BLAKEY's Jazz Messengers. He performed with the group until 1961. One of Blakey's recordings that featured Morgan as a sideman was "The Freedom Rider" (1961).

Morgan worked on his own in Philadelphia and recorded his own album, *The Sidewinder*, in 1963. He returned to New York to work with Blakey from 1964 to 1965. Morgan's second album, *Cornbread*, was released in 1965. Morgan worked closely with Hank Mobley during the mid-1960's, playing on Mobley's 1965 album *Dippin'* and recording with Mobley on his own 1966 album, *The Rajah*. In 1970 and 1971, Morgan was involved actively in the Jazz and People's Movement, an organization led by Roland Rahsaan KIRK that was dedicated to promoting jazz music and African American performers on radio and television. In 1972 Morgan was shot by his mistress during an appearance at Slugs, a New York nightclub, and died at the age of thirty-four.

See also: Freedom rides.

Morgan, Sister Gertrude (1900, Lafayette, Alabama—1980, New Orleans, Louisiana): Self-taught artist. Morgan's paintings reflect her commitment to the fundamentalist sect for which she was a street evangelist. The rhythmic expression that critics note in her painting can be traced to the sect's emphasis on music and dance. Morgan's often richly apocalyptic imagery is also traceable to her religious faith. Morgan claimed to have begun painting in response to a call from God, in 1956. A painter in the "naive" style, Morgan is praised for her instinctive use of color. The relatively late start of her artistic career proved no impediment to her work being widely exhibited during her lifetime.

See also: Painters and illustrators.

Morgan v. Virginia: U.S. SUPREME COURT desegregation case in 1946. It overturned state-mandated segregation of passengers on interstate transportation. Irene Morgan, riding on a bus traveling through VIRGINIA to MARYLAND, refused to give up her seat to a white passenger and move to the back of a bus. She was arrested and fined $10 for violating a Virginia law requiring segregated seating.

Attorneys for the NATIONAL ASSOCIATION FOR THE ADVANCEMENT OF COLORED PEOPLE (NAACP) appealed Morgan's conviction to the Supreme Court. Citing an 1878 case as precedent, they argued that the law placed an undue burden on interstate commerce. On this basis the Court overturned the Virginia statute. Neither appellants nor the Court dealt with the compatibility or incompatibility of the law with the FOURTEENTH AMENDMENT.

In 1947 representatives of the CONGRESS OF RACIAL EQUALITY (CORE) who rode buses through the upper South to test the effects of the *Morgan* decision were arrested for violating state laws. The practical effects of the case were not seen until the 1961 FREEDOM RIDES finally desegregated interstate buses and terminals.

—*George F. Bagby*

Morrison, Toni (Chloe Anthony Wofford; b. February 18, 1931, Lorain, Ohio): Novelist, editor, and PROFESSOR. Toni Morrison was the second of George and Ramah Willis Wofford's four children. As an adult, she was to view her father, who had been a child in GEORGIA in the early part of the twentieth century, as an antiwhite racist but also as someone who encouraged excellence and impressed upon his daughter a positive self-image to help her achieve such excellence. Her mother, on the other hand, maintained an optimistic, integrationist perspective, which was nevertheless tempered by a good deal of suspicion of the violence done by whites against blacks. Although Morrison was reared in OHIO, both of her parents had migrated with their families from the South. The Woffords regaled their children with the folktales, ghost stories, and African American cultural retentions that were to later become an important part of their second child's literary contribution.

Academic Career

An exceptionally bright child, Morrison was the only black student in her class, as well as the first child able to read in the first grade. She studied Latin in high school and graduated with honors from the Lorain Public High School in 1949. She attended HOWARD UNIVERSITY for four years, where she majored in English and started going by the nickname "Toni."

She graduated from Howard in 1953 with a B.A. in English and proceeded to graduate studies at Cornell University, where she wrote her master's thesis on Virginia Woolf and William Faulkner. She graduated from Cornell with a master's degree in English in 1955 and began teaching at Texas Southern University that same year. In 1957 she returned to Howard as an instructor, and she was married to Harold Morrison, a Jamaican-born architect.

Nobel Prize-winning novelist Toni Morrison in 1993. *(AP/Wide World Photos)*

While Morrison was teaching at Howard, her students included Houston A. BAKER, Jr., who later established himself as one of the foremost African American literary critics, and Stokely CARMICHAEL, the BLACK POWER MOVEMENT leader of the 1960's. As a member of a writing group there, she wrote a short story that was eventually to develop into her first novel. In 1962 her first son, Harold Ford Morrison, was born.

Editor

In 1964 she resigned her teaching post at Howard, divorced her husband, and answered an advertisement in *The New York Review of Books* to become a textbook editor at L. W. Singer Publishing Company, a subsidiary of Random House, a job that required her to move to Syracuse, New York. In 1967 Morrison was promoted to senior editor at Random House, where she worked especially on black fiction. In this role, she helped develop the careers of black fiction writers, including Toni Cade BAMBARA and Gayl JONES, as well as the writing career of the black essayist and activist Angela DAVIS.

Novelist

It was while living in Syracuse that Morrison returned to her short story about a black girl who wanted blue eyes. At the encouragement of Alan Rancler, an editor at Macmillan and later Holt, Rinehart, and Winston, she developed the story into a novel that was published by Holt in 1970 as *The Bluest Eye*. The book was generally well received and immediately established Morrison as a writer of great talent.

In 1973 Morrison published her second novel, *Sula*, a study of an intensely individualistic black woman, Sula, and her relationships to her closest friend and to the community from which she is an outcast. *Sula* was also praised (Sarah Blackburn called it "extravagantly beautiful" in *The New York Review of Books*) and was nominated for the National Book Award.

Morrison's third novel, *Song of Solomon*, published in 1977, established beyond any doubt that Morrison was a major American novelist. This powerful and often lyrical novel of a middle-class black man who is coerced by circumstances into searching for his ancestral roots in slavery won for Morrison her largest audience so far and won the National Book Critics Circle Award. Ironically, some of the same black female critics who had been supporters of her first two novels were initially skeptical of this third one, arguing that Morrison had shifted the focus of her writing from the societal forces that threaten black women in order to write a more conventional narrative about a young man growing into wisdom.

Morrison's fourth novel, *Tar Baby* (1981), is perhaps her least often read book and the one that has received the least critical attention. *Tar Baby* traces the relationship between Jadine Childs, a black FASHION model with a European background, and Son, a black fugitive. The conflict between Jadine's rather vague relationship to her African heritage and Son's more direct connection to his emerges as a major theme of the novel; the conflict remains to a large extent unresolved when Jadine and Son separate at the book's end.

Return to Academia

In 1984 Morrison left Random House after twenty years there to become the Albert Schweitzer Professor of the Humanities at the State University of New York at Albany. In 1985 her first play, entitled *Dreaming Emmett*, premiered at Albany, and in 1987 her fifth novel, *Beloved*, was published by Alfred A. Knopf. *Beloved* was widely proclaimed as her finest work to date, and many black writers and critics signed a letter of protest when it was not given the National Book Award. *Beloved* did, however, receive the Pulitzer Prize for fiction. In 1989 Morrison was appointed the Robert F. Goheen Professor of the Humanities at Princeton University.

In 1992 two works by Morrison appeared. Her sixth novel, *Jazz*, set in Harlem in the 1920's, chronicles the harsh existence of a couple whose lives are tragically disrupted by adultery, jealousy, murder, and a bittersweet longing for their lost youth. In her other 1992 work, *Playing in the Dark: Whiteness and the Literary Imagination*, a scholarly volume of literary criticism published by Harvard University Press, Morrison calls for a new critical exploration of the role of black characters in American fiction. That same year she also wrote the lyrics for the operatic piece *Honey and Rue*, performed by Kathleen Battle at Carnegie Hall.

In 1993 Morrison nearly lost many of her original manuscripts and personal papers when her Hudson River home was gutted by fire on Christmas Day. No one in her family was hurt, and the papers, which were stored in her basement, did not suffer serious damage. In 1997 Morrison published the nonfiction work *Birth of a Nation'hood: Gaze, Script, and Spectacle in the O.J. Simpson Case*. Morrison's 1998 novel, *Paradise*, is loosely based on a historical event, the westward migration of a group of former slaves intent on founding an all-black utopian community. The story shifts back and forth over a century of time.

In 1993 Toni Morrison was awarded the Nobel Prize for Literature, thus becoming the eighth woman to receive the prize and the first African American to be so honored. In its announcement of the award, the Swedish Academy of Letters recognized Morrison for creating portraits of black life "characterized by visionary force and poetic import." In addition to this high honor, Morrison was accorded numerous literary awards, including the Pulitzer Prize and the Modern Language Association of America Commonwealth Award in literature. Morrison's novels and criticism have won worldwide acclaim, and she truly earned a position of prominence in African American history and LITERATURE.

Themes and Stature

The central concerns of Toni Morrison's fiction include the history of physical and economic violence against black Americans, the disruption of positive black cultural traditions caused by such violence, and the strategies employed by black Americans to try to preserve their traditions—including those strategies that backfire to some degree. Morrison's focus is primarily on the violence done to, and the cultural traditions of, black women, but her examinations of traditions and violence as they affect black men are also keenly observed and insightful. Through the power of her writing, she succeeded in making these concerns central in American fiction, much as William Faulkner had earlier done with the concerns of the American South. Morrison also engages the same issues in public lectures and in articles that have appeared in *The New York Times Magazine* and elsewhere. Add to this her accomplishments as an editor and influential educator, and Morrison must be ranked with W. E. B. DU BOIS and Langston HUGHES as one of the most important and influential black writers of the twentieth century—and possibly as the most important black female writer in American history.

—Thomas Cassidy
—Updated by Yvonne Johnson

Suggested Readings:

Bjork, Patrick B. *The Novels of Toni Morrison: The Search for Self and Place Within the Community*. New York: Peter Lang, 1992.

Carmean, Karen. *Toni Morrison's World of Fiction*. Troy, N.Y.: Whitston, 1993.

Coser, Stelamaris. *Bridging the Americas: The Literature of Paule Marshall, Toni Morrison, and Gayl Jones*. Philadelphia: Temple University Press, 1995.

Furman, Jan. *Toni Morrison's Fiction*. Columbia: University of South Carolina Press, 1996.

Gates, Henry Louis, and Anthony Appiah, eds. *Toni Morrison: Critical Perspectives Past and Present*. New York: Amistad Press, 1993.

Kubitschek, Missy D. *Toni Morrison: A Critical Companion*. Westport, Conn.: Greenwood Press, 1998.

McKay, Nellie Y., ed. *Critical Essays on Toni Morrison*. Boston: G. K. Hall, 1988.

Morrison, Toni. *Conversations with Toni Morrison*. Edited by Kathleen D. Taylor-Guthrie. Jackson: University Press of Mississippi, 1994.

Peach, Linden. *Toni Morrison*. New York: St. Martin's Press, 1998.

Peterson, Nancy J., ed. *Toni Morrison: Critical and Theoretical Approaches*. Baltimore: John Hopkins University Press, 1997.

Samuels, Wilfred D., and Clenora Hudson-Weems. *Toni Morrison*. Boston: Twayne, 1990.

Soloman, Barbara H., ed. *Critical Essays on Toni Morrison's "Beloved."* New York: G. K. Hall, 1998.

Morrow, E. Frederic (b. April 20, 1909, Hackensack, New Jersey): Political appointee and bank executive. Everett Frederic Morrow received his A.B. degree from Bowdoin College in 1930. From 1942 to 1946, he served in the U.S. Army, attaining the rank of major before receiving his discharge. Morrow enrolled in law school at Rutgers University and graduated with LL.B. and J.D. degrees in 1948.

Morrow's political career began when he was appointed to serve as business adviser to the Department of Commerce from 1953 to 1955. President Dwight Eisenhower then ap-

pointed him to serve as administrative officer for a White House special project group in 1955. With this appointment, Morrow became the first African American to serve as a White House aide. Morrow left the White House in 1961 to serve as vice president of the African American Institute in New York City and then became vice president of Bank of America International in 1964. He wrote a memoir of his years in Washington titled *Black Man in the White House: A Diary of the Eisenhower Years by the Administrative Officer for Special Projects, the White House, 1955-1961* (1963).
See also: Politics and government.

Morrow, John Howard, Sr. (February 5, 1910, Hackensack, New Jersey—January 11, 2000, Fountain Valley, California): Educator and political appointee. Morrow graduated from Rutgers University in 1931 with his A.B. degree. He taught from 1931 to 1935 as a high school instructor of mathematics and Latin before joining the staff of the Bordentown Institute, where he worked as an instructor in English and Latin until 1945. During this time, Morrow studied at the University of Pennsylvania, earning his M.A. degree in 1942.

Morrow's teaching career expanded when he became a professor on the faculty of Talladega College in 1945, serving as the chairman of its foreign languages department until 1954. In 1947 Morrow received a Carnegie grant to study in Europe. He earned his Ph.D. in 1952 from the University of Pennsylvania before joining the faculty of Clark College in Atlanta in 1954. He taught French during summer school sessions at Atlanta University from 1950 to 1956, then moved to North Carolina College, where he served as chairman of the French department until 1959.

President Dwight Eisenhower worked closely with Morrow's brother, E. Frederic Morrow, who was his administrative assistant. Eisenhower appointed John Howard Morrow to serve as the first U.S. ambassador to the Republic of Guinea in 1959. He held this post until 1961, when he was appointed to serve as an alternate delegate to the United Nations and later as U.S. permanent representative to the United Nations Educational, Scientific, and Cultural Organization (UNESCO) in Paris until 1963. From 1963 to 1964, he coordinated the university programs offered to foreign service officers at the State Department's Foreign Service Institute.

John Howard Morrow was the first U.S. ambassador to the West African republic of Guinea, which became independent in 1958. *(AP/Wide World Photos)*

Morrow retired from the foreign service in 1964 to become a professor of romance languages at his alma mater, Rutgers University. After retiring from teaching in 1978, he moved to Southern California, where he was active in a local African Methodist Zion Church until he was incapacitated by Alzheimer's disease. He died in early January, 2000, leaving his wife of sixty-four years.

Morrow ranks with singer Paul ROBESON among the distinguished African American alumni of Rutgers University, which named a new dormitory after him in 1989.
See also: Diplomats.

Morton, Benny (January 31, 1907, New York, New York—December 28, 1985, New York, New York): JAZZ trombonist. Henry Sterling "Benny" Morton grew up in New York City and began playing jazz with friends from high school. His professional career began when he played as an occasional member of Billy Fowler's Orchestra, beginning in 1924. Morton was a member of Fletcher Henderson's Orchestra from 1926 to 1928 and went on to perform in several other top big bands, including those of William "Chick" Webb (1930-1931), Don Redman (1932-1937), and Count Basie (1937-1940). From 1940 to 1943, Morton was trombonist in pianist Teddy Wilson's sextet and appeared briefly in clarinetist Edmond Hall's sextet. He formed his own jazz group in September of 1944. The group disbanded in 1946, and Morgan began working in Broadway theater orchestras for such musicals as *Memphis Bound* (1945), *St. Louis Woman* (1946), and *Jamaica* (1957).

Morton worked as a studio musician in the late 1950's and appeared with various Dixieland and jazz bands in the 1960's. In 1964 he toured in Africa with Paul Taubman's concert orchestra and played in Las Vegas with Ted Lewis. He performed with the Saints and Sinners, a Dixieland group, in 1967 and in 1970, with jazz man Wild Bill Davison in 1968, and with Sy Oliver from 1970 to 1971. Morton toured with the World's Greatest Jazz Band between 1973 and 1974 and resumed touring with the group in 1978 after recovering from a long illness.

Morton, Jelly Roll (October 20, 1890, Gulfport, Louisiana—July 10, 1941, Los Angeles, California): JAZZ pianist, composer, and arranger. Ferdinand Joseph La Menthe "Jelly Roll" Morton was reared by his grandmother in NEW ORLEANS, LOUISIANA. He began his piano-playing career around 1902, performing in VAUDEVILLE and in MINSTREL shows as well as working as a music publisher, tailor, and boxing promoter. Morton also wrote music during his early career, music that had roots in ragtime but foreshadowed the jazz of the 1920's.

Morton made his first recordings in CHICAGO, ILLINOIS, in 1923. His better-known recordings, with the Red Hot Peppers, began in 1926. Much of Morton's reputation rests on this series of recordings with his own band, even though the recordings ended in 1928, when he moved to New York City. By 1930 his favored New Orleans style of jazz was fall-

Pianist Jelly Roll Morton recording classic jazz pieces for the Library of Congress archives in 1938. *(AP/ Wide World Photos)*

ing out of style. His engagements in the late 1920's and early 1930's were limited to lesser clubs and theater pit orchestras.

Morton's career was revived by Alan Lomax, who recorded a series of interviews with Morton for the Library of Congress as well as recording some of Morton's piano solos. It was around this time, in the late 1930's, that Morton made widely publicized claims of being the creator of jazz, in the year 1902. These claims were in response to music critics' naming of W. C. Handy as the originator of jazz and the blues. What Morton probably intended to say was that his work had helped to differentiate jazz from ragtime, but his claims added to his reputation as a braggart.

The recordings Morton made in 1939 and 1940 followed in the New Orleans style but lacked the originality of the Red Hot Peppers songs. He had been an innovator in the 1920's with such songs as "Grandpa's Spells" (1923), "Black Bottom Stomp" (1925), and "Cannonball Blues" (1926), and even earlier with "Jelly Roll Blues" (1905) and "King Porter Stomp" (1906). By the end of Morton's career, his music had fallen behind the times, but he is remembered as a great piano player, composer, and arranger of his era. Numerous writers have chronicled his career, including Alan Lomax in *Mister Jelly Roll* (1950).

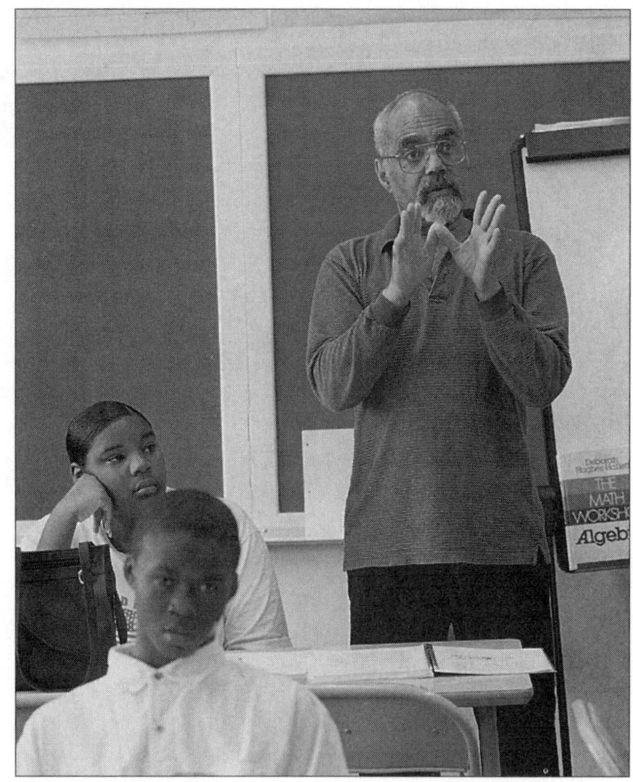

Robert Moses teaching a Jackson, Mississippi, high school math class in 1999. *(AP/Wide World Photos)*

Moses, Robert Parris (b. January 23, 1935, New York, New York): Educator and civil rights leader. Moses attended Hamilton College and later Harvard University. His mother's death, however, cut short his graduate education at the latter. Moses returned to New York City, where he taught high school mathematics.

The beginning of the student sit-in movement in 1960 attracted Moses to Atlanta, Georgia, where he became a volunteer for the Student Nonviolent Coordinating Committee (SNCC). His intellectual manner caused some to suspect—wrongly—that he was a communist. He quickly proved himself, however, and in 1961 he became SNCC's first full-time voter registration worker in the Deep South, undertaking efforts to register black voters in Mississippi. Moses's approach was to build a community base for voter registration efforts that included "freedom schools," in which African Americans could not only learn how to register to vote but also learn about current events and the ways in which community action could combat segregation and discrimination. To Moses, education was a primary weapon in the battle against discrimination.

In Mississippi, Moses directed efforts by an alliance of SNCC and other organizations to win the vote for African Americans. The areas of the civil rights struggle in which he was prominent included the 1963 Freedom Election (a mock election in which all adult African Americans could vote), the Freedom Summer of 1964, and the organization of the MISSISSIPPI FREEDOM DEMOCRATIC PARTY (MFDP), also in 1964. He accompanied the latter to the Democratic National Convention and joined in the MFDP walkout when the convention agreed to seat only two of its members.

Mystery writer Walter Mosley. *(Peter Serling/W. W. Norton)*

Moses's quiet but forceful leadership, which often exposed him to considerable personal danger, made him a legendary figure in the Civil Rights movement. Moses, however, shunned the limelight and disliked being identified as a civil rights leader. Disillusioned by politics after the MFDP was not seated by the Democratic convention, he refused to speak to white people for a brief period. In 1964 he began to use the name Robert Parris, and by 1966, he had retired to private life. For a while, he taught in Africa.

Moses returned to the United States in 1976. He studied philosophy and won a MacArthur Fellowship in 1980. He maintained his dedication to education, founding the Algebra Project, which taught higher math to young black students.

Mosley, Walter (b. January 12, 1952, Los Angeles, California): Novelist. Walter Mosley successfully combines taut, suspenseful plotting with incisive social commentary on the state of race in the United States in his novels. Owing as much to Chester HIMES and Richard WRIGHT as he does to Dashiell Hammett and Raymond Chandler, Mosley picks up a prominent strand of black LITERATURE and marries it with the setting and action of classic hard-boiled DETECTIVE FICTION.

Walter Mosley won the John Creasey Memorial Award and the Shamus Award for outstanding mystery writing and was nominated for the Edgar Award for best first novel. The key to the success of his mystery novels, however, is not a matter of plot but rather one of characterization. Set in and around South Central Los ANGELES in the late 1940's, the 1950's, and the early 1960's, *Devil in a Blue Dress* (1990), *A Red Death* (1991), *White Butterfly* (1992), and *Black Betty* (1994) explore the questionable moral landscape a black man must inhabit in a racist society. A motion picture adaptation of *Devil in a Blue Dress*, directed by Carl Franklin and starring Denzel WASHINGTON and Jennifer Beals, was released in the fall of 1995. Subsequent Easy Rawlins novels include *A Little Yellow Dog* (1996) and *Gone Fishin'* (1997).

Mosley's protagonist, Ezekiel "Easy" Rawlins, is centrally involved in cases that—because of segregationist tendencies and ongoing conflicts between white and black communities—police cannot or will not adequately investigate. His world of crooked cops, corrupt and corrupting politicians, slumming white folks, and exploitative kingpins is, ironically, more insidiously threatening than the more confrontational racism of his native HOUSTON. In true hard-boiled detective fashion, Easy travels through the unforgiving realities of his own and his community's degradation—a journey that does not leave him untouched by contradictory, or compromising impulses to lash out in rage.

A veteran of WORLD WAR II, Easy is all too familiar with the sensation of killing the enemy, an enemy who looked just as white as the men and women who call him "boy" or "son," deny him home loans, and even the dignity that service to country has afforded some of his fellow veterans. The ironies of race are everywhere: While Southern CALIFORNIA booms with real estate development, industrial growth, and the glamour of Hollywood, South Central Los Angeles wallows in despair, unemployment, and violence. This phenomenon is certainly not limited to late 1940's Los Angeles. Thus, Mosley's novels open a window onto the painful ironies of the black experience in the United States. Over the course of the four novels, Easy Rawlins fights with his own personal sense of rage and grows from bachelorhood through marriage and abandonment to fatherhood of an adoptive family founded on trust. Mosley seems to hold out hope for a similar sense of connection for the community at large.

Because his father was a great influence on his work, Walter Mosley dedicated *RL's Dream* (1995) to Leroy Mosley. The author's first novel outside of the mystery genre, it depicts the lives of displaced southerners (one is white, female, and young, the other black, male, and near death) as they re-create the South in New York City through the music of bluesman Robert (RL) JOHNSON. In 1998 and 1999 Mosley published three more novels outside the detective fiction genre, *Blue Light* (1998), *Always Outnumbered, Always Outgunned* (1998), and *Walkin' the Dog* (1999).

In 1999 Mosley donated $100,000 to TRANSAFRICA. He had become involved in supporting the group through the efforts of actor Danny GLOVER, and he served as cochair of a major TransAfrica fund-raising campaign.

Suggested Readings:

Bailey, Frankie Y. *Out of the Woodpile: Black Characters in Crime and Detective Fiction.* Westport, Conn.: Greenwood Press, 1991.

Berger. Roger A. "'The Black Dick': Race, Sexuality, and Discourse in the L.A. Novels of Walter Mosley." *African American Review* 31 (Summer, 1997): 281-294.

Crooks, Robert. "From the Far Side of the Urban Frontier: The Detective Fiction of Chester Himes and Walter Mosley." *College Literature* 22 (October, 1995): 68-90.

Mason, Theodore O., Jr. "Walter Mosley's Easy Rawlins: the Detective and Afro-American Fiction." *Kenyon Review* 14 (Fall, 1992): 173-183.

Mosley, Walter. "How Walter Mosley Discovered His Audience—and the Voice of His Fiction." Interview with Peter Hogness. *Writer's Digest* 76 (March, 1996): 8-9.

Tillery, Carolyn. "The Fiction of Black Crime: It's No Mystery." *American Visions* 12 (April/May 1997): 18-21.

"Walter Mosley." *Current Biography* 55 (September, 1994): 40-44.

Whetstone, Muriel L. "The Mystery of Walter Mosley." *Ebony* (December, 1995): 106-109.

Mossell, Gertrude Bustill (July 3, 1855, Philadelphia, Pennsylvania—January 21, 1948, Philadelphia, Pennsylvania): Journalist. Mossell edited the woman's department of *New York Age*, *Indianapolis World*, and *Woman's Era*, a national magazine for black women. She had initiated that department at *New York Age*. She published her first article, "Woman's Suffrage," in the *New York Freeman*. She often wrote about social and political matters and authored the biographical *The Work of the Afro-American Woman* (1894).

Mossell, Nathan Francis (July 27, 1856, Hamilton, Ontario, Canada—October 27, 1946, Philadelphia, Pennsylvania): Physician. Mossell was the first African American to be graduated from the University of Pennsylvania Medical School. He founded the Frederick Douglass Memorial Hospital in Philadelphia in 1895 and was president of the National Medical Association from 1907 to 1908.
See also: Medicine.

Nathan Francis Mossell. *(National Library of Medicine)*

Moten, Bennie (November 13, 1894, Kansas City, Missouri—April 2, 1935, Kansas City, Missouri): Bandleader. Benjamin "Bennie" Moten became a legendary figure in the development of big band jazz in the lower Midwest. Moten, who studied piano with disciples of Scott Joplin, led his own ragtime trio, known as B.B.& D., in 1918. He spent the majority of his bandleading career in Kansas City, from 1922 until his death. Seminal figures of jazz, such as Walter Page, Count Basie, and Ben Webster, were associated with Moten. Basie's early orchestra, formed after Moten's death, included many of the musicians who had played with Moten.

Moten's ensemble was one of the two dominant swing bands based in Kansas City, the other being the Blue Devils, led by bassist Walter Page. Additional musicians associated with Moten included his brother Buster Moten, who played accordion, singer Jimmy Rushing, trumpeters Hot Lips Page, Joe Keyes, and Ed Lewis, trombonists Eddie Durham and Dan Minor, and saxophonists Eddie Barefield, Harlan Leonard, Jack Washington, and Buster Smith.

Moten's style employed the riff device, which involved the repetition of a particular phrase and contributed to the relaxed swing feeling of the Kansas City style exhibited in such Moten arrangements as "Moten Swing" (1932). Many of Moten's riffs, which eventually were written down, were often originally the result of a "head arrangement," or the spontaneous contribution of a melodic pattern by a band member. This pattern would later become an established part of an arrangement.

Moten's recording career began in 1923,

when a small group which he led was recorded by OKeh Records, one of many recording companies promoting "race records," or recordings by black artists. By 1926 Moten was recording for the Victor label with a somewhat larger ensemble. Moten's recording career developed in the 1920's with such releases as "Elephant's Wobble/Crawdad Blues" (1923), "The New Tulsa Blues" (1927), "Moten Stomp" (1927), and "Kansas City Breakdown" (1928). During the 1930's, he recorded "When I'm Alone" (1930), "Toby/Moten Swing" (1932), "Lafayette" (1932), and "Prince of Wales" (1932).

Constance Baker Motley (right) with Coretta Scott King and Martin Luther King, Jr., at a SCLC banquet in Birmingham, Alabama, in 1965. *(AP/Wide World Photos)*

Motley, Archibald John, Jr. (October 7, 1891, New Orleans, Louisiana—January 16, 1981, Chicago, Illinois): Painter. After studying at the Art Institute of CHICAGO, where he was a Frank G. Logan Medalist and won the institute's J. N. Eisendrath Prize, Motley worked for the Illinois Federal Art Project. His works were exhibited in many institutions and galleries in the United States. His ability to work in different styles was much admired by younger generations of painters, who used his leadership to expand their own artistic horizons.
See also: Painters and illustrators.

Motley, Constance Baker (b. September 14, 1921, New Haven, Connecticut): Judge and CIVIL RIGHTS activist. As a lawyer with the National Association for the Advancement of Colored People Legal Defense and Educational Fund from 1945 to 1965, Motley won nine of her ten major civil rights cases before the U.S. SUPREME COURT. She was elected Manhattan borough president in 1965, becoming the highest-ranking elected black woman in a major American city. She was named as the first black female district judge in 1966.
See also: Judges.

Moton, Robert (August 26, 1867, Amelia County, Virginia—May 31, 1940, Capahosic, Virginia): Educator. Moton grew up in Prince Edward County, VIRGINIA, and in 1885 enrolled in HAMPTON INSTITUTE. He taught for a year in Cottontown, Virginia, before returning to Hampton and being graduated in 1890.

After graduation, Moton became commandant of the male student cadet corps at Hampton. He held this position for twenty-five years, while gradually involving himself off campus. He became active in the NATIONAL NEGRO BUSINESS LEAGUE and was a trustee of the ANNA T. JEANES FUND, an education trust. He traveled extensively raising funds, often with Booker T. WASHINGTON, whose educational ideals he shared.

In 1905 Moton married Elizabeth Hunt Harris of Williamsburg, Virginia, who died childless the following year. He married Jennie Dee Booth in 1908. She was also a graduate of Hampton and active in black women's clubs. The couple had five children, Catherine, Charlotte, Jennie, Robert, and Allen.

When Booker T. Washington died in 1915, Moton was chosen to succeed him as head of TUSKEGEE INSTITUTE. Moton held that position for twenty years, until his retirement. While continuing Washington's emphasis on vocational education, Moton led Tuskegee to begin offering bachelor's degrees in the 1920's. In a joint campaign with Hampton Institute, Moton raised five million dollars for Tuskegee's endowment.

After Booker T. Washington died in 1915, Robert Moton served as president of Tuskegee for twenty years. *(AP/Wide World Photos)*

Moton also adopted Washington's role as adviser to the federal government and to white philanthropic institutions. During WORLD WAR I, he inspected African American troops in France and spoke widely in support of liberty loans. He was instrumental in the federal government's decision to build the Tuskegee Veterans Hospital and, despite opposition from the KU KLUX KLAN, he ensured that the hospital would be staffed at all levels by African Americans. He also held an appointment on the Hoover Commission for the Mississippi Valley flood disaster and chaired the U.S. Commission on Education in Haiti.

Moton's writings include his autobiography, *Finding a Way Out* (1920), and *What the Negro Thinks*, a 1929 book dealing with racial problems more straightforwardly than either he or Washington had done previously. Moton received various honorary degrees, the Harmon Award in Race Relations, and the SPINGARN MEDAL for his work.

See also: Intellectuals and scholars.

Motown: Record company. A highly successful record and music publishing company founded by songwriter Berry GORDY, Jr., in 1959, Motown grew into one of the most profitable black-owned businesses in the United States. The name was taken from a colloquial abbreviation for "motor town," a nickname for DETROIT, MICHIGAN, the location of many automobile factories.

The phrase "the Motown sound" describes the musical style created by the musicians and producers who made the company's first popular recordings in the 1960's. Berry Gordy, who had established himself as a songwriter, was convinced by his young friend and protégé, singer William "Smokey" ROBINSON, that he needed to start a record company if he wanted to earn more money from his songs. Gordy borrowed $800 from his family in order to found Motown Records in a two-story building. Soon Smokey Robinson and the Miracles recorded Motown's first release, "Way Over There," which sold sixty thousand copies. In 1960 "Shop Around," another recording by the Miracles, was released, and it eventually sold a million copies.

Gordy's extended family became involved in the business, which soon included artist management and publishing branches. Singer Marvin GAYE, who had just married Gordy's sister Anna, eventually became one of Motown's most popular stars.

Motown Artists and Hits

The Primes, a young male singing group, and the Primettes, a trio of even younger girls who sometimes opened shows for them, were Detroit residents who became part of the Motown roster and community. The Primes were renamed the Temptations, and their first record was released. In the following year, the Primettes were renamed the SUPREMES and were signed to Motown. At first they were eclipsed by other female Motown acts such as solo artist Mary Wells and the Marvelettes, whose single "Please Mr. Postman" reached number one on the U.S. pop charts in 1961. This achievement was an important measure of status and financial success for Gordy and Motown, since the pop charts represented acceptance by the general population. By contrast, the RHYTHM AND BLUES (R&B) charts were based on record sales in African American communities.

Also in 1961, Gordy signed Steveland Morris, an eleven-year-old blind prodigy who lived in the neighborhood. Gordy gave Morris the stage name "Little Stevie WONDER." Wonder excited audiences by playing keyboards, bongos, and harmonica as well by singing in a joyous, unrestrained style. His first major hit was "Fingertips," which reached number one on the pop and R&B charts in 1963. It was a live recording of his spontaneous interactions with an audience.

Singer Stevie Wonder was given his original stage name, Little Stevie Wonder, by Motown's Berry Gordy. *(AP/Wide World Photos)*

Martha Reeves, working as a secretary at Motown, got an opportunity to record with a female group, who became the Vandellas. Her major hits for Motown were "Heat Wave" (1963) and "Dancing in the Street" (1964). Although the Supremes had been recording with only limited success for some time, their 1984 hits, "Where Did Our Love Go?" "Baby Love," and "Come See About Me," helped to establish them as one of Motown's most valuable groups. After some minor hits, the Temptations also scored big with Smokey Robinson's "My Girl," a relatively slow, sentimental song which went to number one on both the pop and R&B charts in January, 1965, followed by "Get Ready," a driving dance tune.

Throughout the 1960's, Motown remained a dominant force in American popular music, vying with the many groups of the "British Invasion" and adding even more money-making stars such as the Jackson 5, a family group featuring boy soprano Michael JACKSON. Other

Motown groups such as Jr. Walker and the All Stars, the Four Tops, and Gladys Knight and the Pips recorded hit after hit.

In 1967 Gordy started to shift more of Motown's activities to the West Coast, and the company moved to Los Angeles in 1971. During the 1970's and 1980's, Motown entered the film industry, featuring Diana Ross (who had left the Supremes in 1970) and other Motown singers in dramatic roles. Although Motown's most musically productive period was the 1960's, the company continued to expand, and its new groups such as the Commodores (and lead singer Lionel Ritchie) continued to produce hits during this period, along with mainstays Stevie Wonder, Diana Ross, the Temptations, Marvin Gaye, and others. In the 1990's, Motown added more successful artists, including Queen Latifah, Boyz II Men, 702, and 98 Degrees.

Motown founder Berry Gordy, with singer Della Reese, at the 1998 National Association of Black Owned Broadcasters awards banquet, at which Gordy was given a lifetime achievement award. *(AP/Wide World Photos)*

Musical Features

The "Motown sound" was a fascinating study in musical contrasts. It combined the driving beat of rhythm and blues with the lush orchestration of romantic fantasias, the immediacy and vitality of street music with the thoughtfulness of its cleverly constructed melodies and compositions. Most uptempo Motown songs included a bright, crisp guitar (with its treble frequencies emphasized) accenting quarter notes. Vocal music often utilized a traditional African and African American format: while a group sings short rhythmically compelling phrases in a tight homophonic texture, a soloist improvises a more elaborate, freely flowing, and embellished line—sometimes simultaneously, sometimes in a "call and response" pattern.

The electric bass was prominent in the Motown sound, and it was used to drive the music forward by adding exciting rhythmic anticipations. To make the bass lines as clear as possible, bassist James Jamerson (who played on most of Motown's hit recordings of the 1960's) plugged directly into the mixing board rather than into an amplifier, an innovation at the time. Drums (usually played by Benny Benjamin), while typically not soloing, were an important part of the musical texture, and tambourine was sometimes added on the faster pieces. Creative use was made of orchestral strings, which added a sense of urban sophistication and richness to the music, brass, which built upon the foundations for interwoven rhythmic patterns established by earlier innovators such as Count Basie, and woodwinds, especially the bold-sounding blare of the baritone sax. Even purely electronic sounds, which were rare in popular music at the time, appeared in a few pieces such as the Supremes' "Reflections."

Dance Routines
All of the major Motown groups made use of carefully choreographed dance movements, which were synchronized with both the vocal melodies and the accents of the instrumental accompaniment. The movements added a dimension of visual excitement to live and televised performances. Much of the choreography was done by Charles "Cholly" Atkins, a former tap dancing star. Atkins carefully trained his young students in the sophisticated nuances of movement that he had developed during the swing era.

Business
Motown Records grew throughout the 1960's to include the smaller labels Tamla, Gordy, VIP, and Soul. Gordy established Jobete Music as his music publishing firm. (Music publishing companies collect royalties when recordings of the songs they own are sold or played on the radio, and they handle licensing arrangements for song use in films, television, and advertising.)

By the early 1970's, Motown was taking in more than $50 million a year. Motown moved from Detroit to Los Angeles in 1972 and became involved in film and television production as well as music. Motown-produced films included *Lady Sings the Blues* (1972), starring Diana Ross, and *The Bingo Long Traveling All-Stars and Motor Kings* (1976).

Gordy sold a large interest in Motown to MCA in 1984, but he remained chairman of the board. Four years later, he sold Motown to MCA and Boston Ventures, keeping Jobete Music and his production companies. In 1997 he sold half of Jobete to EMI for $132 million. At the time, Jobete was earning roughly $15 million annually.

—*Alice Myers*

See also: Knight, Gladys, and the Pips.

Suggested Readings:
Early, Gerald L. *One Nation Under a Groove: Motown and American Culture*. Hopewell, N.J.: Ecco Press, 1995.
George, Nelson. *Where Did Our Love Go? The Rise and Fall of the Motown Sound*. New York: St. Martin's Press, 1987.
Gordy, Berry, Jr. *To Be Loved: The Music, the Magic, the Memories of Motown*. New York: Warner Books, 1994.
Singleton Berry, Raynoma. *Berry, Me, and Motown: The Untold Story*. Chicago: Contemporary Books, 1990.
Whitall, Susan. *Women of Motown: An Oral History*. New York: Avon Books, 1998.

Mound Bayou, Mississippi: Founded by black entrepreneur Isaiah T. Montgomery and

Residents of Mound Bayou preparing for a celebration of the originally all-black town's founding, in 1997. *(AP/Wide World Photos)*

several others in 1886, Mound Bayou was among the most successful of some sixty or more BLACK TOWNS built across the United States between 1865 and 1900. Incorporated as a MISSISSIPPI town in 1898, with Montgomery as the first MAYOR, Mound Bayou soon boasted sawmills, a cotton oil mill, numerous stores, churches, and a bank. While the town had only four hundred residents in 1904, it served a larger rural area with an almost exclusively African American population of some twenty-five hundred residents. In the early 1990's, Mound Bayou was still known for its black majority population and had about twenty-two hundred residents.

MOVE organization: A small, radical organization of black activists known for its uniquely communal and messianic ideology. The name MOVE is short for movement. Known as the "Family Africa" in the African American community of PHILADELPHIA, where it was formed in 1972, MOVE was founded by John Africa (Vincent Leophart) and at its peak of influence numbered approximately 150 members. By the 1980's, much of the organization's leadership had been either imprisoned or killed as the result of several dramatic confrontations with Philadelphia police, the most notorious of which involved the police bombing of the MOVE headquarters in 1985.

Political Ideology

The characteristic theme of MOVE's politics was its radical rejection of the North American inner-city lifestyle, which it viewed as an evil imposition upon African Americans. In keep-

Aftermath of the Philadelphia police department's bombing of the MOVE organization headquarters in May, 1985. *(AP/Wide World Photos)*

ing with John Africa's teachings, MOVE asserted that Africans living in the United States had become captives of a destructive technology upon which they had grown dependent. Accordingly, the only way out was a radical back-to-nature movement, and MOVE members engaged in a flamboyant pursuit of their goal from within the heart of Philadelphia's African American community.

In pursuing their beliefs, MOVE members formed a highly communal "family" and practiced a vegetarian lifestyle that stressed the benefits of eating raw foods. Aspiring to eat only food that was organically cultivated, the MOVE community took to composting all food refuse to recycle its beneficial elements back into the ground. All forms of life were venerated by MOVE members; the community never killed animals of any kind, including rodents. On the contrary, even verminous animals that strayed onto the community's land were given refuge in makeshift pens, in spite of complaints from neighbors.

Although the group defied many city ordinances, it was MOVE's refusal to send its members' children to school that best symbolized its radical confrontation with the local authorities. MOVE members insisted on freeing their community from what they saw as the larger society's indoctrination. They believed that their children could live healthier and freer lives if they were kept away from the scourge of drugs and the degradation brought on by "plastic consumerism." MOVE members abstained from using diapers on their young, viewing the practice as psychologically and physically harmful. They encouraged their children to engage in religious practices with the group's adults and became known for their dreadlocks and for boasting about their lack of reverence for frequent bathing.

The use of profanity was widespread among MOVE members and was considered symbolic of their belief that real profanity could be identified only with destructive technologies such as nuclear weapons. This became a particular source of friction with neighbors of the MOVE community, given the organization's frequent practice of setting up an outdoor speaker system to denounce local and national authorities and to berate neighbors for collaborating with the white system.

Historical Background

Many of MOVE's founding members had earlier been active in other militant organizations and were accustomed to confrontation with authorities. On March 28, 1976, several members who were celebrating the release from prison of some fellow members were confronted by multiple units of the Philadelphia police, ostensibly in response to neighbor complaints that the celebration was too loud. One member, Janine Africa, was holding a newborn infant in her arms when she was thrown to the ground by police, resulting in the death of her baby, Life Africa. The incident marked the beginning of what would be an increasingly deadly record of engagement with local authorities.

A year later, animosity between the defiant MOVE community and the city intensified, leading to the unprecedented decision of Philadelphia police to blockade the Powelton Village neighborhood, where the MOVE community had set up a virtual compound. At one point, no one was permitted to enter or leave the compound for a period of fifty days, and the area's water was shut off in an unsuccessful attempt to force MOVE members to submit. By August of 1978, a massive police assault with automatic weapons, bulldozers, fire hoses, and a battering ram was unleashed upon the MOVE compound. Arrested MOVE members were brought to trial, and nine were sentenced to from thirty to one hundred years in prison for a police casualty that many people believed was caused by police gunfire.

Various other incidents with the police led to another period of heightened tension begin-

Ramona Africa, the only adult to survive the May, 1985, assault on MOVE, speaks to the press in the midst of her lawsuit against the city a year later. *(AP/Wide World Photos)*

ning in 1982. MOVE members in the Osage Avenue area of Philadelphia formed another compound to house the children of those imprisoned as a result of the 1978 confrontation. Wooden boards were nailed across windows, and wooden bunkers reinforced with railroad ties were constructed out of materials gathered from a nearby park. Neighbors believed that MOVE was constructing underground tunnels in preparation for another long-term siege.

On May 1, 1985, an organized community group opposed to MOVE held a widely publicized press conference in which it threatened to take hostile action on its own if the city government continued to tolerate MOVE activities. Wilson Goode, Philadelphia's first black MAYOR, came under enormous pressure to resolve the MOVE problem.

The MOVE Massacre

On May 13, 1985, police sharpshooters surrounded the MOVE compound, which was now heavily fortified; the organization appeared ready to face off with the police. Later that afternoon, a PENNSYLVANIA state police helicopter approached from the air, and without warning the commander of the Philadelphia police department's bomb disposal unit dropped a bomb on the MOVE compound. Residential windows half a block away shattered as the resulting blast turned the compound's tar roof and wooden foundations into an inferno. The fire quickly raged out of control, and flames spread through sixteen adjacent row houses. Police units positioned on all sides of the block simultaneously fired upon the compound, preventing any easy escape of MOVE members. Of the thirteen people inside the MOVE compound at the time, eleven were burned to death, including five children. One woman and a young boy managed to escape the burning compound and were taken into custody. MOVE founder John Africa was among the dead. Ultimately, more than sixty homes burned completely before the blaze could be extinguished, leaving some 250 people homeless.

Widespread anger over the police bombing of MOVE materialized quickly. Even while surrounding buildings were still ablaze, a group numbering in the hundreds shouted "murderers!" at the authorities and hurled rocks and bottles at police, who were forced to use riot clubs to disperse the crowd. An ensuing political controversy emerged over the city's handling of the affair, focusing mostly on the tactics employed by the police. Even neighbors who had demanded police intervention had lost their homes in the blaze and criticized the police for failing to end the crisis peacefully.

On January 6, 1986, the only adult survivor of the MOVE massacre, Ramona (Johnson) Africa, was brought to trial on charges of aggravated assault, riot, and resisting arrest, among other related charges. Permitted to act as her own attorney in a highly public trial, she defiantly engaged the courtroom in a manner that backfired on the state prosecution; she had won considerable sympathy even from non-MOVE supporters by the time the trial ended. Nonetheless, she was ultimately found guilty of riot and conspiracy charges and was given a seven-year sentence.

Political Significance

The MOVE organization never gained a large following and essentially remained confined to the Philadelphia area. Nevertheless, it took on national significance for two reasons. It represented the unique political development of a counterculture of resistance within the African American urban community. Its radicalism was unprecedented, given the communitarian nature of the movement. Even more significant was the ferocity of official repression that was unleashed to crush the movement. That the unprecedented decision to resort to a civilian bombing was ordered by Philadelphia's first African American mayor contributed still further to the enduring significance of the MOVE confrontation.

Mayor Goode repeatedly defended the police action as necessary to prevent the city from being "held hostage" by a revolutionary terrorist group. Goode was applauded by a number of local and national figures, including Los Angeles police chief Daryl Gates and U.S. Attorney General Edwin Meese III, who called Goode's leadership "exemplary." Yet there was widespread shock and anger within the African American community over the bombing, and the Goode administration was forced within days to establish an impartial commission to investigate the incident. William H. Gray III, an African American congressman representing the area that included the MOVE compound, criticized Goode's approval of the police bombing as "gross negligence," a phrase that proved prophetic when, nearly ten months later, the independent commission concluded that the police bombing was "reckless, ill-conceived, and hastily approved" and had unjustifiably resulted in deaths and widespread property destruction.

—*Richard A. Dello Buono*

Suggested Readings:

Africa, John, "On the Move." In *Hauling Up the Morning: Writings and Art by Political Prisoners and Prisoners of War in the U.S.*, edited by Tim Blunk and Raymond Luc Levasseur. Trenton, N.J.: Red Sea Press, 1990.

Anderson, John, and Hilary Hevenor. *Burning Down the House: MOVE and the Tragedy of Philadelphia*. New York: W. W. Norton, 1987.

Assefa, Hizkias, and Paul Wahrhaftig. *Extremist Groups and Conflict Resolution: The Move Crisis in Philadelphia*. New York: Praeger, 1988.

Blackburne, Laura. "A Framework for Analyzing the Move Conflict." *Conflict Resolution Notes* 4 (September, 1986): 11-12.

Bowser, Charles W. *Let the Bunker Burn: The Final Battle with MOVE*. Philadelphia: Camino Books, 1989.

Boyette, Michael, and Randi Boyette. *"Let It Burn!": The Philadelphia Tragedy*. Chicago: Contemporary Books, 1989.

Harry, Margot. *Attention, Move! This Is America!* Chicago: Banner Press, 1987.

Wagner-Pacifici, Robin E. *Discourse and Destruction: The City of Philadelphia Versus MOVE*. Chicago: University of Chicago Press, 1994.

Moynihan Report: In July, 1965, newspapers throughout the United States began to carry stories about a report that had just been submitted to President Lyndon B. Johnson. The report, which dealt with the structure of African American families and their problems, had been written by Daniel Patrick Moynihan, Johnson's assistant secretary of labor. Moynihan's analysis, which became widely known simply as the Moynihan Report, made a great impact on the ongoing debate about CIVIL RIGHTS and what U.S. policy should be toward minority families.

Why the Report Was Issued

When Lyndon Johnson became president in 1963, he made the passage of civil rights laws a high priority of his administration. Passage of the 1964 Civil Rights Act outlawing RACIAL DISCRIMINATION in housing and public facilities, and the VOTING RIGHTS ACT OF 1965 was speeded by Johnson's resolve. Despite the impact of these laws in overturning legalized segregation, however, the United States was still fraught with racial tension.

In a speech at HOWARD UNIVERSITY, Johnson announced he was convening a conference of civil rights leaders at the White House in the fall of 1965 to discuss what steps needed to be taken on the path to equality for all citizens. So as to have a definite body of materials to discuss at the conference, the president had earlier appointed a commission to prepare a report. This study group had Moynihan as its chairman. In July, 1965, this group produced a seventy-eight-page report entitled *The Negro Family: The Case for National Action*.

The purpose of the report was not to suggest solutions but rather to describe what the study group perceived as problems. The suggestion of solutions was supposed to be the task of the White House conference. Because Moynihan's analysis was a report to a conference and not a policy statement by the government, it was officially a confidential document that was not immediately published in its entirety. Newspaper accounts of the content of the report were thus incomplete and sometimes inaccurate.

What the Report Said

President Johnson said the goal of the report was to develop suggestions that would give "twenty million Negroes the same chance as every other American to learn and grow, to work and share in society, to develop their abilities—physical, mental, and spiritual—and to pursue their individual happiness." The report assumed that mere equality of opportunity would not yield complete equality for blacks for a long time. This condition, the report concluded, was likely to produce more riots such as those that had erupted in New York, NEW JERSEY, CHICAGO, and PHILADELPHIA in 1964. To avoid future violence, steps needed to be taken to help blacks achieve equality of results, the president noted.

Daniel Patrick Moynihan was President Lyndon Johnson's assistant secretary of labor when he undertook his investigation of African American social problems. *(Library of Congress)*

The area identified by the report as weakest, and the most in need of help, was the African American family. The opening words of the report were "at the heart of the deterioration of the fabric of Negro society is the deterioration of the Negro family. It is the fundamental weakness of the Negro community at the present time."

Historically, the report noted, the roots of the weak black family began with SLAVERY. Under slavery, no family stability was possible, since family members could be separated by sale at the pleasure of the slaveowner. Generally, state laws did not consider marriages between slaves to be binding, so there was no legal legitimacy for black families. The RECONSTRUCTION period brought liberty to the former slaves but did not bring equality. Instead, the development of racial segregation emphasized the concept of black inferiority and pressured blacks to be docile merely in order to survive. In the twentieth century, many African Americans left the rural areas where they had traditionally lived, especially in the South, and moved to urban centers, usually in the North.

The report argued that this abrupt shift from rural to urban life had further weakened the traditional base of values in black family life. In these urban settings, the number of children born to African American families made the families so large that even good wages could not provide an adequate living. When a family was forced to go on welfare, family members usually found themselves dealing with female social workers—a fact that further demoralized black men, as this was often perceived to weaken their status. Finally, welfare laws favored aid to families where no able-bodied men were present; African American men thus were subtly encouraged to abandon their families so that their wives and children could get public assistance.

All these factors, the report said, had combined to lead to "a fundamental fact of Negro American family life," the reversal of traditional roles for husbands and wives, creating a matriarchal society. The absence of a strong father figure, the report stated, caused black male children to "flounder and fail." It was noted that young male blacks "are seldom in situations where they have as role models people in skilled occupations."

The report considered the problems of black families to be so serious, and the implications for the nation so dire, that the problem had to be addressed immediately, because it might already be out of control. It was the conclusion of the report that "government policy should enhance the stability of the Negro American family."

Reaction to the Report

Reaction to the report was generally negative. The leaders of the Civil Rights movement felt that Moynihan had given opponents of their cause ammunition with which to attack blacks in their quest for civil rights. This attitude became obvious when the White House Conference on Civil Rights met in November, 1965. To the great disappointment of Johnson, the conclusions of the report about the need for black family stability were dismissed virtually without debate.

Various speakers at the meeting bitterly attacked Moynihan's conclusions. These speakers argued that the report exaggerated black defects. For example, although the report found 38 percent of black families to be headed by women, it made no mention of the 62 percent that followed the traditional male-headed pattern. It was also argued that the report held that the black family was weak primarily because it was different from white families. Critics of the report noted that though it asserted that patriarchal families are stronger than matriarchal ones, no evidence to support this claim was presented. Indeed, Wayne Vasey, the dean of Washington University's School of Social Work, noted that to treat black families as pathological was "to ignore that there can be a lot of strength in a matriarchal pattern."

None of these critics of the report challenged the facts amassed in the document. None denied that many black families faced difficulties. It was accepted that half of all black families were basically middle-class but that the other half were in desperate straits. Civil rights leaders agreed that a new departure was needed to lead the United States to the fulfillment of the promise of equality, but few believed that the report was that departure.

Moynihan defended his conclusions by arguing that the critics of the report were themselves middle-class and thus did not understand the impact of GHETTO life on the family. Moynihan himself came from a ghetto background, and he claimed that he understood the impact such conditions had. This defense did not satisfy critics, who continued to argue that the report placed the blame in the wrong place. Critics contended that the black family was the victim of social wrongs, not the source of these wrongs. James FARMER, the national director of the CONGRESS OF RACIAL EQUALITY (CORE), said in response to Moynihan's findings that "it has been the fatal error of American society for three hundred years to ultimately blame the roots of poverty and violence in the Negro community on Negroes themselves."

The Moynihan Report solved no problems and stimulated no legislation. It did, however, provoke a great deal of discussion and interest in black families and urban ghetto conditions. In that sense, it made a positive contribution.

—*Michael R. Bradley*

See also: Black matriarchy myth.

Suggested Readings:

Bennett, William J. "Reflections on the Moynihan Report Thirty Years Later." *The American Enterprise* 6 (January/February, 1995): 28-32.

Billingsley, Andrew. *Black Families in White America*. Englewood Cliffs, N.J.: Prentice-Hall, 1968.

Bracey, John H., Jr., August Meier, and Elliott Rudwick, eds. *Black Matriarchy: Myth or Reality?* Belmont, Calif.: Wadsworth, 1971.

Ginsburg, Carl. *Race and Media: The Enduring Life of the Moynihan Report*. New York: Institute for Media Analysis, 1989.

U.S. Department of Labor. Office of Policy Planning and Research. *The Negro Family: The Case for National Action*. Washington, D.C.: U.S. Government Printing Office, 1965.

Williams, Walter E., et al. "Sex, Families, Race, Poverty, Welfare: A Symposium Revisiting the Moynihan Report at Its Thirtieth Anniversary." *The American Enterprise* 6 (January/February, 1995): 33-37.

Zollar, Ann C. *A Member of the Family: Strategies for Black Family Continuity*. Chicago: Nelson-Hall, 1985.

Muhammad, Elijah (Elijah Poole; October 7, 1897, Sandersville, Georgia—February 25, 1975, Chicago, Illinois) Leader of the NATION OF ISLAM. Elijah Muhammad represented an important and continuing theme in African American culture, namely the idea that the future of the black community depended on its capacity to determine its own destiny. According to Muhammad, blacks were to accomplish this by separating from the control and influences of white society. Muhammad also altered this historic theme by rejecting the back-to-Africa emphases of earlier African American separatists. Separatism was to occur, instead, in the creation of a distinct black nation on the territory of the United States.

Early Life

Elijah Muhammad was born Elijah Poole in Sandersville, GEORGIA, in 1897, one of thirteen children of poor tenant farmers who had been slaves. His formal education was limited, since he was required to spend much of his childhood working in the fields. He left Georgia at the age of sixteen and traveled randomly, finally settling in DETROIT in 1923. During the GREAT DEPRESSION of the 1930's, he experienced a life-changing encounter when he met and became a follower of Wallace FARD, the founder of the Nation of Islam. Fard encouraged Poole to preach the Nation of Islam's doctrine, open new meeting places, and alter his "slave" name. As a result of Fard's influence, Poole took the name Elijah Muhammad, a name that symbolized his Muslim affiliation and rejection of white culture. He was also appointed supreme minister of the Nation of Islam.

Leadership of the Nation of Islam

Elijah Muhammad's distinctive ideological emphases emerged after Fard mysteriously disappeared in 1934. Muhammad not only claimed to be the messenger of Allah to the Nation of Islam, assuming Fard's organizational leadership, but also reinterpreted Fard. He preached that Fard had been Allah in disguise and had shared with Muhammad secrets known to no one else. Muhammad thus presented himself as the sole custodian of Fard's revelation to the African American community.

This newfound dominance over the religion's adherents, however, did not translate into broader social acceptance. In 1934 Muhammad was arrested for sending his children to a Nation of Islam school rather than to public schools. He lived as a fugitive from 1935 to 1942 and was convicted of encouraging resistance to the draft in 1942; he subsequently spent three years in jail. The effect of Muhammad's absence on the Nation of Islam was organizational disarray, and membership in the religion plummeted. Earlier levels of membership were not regained until MALCOLM X offered his leadership skills to the Nation of Islam and became Muhammad's most visible and effective spokesperson in the 1950's and 1960's. During this era, the Nation of Islam maintained a clear ideology and espoused a workable program.

Belief in Separatism

Muhammad's leadership allowed adherents, commonly called "Black Muslims," to interpret the failures of structural assimilation in American society. The perceived impossibility of an integrated society was explained as both the negative work of whites and a positive possibility for blacks. For Muhammad, separatism was not synonymous with segregation; it was not the result of an imposition by whites but a choice that blacks made in order preserve their identity. While segregation was forced, separatism was the willed means by which the group could determine its own future.

This idea of a positive social divorce from the larger society can be traced historically to the AMERICAN COLONIZATION SOCIETY in the early 1800's and, later, to Marcus GARVEY's back-to-Africa movement of the early twentieth century. Garvey had a direct influence on Muhammad's thought; Muhammad, however, significantly distinguished between being separated and returning to Africa. He refused to romanticize Africa; he interpreted black Americans as an Asiatic rather than an African race and developed a reparations scheme according to which the U.S. government would offer several southern states to the Nation of Islam as territory in which to form a separate geographic and political entity.

The practical beginnings of this separatism can be found in the Nation of Islam's alternative institutions: a university, schools, farms, small businesses, and houses of worship, all of which function as concrete evidences of the ideology of separatism. Muhammad sought not only to alter historic separatist world-

Elijah Muhammad addresses a Chicago assembly of the Nation of Islam in February, 1978, as boxer Muhammad Ali (lower left) listens. *(AP/Wide World Photos)*

views but also to establish institutions that could give practical force to his philosophy. Muhammad's structures differed from many black sects and cults in that they included economic and educational enterprises and offered Nation of Islam followers a sense of community.

Doctrine

Elijah Muhammad's strong sense of community among blacks emphasized a stringent socialization process. Black Muslims made public declarations of their faith, regularly attended temple meetings, observed dietary regulations, and were committed to obeying specific ethical rules. Black Muslims could not use tobacco, alcohol, or narcotics, could not gamble, and were reprimanded if they lied, stole, or were discourteous.

The effort toward community was especially rigid in regulations regarding the sexes. Women were particularly respected in Muhammad's ideology; they were considered the most valuable property of the Nation of Islam and deserving of respect from men. Muhammad abhorred the practice of women heading households. He claimed that the black man would never experience self-worth until he took responsibility for the protection, care, and oversight of women within the home. Adultery was firmly denounced by Muhammad. The home was to be a male-led institution in which women and children were secure, safe, and appropriately led. The stable family ethic related to other of Muhammad's institutional emphases: The home would be secure only as better educations were acquired, economic ventures were successful, superior employment was attained, and values were practiced that avoided criminal acts and immoral behavior. Muhammad's family-oriented moral system interrelated with and reinforced the ethics of the entire Nation of Islam community.

The ethics proclaimed by Muhammad were in stark contrast to his interpretation of the white community's immoralities. The collective "white man" was perceived as the devil and the incarnation of evil; whites, Muhammad said, could not provide blacks with any alternatives to antagonism. This was not because of special historical events, according to Muhammad, but because devils could only offer a society that was racist by nature. It was out of this structural racism that the exploitation and denigration of the black person occurred. Muhammad particularly emphasized the practical results of this evil: Perpetual discrimination against blacks provided the necessary labor for the functioning of the white-directed economy. Only whites could benefit from such a system, while blacks had to separate from it if they were to regain their identities and self-esteem. In addition, Muhammad argued, separation from white immorality was a necessity if blacks were to function effectively as authentic humans.

The teachings of Elijah Muhammad gained wide exposure when Malcolm X was interviewed on national television and his statements were discussed in the white media. White society perceived the Muslim antipathy toward it as a threat. Many African Americans, however, were attracted by Muhammad's ideologies and found them consistent with their interpretations of their own life experiences. Some also found Muhammad's demands for sacrifice, discipline, and self-denial appealing as a means of addressing social frustration and of establishing an alternative lifestyle. While the exact membership figures for the Nation of Islam have always been kept secret, it is probable that they were highest when Malcolm X was Muhammad's main spokesperson. The influence of Muhammad's ideas has extended far beyond official membership in mosques; the themes of disjunction and separate group control have been dispersed among groups not affiliated with the organization.

Legacy

Since Elijah Muhammad's death in 1975, his legacy has continued in two distinct ways. His son, Wallace Deen MUHAMMAD (also known as Iman Wareet Deen Muhammad), established the American Muslim Mission, which had between 135 and 145 local mosques before it was decentralized in 1985. The mission's theology was close to that of the worldwide Muslim faith, and it deemphasized Elijah Muhammad's teachings that African Americans are a separate nation. It was through Minister Louis FARRAKHAN, who disassociated from Wallace Deen Muhammad, that the ideology of Elijah Muhammad was maintained. Farrakhan's reiteration of traditional Black Muslim orthodoxies includes interpretations of collective white devilry and the need for African Americans to control their destiny through separation.

—*William T. Osborne*

See also: Islam; Religion.

Suggested Readings:

Clegg, Claude A. *An Original Man: The Life and Times of Elijah Muhammad*. New York: St. Martin's Press, 1997.

Essien-Udom, Essien U. *Black Nationalism: A Search for an Identity in America*. New York: Dell, 1964.

Lincoln, C. Eric. *The Black Muslims in America*. Rev. ed. Westport, Conn.: Greenwood Press, 1982.

Marsh, Clifton E. *From Black Muslims to Muslims: The Transition from Separatism to Islam, 1930-1980*. Metuchen, N.J.: Scarecrow Press, 1984.

Muhammad, Elijah. *Message to the Blackman in America*. Chicago: Muhammad Mosque of Islam Number 2, 1965.

Perry, Bruce. *Malcolm: The Life of a Man Who Changed Black America*. Barrytown, N.Y.: Station Hill Press, 1991.

Muhammad, Wallace D. (also known as Imam Warith Deen Muhammad; b. October 30, 1933, Detroit, Michigan): Religious leader. The son of Muslim leader Elijah MUHAMMAD (formerly Elijah Poole) and Clara Muhammad, Muhammad had vocational training in welding and attended the Muhammad University of Islam. Following the death of his father in 1975, Muhammad became the leader of the NATION OF ISLAM. He changed the name of the organization to the World Community of Islam in the West (1975) and again, in 1980, to the American Muslim Mission. Muhammad also brought about doctrinal and structural changes in the American Muslim Mission.

Before he succeeded his father, the organization had preached strict racial separation and the establishment of an African American nation, with a moral obligation on the part of the United States to support the new nation economically until it could survive on its own. Muhammad fought against separatism in religion by preaching that God is nonracial and should not be given a racial image; he also opened the American Muslim Mission to white membership. He changed the name of the journal *Muhammad Speaks* to *Bilalian News*.

Muhammad's leadership brought the American Muslim Mission toward Orthodox Islam and to full acceptance and recognition by the Islamic headquarters in Mecca, Saudi Arabia, and by international Islamic organizations. He conducted pilgrimages to Mecca and improved the image and welfare of the American Muslim Mission by operating educational institutions, businesses, and hospitals. Muhammad himself operated mostly as an independent Muslim lecturer and as a scholar of Arabic and Islamic studies.

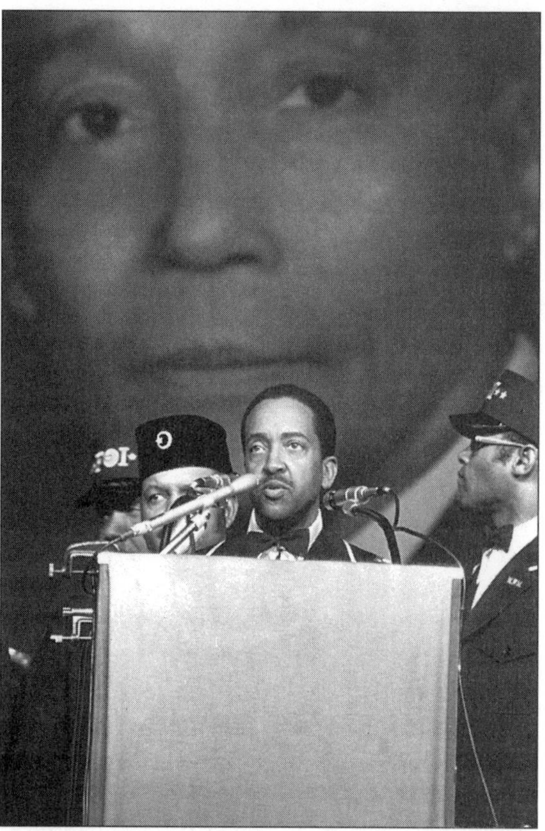
Wallace D. Muhammad speaking under a huge picture of his father shortly after succeeding him as spiritual leader of the Nation of Islam in early 1975. *(AP/Wide World Photos)*

In 1985 Muhammad further reorganized the American Muslim Mission by decentralizing it, removing himself as the leader of the national organization, and allowing local centers and their imams (ministers) to guide and foster the affairs of each local temple, mosque, or congregation. Although he remained the minister of the PHILADELPHIA Temple, he also maintained the CHICAGO headquarters. It was there that the official journal of the American Muslim Mission, *Muslim Journal*, was published.

In the 1980's and 1990's, there were two major African American leaders of Muslim groups in the United States, Wallace Muhammad and Louis Abdul Farrakhan. Farrakhan had been a figure in the original Nation of Islam under Elijah Muhammad's leadership. He left the group after Wallace Muhammad changed the direction and name of the organization. Farrakhan founded a new group in 1978 and named it the Nation of Islam. In a number of speaking engagements in the 1990's, Muhammad was highly critical of Farrakhan and warned his audiences of following a leader with what he saw as messianic ambitions. In the late 1990's, however, there were signs that relations between Muhammad and Farrakhan—which had long been cool and sometimes hostile—were becoming more cordial.

See also: Islam; Religion.

Muhammad Speaks: Tabloid-sized newspaper published by the NATION OF ISLAM during the era when Elijah MUHAMMAD was the spiritual leader of the organization.

Malcolm X holds a copy of *Muhammad Speaks* at a Nation of Islam rally in New York City in July, 1963. *(AP/Wide World Photos)*

Muhammad Speaks was first published in May, 1960, in the Harlem section of New York City. Originally it was a monthly newspaper that sold for fifteen cents. Later it was published in a printing shop in Chicago owned by the Nation of Islam (Black Muslims). It also became a weekly newspaper which sold for a quarter. The paper was named after Elijah Muhammad, who was the leader of the Nation of Islam from the mid 1930's until his death in 1975.

Under the leadership of Elijah Muhammad, the Nation of Islam followed a doctrine which combined elements of Islam with a belief in black separatism and self-sufficiency. The newspaper described itself as a paper dedicated to "Freedom, Justice and Equality for the so-called Negro" and stated, "The Earth Belongs to Allah." *Muhammad Speaks* published news of interest to African Americans in general and members of the Nation of Islam in particular. It also carried advertisements for businesses that served the African American community. Each issue of the paper also had a full page devoted to the program of the Nation of Islam as espoused by Elijah Muhammad, who was called the Messenger of Allah. The program included a list of what the Muslims wanted and what they believed. Both these lists evolved over time.

In addition to serving as an information source for the Nation of Islam *Muhammad Speaks* also was a major source of revenue for the movement. Members of the organization would aggressively sell the paper to African Americans in the communities where the movement was active. At one time the paper had a circulation estimated to be over 600,000 through subscriptions and street sales. This figure made it the most widely read paper in the African American community.

Following the death of Elijah Muhammad in 1975, his son Wallace Muhammad became leader of the Nation of Islam. Soon thereafter, Wallace dropped the movement's traditional demand for a separate state for African Americans and ceased to list the demands of the Nation of Islam in every issue of the paper. In October, 1976, the Nation of Islam under Wallace Muhammad ceased to exist when he christened his organization the World Community of Islam in the West and aligned it with the orthodox nonracial policies of contemporary Islam.

In 1978 Louis Farrakhan resurrected the traditional beliefs of the movement and reestablished the Nation of Islam. Farrakhan revived the movement's paper, renaming it *The Final Call*. This paper once again published Muslim beliefs and demands.

While the Nation of Islam has had numerous publications during its history, no other has had the impact or circulation of *Muhammad Speaks*. For African Americans living in the urban areas of the United States in the 1960's and 1970's, it was a well-known publication which provided the black community with information and a sense of identity. For the Nation of Islam, *Muhammad Speaks* was not only its propaganda organ but also a major source of income.

—*William V. Moore*

See also: Religious publishing.

Mulattoes: Persons with one black and one white parent, or, as popularly construed, people with mixed black and white ancestry. Although skin colors vary widely, mulattoes are marked by any color lighter than ebony. The amount of sexual exploitation by white masters of black female slaves is evident from the large numbers of mulattoes that could be found on southern PLANTATIONS.

See also: Biracial and mixed-race children; Miscegenation.

Murphy, Eddie (b. April 3, 1961, Brooklyn, New York): FILM actor and comedian. By the 1990's, Murphy's films had grossed more than one billion dollars in worldwide sales, making Murphy among the most celebrated and powerful of African American entertainers. As a television performer, stand-up comedian, singer, actor, writer, producer, and entrepreneur, Murphy emerged as a leading figure in the so-called African American renaissance in the popular arts. Murphy headed a production company that supported the creative work of other African American performers and writers; moreover, his meteoric rise to superstar status demonstrated an appeal that goes beyond once-rigid ethnic boundaries.

Early Life

Edward Regan "Eddie" Murphy was the son of a New York policeman and his wife, a telephone operator. When Murphy was three years old, his father died; six years later, his mother remarried, and the family moved to Roosevelt, a predominantly African American community on Long Island. At the age of fifteen, Murphy began to perform at a local youth center. As a young stand-up comedian, he imitated the street-wise and often profane satiric comedy of his hero, Richard PRYOR. Murphy soon began to perform at other Long Island comedy clubs, earning between twenty-five and fifty dollars a performance. Continually refining his act in the basement of the family home, Murphy began to incorporate more of his own material into his act, adding improvisations and his own brand of insult comedy. In less than two years, Murphy had become a regular at such Manhattan comedy clubs as the Improvisation and the Comic Strip. In 1980, at the age of nineteen, Murphy faced a choice: to enroll at Nassau Community College to study theater or to attend an audition for an opening on NBC's *Saturday Night Live*.

Television and Film Beginnings

After six auditions, Murphy was finally given the role of featured player on the irreverent comedy series; he made his first appearance on the show on November 15, 1980. In January of 1981, he was made a permanent member of the cast, earning $4,500 an episode. *Saturday Night Live* was the perfect vehicle for Murphy to showcase his impressive comedic talents, and he quickly gained a national following. The youthful Murphy's blend of infectious charm, witty improvisations, and sharp-edged satire revived the show's flagging ratings and made his gallery of comic impersonations a central feature of the show's popularity.

Murphy's comic creations became part of the national television culture: Mr. Robinson, a ghetto-like version of Mr. Rogers; Tyrone

Green, a convict and white-hating author; Little Richard Simmons, a bizarre synthesis of the exercise personality Richard Simmons and the black musician Little Richard; Raheem Abdul Muhammad, an aggressive film critic; and Velvet Jones, an exaggerated and stereotypical pimp. Murphy also parodied such leading black figures as Bill COSBY, James BROWN, Stevie WONDER, Michael JACKSON, and South African bishop Desmond Tutu.

As a result of his phenomenal popularity, Murphy was able to make the transition from television to film in less than two years. In December, 1982, he made his film debut in the action comedy *48 HRS.* Playing opposite Nick Nolte, Murphy impressed both audiences and critics with his easy confidence and comic ability. By capitalizing on those same talents that had made him a television star, Murphy's performance guaranteed both the critical and popular success of the film and of his future career in films. His demonstrated popularity in *48 HRS.* would lead Murphy away from television and into the high-profile world of American cinema.

The Growth of a Superstar

Murphy's next film was the John Landis comedy *Trading Places* (1983). Similar in structure to *48 HRS.*, with Murphy again playing costar to a white lead, this sophisticated social comedy of manners once again highlighted Murphy's astonishingly varied comic resources. Not until the 1984 release of *Beverly Hills Cop*, however, did Murphy truly emerge as one of the biggest box-office attractions of the 1980's. Produced by Don Simpson and Jerry Bruckheimer and directed by Martin Brest, the film provided Murphy with his first starring role: Murphy himself would be responsible for the success or failure of the film. As the hip, fast-talking, and likable DETROIT detective Axel Foley, Murphy gave the performance of a mature and polished comic actor. Playing in just over two thousand theaters, the film grossed

Eddie Murphy's acting career rose to a new level when he created the character of Detroit police officer Axel Foley in *Beverly Hills Cop* in 1984. *(Arkent Archive)*

$19.8 million in five days; after twenty-three days, the film had grossed $64.5 million, making it Paramount's highest-grossing winter release in history. After only three films, Murphy had established himself as one of Hollywood's most powerful performers.

In 1986 Murphy starred in *The Golden Child*, a rather uninspired action-adventure film that bordered on the whimsical. *Beverly Hills Cop II* was released in 1987; opening in a record-breaking 2,326 theaters, the film took in the largest single-day earnings in cinema history—$9.7 million. Although the film was reviewed far more critically than the original, the sequel grossed more than $33 million in four days. Murphy's exclusive contract with Paramount in August, 1987, signed fast on the heels of this huge hit, guaranteed Murphy creative and financial control over all his future film projects.

Box-Office Hits

The 1987 film of Murphy's raunchy stand-up routine, *Eddie Murphy Raw*, proved another commercial success, although a number of critics suggested that Murphy fell considerably short of the genius of Richard Pryor. *Coming to America*, released in the summer of 1988, reunited Murphy with director John Landis and demonstrated the entertainer's growing maturity. Echoing some of the romantic comedies of the 1930's, this romantic fairy tale highlighted Murphy's talents as a film actor. The film also illustrated Murphy's commitment to the use of African American performers who in the past were marginalized by Hollywood filmmakers; the film features such African American actors as John Amos, James Earl Jones, Madge Sinclair, and Arsenio Hall.

In 1989 Murphy's production company produced *What's Alan Watching?*, a highly innovative television comedy, for CBS. The end of the decade saw Murphy release two more films: *Harlem Nights* (1989), which Murphy wrote, produced, and directed, and *Another 48 HRS.* (1990). Both were box-office successes, but both were also the subject of some very hostile reviews. In *Boomerang* (1992), Murphy was cast as a suave marketing executive who meets his match when he falls in love with his new female boss. Although the film succeeded in giving Murphy a new image as a romantic leading man, some critics were offended by what they saw as the script's sexist themes. Other Murphy films in the 1990's included *Vampire in Brooklyn* (1995), *The Nutty Professor* (1996), in which he played more than five roles, and *Dr. Doolittle* (1998). In 1999 he appeared in *Life* and *Bowfinger*; in the latter he costarred with Steve Martin.

Critical Ambivalence

Murphy always received negative critical commentaries as well as accolades. His critics identified a number of aspects of Murphy's comic and filmic vision that they found troubling: his apparent hostility toward women, his lack of interest in exploring social or political issues, his unrelenting profanity, his insensitive treatment of homosexuals, and his seeming endorsement of a new African American stereotype.

Yet Murphy's accomplishments are enormous. He successfully marketed his considerable personal charm and likability in a number of ventures outside his usual film projects. He produced best-selling comedy albums and even recorded music albums, one of which, *So Happy* (1989), proved quite successful. He became one of the most popular performers in America, appealing to urban and rural, African American and white audiences alike. As a business figure, Murphy led his production company into the television market, producing the series *The Royal Family*, and he bought the rights to August Wilson's acclaimed drama *Fences*. In 1999 his company helped to produce the claymation program *The PJs*. Other projects with which Murphy was involved as producer included the films *Life* and *Vampire in Brooklyn*; for the latter, he also was involved in creating the story.

—*Michael John McDonough*

See also: Comedy and humor; Comics, stand-up.

Suggested Readings:

Allen, Bonnie. "Eddie Murphy: Serious Business." *Essence* (December, 1988): 44.

Collier, Arlene. "Eddie Murphy." *Ebony* (July, 1985): 40.

Grossberger, Lewis. "Eddie: The Unauthorized, Unexpurgated, and Unsolicited Biography." *Esquire* (December, 1985): 335.

Mitchell, Elvis. "The Prince of Paramount: Eddie Murphy." *Interview* (September, 1987): 60.

Murphy, Eddie. "Eddie Murphy: The Rolling Stone Interview." *Rolling Stone* (August 24, 1989): 50.

Sanello, Frank. *Eddie Murphy: The Life and Times of a Comic on the Edge*. Secaucus, N.J. : Carol, 1997.

Murphy, Isaac (Isaac Burns; April 16, 1856, Frankfort, Kentucky—February 12, 1896, Lexington, Kentucky): Jockey. Murphy won his first of three Kentucky Derbys in 1884, riding Buchanon. He also won in 1890 and 1891. His most famous race came in 1890, in a match between Salvator and Tenny. Murphy rode Salvator, while Snapper Garrison rode Tenny in one of the most publicized races of the late nineteenth century, amid debates of whether Murphy or Garrison, a white man, was the better jockey. Murphy won in a head-to-head finish. Murphy was victorious on 628 of 1,412 mounts. He was named to the Jockey's Hall of Fame in 1956.

Murray, George Washington (September 22, 1853, near Rembert, South Carolina—April 21, 1926, Chicago, Illinois): U.S. representative from South Carolina. Born into slavery and orphaned by the time of the Emancipation Proclamation, Murray took advantage of postwar opportunities for education and attended both the University of South Carolina and the State Normal Institute at Columbia, receiving his degree in 1876. After graduation, Murray returned to Sumter County to work as a farmer, schoolteacher, and lecturer for the Colored Farmers' Alliance.

Murray's efforts as local county chairman of the Republican Party were rewarded when he was appointed as customs inspector for the port of Charleston in 1890. That year, he ran unsuccessfully for the Republican nomination to Congress from the Seventh District. In 1892 he ran again and won the nomination. Although his election victory was jeopardized by the "eight-ballot box" rule—a discriminatory practice designed to reduce black voting—the state board of election canvassers declared Murray the winner over his Democratic opponent.

Murray took office on March 4, 1893, and was appointed to the House Committee on Education. He fought against Democratic efforts to annul Reconstruction laws safeguarding blacks' right to vote and highlighted black achievements by providing Congress with a partial list of black-held patents for inventions (including patents held by Murray himself for agricultural tools). He ran for reelection in 1894 in the newly reapportioned First District and was defeated. Murray appealed to the state board of election canvassers, which rejected his appeal. The House Committee on Elections conducted its own investigation and declared Murray the winner. He officially commenced his second term on June 4, 1896, and was made a member of the House Committee on Expenditures in addition to his previous committee assignment.

A state constitutional convention revised South Carolina's 1868 constitution and instituted residency requirements, poll taxes, literacy tests, and other measures designed to disfranchise black citizens. Reduced black registration and a divided state Republican Party combined to defeat Murray's bid for a third term in 1896. After his loss, Murray returned to farming. In 1905 he was convicted of forgery in a contract dispute with farm tenants and moved to Chicago, Illinois, to avoid the mandatory sentence of three years of hard labor. In Chicago, Murray became active in local politics and authored two books on race relations.

See also: Congress members; Politics and government.

Murray, Pauli (November 20, 1910, Baltimore, Maryland—July 1, 1985, Pittsburgh, Pennsylvania): Civil rights activist and cleric. Murray was active in the campaigns for

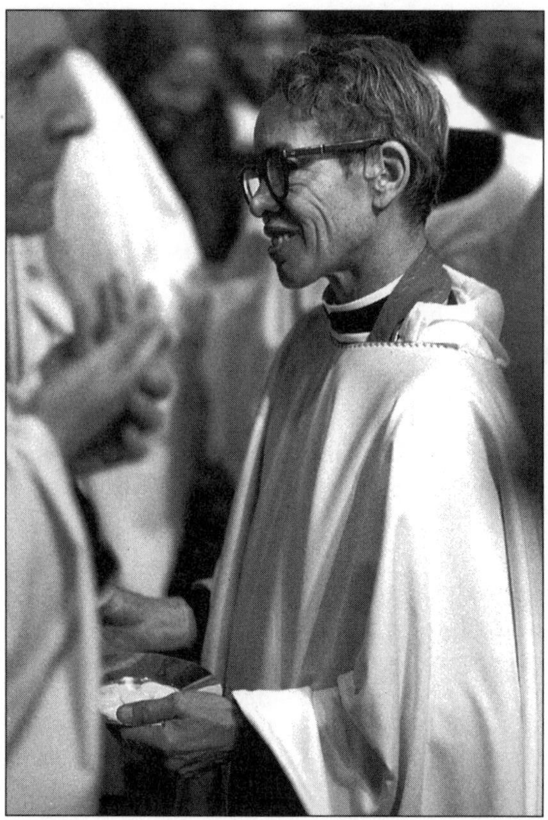

Pauli Murray at her ordination as an Episcopal priest in early 1977. *(AP/Wide World Photos)*

women's rights and civil rights. She served as deputy attorney general of CALIFORNIA in 1946 and taught law at Brandeis and Boston Universities. She helped found the National Organization for Women and, in 1977, was the first African American woman to be ordained as an EPISCOPALIAN priest. Murray was also a writer; she published nonfiction, fiction, and poetry.

Museum programs: Every region and nearly every state of the country has African American historic landmarks, including museums, houses, gravesites, colleges, and monuments. Each offers an opportunity for people of all ages and backgrounds to look into different aspects and time periods of the African American past, beginning with SLAVERY and progressing through the CIVIL RIGHTS movement to more current events.

The Midwest

The Henry Ford Museum and Greenfield Village is located in Dearborn, MICHIGAN. An African American Inventor's museum is found there along with three historic building sites that are interpreted in a village scene. The village contains the Hermitage Plantation Slave Houses (1850), the Mattox Farmhouse (1930), and the George Washington CARVER Memorial Cabin with exhibits depicting Carver's life from 1865 to 1943. The intention of the village is to depict the lives of African Americans up through the 1940's.

The city of DETROIT, MICHIGAN, is filled with the life stories of its large African American population. The Detroit Historical Museum established a program that brings the past to life through several individual tours, including one that traces the Detroit stations of the UNDERGROUND RAILROAD, another that discusses Detroit's role as a destination for waves of settlers moving northward during the "GREAT MIGRATION" of the early twentieth century, and an interdisciplinary heritage tour of Detroit designed for high school students. The museum also hosts African American cultural events and workshops for people of all ages.

Businessman Berry GORDY, Jr., took a gamble in the 1950's when he decided to open a recording business called Hitsville, U.S.A., in Detroit. Gordy wanted to create a new urban music that would appeal to young black listeners and attract white listeners as well. In 1958 he finally found the sound he was looking for in singer-songwriter Smokey ROBINSON and his group, the Miracles. The group's 1959 song, "Shop Around," shot up to number two on the nation's popular music charts. Soon after, Gordy changed the name of his record company to MOTOWN. In 1971 Gordy moved to LOS ANGELES, but the history of Motown remains in Detroit in the same building where the Four Tops, the Temptations, Mary Wells, the Supremes, Marvin Gaye, and many other famous musicians recorded. The Motown Museum has mementos of the famous stars and has been restored to look as it did in the 1960's when Motown was at the height of its popularity.

The Indiana community of Fountain City was the home of white abolitionist Levi Coffin and was considered the "Grand Central Station" of the Underground Railroad. With the cooperation of other residents in the area, Coffin aided several thousand slaves in gaining their freedom. Harriet Beecher Stowe was a great admirer of Coffin and refers to him in her book, Uncle Tom's Cabin (1851). Coffin's house has been restored to its appearance during 1840's and 1850's. Tours can be taken to see the house and its furnishings and learn a little of the history of the Underground Railroad.

The Great Plains

Although Nebraska does not have a large black population, it did play a significant role during the years of the Underground Railroad. Allen B. Mayhew of Nebraska City helped fugitives flee to safety in Canada by way of his cabin, which was connected with caves along the Missouri River. The caves the slaves used as hiding places are still known as John Brown's caves. A museum in Nebraska City tells the story of the years the cabin and caves were used as a station in the Underground Railroad. In addition, the Great Plains Black History Museum in Omaha provides a historical overview of the role of black settlers and pioneers in the northern plains states of Nebraska, North and South Dakota, Montana, and Wyoming.

Kansas City, Missouri, has several museums relating to African American history and culture. The Black Archives of MidAmerica features displays on the buffalo soldiers (particularly the Ninth and Tenth Cavalry units organized in Kansas) and on notable figures in the development of Kansas City jazz, including the famous black band leader Count Basie. In 1991 the Negro League Museum was opened to the public, preserving more than a century of black baseball history with special focus on the activities of the all-black teams that competed in the league from 1920 through the 1950's. Located in Kansas City's historic 18th and Vine street district not far from the place where Andrew "Rube" Foster founded the league in 1920, the museum displays a rich array of artifacts and highlights

The Black Archives of MidAmerica in Kansas City, Missouri. *(Black Archives of MidAmerica)*

the achievements of the Kansas City Monarchs, one of the most outstanding teams that competed in the segregated Negro Leagues.

The Mid-Atlantic Region

In 1977 the Afro-American Historical Museum was founded in New Jersey under the Jersey City Branch of the National Association for the Advancement of Colored People (NAACP). The museum holds a large collection of artifacts including artwork, books, photos, and other historical documents.

The Bethune Museum and Archives, located in Washington, D.C., is named for the famous black educator Mary McLeod Bethune. The museum is devoted to interpreting the lives of African American women and the organizations they helped develop. The museum contains one of the largest collections of African American women's manuscripts on topics such as civil rights, education, employment, health, housing, military, and women's rights. The exhibits explore the lives and experiences of African American women and topics relating to women that have been neglected in the past.

The Howard University Museum in Washington, D.C., took as its mission the preservation of the history and heritage of African Americans. At the urging of scholars such as W. E. B. Du Bois, Kelly Miller, and Alain Locke, the National Negro Museum and Library was finally approved on October 25, 1938. In the 1990's, the museum continued to house artifacts and rare documents relating to black history.

The life and legacy of one of the greatest African American abolitionists, orators, suffragists, and civil rights activists is portrayed in the Frederick Douglass National Historic Site, in Washington, D.C. The site, Cedar Hill, was Douglass's home and is filled with arti-

The collections of the African American Museum in Philadelphia specialize in art and local regional culture.

In 1999 Colonial Williamsburg staged a program titled "Enslaving Virginia" that featured live reenactments of master-slave relationships. *(AP/Wide World Photos)*

facts from his life. The tours include a walk through the first floor of the home, the gardens, and the Growlery. A film about Douglass is also shown to educate visitors about his achievements and his life.

New England

The Museum of Afro-American History and the African Meeting House are found in BOSTON, MASSACHUSETTS. The museum offers visitors a chance to get a glimpse of the life of an African American in New England in the eighteenth, nineteenth, and early twentieth centuries. The African Meeting House, which was completed in 1806, is the oldest black church edifice still standing in the United States. The brick structure, located on Beacon Hill, played an important role in the abolitionist era and hosted a great many famous orators, including William Lloyd Garrison, Frederick Douglass, and Charles Sumner. The meeting house has been restored to its 1850's appearance and offers free tours to visitors.

The Southeast

The National Civil Rights Museum in MEMPHIS, TENNESSEE, offers an interpretive exhibit displaying critical events in the Civil Rights movement beginning with the U.S. SUPREME COURT's 1954 decision in *Brown v. Board of Education*. Each exhibit uses a variety of forms of media to re-create the atmosphere of the volatile 1950's and 1960's.

Colonial Williamsburg in VIRGINIA contains nearly one hundred historic buildings, live craft demonstrations, and living history exhibits. Among the museum's personnel are several African American guides, called interpreters, who reenact typical scenes and expe-

(continued on page 1766)

Museums and Research Centers

African American Museum

Address: 1765 Crawford Rd., Cleveland, OH 44106. Phone: (216) 791-1700; FAX: (216) 791-1774. Web site: www.ben.net/aamuseum

Dedicated to local and regional history as well as hosting special and traveling exhibits, this museum was established in 1953. Among its many artifacts and displays, the museum showcases the achievements of inventor Garrett A. MORGAN, a resident of Cleveland. Morgan's inventions included a safety helmet/gas mask used by firefighters and soldiers and the first automatic traffic light.

African American Museum in Philadelphia

Address: 701 Arch St., Philadelphia, PA 19106-1557. Phone: (215) 574-0380; FAX: (215) 574-3110. Web site: aampmuseum.org

Established in 1976 as one of the first modern museums of black culture, the facility contains art exhibits as well as a permanent collection of materials related to black culture in Philadelphia and the Delaware Valley as well as throughout North America.

African-American Panoramic Experience (APEX) Museum

Address: 135 Auburn Ave. NE, Atlanta, GA 30303. Phone: (404) 523-2739; FAX: (404) 523-3248. Web site: www.apexmuseum.org

Museum of local black history founded in 1978. Serving as a gateway to the Martin Luther King, Jr., National Historic District, this museum features exhibits by Atlantans and nationally known artists but concentrates on material relevant to the local culture.

African Art Museum of Maryland

Address: 5430 Vantage Point Rd., Columbia, MD 21044. Phone: (410) 715-3047.

Founded in 1980 and located on the grounds of the historic Oakland Manor estate, the museum displays a choice collection of traditional African artifacts, including textiles, masks, gold weights, jewelry, musical instruments, and household items.

African Art Museum of the S.M.A. Fathers

Address: 23 Bliss Ave., Tenafly, NJ 07670. Phone: (201) 894-8611; FAX: (201) 541-1280. Web site: www.smafathers.org

Established in 1978, the museum is affiliated with the Society of African Missions, a French missionary society that collected and preserved West African cultural artifacts. The museum displays works created in ivory, bronze, wood, gold, and brass in sub-Saharan Africa.

Afro-American Cultural Center

Address: 401 N. Myers St., Charlotte, NC 28202. Phone: (704) 374-1565; FAX: (704) 374-9273. Web site: www.aacc-charlotte.org

Founded in 1974 and located in a historic former church, the center features exhibits and educational programs that showcase the region's African American history and culture. It includes a performing arts department that offers theater, music, and dance events.

Afro-American Historical Museum

Address: 1841 John F. Kennedy Blvd., Jersey City, NJ 07305. Phone: (201) 547-5262; FAX: (201) 547-5392

Founded in 1977 and located on the second floor of the Greenville Public Library, the Afro-American Historical Museum emphasizes the history of African Americans in New Jersey. Permanent artifacts and exhibits are particularly related to local black fraternal organizations, New Jersey-born blacks involved in sports and entertainment, and black women of New Jersey. The museum also houses a library containing five hundred volumes related to African American history.

America's Black Holocaust Museum

Address: 2233 N. Fourth St., Milwaukee, WI 53212. Phone: (414) 264-2500; FAX: (414) 264-0112.

Founded in 1988, the museum includes exhibits on SLAVERY, civil rights, and the Middle Passage. Because of the graphic nature of the atrocities portrayed in the 12,000-square-foot exhibit space, the museum recommends that visitors be older than eight years of age.

***Amistad* replica**

Address: Connecticut Afro-American Historical Society, 444 Orchard St., New Haven, CT 06511-4111. Phone: (203) 432-4131. Web site: www.amistadamerica.org

Launched as a joint venture by the Connecticut Afro-American Historical Society and the Mystic Seaport Museum with funding from the state of Connecticut, the replica is an exact re-creation of the 64-foot, two-masted schooner *Amistad* that set sail from Havana in 1839 and concluded its journey off the coast of Long Island Sound with its rebellious slave passengers transported to New Haven, Connecticut. The ship replica is intended to sail to port cities in Connecticut and other states to provide instruction to students about the slave trade, the abolitionist movement, and the impact of the *Amistad* rebellion and the resulting court case in which former president John Quincy Adams pleaded the slaves' cause before the U.S. SUPREME COURT.

Amistad Research Center

Address: Tilton Hall, Tulane University, 6823 St. Charles St., New Orleans, LA 70118-5698. Phone: (504) 865-5535; FAX: (504) 865-5688. Web site: www.tulane.edu/~amistad

Founded in 1966 by the American Missionary Association, the center is located on the campus of Tulane University. One of the largest manuscript archives in the United States, the center houses more than eight million documents. The vast majority of these records pertain to the history and culture of African Americans, while additional documents are related to other ethnic minorities, race relations, civil rights, and the history of the United Church of Christ. The center makes its resources available to anyone doing research in these fields.

Anacostia Museum

Address: 1901 Fort Place SE, Washington, DC 20020. Phone: (202) 287-3306; FAX: (202) 287-3183. Web site: www.si.edu/anacostia

Founded in 1967, this museum affiliated with the Smithsonian Institution also serves as a research center. The museum focuses on the primarily black Anacostia neighborhood of Washington, D.C., and includes artifacts and materials from areas of the rural South that have been historically significant to generations of African Americans.

Avery Research Center for African American History and Culture

Address: 125 Bull St., Charleston, SC 29424. Phone: (843) 953-7609; FAX: (843) 953-7607. Web site: www.cofc.edu/~averyrsc

Located on the campus of the College of Charleston, the center is the largest research facility devoted to the Gullah culture and language. Its holdings document the history and culture of African Americans in Charleston, the South Carolina Low Country, and the southern United States.

Banneker-Douglass Museum

Address: 84 Franklin St., Annapolis, MD 21401. Phone: (410) 974-2893. Web site: http://www.ari.net/mdshpo/bdm.html

Dedicated to two Maryland residents, scientist Benjamin BANNEKER and abolitionist Frederick DOUGLASS, the museum is located in Annapolis in the old Mt. Moriah Church. This state-operated museum contains exhibits related to African American life and history. Maryland's black culture receives special attention in temporary exhibits.

Beck Cultural Exchange Center

Address: 1927 Dandridge Ave., Knoxville, TN 37915-1997. Phone: (423) 524-8461.

Founded in 1975, the center houses a collection of books, periodicals, and audio recordings that are related to the history of African Americans in Knoxville and eastern Tennessee. One room contains the personal memorabilia of William H. HASTIE, the first African American federal judge and first black governor of the U.S. Virgin Islands.

Bethune Museum and Archives

Address: 1318 Vermont Ave. NW, Washington, DC 20005. Phone: (202) 673-2402; FAX: (202) 673-2414. Web site: www.nps.gov/ mamc

Located in the Bethune Council House, the former home of Mary McLeod BETHUNE and headquarters of the NATIONAL COUNCIL OF NEGRO WOMEN, the museum houses exhibits and programs that emphasize the contributions of black women to American life. Memorabilia pertaining to Bethune's life are part of the permanent collection. The museum building is a National Historic Site.

Black American West Museum and Heritage Center

Address: 3091 California St., Denver, CO 80205. Phone: (303) 292-2566; FAX: (303) 382-1981. Web site: www.coax.net/people/lwf/ bawmus.htm

Founded by Western enthusiast Paul Stewart in 1971, the museum exhibits and preserves artifacts, documents, and other memorabilia that tell the history of black pioneers. As one of the most comprehensive sources of historic materials on this subject, the museum attempts to chronicle accurately the contributions African Americans made to the settling of the West and to its culture.

(continued)

Black Archives History and Research Foundation

Address: Joseph Caleb Community Center, 5400 NW 22nd Ave., Bldg. B, Suite 101, Miami, FL 33142-3009. Phone: (305) 636-2390.

This research center focuses on black involvement in southern Florida. Miami has become home to black people of Caribbean, South American, West Indian, and other backgrounds. Exhibits at the archives emphasize the contributions of these various groups to the local culture.

Black Archives of MidAmerica

Address: 2033 Vine St., Kansas City, MO 64108. Phone: (816) 483-1300. Web site: www.blackarchives.org

This museum and library collection, located near the historic 18th and Vine District in what was once the first black firehouse in Kansas City, focuses on black history in Missouri, Kansas, Nebraska, and Iowa. It holds an extensive documents collection, including displays on the black military units (the BUFFALO SOLDIERS) that served there and the Kansas City style of JAZZ music.

Black Archives, Research Center, and Museum

Address: Carnegie Library, Florida A & M University Campus, Tallahassee, FL 32307. Phone (904) 599-3020; FAX: (904) 561-2604. Web site: www.freenet.fsu.edu/ Historic_Preservation/black_archives.html

Since 1975 Florida A&M's original Carnegie Building has housed the Black Archives, Research Center, and Museum, which features an extensive collection of African American cultural artifacts, including visual art.

Black History Museum and Cultural Center of Virginia

Address: Clay St. (between First and Adams), Richmond, VA 23219. Phone: (804) 780-9093.

Founded in 1981 and housed in a building in the Jackson Ward historic district long associated with Richmond's black community, the museum contains a collection of some 5,000 artifacts and documents relating to African American history in Virginia. Among its holdings are the papers of historian-educator Carter G. WOODSON and the collection of Colonel Charles Young.

California African-American Museum

Address: 600 State Dr., Los Angeles, CA 90037. Phone: (213) 744-7432; FAX: (213) 744-2050. Web site: www.caam.ca.gov

Founded in 1981 and located at Exposition Park near the historic Los Angeles Coliseum, the California Afro-American Museum offers exhibits that explore the art, history, and culture of African Americans and the heritage of the African DIASPORA in the New World. The paintings, sculptures, photographs, and other visual arts displayed in the museum's exhibit space demonstrate the creative spirit and unique vision found among African American and Afro-Caribbean artists. The museum's holdings include a substantial library of books, periodicals, and audio tapes, and video cassettes related to African and African American culture.

Carter's Grove Slave Quarter at Colonial Williamsburg

Address: 8 miles southeast of Williamsburg, Virginia, on U.S. 60. Phone: (804) 229-1000 ext. 2973 (ticket information).

As one of several sites where the Colonial Williamsburg Foundation presents interpretive programs that re-create the life experiences of African Americans in eighteenth century Virginia, Carter's Grove features a reconstructed slave quarters on the original site where slave cabins once stood. Costumed interpreters from the museum's Department of African American Interpretation and Presentations guide visitors through the site and present stories based on historical research about the slaves who once lived and worked at Carter's Grove.

Chattanooga African-American Museum

Address: 200 E. Martin Luther King Blvd., Chattanooga, TN 37403. Phone: (423) 266-8658; FAX: (423) 267-1076. Web site: www.anet-stl.com/~afields/caam/caam.html

Founded in 1983 and formerly known as the Afro-American Museum, this museum has a collection that focuses primarily on local people and events. The museum's main attraction is its collection of artifacts related to singer Bessie SMITH, a native of Chattanooga.

Delta Blues Museum

Address: 114 Delta Ave., Clarksdale, MS 38614. Phone: (601) 627-6820; FAX: (601) 627-7263. Web site: www.deltabluesmuseum.org

Founded in 1979 and designated as part of the Carnegie Public Library, the museum preserves and presents the work of many of the area's BLUES musicians in addition to that of noted blues guitarist Muddy WATERS. Visitors have access to recordings, photographs, archival documents, and other memorabilia that pertains to blues music and its influence on jazz, country, rock and roll, and popular music in general.

Du Sable Museum

Address: 740 E. 56th Place, Chicago, IL 60637. Phone: (773) 947-0600; FAX: (773) 947-0677. Web site: www.dusable.org

One of the oldest and largest museums of African American culture in the United States, the Du Sable Museum was founded in 1961 by Margaret Burroughs as the Ebony Museum of Negro History and Art. It was renamed to honor Jean Baptiste Pointe DU SABLE, a Haitian-born pioneer of mixed African and French heritage who is credited as the founder of Chicago. The museum houses more than ten thousand books, artifacts, manuscripts, art works, and other items relating to African and African American history and culture. The museum also offers a variety of outreach programs for schools and the black community.

Ebony Museum of Art

Address: 30 Jack London Village, Oakland, CA 94607. Phone: (510) 763-0745.

Celebrating both African and African American art, this museum was founded in 1980 and is housed in a three-story Victorian home in one of the historic districts of OAKLAND, CALIFORNIA. The collection includes ancient tribal artifacts as well as a host of contemporary African crafts and African American artifacts. The museum also features the Degradation Room, with its collection of artifacts from pre- and post-slavery days. Concerned with encouraging and supporting cultural pride in the African American artistic vision, the museum sponsors a bimonthly show of the works of contemporary African American artists and art competitions at local schools, and also holds student-based art workshops.

Eubie Blake Cultural Center. *See main text entry.*

Freetown Village of Indiana State Museum

Address: 202 N. Alabama St., Indianapolis, IN 46204-2185. Phone: (317) 232-1641; (317) 631-1870.

Freetown Village is a living-history exhibit within the Indiana State Museum. Using the museum's resources and artifacts, a group of actors, interpreters, and storytellers present vignettes, plays, and workshops that re-create the life experiences of African Americans in Indiana after the Civil War.

Great Blacks in Wax Museum

Address: 1601 E. North Ave., Baltimore, MD 21213-1409. Phone: (410) 563-3404.

The museum's displays depict the black struggle from early history through the Civil Rights Movement. More than 100 wax figures are portrayed, including Booker T. WASHINGTON; Ida Barnett WELLS; Mary Church TERRELL; Martin Luther KING, Jr.; MALCOLM X; Carter G. Woodson; Bessie COLEMAN; and Dr. Charles DREW.

Great Plains Black History Museum

Address: 2213 Lake St., Omaha, NE 68110. Phone: (402) 345-2212; FAX: (402) 345-2256. Web site: members.aol.com/asmith8955/ ahist.htm

Founded in 1975, this museum is dedicated to preserving the history of African Americans in the Midwest from the pre-Civil War era to modern times. Focusing on the achievements of black homesteaders and pioneers, particularly black women, the museum contains photographs, artifacts, and other historical materials and hosts temporary exhibits and community programs.

Harriet Tubman home. *See main text entry.*

Jordan House Museum

Address: 2001 Fuller Rd., West Des Moines, IA 50265-5528. Phone: (515) 225-1286.

Housed within a residence that served as an actual station on the UNDERGROUND RAILROAD, this museum features displays that tell the stories of fugitive slaves and the abolitionists who assisted them on their routes to freedom in the northern United States and Canada.

Karamu House

Address: 2355 E. 89th St., Cleveland, OH 44106-3403. Phone: (216) 795-7070. Web site: little.nhlink.net/nca/karamu.htm

Best known for its theater and its art center, Karamu House was founded in 1915 by Russell and Rowena Jelliffe as the first professional black theater outside New York City. *Karamu* is a Swahili word for festivity, banquet, communal gathering, or entertainment. The center provides education in the performing, vi-

(continued)

sual, and cultural arts, while the theater offers opportunities for black performing artists and playwrights. Charles Gilpin, Langston HUGHES, Robert Guillaume, and others who became famous in film, theater, and television have been associated with Karamu House.

Motown Museum/Hitsville, U.S.A.

Address: 2648 W. Grand Blvd., Detroit, MI 48208-1285. Phone: (313) 875-2264, (313) 875-2266.

Founded in 1985, the Motown Museum was designated as an official historic site in 1987. The museum is housed in the original building used by company founder Berry GORDY, Jr., as a makeshift recording studio when the label was founded in 1959. The museum's contents serve as a tribute to Gordy and the stable of recording artists who created the "Motown sound." During the 1960's, Motown entertainers such as the TEMPTATIONS, the SUPREMES, the FOUR TOPS, Marvin GAYE, Mary Wells, the Jackson 5, and Smokey ROBINSON created albums that established the international popularity of African American rhythm-and-blues and pop music.

Museum of African-American Life and Culture

Address: 3536 Grand Ave., Dallas, TX 75210. Phone: (214) 565-9026; FAX: (214) 421-8204.

Founded in 1972 and located on the grounds of Dallas Fair Park, this museum showcases traditional African ceremonial artifacts, African American folk art, and various materials on African American history. Among its community programs, it sponsors a black history summer camp for children.

Museum of Afro-American History

Address: 46 Joy St., Boston, MA 02114-4005. Phone: (617) 742-5415.

Although there is no single building that contains permanent museum exhibits, this museum administers several sites on the Black Heritage Trail in Boston that collectively present a panoramic view of the region's African American cultural heritage.

Museum of the National Center of Afro-American Artists

Address: 300 Walnut Ave., Boston, MA 02119. Phone: (617) 442-8614, 442-8014; FAX: (617) 445-5525.

Founded in 1969 and located within a nineteenth-century house, the museum houses paintings, prints, and graphics by African American artists, Afro-Caribbean art, and African art.

National Afro-American Museum and Cultural Center

Address: 1350 Brush Row Rd., Wilberforce, OH 45384-0578. Phone: (937) 376-4944; FAX: (937) 376-2007. Web site: winslo.ohio.gov/ohswww/places/afroam/index.htm

Established in 1972 and funded by a 1971 act of Congress, the museum is located on the original campus of Wilberforce University. The university itself moved to a different site nearby. The historic original campus site, dating to the 1860's, is part of the museum's conference center. The museum approaches the civil rights revolution from an everyday perspective, with exhibits on typical businesses, churches, and homes of African Americans of the 1950's as well as other exhibits dealing with the larger issues of the era.

National Civil Rights Museum

Address: 450 Mulberry St. Memphis, TN 38103. Phone: (901) 521-9699; FAX: (901) 521-9740. Web site: www.mecca.org/~crights/ ncrn.html

Dedicated in 1991, this museum is housed in the former Lorraine Motel, the site of the assassination of Martin Luther King, Jr., on April 4, 1968. As the site of King's death, the Lorraine Motel is a most appropriate location for a museum dedicated to preserving the history of the Civil Rights movement. The National Civil Rights Museum brings to life the actual movement from the mid-1950's through the end of the 1960's. Sixteen interpretive vignettes present the principal events in the Civil Rights movement through photographs, documents, audiovisual material, graphics, and artifacts. The museum also sponsors children's story hour programs, holds monthly local history panel discussions, hosts conferences, and offers performances, films, and lectures in its large auditorium.

National Museum of African Art

Address: 950 Independence Ave. SW, Washington, DC 20560. Phone: (202) 357-4600; FAX: (202) 357-4879. Web site: www.si.edu/nmafa

The museum is part of the Smithsonian Institution. Formerly a private collection, it was taken over by the Smithsonian in the 1970's and moved to its present location. The only major museum in the United States devoted to the acquisition and exhibition of this type of art, the collection contains more than six thousand pieces of sub-Saharan African art. Its wood, bronze, and ivory sculptures are considered to be the best collective source for research on the influence of African art on European artists.

National Museum of the Tuskegee Airmen

Address: 6325 W Jefferson Ave, Detroit, MI 48209. Phone: (313) 843-8849: FAX: (313) 843-1540. Web site: pw1.netcom.com/~chehaw/taimuseum.htm

Founded in 1987 as a repository for the archives and memorabilia of the National Tuskegee Airmen, Inc., the museum displays the accomplishments of African Americans who served in the segregated 332nd Fighter Group and the 477th Composite Fighter-Bomber Group during World War II. With assistance from the city of Detroit, the Tuskegee Airmen dedicated former enlisted men's quarters at historic Fort Wayne as the National Historical Museum of the Tuskegee Airmen. Among its collections are model aircraft, equipment, supplies, uniforms, and photographs that highlight the contributions of African Americans in aviation.

National Voting Rights Museum and Institute

Address: 1012 Water Ave., Selma, AL 36702-2516. Phone: (334) 418-0800; FAX: (334) 418-0278. Web site: www.olcg.com/selma/ nvrm.html

Founded in 1992, the museum is housed in the former headquarters of the White Citizens Council of Alabama at the foot of the Edmund Pettus Bridge, site of the "bloody Sunday" altercation during the Civil Rights movement. The museum's exhibition rooms include displays on Reconstruction, black suffrage, and the Civil Rights movement.

Negro League Museum

Address: 1601 E. 18th St., Kansas City, MO 64108-1600. Phone: (816) 221-1920.

Opened to the public in January of 1991, this museum is dedicated to preserving and illuminating the history of African American baseball. Located in Kansas City's 18th and Vine Street Historic District, the museum displays photographs and artifacts and has interactive exhibits on the history of African American baseball. Exhibits cover more than a century of African American baseball. The accomplishments of the great teams and players of the Negro Leagues are highlighted. The museum pays special tribute to the Kansas City Monarchs, the great Negro League team on which Satchel Paige, John "Buck" O'Neil, and Jackie Robinson played.

North American Black Historical Museum and Cultural Centre

Address: 277 King St., Amherstburg, Ontario, N9V 2C7 Canada. Phone: (519) 736-5433; (519) 736-7353.

Opened to the public in 1981, the museum contains artifacts and exhibits that illustrate the history of the Underground Railroad, abolitionist efforts, and the growth of the black community in Amherstburg and other Canadian cities. As one of the northern terminals of the Underground Railroad, Amherstburg had a thriving black community in the 1850's. Descendants of these escaped slaves began raising funds in 1966 to establish a museum to commemorate the history of their community. The museum complex includes a restored house and the Nazrey African Methodist Episcopal (AME) Church.

Schomburg Center for Research in Black Culture.
See main text entry.

Studio Museum of Harlem

Address: 144 W. 125th St., Harlem, NY 10027. Phone: (212) 864-4500; FAX: (212) 666-5753. Web site: www.studiomuseum.org

The most important repository in the United States for contemporary black art and African and Caribbean folk art. Incorporated in 1967 as a gathering place for artists who needed working space, the studio became known as a cultural center. It expanded to become a concert hall, lecture hall, and assembly hall. The studio moved in 1980 from its original location into a former office building, giving it the opportunity to expand its renowned programs.

University of Mississippi Blues Archive

Address: Farley Hall Room 340, University of Mississippi, Grove Loop, University, MS 38677. Phone: (601) 232-7753.

Established in 1984, the archives include three major collections: a southern music and folklore collection; the B. B. King Collection of materials, artifacts, and phonograph recordings; and the Living Blues Collection of thousands of classic phonograph records. The collections include gospel as well as blues recordings, along with videotapes, film footage, television documentaries, and taped interviews with blues performers.

W. E. B. Du Bois Library, Special Collections, and Archives

Address: University of Massachusetts, 154 Hicks

(continued)

Way, Amherst, MA 01003. Phone: (413) 545-2780, (413) 545-0150.
Dedicated in 1996, the library contains archival documents and records belonging to historian, writer, and social activist W. E. B. Du Bois (1868-1963). The collection includes manuscripts and printed versions of Du Bois's speeches, articles, newspaper columns, pamphlets, essays, book reviews, and books.

Wisconsin Black Historical Society Museum
Address: 2620 W. Center St., Milwaukee, WI 53206-1115. Phone: (414) 372-7677; FAX: (414) 372-4882.
In addition to dramatic murals portraying black history from slavery through the 1990's, the museum displays artifacts within rooms that represent typical living quarters for the many African American families who moved to Wisconsin in the 1930's and 1940's to work in local factories and businesses.

riences of blacks who lived in the state's colonial capital. One special program is called "The Other Half," a living history demonstration that provides a glimpse of how African Americans worked and lived in Williamsburg before the capital was moved to Richmond in 1780.

The George Washington Carver Museum is a national historic site located in ALABAMA. It was established by the Tuskegee Institute in 1938. George Washington Carver was employed at the Tuskegee Institute for more than forty years and worked tirelessly to improve the living conditions of those in the surrounding area. Through his scientific research, particularly in the field of agriculture, he sought to improve the life of humankind. The museum is split in two sections, one part containing Carver's laboratory equipment as well as artifacts from his life. The second part of the museum tracks the growth of the Tuskegee Institute from its beginnings in 1881 up through the late twentieth century.

The West

The California African-American Museum in Los Angeles focuses its exhibits around the history, culture, and art of black Americans paying particular attention to those in Southern CALIFORNIA. Located near the famous Los Angeles Coliseum and Exposition Park, the museum offers a variety of exhibits through the year as well as special workshops that encourage community participation.

Denver's Black American West Museum and Heritage Center, located near the city's downtown district, highlights the role of the black cowboy in the Old West. One of the most notable figures whose life is depicted at the museum is Nat Love, also known as "Deadwood Dick," who was famous for his tall tales about his exploits as a cowboy and gunfighter.

These are only a few of the museums with African American emphases that can be found in each area of the country. Many more monuments, grave sites, and areas of African American historical importance are located in nearly every state. The museums differ in their content, making each visit to another site an exciting adventure filled with new people and different subjects.

—*Jeri Kurtzleben*

See also: Historic landmark and neighborhood preservation.

Suggested Readings:

"Black Museums: Keeping the Legacy Alive." *Ebony* (March, 1994): 36-39.

Cantor, George. *Historic Landmarks of Black America*. Detroit: Gale Research, 1991.

Estell, Kenneth, ed. *The African-American Almanac*. 6th ed. Detroit: Gale Research, 1994.

Fleury, Eric M. "Emergence of Museums and Institutes for African-American Civil Rights, History, and Culture." *The Black Collegian* 28 (February, 1998): 143-145.

Perry, James A. "A Virtual Tour: Birmingham and Memphis Civil Rights Institutes." *The*

Black Collegian 27 (February, 1997): 152-155.

Profile of Black Museums. Washington, D.C.: African American Museums Association, 1988.

Ruffins, Faith D., and Paul Ruffins. "Recovering Yesterday." *Black Issues in Higher Education* 13 (February 6, 1997): 16-22.

Williams, Arlene. "Museums in Crisis." *American Visions* 7 (February-March, 1992): 22-25.

Music: Among the major contributions that African Americans have made to the development of American culture is a musical legacy. Evolving from traditions on the African continent and enhanced by the enslavement experience in the Americas, many unique and distinctive musical genres can be attributed to African Americans.

African Heritage

On the African continent, there are between eight hundred and one thousand different languages and ethnic groups. Because many cultural groups were intermingled through the enslavement experience in the New World, African influences on the African American musical legacy must be addressed in collective terms. Certain collective practices and techniques in traditional African music survived in varying degrees in African American music. Such practices include the collective (or group) performance of certain music and the functional use of certain musical genres (for example, music commonly associated with a particular event or situation, such as work songs). There is also the improvisational nature of certain genres and styles and the prodigious use of call-and-response, or the alternation or overlapping of two musical sources in a performance. Many instrument-making practices were retained from the African continent, construction of the banjo, marimba, and berimbau (in South America) being some of the most prominent.

In identifying Africanism in African American musical traditions, the focus of scholarly attention traditionally has been on rhythmicity. Rhythm is the most researched aspect of African music. Because of its relation to African American traditions, there is no shortage of articles, essays, and books that examine this aspect of African American music. Although a rhythmic approach to sound is manifested clearly in many traditions, there are other aspects of these musical styles which deserve greater focus.

The similarity of vocal styles between African and African American musical traditions is much less commented upon. These phenomena are of particular interest because most music on the African continent is vocally conceived and oriented, as are most musical genres in African American traditions. Stylized vocal effects such as screams, glissandi, falsetto, yodels, slides, and raspy voice are found in abundance among many ethnic groups on the African continent and similarly are found in many African American traditions. Whereas the elaborate and virtuosic drumming found on the African continent is mostly a West African phenomenon, the vocal styles are found across the continent. The vocal basis of many African American genres is a necessary area of consideration because it broadens the range of examination of these styles.

African Diaspora in the New World

Of the fifteen million Africans who were brought to the New World, the vast majority were enslaved from the sixteenth through much of the nineteenth century. Despite enslavement, they maintained and practiced some variation of their African beliefs, culture, and musical traditions. An area that combined these customs with European influences was religious practice. Many Africans in the New World, especially in areas colonized by Catholics, became nominal Christians but continued to practice their traditional African belief sys-

The importance of music to African Americans is reflected in this late nineteenth century family's inclusion of instruments in their family portrait. *(Library of Congress)*

tems with adaptations to Catholicism, for example. These adapted religions were fertile ground for maintaining many ritualized African chanting practices and sung styles. Examples of such syncretized religions are Candomble in Brazil, SANTERÍA in CUBA and PUERTO RICO (also practiced by many Puerto Rican Americans in New York), VOODOO in HAITI, and, to a lesser extent, Kumina in JAMAICA. Rich musical traditions are associated with many of these religious beliefs.

Colonial and Antebellum Era

Most musical activity in colonial society was vocal, although there are late eighteenth-century paintings that depict enslaved Africans dancing and playing stringed instruments. Because much of colonial society (both black and white) was preliterate, collective song teaching, as in a church service for example, was done by a technique called "lining out." This process involved a leader singing a line or two of a song or hymn, sometimes over-enunciating the words. The congregation followed by singing the same line after the leader. This method still is used in some African American churches. Other indications of African American musical activity during the eighteenth century come from accounts in news journals in MASSACHUSETTS, NEW YORK, and VIRGINIA. When papers in these areas reported missing or fugitive Africans, they frequently commented on musical ability (on a particular instrument, for example) as well as giving a physical description.

Records from the AMERICAN REVOLUTION era show African Americans not only as fighting personnel but also as musicians. Specific statutes (for example, the Virginia Act of 1776) allowed for the recruitment of African American musicians during the war. During and immediately following the American Revolution, several northern states formally or gradually abolished African slavery. Some freed Africans who had fought for the Loyalist forces were removed to areas in the Caribbean or to Canada, and some were repatriated to Africa.

The period after the revolution saw the emergence of two important African American institutions, the self-help benevolent societies and the African independent churches. The benevolent societies, such as the African Union Society (RHODE ISLAND), FREE AFRICAN SOCIETY (PHILADELPHIA, PENNSYLVANIA), Brown Fellowship (Charleston, SOUTH CAROLINA), and the African Society of BOSTON, were among several pseudoreligious moral aid groups that formed to help recently freed blacks. By the late eighteenth and early nineteenth century, several independent African churches had emerged in both southern and northern states. Many churches in the South, however, were either very closely scrutinized or shut down because of uprisings that were planned or carried out by religious leaders such as GABRIEL Prosser, Denmark VESEY, and Nat TURNER.

By the late eighteenth century, Methodism had claimed large numbers of African Americans because of its antislavery stance. Richard ALLEN, a celebrated religious leader and founding member of the Free African Society, founded the AFRICAN METHODIST EPISCOPAL CHURCH in 1794. In 1816 he established the AME Church as a body independent from the mother METHODIST Church. In 1801 Allen published a collection of religious song lyrics that became widely used in African American Protestant churches around the country.

Another religious phenomenon of the early nineteenth century that involved African Americans was the camp meeting. These outdoor continuous religious services were inspired by the Second Great Awakening religious movement that spread around the United States. African American participants were known to do dances such as the "ring shout" and "shuffle step" at camp meetings.

Spirituals were the most significant musical contribution of the enslaved population of the nineteenth century. It is still difficult to define this large body of religious music, but the genre is unique because it represented a musical manifestation of the African American enslavement experience under Protestant Christianity. Another factor adding to its musical uniqueness is that a similar tradition did not develop on the African continent or anywhere else in the diaspora. There are few absolute features that can be pointed to when trying to distinguish one spiritual from another. Up-tempo songs such as "A Great Camp Meetin'" might have been a jubilee, while an equally spirited "I'm Gonna Lift Up a Standard for My King" might have been regarded as a shout.

An apparently standard feature of the spiritual was its employment of African American dialect. The earliest compilation of spirituals was *Slave Songs of the United States* (1867), a collaborative work of William Allen, Charles Ware, and Lucy McKim Garrison. In the preface to the work, they comment on the uniqueness of African American vocal styles and the inability of conventional Western musical notation to transcribe accurately unique vocal effects such as screams, yodels, falsetto, and glissandi.

Related to spirituals, but functioning in an entirely different capacity, were the alert and map songs. Although their texts ostensibly were religious, the alert songs encoded messages or signals about escape attempts or secret meetings. Examples of such songs are "Steal Away to Jesus," "Good News the Chariots Comin'," "Wade in the Water," and "I'm Packin' Up." Map songs were designed to give directions to fugitive or runaway Africans. In the song "Sheep, Sheep, Don't You Know the Road?," the use of the word "road" could have encoded some message about a specific escape route. "Follow the Drinking Gourd" was another map song. It a was a metaphoric allusion to the Big Dipper constellation, indicating that escapees were to follow the Big Dipper north.

Minstrelsy

Minstrelsy was a nineteenth-century form of popular theatrical entertainment in which MINSTREL actors (mostly but not exclusively white) went on stage in BLACKFACE (with burnt cork or charcoal) and sang songs, danced, told jokes, or mimicked slaves. An antecedent of minstrel songs, the so-called "Negro songs," had been in circulation since the mid-eighteenth century. By the early nineteenth century, songs that mimicked, ridiculed, or mocked the slaves began to gain popularity. Songs such as "Three-Fingered Jack" (1812), "The Negro and the Buckra Man" (1816), and "The Guinea Boy" (1816) are examples of early songs that included a thick southern dialect mimicking that of many enslaved blacks.

Following the CIVIL WAR and emancipation, African Americans' musical presence was felt most strongly on the minstrel stage. This form of theatrical entertainment began in the 1820's, when white men (and a few blacks) performed on stage in blackface and told jokes and sang songs about slave life. There were several common caricatures that depicted African American men as lazy, loud-laughing, shuffling Sambos, as oversexed dandies, or as violent brutes. After the Civil War, African Americans came to dominate the tradition. Notable African American minstrels were George B. Hicks and his Georgia Minstrels, Samuel Lucas, and James A. Bland. Bland's works were among the most popular minstrel songs. His more than seven hundred compositions include "Carry Me Back to Old Virginny" (1878), "Oh Dem Golden Slippers" (1879), and "Hand Me Down My Walking Cane" (1880).

James A. Bland, composer of Virginia's state song, "Carry Me Back to Old Virginny." *(Dover Publications)*

Coon Songs and Ragtime

The last decades of the nineteenth century were a fertile period for African American music. An outgrowth of the minstrel song tradition was the generic "coon song" (coming from "raccoons," a pejorative term for black men). It was a genre of comic song popular between 1880 and 1920. African American composers within this tradition include Ernest Hogan, who composed the trend-setting "All Coons Look Alike to Me," Gussie Lord Davis, writer of "When I Do the Hoochy-Coochy in de Sky," and brothers James Weldon and J. Rosamund JOHNSON, who wrote "Under the Bamboo Tree." The most prolific of the coon song composers was musical stage composer Bob Cole, whose "I Wonder What Is Dat Coon's Game?" and "No Coons Allowed" were among the most popular. The Johnson brothers turned to more constructive songwriting when, in 1901, they collaborated to produce "Lift Every Voice and Sing," commonly known as the black national anthem.

Rag piano music, or RAGTIME, was the first African American musical tradition to achieve widespread international appeal. It had emerged as a genre by the early twentieth century. The term "rag" apparently had some connection with a dance tradition. Its major features included the employment of a syncopated melodic line played by the right hand on the keyboard and a repeated bass (regular moving bass line) played by the left

A prodigious lyricist, James Weldon Johnson collaborated with his brother, Rosamond Johnson, to create such standards as "Lift Every Voice and Sing." *(Arkent Archive)*

hand. The latter seems to have developed from an earlier brass band tradition. The first African American to publish a piano work that included "rag" in its title was Thomas Turpin, with "Harlem Rag" (1897). The most celebrated rag music composer, Scott Joplin (1868-1917), preferred the term "syncopated piano music." "Maple Leaf Rag" (1899), "The Entertainer" (1902), "Bethena Waltz" (1905), "Gladiolus Rag" (1907), and "Magnetic Rag" (1914) are among his most enduring piano works. Joplin also composed a folk ballet, *The Ragtime Dance* (1899), and two rag operas—*A Guest of Honor* (1903, now lost) and *Treemonisha* (1911), which was not performed in its full form until 1972. Other important composers of rag music include Arthur Marshall (1881-1968), Scott Hayden (1882-1915), and James Scott (1885-1938).

Blues

Vocal blues developed at the beginning of the twentieth century. Blues directly or indirectly influenced many other genres, including jazz and gospel music. The vocal antecedents of the blues were eighteenth and nineteenth-century African work songs, field hollers, and stylized vocalities such as falsetto, glissandi, screams, growls, moans, whoops, raspy voice, and vocal slides. Various musicians such as W. C. Handy, Gertrude "Ma" Rainey, and William Geary "Bunk" Johnson recalled hearing the blues, either in a cohesive or some prototype form, at the turn of the century (in Johnson's case, as early as the 1880's). The fact that these blues "citings" are from different parts of the South makes it difficult to trace the genre to a specific geographical region.

There are three principal styles of the blues, although there are several subcategories with geographical identities. The earliest of the cohesive blues styles was the country blues, also known as down-home blues. This tradition featured a singer (usually self-accompanied on guitar) and use of vocal effects such as growls, taut or raspy voice, screams, and occasional spoken lines in the song. This tradition was dominated in early years by men such as Charley Patton, Blind Lemon Jefferson, "Mississippi" John Hurt, and John Adam Estes, and later by practitioners such as Eddie "Son" House, Robert Johnson, Willie Brown, Lonnie Johnson, and "Memphis" Minnie Douglas. Between 1910 and 1920, the blues developed a more cohesive structural form. The twelve-bar metric structure popularized by W. C. Handy in his notation of blues songs such as "Memphis Blues" (1912) and "St. Louis Blues" (1914) became known as the blues form. The

(continued on page 1775)

Notable Pop, Motown, and Modern R&B Groups

Bell Biv DeVoe (Ricky Bell, Michael "Biv" Bivins, and Ronnie DeVoe). Rhythm-and-blues/hip-hop trio. The group's members were part of the founding lineup of the group New Edition. Bell Biv DeVoe's debut album, *Poison,* (1990) sold more than three million copies. In 1991 they performed on the nationwide "Triple Threat" tour with pop singers Keith Sweat and Johnny Gill, another former member of New Edition. In that same year, RCA Records released a remix album of their music entitled *WBBD—Bootcity!*

Boyz II Men (Nathan "Alex Vanderpool" Morris, Wanya "Squirt" Morris, Michael S. "Bass" McCary, Shawn "Slim" Stockman). Nate Morris (pictured) created the group's name as a variation on a song title "Boys to Men" by the pop music group New Edition. Boyz II Men's first album, *Cooleyhighharmony* (1981), sold more than 7.5 million copies. In 1994 Boyz II Men released their second album, *II,* which reached number one on the Billboard pop album chart and stayed there for ten weeks. In December of 1994, their ballad "I'll Make Love to You" set a new record for consecutive weeks at number one on the pop singles chart. It was soon replaced by their next single, "On Bended Knee."

AP/Wide World Photos

Cameo. Twelve-piece FUNK group. Cameo's first two albums contained the hit singles "Rigor Mortis," "It's Serious," and "It's Over." In 1978 Cameo released *Ugly Ego,* with the hit singles "Insane" and "Give Love a Chance." *Secret Omen* (1979) contained two more hit singles, "I Just Want to Be" and "Sparkle." Singles from the 1980 albums, *Cameosis* and *Feel, Me* contained singles that became pillars of the rhythm-and-blues charts: "We're Goin' Out Tonight," "On the One," "Shake Your Pants," and "Keep It Hot."

Chantels (Arlene Smith, Lois Harris, Sonia Goring, Jackie Landry, and Rene Minus). First successful all-female vocal group. The Chantels adapted their group's name from that of a rival high school, St. Francis de Chantelle, in 1956. Two years later, their hit singles included "I Love You So" and "If You Try."

Chiffons (Barbara Lee, Patricia Bennett, Sylvia Peterson, and Judy Craig). Female rock-and-roll vocal group. Beginning with "He's So Fine," the Chiffons released a series of top songs including "One Fine Day" (1963), "Sailor Boy" (1964), "Nobody Knows What's Going On" (1965), and "Sweet Talkin' Guy" (1966).

Crystals (Dolores "Lala" Brooks, Mary Thomas, Barbara Alston, Pat Wright, and Dee Kennibrew). Female vocal group. The Crystals were the first group to sign a contract to record for Phil Spector's Philles Records label. The group's first hit single, "There's No Other (Like My Baby)" (1961), reached the top twenty on the rhythm-and-blues chart. The group's second hit, "Uptown," reached number thirteen. Spector released the number-one hit single "He's a Rebel" under the Crystals's name, though none of the original group members performed on the recording. The group did record "Da Doo Ron," which hit number three on the rhythm-and-blues chart, and "Then He Kissed Me," which reached number six.

Delfonics (William and Wilbert Hart, Randy Cain, and Ritchie Daniels). In 1968 their million-selling "La Means I Love You" brought them national fame. Their other hit songs include "Ready or Not, Here I Come," "Break Your Promise," "Tell Me This Is a Dream," and "Didn't I (Blow Your Mind This Time)."

Dynasty (Nidra Beard, Linda Carriere, Kevin Spencer, William Shelby, and Leon Sylvers III). Disco group. Beard and Carriere had belonged to early disco groups DeBlanc and Starfire. The group's music, especially the album *Your Piece of the Rock,* is exemplary of the late 1970's interest in finely produced dance music.

En Vogue (Terry Ellis, Cindy Herron, Maxine Jones, and Dawn Robinson). Quartet. The group's members answered an open call to audition for Los Angeles producers Denzil Foster and Thomas McElroy in 1988. En Vogue released the debut album *Born to*

Sing in 1990. The album's single "Hold On (to Your Love)" went platinum, and the album sold more than one million copies. *Remix to Sing* was released in 1991, followed by their 1992 hit album *Funky Divas*.

Fifth Dimension (Lamonte McLemore, Billy Davis, Jr., Ron Towson, Marilyn McCoo, and Florence LaRue). McLemore organized the group as the Versatiles in 1963. The group changed its name to the Fifth Dimension before its first major hit, "Go Where You Wanna Go" in 1967. Dozens of hits and fourteen gold records followed over the next decade, among them "Up, Up, and Away" (which won a Grammy Award as best record in 1967), "One Less Bell to Answer," "Stoned Soul Picnic," and "Aquarius/Let the Sunshine In" (which won a Grammy Award in 1969).

Four Tops. *See main text entry.*

Jackson 5 (Jermaine, Tito, Marlon, Michael, and Jackie Jackson; later, Randy Jackson). The Jackson 5's early and best works remain their hit singles, including "ABC" (1970), "I Want You Back" (1970), "I'll Be There" (1970), and "Dancing Machine" (1974), all marked by extensive harmonies with Michael as lead vocalist. He began a solo career in 1971 but continued to sing with the group until 1986, when his participation made the group too expensive. The group changed its name to the Jacksons in 1976.

Jodeci (Joel "Jo-Jo" Hailey, Cedric "K-Ci" Hailey, Dalvin DeGrate, Donald "DeVante Swing" DeGrate, Jr.). Rhythm-and-blues-influenced group. Jodeci comprises two pairs of brothers. The group's debut album, *Forever My Lady* (1991), sold more than two million copies and featured a top-twenty pop hit, "Come and Talk to Me." After releasing the album *Diary of a Mad Band* (1993), the group reached the top of the rhythm and blues charts in early 1994 with the hits "Cry for You," "What About Us," and "My Heart Belongs to You." In 1995 they released the album *The Show the Party after the Hotel*, which included "Love U 4 Life."

Knight, Gladys, and the Pips. *See main text entry.*

Lakeside (Fred Alexander, Norman Beavers, Marvin Craig, Fred Lewis, Tiemeyer McCain, Thomas Shelby, Stephen Shockley, Otis Stokes, and Mark A. Wood). Their debut album, *Lakeside*, was released by ABC Records. Their next two albums, *Rough Riders* and *Shot of Love*, appeared in 1979 on Solar Records and RCA Records, respectively. The group's second album with RCA Records was *Fantastic Voyage* (1980), and its title single hit number one on the *Cash Box* black contemporary chart that year.

AP/Wide World Photos

Levert (Gerald Levert, Sean Levert, and Marc Gordon). Rhythm-and-blues-influenced trio. Levert's albums include *Bloodline*, *The Big Throwdown*, *Just Coolin'*, and *Rope A Dope Style*. Gerald and Marc wrote most of the group's songs and served as the group's producers. In 1992 Gerald recorded a solo album, *Private Line*, which featured a father-son duet on the single "Baby Hold on to Me."

Living Colour (Vernon Reid, Will Calhoun, Corey Glover, and Muzz Skillings). Hard rock band. The group signed with Epic records in 1987 and released its debut album, *Vivid*, in 1988. A single from that album, "Cult of Personality," won a Grammy Award for best hard rock performance. The group's next album was entitled *Time's Up*.

Martha and the Vandellas. *See main text entry.*

Marvelettes (Gladys Horton, Katherine Anderson, Georgeanna Tillman, Juanita Cowart, and Wanda Young). The group played a prominent part in the rise of Motown Records. Its hits included "Please Mr. Postman," "Beechwood 4-5789," and "Too Many Fish in the Sea."

AP/Wide World Photos

Midnight Star (Reggie Calloway, Vincent Calloway, Belinda Lipscomb, Melvin Gentry, Bo Watson, and others). Funk band. Midnight Star's fourth album, *No Parking on the Dance Floor* (1983), generated the group's

(continued)

first top-ten rhythm-and-blues hit, "Freak-A-Zoid," which went double platinum. The group's next hit single, "Operator," was released from its album *Planetary Invasion* (1984) and reached number one on the rhythm-and-blues singles chart. Reggie and Vincent Calloway left to form a duo in 1986. The remaining members released *Headlines* in 1986.

Mills Brothers (Herbert, Harry, and Donald Mills). The principal members were accompanied by brother John Mills, Jr., until his death in 1936, when his place was taken by his father. They had their own network radio program in 1931 and appeared in the films *The Big Broadcast* (1932), *Twenty Million Sweethearts* (1934), and *Broadway Gondolier* (1935). Among their many hits, "Paper Doll" (1942) stands out as their biggest success, selling six million copies during its time.

Miracles (Ronnie White, Bobby Rogers, Warren "Pete" Moore, and Marv Tamplin). The Miracles achieved their greatest success as backup to Smokey ROBINSON, with hits such as "The Tears of a Clown" and "Shop Around." Robinson left the group in 1972 and was replaced by Billy Griffin. The Miracles had several pop hits after Robinson's departure.

Neville Brothers (Aaron, Arthur, Charles, and Cyril Neville). NEW ORLEANS rhythm-and-blues band. The group's music features four-part vocal harmonies and combines rhythm and blues, gospel, reggae, and the "Mardi Gras Indian" music developed by New Orleans's African American "tribes." The Neville Brothers gained national prominence with their albums *Yellow Moon* (1989) and *Brother's Keeper* (1990).

New Edition (Ralph Tresvant, Ronald DeVoe, Michael Bivins, Bobby Brown, and Ricky Bell). New Edition had a major hit record with their first release, *Candy Girl*. Tresvant and Brown went on to successful solo careers, and the remainder of the group reorganized themselves as the more HIP-HOP-oriented Bell Biv DeVoe.

MCA Records

Persuaders. The Persuaders updated the doo-wop sound of the 1950's by combining it with the smooth soul style developed in the early 1970's. The group's debut album, *Persuaders*, was released on Atlantic records in 1971. Its follow-up album, *Thin Line Between Love and Hate* (1971), produced a hit title single. Its next album, *Best Thing That's Happened to Me*, produced the hit "Some Guys Have All the Luck."

Persuasions (Jimmy Hayes, Jerry Lawson, Herbert "Tubo" Rhoad, Joseph "Jesse" Russell, and Jayotis Washington; later, Willie Daniels). A cappella vocal group. A 1967 performance, taped by a fan, was released on Frank Zappa's Straight records label in 1968 as *A Capella*. The Persuasions then released three albums with Capitol—*We Came to Play* (1971), *Street Corner Symphony* (1972), and *Spread the Word* (1972)—and *We Still Ain't Got No Band* (1973) for MCA Records. In the mid-1970's, tenor Jayotis Washington was replaced by Willie Daniels. *More than Before* and *I Just Want to Sing with My Friends*, which contained instrumental backups on some tracks, were released in 1974. In 1977 Daniels left and Washington returned for the albums *Chirpin'* and *Comin' at Ya* (1981).

Pointer Sisters. *See main text entry.*

Ronettes (Ronnie and Estelle Bennett and Nedra Talley). Female vocal group. Formed in 1959, the Ronettes, were promoted and packaged by record producer Phil Spector, the husband of lead singer Ronnie Spector. The group's hits included "Be My Baby" and "Baby, I Love You" (1963), "Walking in the Rain" (1964).

Shalamar (Jody Watley, Jeffrey Daniels, and Howard Hewett). Watley and Daniels, dancing partners on the television music show *Soul Train*, were joined by Hewett to form a vocal group for Shalamar records in 1978. Live shows featured Watley's and Daniels' dancing as well as singing talents. Shalamar moved to Solar Records and released a number of hits, including "The Second Time Around." An album of outtakes was released in 1981, followed by *Friends* (1982), which featured higher, more polished production values.

Shirelles. *See main text entry.*

Supremes. *See main text entry.*

Temptations. *See main text entry.*

TLC (Lisa "Left Eye" Lopes, Rozonda "Chilli" Thomas, and Tionne "T-Boz" Watkins). Rhythm and blues/hip-hop group. TLC released their first album in 1992. *Ooooooohhh . . . On the TLC Tip* sold 2.8 million copies and established the group's reputation for melodic urban love songs from a strong, female perspective. TLC's second album, *CrazySexyCool* was released in 1994.

AP/Wide World Photos

twelve-bar metric structure of the blues can be divided into three lines. The first two measures of each line represent the vocal call, and the last two represent the instrumental response. The call and response between voice and instrument is significant because the instrumental response is, in effect, acting in a vocal capacity. This principal, of instruments imitating voice, was explored even further with the emergence of jazz.

The next major style of blues emerged at the beginning of the 1920's, when cabaret singer Mamie Smith (1883-1946) recorded "You Can't Keep a Good Man Down" and "This Thing Called Love." This tradition of the blues, which was dominated by women, was called classic blues or sometimes city blues. This style featured a singer with a piano or small accompanying ensemble. Names associated with this tradition include Bessie Smith, Gertrude "Ma" Rainey, Clara Smith, Alberta Hunter, Ida Cox, Victoria Spivey, and Beulah "Sippie" Wallace.

A more recent style of the blues is known as the contemporary or urban blues. Chicago is considered the home of this tradition. As many musicians migrated to urban areas in the North during the 1930's and 1940's, Chicago became, in many ways, a base for the more recent contemporary or urban blues. This tradition includes singers and instrumentalists. Its form tends to be more notated and arranged than the earlier traditions, and it tends to use more electric or amplified instruments. Practitioners include B. B. King, Willie Mae "Big Mama" Thornton, Koko Taylor, Bobby Bland, John Lee Hooker, Howlin' Wolf (Chester Burnett), and Muddy Waters.

Jazz

Jazz represents a mixture of at least three preceding musical traditions. Nineteenth-century all-black brass bands, which by the turn of the century were known as syncopated dance bands and society orchestras, among other names, provided the basis for the jazz ensemble. Another influence was from rag music, particularly with the presence of the piano in the ensemble. The most influential tradition on jazz was the blues. Jazz developed as a vocally oriented music in which the instruments tried to imitate the vocal effects found in the blues. New Orleans, Louisiana, is frequently cited as the birthplace of jazz, but the traditions that coalesced into its emergence were practiced in other parts of the country as well. What distinguished New Orleans from other places was that at the beginning of the twentieth century it was a significant musical center, attracting many musicians from other parts of the country.

The earliest of the cohesive styles of jazz, known as Dixieland or New Orleans jazz, fea-

(continued on page 1783)

Notable Pop, Motown, and Modern R&B Musicians

Aaliyah (b. Jan. 16, 1979; Brooklyn, N.Y.). Rhythm-and-blues singer. Aaliyah, with her velvet voice and gangster femininity, debuted in 1994, at the age of fifteen, with her album *Age Ain't Nothing but a Number.*

Adams, Oleta (b. 1961?). Rhythm-and-blues singer. Adams performed as a featured vocalist on the 1989 Tears for Fears album *Sowing the Seeds of Love*. Her debut album, *Circle of One* (1990), contained the hit single "Get Here."

Ashford and Simpson. *See main text entry.*

Austin, Patti (b. Aug. 10, 1948, New York, N.Y.). After making a career singing commercial jingles, Austin released a duet with George Benson, "Give Me the Night," thus beginning a working relationship with her godfather, Quincy Jones. *Every Home Should Have One*, released in 1981, launched Jones's own record label, Qwest. Austin's duet with James Ingram, "Come to Me" (1982), was used as the love theme for the daytime drama *General Hospital*.

Bailey, Pearl. *See main text entry.*

Baker, Anita (b. Jan. 26, 1958, Toledo, Ohio). Rhythm-and-blues singer. Baker's albums include *The Songstress* (1983), *Rapture* (1986), *Giving You the Best That I Got* (1988), and *Compositions* (1990), and she received a number of Grammy Awards and American Music Awards. Baker also wrote, arranged, and produced many of the songs on her albums.

AP/Wide World Photos

Belafonte, Harry. *See main text entry.*

Benton, Brook (Benjamin Franklin Peay; Sept. 19, 1931, Camden, S.C.—Apr. 9, 1988, New York, N.Y.). Singer and songwriter. Benton's songs were recorded by artists such as Nat "King" Cole, Patti Page, Roy Hamilton, and Clyde McPhatter. In 1959 he began recording his own compositions, including the singles "It's Just a Matter of Time" and "The Boll Weevil Song." He also recorded duets with Dinah Washington. In 1970 he released the hit "Rainy Night in Georgia." Benton was among the first African American singers and writers who established themselves as album artists.

Berry, Chuck. *See main text entry.*

Braxton, Toni. *See main text entry.*

Brown, Bobby (b. 1969, Boston, Mass.): A teen idol of the 1980's and early 1990's, Brown combines hip-hop and rap with older traditions of soul and rhythm and blues in his singing. Sales of his albums have been helped by his athletic dancing and sexual stage presence. In 1992 he married singer Whitney Houston.

Brown, Joyce (b. Dec. 1, 1920, New York, N.Y.). Brown was the first black woman to conduct the opening of a Broadway musical, which she did for *Purlie* on March 15, 1970. She was musical director of the Alvin Ailey Ballet Company.

Bryson, Peabo (b. Apr. 13, 1951, Greenville, S.C.). Soulful balladeer. Bryson's first single, "Underground Music," was released in 1975. His first album, *Peabo*, came out later that year. He released *Reaching for the Sky* and *Crosswinds* (1979) before recording a duet with Roberta Flack on the live album *Live and More*. Other work includes an appearance in the musical comedy a *Woman Like That* in 1991 and an album, *Can You Stop the Rain*, released the same year.

Burrows, Vinie (b. Nov. 15, 1928, New York, N.Y.). Burrows created a solo performance work, *Walk Together Children* (1968), which explored the African American condition in the United States with music, poetry, and prose.

AP/Wide World Photos

Campbell, Tevin (b. 1977, Dallas, Tex.). Singer. At the age of thirteen, Campbell topped the rhythm-and-blues charts with "Tomorrow (A Better You, a

Better Me)." "Round and Round" appeared on the soundtrack of PRINCE's film *Graffiti Bridge* (1990). Campbell's debut album, *T.E.V.I.N.*, was released in 1991.

Cara, Irene (Irene Escalera; b. Mar. 18, 1959, Bronx, N.Y.). Singer, dancer, and keyboardist. In the early 1970's, Cara was a cast member of the Broadway musical *The Me Nobody Knows*, which won an Obie Award in 1970. Her recording of the title song from the film *Fame* (1980) reached the top five on the charts, and another song from the sound track, "Out Here On My Own," was also a hit. *Fame* won an Academy award in 1980 for best original song, and the sound track album went platinum. Her single "What a Feeling," from the film *Flashdance* (1983), was a top-selling hit for which she won two 1983 Grammy Awards.

AP/Wide World Photos

Carey, Mariah. *See main text entry.*

Carter, Nell (b. Sept. 14, 1948, Birmingham, Ala.). Singer. Carter first gained popular and critical recognition for her role in *Ain't Misbehavin'* (1978) for which she earned a Tony Award. In 1991 she starred in the Long Beach Civic Light Opera's production of *Hello, Dolly!*

Chapman, Tracy. *See main text entry.*

Charles, Ray. *See main text entry.*

Chenier, Clifton. *See main text entry.*

Cole, Nat "King." *See main text entry.*

Cole, Natalie (b. Feb. 6, 1949, Los Angeles, Calif.). The daughter of singer-pianist Nat "King" Cole, Natalie Cole released a number of top-selling albums, beginning with *Inseparable* (1975). After a lull in her singing career, she released the successful *Unforgettable* (1991), a collection of her father's memorable songs; on the title song, she sang a duet with her father's voice.

Cooke, Sam. *See main text entry.*

Cotton, Elizabeth. *See main text entry.*

Davis, Sammy, Jr. *See main text entry.*

Day, Morris (b. 1957, Springfield, Ill.). Day was the lead singer of the group the Time, which released its debut album in 1981. Its second release, *What Time Is It*, was released in 1982. In 1984 Day played the foil to Prince's lead role in *Purple Rain*. After the release of *Jungle Love*, Day left the Time to pursue both an acting and a solo singing career. He appeared in another Prince film, *Graffiti Bridge* (1990), and recorded *The Color of Success* in late 1985. In 1990 the Time reunited and released *Pandemonium*.

Domino, Fats. *See main text entry.*

Duncan, Todd. *See main text entry.*

Flack, Roberta. *See main text entry.*

Gaye, Marvin. *See main text entry.*

Gaynor, Gloria (b. Sept. 7, 1949, Newark, N.J.). Singer often dubbed the "queen of American disco music." Gaynor's first album, *Never Can Say Goodbye* (1975), featured a cover of the Jackson 5's song of the same name, the MOTOWN hit "Reach Out," and her own single, "Honey Bee." In 1979 she released a powerful remake of the Perren/Fekaris song "I Will Survive." This anthem to female power reached the number-one position on the pop charts. She released *Gloria Gaynor* in 1982.

AP/Wide World Photos

Grant, Micki (M. Louise Perkins; b. June 30, 19??, Chicago, Ill.). Grant wrote the lyrics for Vinnette Carroll's 1971 Broadway play *Don't Bother Me, I Can't Cope* and cowrote the play *Your Arms Too Short to Box with God*, which appeared on Broadway in 1976 and 1980. In 1972 she won a Grammy Award, a National Association for the Advancement of Colored People IMAGE AWARD, an Obie, and two Tony nominations.

(continued)

Harney, Ben (b. 1953). Singer and actor. Harney is well known for his numerous Broadway performances, including roles in *The Wiz*, *Ain't Misbehavin'*, *Purlie*, and *Pippin*. In 1982 he won a Tony Award for his role as Curtis Taylor in *Dreamgirls*.

Havens, Richie. *See main text entry.*

Hendrix, Jimi. *See main text entry.*

Hewett, Howard. Hewett began his pop singing career as a founding member of the group Shalamar. He cowrote and coproduced eight of the nine songs that appeared on his debut solo album, *I Commit to Love* (1986). Hewett released his second album, *Forever and Ever*, in 1988.

Holloway, Brenda (b. June 21, 1946, Atascadero, Calif.). Pop vocalist. Holloway's first hit single was the soul-flavored ballad "Every Little Bit Hurts" (1964), which sold more than one million copies. She composed the song "You've Made Me So Very Happy" and released the single in 1967.

Holman, Eddie. Pop vocalist. Holman released the singles "This Can't Be True" and "Am I a Loser" in 1966. Three years later he had a huge hit with "Hey There Lonely Girl" (1969). Holman also hit the charts with "Don't Stop Now" (1970) and "Cathy Called" (1970).

Horne, Lena. *See main text entry.*

Houston, Whitney. *See main text entry.*

Howard, Miki. Howard's rhythm-and-blues singing style has been compared to that of Anita Baker. Her single "Come Share My Love" (1986) reached the *Billboard* top twenty chart for black singles.

AP/Wide World Photos

Hyman, Phyllis (b. 1950, Philadelphia, Pa.). Singer. Hyman's first album, *Phyllis Hyman*, was released in 1977. She then recorded *Somewhere in My Lifetime* (1979) and *You Sure Look Good to Me* (1980). She made her Broadway debut in 1981 in *Sophisticated Ladies*, for which she received a Tony Award nomination. Her Broadway performance coincided with her next Arista album, *Can't We Fall in Love Again?* (1981). The album *Prime of My Life* was released in 1991.

Ingram, James (b. Feb. 16, 1956, Akron, Ohio). Singer and songwriter. In 1980 Quincy Jones asked Jones to record "Just Once" and "One Hundred Ways," for his own album *The Dude* (1981). In 1982 Ingram recorded a duet with Patti Austin entitled "Baby Come to Me" for Jones's Qwest Records. This track reached number one on the pop charts and won Ingram his first Grammy Award. The pair released another duet on Qwest in 1983, "How Do You Keep the Music Playing," which reached the top ten. Toward the end of 1983, Ingram released his first solo album, *It's Your Night*, which spawned the blockbuster single "Yah Mo Be There." In 1986 Ingram released his second solo work, *Never Felt So Good*, and *It's Real* was released in 1987.

Ink Spots. *See main text entry.*

Jackson, Freddie (b. 1958). Rhythm-and-blues vocalist. Jackson's debut album, *Rock Me Tonight*, was released in 1985 and went platinum. *Just Like the First Time* (1987), a multiplatinum album, and *Don't Let Love Slip Away* (1988) followed.

Jackson, Janet. *See main text entry.*

Jackson, Michael. *See main text entry.*

Johnson, Jesse (b. 1961, Rock Island, Ill.). Singer and musician. Johnson appeared in Prince's film *Purple Rain* (1984) and cowrote the hit "Jungle Love." He left his previous group the Time in 1984 and recorded two 1985 hit singles, "I Want to Be Your Man" and "Can You Help Me." He wrote two songs for Janet Jackson's *Dream Street* album and cowrote "Shortberry Strawcake" for Sheila E.'s debut album. Johnson also sang "Heart Too Hot to Hold" for the sound track to the 1985 film *The Breakfast Club*. His 1989 album, *Jesse Johnson's Revue*, featured the single "I Want My Girl."

Jones, Quincy. *See main text entry.*

Kendrick, Eddie (Dec. 17, 1939, Union Springs, Ala.—Oct. 5, 1992, Birmingham, Ala.). Singer and songwriter. Kendrick, who dropped the "s" from "Kendricks" in the late 1970's, was an original member of the TEMPTATIONS, whose hits include "The Way You Do the Things You Do" (1964). His solo singles include the number one hit "Keep on Trucking" (1973).

Khan, Chaka (Yvette Marie Stevens; b. Mar. 23, 1953, Great Lakes, Ill.). Singer and songwriter. As vocalist for the band Rufus, Khan's first great success was with the crossover hit, "Tell Me Something Good," a gold record that also won a Grammy Award for best vocal performance in 1974. This success was followed by another gold record, *Rags to Rufus* (1974). Khan went solo in 1978; she had the hit "Ain't Nobody" in 1983, and her 1984 release *I Feel for You* went gold. "Own the Night" enjoyed considerable success in 1985.

Reprise Records

King, Evelyn "Champagne" (b. July 1, 1960, The Bronx, N.Y.). Pop singer. King's *Smooth Talk* appeared in 1977, in the disco era, and its single "Shame" became one of the biggest hits of the year. Nicknamed "Champagne" because of her bubbly personality, King soon became a staple of dance-club deejays nationwide. Her second album, *Music Box*, went gold in 1979 and produced several hit singles for 1980 and 1981. *Get Loose* (1982) also went gold.

Kitt, Eartha. *See main text entry.*

Kravitz, Lenny (b. 1964?, New York, N.Y.). Multi-instrumentalist and singer. Kravitz's 1989 album, *Let Love Rule*, boasted an eclectic musical style that critics compared to those of both Prince and John Lennon. The album *Mama Said* followed in 1991 to enthusiastic reviews; it contained the number-two single "It Ain't Over 'Till It's Over." Sometimes called a "retro-rocker," Kravitz consciously tried to attain a 1960's or early 1970's sound on some of his recordings in the 1990's. He had a hit in 1999 with a remake of "American Woman," featured in the film *Austin Powers: The Spy Who Shagged Me*.

LaBelle, Patti. *See main text entry.*

Lattisaw, Stacy (b. Nov. 25, 1966, Washington, D.C.). Singer. Lattisaw's first album, *Young and in Love* (1979), was released when she was twelve years old. *Let Me Be Your Angel* (1980), *With You* (1981), and *Sneakin' Out* (1982) followed. The title track from *Let Me Be Your Angel* hit the top spot on the rhythm-and-blues chart and the top forty on the pop chart.

Lincoln, Abbey. *See main text entry.*

Little Eva (Eva Narcissus Boyd; b. June 29, 1945, Bell Haven, N.C.). Singer. At the age of seventeen, Little Eva was immortalized with a single hit, one of the most-loved dance tunes of all times, "The Loco-Motion." In 1962 the single went to number one on both the rhythm-and-blues and pop charts.

Little Richard. *See main text entry.*

Mathis, Johnny. *See main text entry.*

McFerrin, Bobby, Jr. (b. Mar. 11, 1950, New York, N.Y.). Vocalist. The son of opera singers Robert and Sara McFerrin, McFerrin is best known for his improvised singing. His highly original singing relies on his powerful vocal range as well as his ability to use his voice as a musical instrument. His concerts, which often make effective and powerful use of audience participation, have featured duets with horn players Wynton MARSALIS and Wayne SHORTER. His "Don't Worry Be Happy" (1988) was a number-one hit.

AP/Wide World Photos

Mitchell, Abbie (Sept. 25, 1884, Baltimore, Md.—Mar. 16, 1960, New York, N.Y.). Singer. Mitchell rose to prominence performing with VAUDEVILLE stars Bert WILLIAMS and George WALKER. Apart from her versatile performances in musical comedy, drama, and opera, Mitchell is remembered for nurturing many American talents when she taught and directed music at TUSKEGEE INSTITUTE.

(continued)

Nash, Johnny (b. Aug. 19, 1940, Houston, Tex.). Singer. Nash came to the attention of Arthur Godfrey in the mid-1950's and became a regular on Godfrey's television and radio shows in 1956. With the release of "I Can See Clearly Now" (1972), Nash won sudden national acclaim, and his song was number one on the record charts. "Tears on My Pillow" gave him a second number-one hit.

Neville, Aaron (b. 1941, New Orleans, La.). Rhythm-and-blues singer. Known for his distinctive falsetto, Neville first had a major hit record with "Tell It Like It Is" in 1966. In 1977 he joined his brothers Art, Cyril, and Charles to form the Neville Brothers. In 1990 he won a Grammy Award for his duet with Linda Ronstadt, "Don't Know Much."

O'Neal, Alexander. Pop vocalist. O'Neal was discovered in Minneapolis by Prince, who helped promote his career. His debut album, *Alexander O'Neal* (1985), was produced in collaboration with former Time members Monte Moir, Terry Lewis, and Jimmy Jam. O'Neal's second album, *Hearsay* (1987), produced the hit single "Fake."

Parker, Ray, Jr. (b. May 1, 1954, Detroit, Mich.). Singer and songwriter. Parker began his career as a session musician and songwriter. His band Ray Parker, Jr., and Raydio released several gold albums before Parker went solo in 1982. *The Other Woman* was followed by a collection album and *Woman Out of Control* (1983). In 1984 Parker's title track to the film *Ghostbusters* went multiplatinum. In 1985 *Sex and the Single Man* was also a hit.

Jon Abeyta/MCA Records

Paul, Billy (Paul Williams; b. Dec. 1, 1934, Philadelphia, Pa.). Rhythm-and-blues singer. In November, 1972, Paul released his multimillion-selling hit, "Me and Mrs. Jones." He later recorded "Am I Black Enough for You?" (1973), "Thanks for Saving My Life" (1974), and "Let's Make a Baby" (1976), all singles that made it onto the soul charts.

Pendergrass, Teddy (b. Mar. 26, 1950, Philadelphia, Pa.). Singer. Pendergrass joined Harold Melvin and the Blue Notes, a Philadelphia rhythm-and-blues group, in 1970. Their major hit was "If You Don't Know Me by Now" (1972). In 1976 Pendergrass left the group for a successful solo career. He was paralyzed from the neck down as the result of an automobile accident in 1982.

Pride, Charley (b. Mar. 18, 1938, Sledge, Miss.). Country music singer. Pride was the first African American to become a superstar in country and western music. In 1967 he became the first black country singer to appear at the Grand Ole Opry. He won numerous awards, including three Grammy Awards.

AP/Wide World Photos

Prince. *See main text entry.*

Reese, Della (Dellareese Taliaferro; b. July 6, 1932, Detroit, Mich.). Vocalist. By age thirteen, Reese was touring with Mahalia Jackson. Her biggest hit was "Don't You Know" in 1959. She had moderate success as a pop and cabaret singer in the 1960's, 1970's, and 1980's. Also an actor, Reese appeared on the television series *Touched by an Angel* in the 1990's.

Richie, Lionel (b. June 20, 1949, Tuskegee, Ala.). Singer. Richie's musical career began with the Commodores, a group that enjoyed great success in the late 1970's, with Richie writing some of its most successful songs, such as "Easy" (1977) and the number-one hit "Three Times a Lady" (1978). He left the group permanently in 1982. He wrote the number-one hit "Lady" for Kenny Rogers in 1980 and the theme song for the 1981 film *Endless Love*. Diana Ross recorded the song with him, and it became a number-one hit in 1981. *Can't Slow Down* (1984) produced five hit singles, including "All Night Long." In 1984 he teamed with Michael Jackson to write "We Are the World," and in 1985 Richie won an Academy Award for his "Say You, Say Me" from the film *White Nights*.

Riley, Cheryl "Pepsii" (b. 1962, New York, N.Y.). Singer. Riley's hit single "Thanks for My Child"

(1988) brought attention to the plight of single parents but was criticized for supposedly advocating single parenthood. Her album *Chapters* was released in 1990.

Riperton, Minnie. *See main text entry.*

Robinson, Smokey. *See main text entry.*

Ross, Diana. *See main text entry.*

Rucker, Darius (b. 1966?, Charleston, S.C.). Singer and songwriter. Rucker achieved fame as the lead singer and songwriter with the rock group Hootie and the Blowfish. *Cracked Rear View* was released in 1994. The album's first single, "Hold My Hand," reached the top ten on *Billboard* magazine's pop music charts. By January of 1996, more than twelve million copies of the album had been sold. Rucker and his fellow band members released their second album, *Fairweather Johnson*, in 1996, and *Musical Chairs* in 1998.

AP/Wide World Photos

Ruffin, David (Jan. 18, 1941, Meridian, Miss.—June 1, 1991, Philadelphia, Pa.). Singer. Ruffin was the lead singer and one of the original members of the Motown group the Temptations. He left in 1968 to embark on a solo singing career and met with moderate success. He rejoined the Temptations in 1982 for the *Reunion* album and was inducted into the Rock and Roll Hall of Fame in 1989 with four other members of the group.

RuPaul (RuPaul Andre Charles; b. Nov. 17, 1960, San Diego, Calif.). In 1990 disco drag queen Ru Paul performed in the video of the B-52's hit song "Love Shack." His debut album was called *Supermodel of the World* (1993). RuPaul's single "Supermodel (You Better Work)" spent five months on *Billboard* magazine's Hot 100 list and reached number two on the magazine's dance chart in March of 1993. The album's second single, "Back to My Roots," was a tongue-in-cheek homage to black fashions and hairstyles over the years.

Rushen, Patrice (b. Sept. 30, 1954, Los Angeles, Calif.). Vocalist, film composer, and music director. As a vocalist, Rushen recorded numerous albums that produced singles such as "Haven't You Heard," "Never Gonna Give You Up," "Don't Blame Me," "Remind Me," "Feels So Good," and "Forget Me Nots." She composed the score for the films *Without You I'm Nothing* (1990) and *Hollywood Shuffle* (1987). Rushen was the first African American and the first woman to be the musical director of television's Emmy Awards (1991, 1992). She served as musical director, conductor, and arranger of television's *The Midnight Hour* and was the musical director of *Comic Relief V* in 1992.

Scott-Heron, Gil (b. Apr. 1, 1949, Chicago, Ill.): Scott-Heron's compositions depicting racial and social issues spurred further generations of socially conscious artists. A published author as well a performer, Scott-Heron managed to fuse JAZZ stylings with a running dialogue that many consider to be a precursor to the RAP and HIP-HOP styles of the 1980's and 1990's. Releases include *Pieces of a Man* (1973), which included the poem "The Revolution Will Not Be Televised; Scott-Heron performed "We Almost Lost Detroit" in 1979 at an antinuclear power benefit concert at Madison Square Garden.

Sheila E. (Sheila Escovedo; b. Dec. 12, 1959, San Francisco, Calif.). Singer and percussionist. Proficient on ten different percussion instruments as well as guitar and piano, Sheila E. was a successful studio musician until Prince encouraged her to write and record her own music. In 1984 she released *The Glamorous Life*. Two other albums, *Romance 1600* and the self-titled *Sheila E.*, soon followed. In 1985 she starred in producer Michael Schultz's film *Krush Groove*.

Simone, Nina. *See main text entry.*

Snow, Phoebe (b. July 17, 1952, New York, N.Y.). Singer, guitarist, and composer. Snow attracted fans in the 1970's with original songs such as "Poetry Man," "I Don't Want the Night to End," "No Show Tonight," "Shine, Shine, Shine," and "Harpo's Blues."

Summer, Donna. *See main text entry.*

Sylvester (Sylvester James; c. 1946, Los Angeles, Calif.—December, 1988, Oakland, Calif.). Singer. Flam-

(continued)

boyant disco star Sylvester's brand of high-camp style enabled him to cross over from gay disco fame to mainstream appeal at the peak of the disco craze. His second album, *Step Two,* was released in 1978 and included two hit singles, "(You Make Me Feel) Mighty Real" and "Dance (Disco Heat)."

Syreeta (Syreeta Wright; b. 1946, Pittsburgh, Pa.). Singer. Syreeta began writing songs with Stevie WONDER in the early 1970's. Her fourth album, *Rich Love, Poor Love* (1977), featuring G. C. Cameron, yielded several hit singles. Billy Preston and Syreeta sang a duet together for the sound track to the film *Fast Break* (1979). They completed an album in 1981, *Billy Preston and Syreeta,* and had several hit singles, including "It Will Come in Time" and "With You I'm Born Again."

Terrell, Tammi (Thomasina Montgomery; 1946, Philadelphia, Pa.—Mar. 16, 1970, Philadelphia, Pa.). Singer. Motown paired Terrell with Marvin GAYE, and their three-year singing partnership put them at the top of the charts. "Ain't No Mountain High Enough" and "Your Precious Love" were released in 1967. "Ain't Nothing Like the Real Thing" and "You're All I Need to Get By" are classics in pop music.

Turner, Tina. *See main text entry.*

Vandross, Luther (b. Apr. 20, 1951, New York, N.Y.). Singer. Vandross recorded his first million seller, *Never Too Much,* in 1981. Subsequent releases on Epic, *Forever, for Always, for Love; Busy Body;* and *The Night I Fell in Love,* followed. Hits include "Here and Now" (1990) and, with Mariah Carey, "Endless Love" (1994).

AP/Wide World Photos

Vanity (Denise Matthews; b. 1958, Niagara Falls, Ontario, Canada). Singer. The name "Vanity" was assigned to Matthews by Prince, who teamed her with Susan Moonsie and Brenda Bennett, dressed the three in camisoles, and billed them as Vanity 6. In 1983 Vanity left the group and later released *Wild Animal.* Two singles, "Pretty Mess" and "Mechanical Emotion," each reached the top twenty-five on the rhythm-and-blues charts in 1984. Vanity has also appeared in occasional films, including *The Last Dragon* (1985).

Warwick, Dionne. *See main text entry.*

Waters, Ethel. *See main text entry.*

Watley, Jody (b. Jan. 30, 1961, Chicago, Ill.). Singer and dancer. A former *Soul Train* dancer, Watley joined with dancing partner Jeffrey Daniels and Howard Hewett to form the group Shalamar. They enjoyed great success in the late 1970's and early 1980's before Watley left the group in 1983 to pursue her solo career. Her second album, *Larger than Life,* produced six top-ten singles, and she won a 1988 Grammy Award as best new artist. Her album *Affairs of the Heart* came out in 1991 and soon went platinum. She released an exercise video, *Dance to Fitness,* the same year.

Wells, Mary (May 13, 1943, Detroit, Mich.—July 26, 1991, Los Angeles, Calif.). Pop singer. From 1961 to 1964, Wells made such top-ten records as "You Beat Me to the Punch" (1962), "Two Lovers" (1962), and "My Guy" (1964, written by Smokey Robinson), a number-one hit that became her signature song. In 1964 Wells recorded two hit duets with singer Marvin Gaye.

Williams, Deniece (b. June 3, 1951, Gary, Ind.). Singer and songwriter. Williams's first album, *This Is Niecey* (1977) produced a worldwide hit single, "Free." The follow-up single, "That's What Friends Are For," was also was a big hit, while a number of her songs were recorded by other artists. In 1978 she released a duet with Johnny Mathis, "Too Much, Too Little, Too Late," which became a number-one hit. She produced several gospel records, which garnered her three Grammy Awards. Her album *I Can't Wait* was released in 1988, and a duet album featuring Williams, *Better Together,* appeared in 1992.

Williams, Vesta. Pop vocalist. Williams's 1986 album *Vesta* contained the hit single "Once Bitten Twice Shy," and her follow-up album, *Special* (1991), was also a best-seller.

Wilson, Jackie. *See main text entry.*

Wilson, Shanice (b. 1973). Pop vocalist. Wilson's debut album, *Discovery*, was praised by critics but failed to achieve commercial success. Her second album, *Inner Child* (1991), was produced by Narada Michael Walden, who had produced records for Aretha Franklin and Whitney Houston. Wilson cowrote eight songs on the album, mostly with Walden.

Wonder, Stevie. *See main text entry.*

Wright, Betty (b. Dec. 21, 1953, Miami, Fla.). Rhythm-and-blues singer. Wright's first hit single, "Girls Can't Do What the Guys Do," was released in 1968. In 1971 the single "Clean Up Woman" sold more than a million copies. She is best known for her 1975 hit single, "Where Is the Love."

Yancey, Jimmy. *See main text entry.*

tured a small ensemble of five to eight instruments including cornet, clarinet, trombone, trap drum set, piano, banjo (or guitar), and on occasion tuba. The ensemble was divided into a melodic section called the front line (cornet, clarinet, and trombone), which collectively improvised the melody, and an accompanying section called the second line or rhythm section. Major practitioners within this tradition were Joseph "King" OLIVER, Freddie Keppard, Ferdinand "Jelly Roll" MORTON, Edward "Kid" ORY, and Sidney BECHET.

The Swing Era

From the mid-1920's, the size of the jazz ensemble began expanding. As the size of the ensemble increased, musicians were required to read music (which was not a requirement within the New Orleans jazz tradition) and tended to have more formal musical training. By the mid-1930's, African American big band leaders included Cabbell "Cab" CALLOWAY, William "Count" BASIE, Jimmie LUNCEFORD, and Edward Kennedy "Duke" ELLINGTON. Ellington was one of the most prolific composers in U.S. history, with such popular works as "Mood Indigo" (1930), "Sophisticated Lady" (1933), and "Black, Brown, and Beige" (1943). Swing music had an overall rhythmic drive, and the melodic line was divided among solo instruments or sections within the ensemble, such as the brass section, woodwinds, or rhythm section. Within the swing tradition, the terms "hot" and "sweet" took on racial connotations. "Hot" jazz had an excited or wild style associated with African American musicians. The more tuneful, relaxed, "sweet" style was more commonly associated with white musicians. Sweet jazz was seen as lacking the bite of the original "hot" style.

Bebop

Although there were many well-known African American swing musicians, most of the attention and playing engagements went to white big band leaders such as Benny Goodman, the Dorsey brothers (Tommy and Jimmy), Guy Lombardo, and Lawrence Welk. Except for Count Basie and Duke Ellington, most African American big band leaders found it increasingly difficult to earn a living. RACIAL DISCRIMINATION regarding musical engagements in jazz produced much resentment among African American jazz musicians, who developed a new style of music partly in response.

The beginnings of the BEBOP movement centered around after-hours jam sessions in two Harlem nightclubs, MINTON'S PLAYHOUSE AND, TO A LESSER EXTENT, MONROE'S. Leading these after-hours sessions were musicians such as electric guitarist Charlie CHRISTIAN, TRUMPETER DIZZY GILLESPIE, pianist Clyde Hart, string bass player Jimmy Blanton, and saxophonists Charlie PARKER AND LESTER YOUNG. Bebop, as a new form of jazz, came to the public attention through the recordings of Parker and Gillespie in the mid-1940's. The music was fast, rhythmic, asymmetrical, and more esoteric than swing. Black innovators in this style wanted music that demanded more from them and would be difficult for white musicians to copy. The musicians manifested an antientertainer attitude (for example, by smoking on stage, wearing sunglasses, turning away from the audience, and failing to acknowledge applause). Since the bebop ensemble was much smaller than the average big band (generally four or five players), it also was more economical.

Rhythm and Blues

RHYTHM AND BLUES emerged in the late 1940's and early 1950's. Rhythm and blues grew out of the urban blues tradition. In the traditional blues, the focus was on the singer, but within rhythm and blues, the instrumentalist or the entire ensemble gained prominence. Generally, the music was up-tempo, with an emphasis on rhythm that made it easy to dance to. Major exponents of this tradition were Arthur "Big Boy" CRUDUP, Joe Turner, "LITTLE RICHARD" Penniman, Bo DIDDLEY, Ruth BROWN, and Chuck BERRY. Many rhythm-and-blues artists later took up rock and roll.

Cool Jazz and Hard Bop

During the mid-1950's and early 1960's, jazz experienced changes as well. There were musicians, mostly white, who believed that bebop had become esoteric, abstract, and undanceable. A cool or more relaxed and tuneful style of jazz emerged. This movement gained some recognition, mostly on the West Coast, but it was largely unsuccessful. Cool jazz did lead, however, to another movement in jazz by African American musicians on the East Coast. Hard bop was stylistically similar to the original bop style. In addition to Dizzy Gillespie and Miles DAVIS, other prominent names in hard bop were Thelonious MONK, Charles MINGUS, Art BLAKEY, Horace Silver, Julian "Cannonball" ADDERLEY, and Quincy JONES.

By the early 1960's, the standard bop formula (the ensemble playing at the beginning and end of a work and between improvisatory solos) had become stagnant. Some musicians, such as tenor saxophonist John COLTRANE, experimented with African and eastern musical influences and moved into free jazz. Ornette COLEMAN expanded stylistic parameters in his thirty-seven-minute improvisatory recording, *Free Jazz* (1960).

Popular Styles

By the early 1960's, several types of groups and of individual African American musicians had appeared. All-male groups such as the Four Tops, the Temptations, and Smokey ROBINSON and the Miracles were outgrowths of the 1950's rhythm-and-blues and doo-wop quartets. Their female counterparts were groups such as the SUPREMES, MARTHA AND THE VANDELLAS, and the Marvelettes. Many of these groups were associated with music labels owned by Berry GORDY, Jr., including MOTOWN Records. The new style of music, involving either a strong dance rhythm or slow, romantic balladeering, became known as the Motown sound.

Solo artists such as Ray CHARLES, Aretha FRANKLIN, Jackie WILSON, Mary Wells, James BROWN, and Marvin GAYE also emerged during this period. Many came from religious (gospel) music backgrounds and made a transition from rhythm and blues to popular music, which generally was aimed at younger audiences. In the context of the Civil Rights movement of the 1960's, James Brown recorded "Say It Loud, I'm Black and I'm Proud" (1968), which became a rallying cry for many young African Americans of that era.

In the 1970's, African American musicians became more conscious of social issues, as manifested in Marvin Gaye's *What's Going On?* (1971), a commentary on the Vietnam War and other social ills. A second generation of

(continued on page 1786)

Producers, Songwriters, and Music Executives

Bradford, Perry "Mule." *See main text entry.*

Dr. Dre. *See main text entry.*

Gamble and Huff. Songwriting and producing team Kenny Gamble and Leon Huff were responsible for establishing PHILADELPHIA as a major center for soul music during the early 1970's and are credited with creating the "Philadelphia sound." The duo formed Philadelphia International Records, writing and producing million-selling hit records for artists such as the O'Jays, Billy Paul, Harold Melvin and the Blue Notes, the Intruders, and the Three Degrees.

Gordy, Berry, Jr. *See main text entry.*

Harrell, Andre O'Neal (b. 1962?, Bronx, N.Y.). RAP performer and record company executive. Harrell joined with Alonzo Brown to form the rap duo Dr. Jekyll and Mr. Hyde. The duo had three hits: "Genius Rap," "Fast Life," and "AM/FM." In 1983 Harrell began working for Russell Simmons's Rush Communications company, leaving in 1987 to start his own recording company, Uptown Records. Harrell discovered and produced performers such as Heavy D and the Boyz, Jodeci, Father MC, Christopher Williams, Al B. Shure!, and Mary J. Blige. In the 1990's Harrell branched out into television and film production. He succeeded Jheryl Busby as head of MCA's Motown Records division.

AP/Wide World Photos

Holland-Dozier-Holland. Songwriting and record producing team composed of brothers Brian and Eddie Holland and Lamont Dozier. The three joined MOTOWN Records early in its history. The trio often wrote and produced for the Supremes and Four Tops. At their peak, from 1963 to 1966, the team produced twenty-eight top-ten records, twelve of which were number-one hits. They left Motown in 1968 to form their own Invictus and Hot Wax recording labels.

Jones, Quincy. *See main text entry.*

Jones, Richard Myknee (June 13, 1889, Donaldsville, La.—Dec. 8, 1945, Chicago, Ill.). Jazz pianist, songwriter, and producer. In 1919 Jones became manager of the Clarence Williams Publishing Company. In the 1920's OKeh Records hired him to serve as recording director of the label's "race records." Jones made his first recording in 1923. He toured and recorded with his group the Jazz Wizards, later known as the Chicago Cosmopolitans. In the 1930's, Jones worked as a talent scout for Decca Records, later scouting for Mercury. He was best known for his songs "Jazzin' Babies Blues" (1924), "Riverside Blues" (1925), and the blues standard "Trouble in Mind" (1926).

Lewis, Terry, and James "Jimmy Jam" Harris III. Pop songwriters and producers. Harris and Lewis began writing songs and producing albums for the group the Time, including *The Time* (1981) and *What Time Is It.* (1982). They formed their own production company called Flyte Tyme Productions. Between 1983 and 1985, Jimmy Jam and Lewis were busy working with performers such as the SOS Band, Cherrelle, Alexander O'Neal, and Force M.D.'s. Their greatest success came in collaboration with Janet Jackson on her hit album *Control* (1986).

Shocklee, Hank (Hank Boxley; b. 1960?). Early rap music producer. Shocklee and PUBLIC ENEMY's Chuck D. grew up together, and Shockley produced Public Enemy's debut album in 1987. Public Enemy, Ice Cube, and many other artists on the Def Jam Records label were developed as a result of Shocklee's efforts as a producer and remixer. In 1990 he founded the S.O.U.L. (Sound of Urban Listeners) label. The sound track to the film *Juice* (1992) was scored, assembled, and produced by Shocklee.

Simmons, Russell (b. 1957?, Hollis, Queens, N.Y.). Rap music manager, producer, and record executive. With Rush Productions and later with his Rush Artist Management company, Simmons directed the careers of such popular rap artists as L.L. COOL J, Public Enemy, and the Beastie Boys. Simmons, with Rick Rubin, cofounded Def Jam Records in 1985. Simmons also served as associate producer of the rap films *Krush Groove* (1985) and *Tougher than*

(continued)

Leather (1988). When Simmons and Rubin eventually dissolved their partnership, Simmons maintained creative control of the majority of artists signed to Def Jam. His multimillion-dollar entertainment company—embracing music, film, and television—became the largest black-owned music business in the United States.

Toussaint, Allen (b. Jan. 14, 1938, New Orleans, La.). Songwriter, producer, and arranger. An accomplished pianist, Toussaint wrote and produced songs and albums for artists such as Joe Cocker, Dr. John, and the Pointer Sisters. Among the songs he wrote are rock and soul classics from the 1960's such as "Mother-in-Law," "Workin' in a Coal Mine," and "Sea Cruise." His "Whipped Cream" was a hit for Herb Alpert. Toussaint made his own instrumental album for RCA, entitled *Wild Sounds of New Orleans* (1958) and released under the name of Al Tousan.

AP/Wide World Photos

Whitfield, Norman (b. 1943, New York, N.Y.). Songwriter and producer. Coauthor of "I Heard It Through the Grapevine" (1968), a top-ten single for Marvin Gaye, Whitfield, along with his collaborator Barrett Strong, pioneered Motown's shift from the lyrical purity of the Holland-Dozier-Holland writing team to the "psychedelic soul" sound. After he left Motown in the mid-1970's, Whitfield wrote for and produced acts such as Rose Royce and the Undisputed Truth.

Motown recording artists appeared with the Jackson 5, a group discovered by Diana Ross of the original Supremes. By the early 1970's, Michael Jackson, lead vocalist of the Jackson 5, had launched a successful solo career, and by the late 1980's he had become the world's most popular contemporary musician.

Rap Music

In the mid-1970's, New York City disc jockeys began experimenting with recordings using two turntables, a mixer, and speakers to talk over the background beat from the turntables. This style was first called jazz mixing but later became known as rap music. Some pioneers in the genre were Grandmaster Flash (Joseph Saddler), Cool DJ Herc (Clive Campbell), Kurtis Blow, and Afrika Bambaataa. Rap is less distinctive as a musical art than it is as a verbal art. Its poetry combines rhymed couplets (some of which are improvised) over a fast background beat, with occasional effects being interjected by a scratcher (turntable operator). By the late 1980's and early 1990's, artists including Queen Latifah, Ice Cube, M. C. Hammer (also a dancer), Will Smith, and Kool Moe Dee had begun infusing social and political messages into their rap songs. Still others, most notably Luther Campbell of 2 Live Crew and Chuck D. of Public Enemy, generated public controversy in the early 1990's because of the sexually explicit nature of their rap lyrics.

Gospel Music

Gospel music emerged from religious roots in the late nineteenth-century African American Holiness and Sanctified Christian practices. The term "gospel music" in reference to an African American sacred music genre did not become standard before the late 1930's. An early pioneer of gospel songs was the Reverend Charles Albert Tindley, whose religious compositions "Stand By Me," "I Do, Don't You," and "Nothing Between" included both words and music. Within the Church of God and Christ and Pentecostal denominations (both within the Holiness tradition), the genre took greater shape in urban areas. It frequently used the growls, hums, falsetto, screams, and bent notes that were the vocal basis of the blues. The blues influence was infused within the gospel music tradition even more with the emergence of Thomas A. DORSEY, the acclaimed "father of gospel music." As a former blues pianist and composer, Dorsey was a prime promoter of gospel music and was responsible for many traditions that became associated with it. Several of his "disciples," such as Sallie MARTIN and Roberta Martin (no relation) and Willie Mae Ford SMITH, influenced the next generation of gospel singers as the genre became more professional and commercial. One of Smith's protégés, Mahalia JACKSON, was in large part responsible for spreading gospel music outside the U.S. borders.

Gospel music enjoyed a "golden age" during the mid-1940's and 1950's, when women such as Queen C. Anderson, Clara WARD, Ruth Davis, Dorothy Love Coates, Edna Gallmon Looke, and Bessie Griffin, along with men such as Julius Cheeks, Archie Brownlee, Alex Bradford, James CLEVELAND, Claude Jeter, Brother Joe May, and Ira Tucker, were among the most celebrated names in the business. Gospel music's close association with the CIVIL RIGHTS movement of the 1950's and 1960's exposed white Americans to the tradition. Because of its spread throughout Protestant African American congregations around the United States, gospel music enjoys enduring success.

Gospel is only one of the forms of African American music with roots back to the nineteenth century or even further. All modern forms of black music, in fact, can trace at least a small part of their heritage back to the African continent.

—*Christopher Brooks*

See also: Chicago blues; Chicago jazz; House music.

Suggested Readings:

Barlow, William, and Cheryl Finley. *From Swing to Soul: An Illustrated History of African American Popular Music from 1930 to 1960*. Washington, D.C.: Elliott & Clark, 1994.

Caldwell, Hansonia L. *African American Music: A Chronology, 1619-1995*. Los Angeles: Ikoro Communications, 1995.

Floyd, Samuel A. *The Power of Black Music: Interpreting Its History from Africa to the United States*. New York: Oxford University Press, 1995.

Haskins, James. *Black Music in America: A History Through Its People*. New York: Thomas Y. Crowell, 1987.

Jackson, Irene V., ed. *More than Dancing: Essays on Afro-American Music and Musicians*. Westport, Conn.: Greenwood Press, 1985.

Kebede, Ashenafi. *Roots of Black Music: The Vocal, Instrumental, and Dance Heritage of Africa and Black America*. Trenton, N.J.: Africa World Press, 1995.

Merlis, Bob, and Davin Seay. *Heart and Soul: A Celebration of Black Music Style in America, 1930-1975*. New York: Stewart, Tabori & Chang, 1997.

Morgan, Thomas L., and William Barlow. *From Cakewalks to Concert Halls: An Illustrated History of African American Popular Music from 1895 to 1930*. Washington, D.C.: Elliott & Clark, 1992.

Neal, Mark A. *What the Music Said: Black Popular Music and Black Public Culture*. New York: Routledge, 1999.

Shaw, Arnold. *Black Popular Music in America: From the Spirituals, Minstrels, and Ragtime to Soul, Disco, and Hip-Hop*. New York: Schirmer Books, 1986.

Small, Christopher. *Music of the Common Tongue: Survival and Celebration in African American Music*. Hanover, N.H.: University Press of New England, 1998.

Southern, Eileen. *The Music of Black Americans: A History*. 3d ed. New York: W. W. Norton, 1997.

Spencer, Jon M. *Researching Black Music*. Knoxville: University of Tennessee Press, 1996.

Stewart, Earl L. *African American Music: An Introduction*. New York: Schirmer Books, 1998.

N

Nabrit, James Madison, Jr. (September 4, 1900, Atlanta, Georgia—December 27, 1997, Washington, D.C.): Lawyer and government official. On August 25, 1965, Nabrit was appointed as ambassador to the United Nations and was the highest-ranking African American to serve in any U.S. delegation to the United Nations up to that time. He served as a deputy representative on the United Nations Security Council.

Nabrit earned his B.A. at Morehouse College in 1923 and his J.D. at Northwestern University in 1927. He taught English at Leland College from 1925 to 1928 and was dean of Arkansas State College from 1928 to 1930. In 1930 Nabrit set up a law practice in HOUSTON, TEXAS, handling CIVIL RIGHTS cases, many involving the right to vote. Nabrit joined the HOWARD UNIVERSITY School of Law faculty in 1936. He taught the first course in civil rights ever offered at a law school in the United States. In addition to his teaching responsibilities, Nabrit was the director of public relations from 1940 to 1950 and from 1955 to 1958, secretary of the university from 1939 to 1960, and dean of the school of law from 1958 to 1960. Howard University named Nabrit as its president in 1960. He served in that position until 1969, when he resigned after conflicts with militant students on campus.

Nabrit served in various governmental positions while at Howard University. During WORLD WAR II, he was on the Selective Service Board, and he was chair of the Price Control Board for the Northwest Area of the District of Columbia. In 1954 he was legal adviser to the governor of the VIRGIN ISLANDS, at a time when the executive branch of the territory's government was being reorganized. From 1954 to 1961, he was a member of the President's Committee on Government Contracts, which was created to end job discrimination in companies holding government contracts. Nabrit was twice a delegate to the International Labor Conference in Geneva, Switzerland.

While at Howard, Nabrit continued his participation in civil rights cases and was counsel in many of the important civil rights cases between 1945 and 1960. He discontinued participation with these cases when he became university president, but he affirmed his duty to prepare others to fight for equal rights. In addition, he tried to raise Howard University's academic standards, which were low, he said, because of the inadequate preparation many students had received in segregated high schools.

Nabrit participated in the case NIXON V. HERNDON (1927), which ruled unconstitutional a TEXAS statute prohibiting African Americans from voting in primary elections. MCLAURIN V. OKLAHOMA STATE REGENTS (1950) prohibited the state from discriminating against a student of any racial group at a state-supported institution. *Bolling v. Sharpe* (1954) was possibly Nabrit's most important case, argued before the U.S. SUPREME COURT. The ruling in that case prohibited racial discrimination in public schools in the District of Columbia. This case, with others, led to the Supreme Court's declaration that public school segregation is unconstitutional.

See also: Diplomats; Segregation and integration.

Nabrit, Samuel (b. February 21, 1905, Macon, Georgia): Educator. Nabrit earned his B.S. from Morehouse College and, in 1932, became the first African American to earn a Ph.D. from Brown University. In 1966 Nabrit became the first African American appointed to the U.S. Atomic Energy Commission. He served as president of Texas Southern University from 1955 to 1966. He also served as executive director of the Southern Fellowships Fund of the Council of Southern Universities and as chair of the Institute for Services to Education.

Names: African Americans have a unique history of choosing personal names, and naming traditions have been influenced by a variety of factors. The earliest influence is West African naming traditions, as most of the slaves in America were brought from this region. Subsequently, names were assigned to enslaved people by their masters. After emancipation, some of these names were retained, but many former slaves adopted new names. Twentieth century naming practices include continuing the tradition of keeping certain names in the family, making up entirely new names, and renaming oneself for religious reasons.

The original personal names of enslaved Africans in America reflected the African culture or ethnic group, usually West African, from which an individual came. Cuffey was a common African name, as were Cudjo, Quashie, Jacco (Jocko), Juba, Catto, Sambo, Mingo, Mina, Cuba, Phibee (Fibi), Binta, and Benah. Some of these names symbolize the traditional African custom of calling children after a significant event corresponding to the day of the week or season a child was born. Cuffey signifies Monday in one West African language; Cudjo means the same in another. Quashey connotes Sunday in the Akan language, and Phibee indicates Friday. Cuba, Quaco, or Jacco mean Wednesday.

Naming During the Slavery Era

One aspect of the enslavement process was the stripping of African names and their replacement with names originating in Europe. In the British colonies, African names were anglicized; Cuffey or Cuffee evolved into Coffee, Cudjo became Joe, Jacco resulted in Jack, Phibee became Phoebe, and Catto or Keto (a noun in the Bambara, Yoruba, and Hausa languages) was transformed into Cato after the ancient Roman statesman. The names of many of the thirty-one Africans executed in the alleged 1741 New York City slave revolt illustrate this transition; their names included Quaco, Kips' Negro, Caesar, Cuffee, Prince, Jack, Jamaica, Albany, and Tickle.

Several of the early African names continued in the black community, however, and they identified the bearer as being of African ancestry. Paul CUFFE, a wealthy merchant and sea trader in MASSACHUSETTS, lived during the eighteenth century. Octavius Catto was a prominent educator and political activist in PHILADELPHIA in the late 1800's. Benjamin BANNEKER's grandmother, an Irish indentured servant, took his African grandfather's name, Banakry, when the two married in colonial VIRGINIA. These celebrated names have been retained by descendants and grace buildings and organizations.

Often the names given to enslaved Africans by slaveholders were facetious or mocking. Appellations such as Caesar, Scipio, Neptune, Prince, Pompey, and Hannibal are examples. Common names among enslaved African women were Sukey, Lucy, Dicey, Dilsey, and Dinah. Such labels were badges of enslavement and inferiority. They became associated primarily with African Americans so that Elizabeth Cady Stanton could say, as she fought for women's suffrage, that white women wanted Bridget and Dinah (white and black women) to be able to vote rather than Patrick and Sambo (white and black men). It was understood that she was using common stereotypical names for blacks. That these names were considered insulting can be seen in the fact that most did not survive after SLAV-

ERY ended and African Americans were free to choose their own names.

Africans changed what they felt to be negative names when they obtained freedom in order to demonstrate their new condition. In 1820 a black man in Sumterville, SOUTH CAROLINA, had his name changed legally from "April" to "William" Ellison after being freed because "April" stigmatized him as a person who had been enslaved. Escape from enslavement also occasioned name changes, as fugitives altered their names to avoid detection by slave catchers. Frederick Bailey, therefore, became Frederick DOUGLASS. When Henry Highland GARNET's entire family escaped, his father, a native of Africa, held a renaming ceremony in which he assigned them all the same surname, Garnet, and each one a different first name.

In the early years of slavery, enslaved Africans were given only first names. Sometimes, in order to distinguish between slaves with similar names, slaveowners categorized a person by whom his or her parents were or by some type of diminutive equivalent to a physical description or perceived origin. For instance, "Sally's Mingo" would have meant that Mingo was the son of Sally. Yellow Lucy, Big Minah, Little Dilsey, and Blind Tom are illustrations of physical diminutives. The names Gullah Jack, a leader in Nat Turner's Virginia rebellion, and Congo Joe are derived from African locations. Later, as the African population grew, surnames were assumed and used by the enslaved and enslavers. Runaway slave announcements often gave first and last names of fugitives and noted the names by which they called themselves.

Newly freed Africans also supplied themselves with surnames. Amos Beman, a well-known nineteenth-century abolitionist, chose his own last name after he was freed because he wanted to "be a man." In a another famous case, Isabella Baumfree stated that when she left enslavement, she left everything behind,

After winning her freedom, Isabella Baumfree changed her named to "Sojourner Truth" in the belief that God wanted her to travel to spread the Christian faith. *(Arkent Archive)*

including her slave name. She said that God gave her a new name, Sojourner, because she was to travel about and proselytize the Christian gospel. She asked God for a surname. He gave her the last name of Truth because she was to bring the truth to people. She became the acclaimed abolitionist Sojourner TRUTH.

Countless enslaved Africans retained traditional African naming practices. For example, in addition to the name that the slaveowner gave them, slaves frequently had a secret pet name or nickname by which they were known in their own families or among friends. Elizabeth Botume, a white woman who worked as a missionary among the newly freed Africans in the Sea Islands of South Carolina, gave an illustration of the confusion of such names in her book *First Days Amongst the Contrabands* (1893). She reported that it was difficult to record the names of the freed people because they used various names for themselves and others in addition to their given names. The conferring of pet names remains common in black culture.

African Americans also named their children after kin, as was customary in Africa, so that many families recirculated the same names over and over. Children were regularly named for dead or separated family members, including siblings. This was especially true for boys, who were often given their fathers' or grandfathers' names. This familial tie was strengthened after the Civil War, when some African American sons took the last names of their fathers, even if they already had a surname, in order to make it their family name. During the period of enslavement, fathers were often separated from their families because of the nature of slaveholding; mothers and fathers often lived on different plantations, and the names of enslaved fathers were rarely noted in slaveholders' records. The custom of christening sons and, sometimes, daughters after their fathers established a bond that could not be broken by enslavement.

The sale of Africans to different owners occasionally prompted name changes, as the enslaved person came to be known by the new slaveowner's last name or the owner simply decided to change the enslaved's name. In one 1856 bill of sale, a slaveowner is selling "a negro boy I named Nathen aged eighteen." Olaudah Equiano says in his 1789 narrative, *The Interesting Narrative of the Life of Olaudah Equiano: Or, Gustavus Vassa, the African*, that he was forced to accept a series of European names as his masters changed. He was called Jacob, Michael, and then Gustavus Vassa on the whim of each master.

Naming After Emancipation

The acquiring of new surnames on a massive scale by black people is apparent in CIVIL WAR pension records and RECONSTRUCTION records. As they attempted to assume the mantle of American citizenship, African Americans often used last names with which they were familiar, sometimes those of slaveholders. Others assumed European names to represent their changed situation, rejecting specific names reminiscent of their particular experience of enslavement. Most African American surnames therefore are little distinguishable from white American names, especially British, Irish, Scots-Irish, and Welsh-derived names, since these groups were the primary slaveholders in the United States. Last names such as Jones, Williams, and Brown are commonplace among the black population.

Name variations posed difficulties as families attempted to reunite after emancipation. *The Christian Recorder*, a leading nineteenth-century African American newspaper, carried poignant advertisements from persons seeking family members. Notices asking for information about persons described the names they were known to use in enslavement, the owners' names, and locations where they were last seen. The people placing the ads often gave the different names by which they were known as well.

Twentieth-Century Naming

Early twentieth century African American male names reflected the honor that African Americans gave to specific people who were considered to be supporters of the black community. George Washington, Benjamin Franklin, Thomas Jefferson, Ulysses Grant, Abraham Lincoln, Booker T. WASHINGTON, and later Franklin D. Roosevelt have all been venerated by the extensive christening of male children with these names. These appellations, in their full forms such as Benjamin Franklin Jones, are almost exclusively trademarks of African American names.

The activism and self-definition of the Civil Rights and Black Power movements of the 1960's are evident in current African American names. A custom of creating first names associated with, or loosely based on, African, French, or Spanish words emerged from these movements, and these types of names have become uniquely identified with African American culture. Names such as Kiya, Shaquita, DuShawn, Shanaynay, Laquita, Tameka, Shameka, Malika, DeJuan, Shonda, Keisha, LaVeta, Shanika, Colita, Shawniqua, Moesha, and many other derivatives and variations typically identify the bearer as an African American.

Many African Americans assume African or Arabic names as a symbol of their commitment to self-definition. Names such as Kamil, Ali, Kwame, Amir, Nzinga, Ra, Halima, Kareem, Khadijah, Jamal, Kamal, Rashid, and Muhammad are common. Adherents of the NATION OF ISLAM reject "slave" names, the European names originating in the period of enslavement. They initially take the surname of "X" to represent the names that Africans were stripped of during the enslavement process. They later take Arabic names to manifest the Muslim religion they observe. Malcolm Little became the well-known MALCOLM X, and after his pilgrimage to Mecca he took the name of Al Hajj Malik-El Shabazz.

—*Ella Forbes*

See also: African cultural transformations; African heritage; African languages and American English.

Suggested Readings:

Asante, Molefi K. *The African American Book of Names and Their Meanings*. People's Publishing Group, 1999.

Blassingame, John W. *The Slave Community*. New York: Oxford University Press, 1979.

Gutman, Herbert G. *The Black Family in Slavery and Freedom, 1750-1925*. New York: Vintage Books, 1976.

Holloway, Joseph E. *The African Heritage of American English*. Bloomington: Indiana University Press, 1997.

_______, ed. *Africanisms in American Culture*. Bloomington: Indiana University Press, 1990.

Johnson, Michael P., and James L. Roark. *Black Masters: A Free Family of Color in the Old South*. New York: Norton, 1984.

Stuckey, Sterling. *Slave Culture*. New York: Oxford University Press, 1987.

Umar, Warithu-Dean. *The Name Game: The Book of Lost Names and Commentary, What Every Black African-American Should Know About Their Names*. Glenmont, N.Y. Muslim Broadcasting Syndicate, 1991.

Nash, Charles Edmund (May 23, 1844, Opelousas, Louisiana—June 21, 1913, New Orleans, Louisiana): Legislator and MILITARY hero. Nash enlisted in the Union army in 1863. During the battle of Fort Blakely, LOUISIANA, he lost the lower third of one leg. After the war, he worked for the NEW ORLEANS customs office. Political ties developed in that post helped him win election to the U.S. House of Representatives in 1874. He served one undistinguished term and lost his reelection bid. He served briefly as a postmaster before returning to his original occupation of bricklaying.

National Advisory Commission on Civil Disorders: Appointed by President Lyndon B. Johnson to investigate the causes of urban rioting in the mid-1960's. Otto Kerner, the governor of Illinois, chaired the commission, which included John V. Lindsay, mayor of New York City, as vice chair as well as nine other members representing government, the police, industry, labor, and civil rights groups. The members included Roy WILKINS of the NATIONAL ASSOCIATION FOR THE ADVANCE-

MENT OF COLORED PEOPLE (NAACP) and African American senator Edward BROOKE. Named on July 29, 1967, the commission delivered its final report, known as the KERNER REPORT, on March 1, 1968.

President Johnson instructed the commission to ignore political considerations and to focus exclusively on the causes of urban rioting as a threat to the health and safety of Americans. He gave the commission three basic topics to consider as guidelines for its work: the facts concerning what actually occurred in the riots, the causes of the riots, and how future outbreaks of rioting could be prevented. Within weeks, the commission recommended increasing the number of African Americans in the Army and the National Guard, reviewing procedures for promotion in both bodies, and increasing training in riot control for members of the National Guard.

The commission's starting point was an examination of racism in its historical context. Even before the commission had issued its report, President Johnson pledged to use national resources to remedy historical racism and social injustice. Johnson and the commission saw the United States dividing into two nations, partly as a result of white racism directed against African Americans and partly as a result of black nationalist rhetoric as delivered by such figures as Stokely CARMICHAEL and H. Rap BROWN. The commission also looked at the day-to-day encounters of police officers and citizens. Members decided that these encounters needed to involve discretion, rather than simply a decision of whether to arrest a suspect or to do nothing. Formally, officers were not given such discretionary powers. The commission recommended that police departments draw up guidelines for officers that would spell out intermediate measures, especially for officers working in disadvantaged areas.

See also: Johnson administration; Race riots.

National Association for the Advancement of Colored People: The National Association for the Advancement of Colored People (NAACP) was formed on February 12, 1909, the one hundredth anniversary of the birth of Abraham Lincoln. The NAACP was brought into being by a group of white and African American socialists. In a real sense, the NAACP was an outgrowth of a larger dissatisfaction with the policies of Booker T. WASHINGTON, the "wizard" of Tuskegee, ALABAMA, whose policies of accommodation to segregation and JIM CROW LAWS were meeting with growing resistance. This dissatisfaction led in 1905 to the creation of the NIAGARA MOVEMENT, a group of black intellectuals who opposed Washington's policies and who were led by W. E. B. DU BOIS. The Niagara Movement folded, but its members formed the core of the later association. The NAACP was, as well, a response to a spate of pogroms launched against African American communities in ATLANTA, Springfield, Illinois, and elsewhere.

Founders

The whites involved in the NAACP's founding included William English Walling, a southerner, Mary White Ovington, an affluent woman who had participated in the early stages of the Niagara Movement as a reporter for the *New York Evening Post*, and Henry Moskowitz, a New York social worker. The most prominent African American involved was Du Bois.

Originally, the organization they founded was to be called the "National Negro Committee," but in 1910 the present name was adopted, and the group was incorporated in New York City. The NAACP was quick to establish chapters nationwide and to establish a magazine, THE CRISIS, that quickly gained prominence as the leading journal of opinion among African Americans.

The NAACP was able to attract a number of prominent African American leaders over the years. There was James Weldon JOHNSON, a novelist who also helped write "Lift Every Voice and Sing," the "Negro national anthem," and who served the U.S. government as a diplomat in Latin America. There was William Pickens, a graduate of Yale University and a linguist, who also went on to work for the federal government. There was Walter WHITE, who lived through the bloody Atlanta race riot of 1906 that helped to inspire the association. White rapidly achieved notoriety because of his light skin, blond hair, and blue eyes, which allowed him to infiltrate white racist organizations and report graphically on their atrocities. He was also a novelist of note who played a key role in bringing into being the HARLEM RENAISSANCE of the 1920's. There was also Roy WILKINS, a journalist from the Midwest who joined the NAACP's staff in the 1930's and led the organization throughout the tumultuous 1960's, where he came to be known as a leading opponent of black power and other forms of militance.

Du Bois's Leadership

The most prominent NAACP leader was W. E. B. Du Bois. A sociologist, historian, novelist, and journalist, Du Bois was born in 1868, in the midst of RECONSTRUCTION, and died in 1963, as the MARCH ON WASHINGTON was setting a new stage in the African American struggle for equality. He edited *The Crisis* from 1909 until 1934, when he left the organization after a dispute over the efficacy of black solidarity efforts that were termed by some "self-segregation."

During Du Bois's tenure—which coincided with the leadership of Johnson, Pickens, and White—the NAACP pioneered in bringing court battles against legalized segregation. The court struggles were an interracial effort; one of the NAACP's top lawyers was Moorfield Storey, who was white. Particular targets of the NAACP's legal attack were such institutions as the "white primary," which prevented African Americans from voting in party primaries; in the one-party-dominated South, where most African Americans lived, this effectively barred them from political life. It was not until 1944, with the U.S. SUPREME COURT ruling in SMITH V. ALLWRIGHT, that the white primary was ruled unconstitutional. The NAACP also litigated against other measures that barred African Americans from voting, such as poll taxes and the grandfather clause. The NAACP also brought suit against zoning laws that perpetuated residential segregation and against laws that mandated "SEPARATE BUT EQUAL" education.

NAACP Lawyers

There were also African American lawyers who led these litigation efforts. Charles Hamilton HOUSTON, a graduate of Amherst College and Harvard Law School, trained a generation of civil rights lawyers during his tenure at the law school of HOWARD UNIVERSITY. One of the lawyers he trained was Thurgood MARSHALL, who was lead counsel during the most celebrated NAACP legal victory, the 1954 BROWN V. BOARD OF EDUCATION decision, in which the Supreme Court ruled that segregated education was unconstitutional. Marshall was later appointed to the Supreme Court by President Lyndon B. Johnson; he held his post until 1991. Another prominent NAACP lawyer was Constance Baker MOTLEY, who also was appointed to a federal judgeship.

Dissension in the Ranks

Though hailed as the oldest and largest civil rights organization, the NAACP also has been criticized over the years. Some of that criticism was directed by the NAACP's most noted leader, Du Bois. After leaving the organization in 1934, he returned in 1944 to coordinate the NAACP's international efforts, focusing specifically on the decolonization of Africa. In 1948, however, Du Bois was fired from the

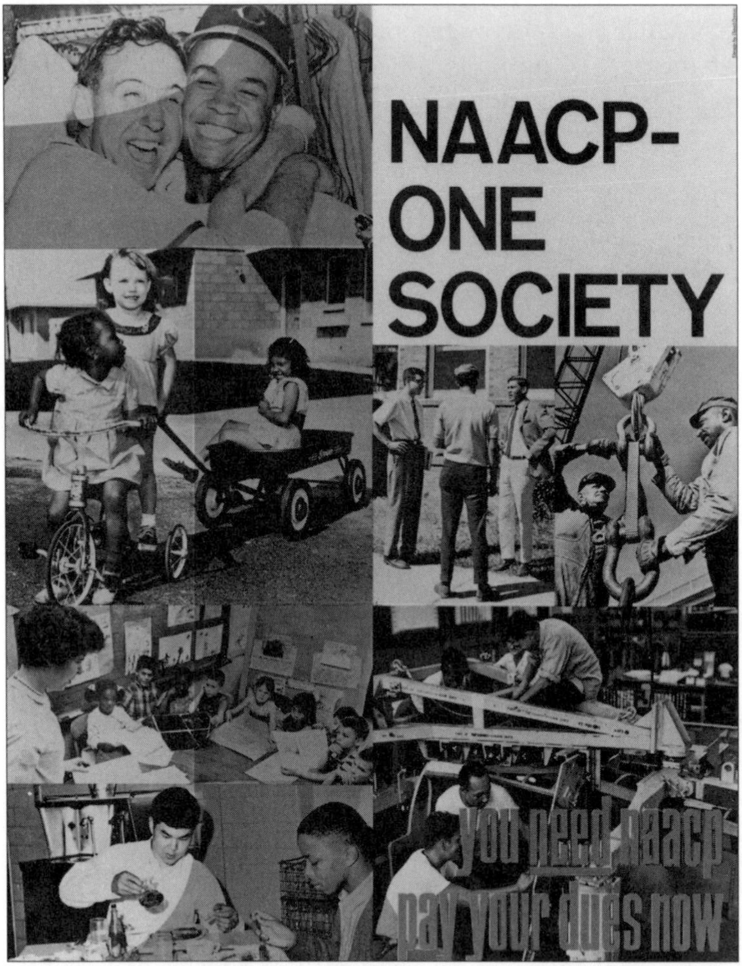

Recruitment poster for the NAACP. *(Library of Congress)*

NAACP, because of his desire to take the plight of African Americans before the United Nations—a move viewed by the NAACP leadership as a pro-Soviet gesture—and because of his reluctance to support Harry S Truman, the choice of Roy Wilkins, Walter White, and most of the NAACP leadership, in Truman's presidential campaign. The firing of Du Bois signaled a retreat by the NAACP from the taking of positions on international questions, at a time when Cold War policies sent tax dollars needed to solve domestic ills to fight wars elsewhere.

Though the NAACP was congratulated for its victory in the *Brown* case, a victory that helped set the stage for the 1960's Civil Rights movement, the organization was criticized during this period for relying too heavily on the courts, which increasingly were dominated by conservatives not friendly to the movement. The NAACP also was criticized for not wielding its mass membership more expertly; some argued that this weakness made the rise of Martin Luther King, Jr., and the Southern Christian Leadership Conference (SCLC) both inevitable and necessary.

The NAACP also was criticized in 1973 for refusing to go along with a decision by the African American leadership of Atlanta to sacrifice desegregation of public schools in return for black administration of the Atlanta school system. There were those who felt that the association was insufficiently flexible and wedded unduly to the notion of integration. Others, though, felt that the NAACP made the proper decision in opposing the deal. Julian Bond, who rose to leadership of the NAACP's Atlanta branch in 1973 because of his support of the arrangement, later came to the conclusion that the national NAACP's opposition was proper.

Lobbying Efforts

In addition to its court struggles, the NAACP became known for its lobbying efforts, emanating from the organization's Washington, D.C., office. For years, this office was headed by Clarence Mitchell, who was nicknamed the "101st senator" and who played a key role in the passage of the Civil Rights Act of 1964 and the Voting Rights Act of 1965. The NAACP Washington office has continued with the traditional civil rights agenda—it played a pivotal role in the passage of the Civil Rights and Women's Equity Act of 1991—but also has broadened that agenda by becoming involved in issues such as the status of Haitian refugees, police misconduct, and questions of economic parity and development.

The national office of the NAACP is based in Baltimore and in the 1980's was headed by Benjamin Hooks, a former commissioner of the Federal Communications Commission and a lifelong Republican. The national office is responsible for coordination of the organization's fifteen hundred branches and 400,000-plus membership. The archives of the NAACP are housed in the Library of Congress in Washington, D.C. In February of 1992, Hooks announced his intention to retire as executive director of the NAACP; he stepped down in 1993 after serving for fifteen years. Benjamin Chavis was chosen as his replacement.

Challenges in the 1990's

In the 1990's, the nation's oldest civil rights group faced a variety of internal problems and challenges, some of which threatened to put a halt to the organization's operations. Bitter internal divisions hampered the NAACP's struggle to regain the prestigious leadership role that made the organization a symbol of justice for African Americans during the Civil Rights movement. The NAACP faced a serious financial crisis when it was revealed that the organization was operating with an estimated deficit of $4 million, much of which was attributed to losses associated with televising the annual Image Awards ceremonies in Hollywood.

Myrlie Evers-Williams addressing reporters after being elected to the chair of the NAACP in early 1995. *(AP/Wide World Photos)*

Financial mismanagement charges were directed at executive director Chavis, who was fired in August of 1994 after serving little more than a year in office. Chavis had alienated many NAACP supporters through his casual slighting of influential black labor leaders as well as his high-profile overtures to Nation of Islam leader Louis Farrakhan. Before he was fired, Chavis revealed that he had agreed to pay more than $300,000 as part of a private settlement of a sexual harassment claim filed against him by Mary Stansel, a former NAACP employee. Other female staff members had filed a class-action suit charging the national headquarters

President Bill Clinton (left) watches as Kweisi Mfume (hand raised) is sworn in as president of the NAACP in January, 1996. *(© Roy Lewis Archives)*

with allowing gender discrimination and fostering the creation of a hostile workplace.

Like Chavis, NAACP board chairman William Gibson was accused of using organization funds to cover personal expenses. Many nationally prominent African Americans, including Julian Bond, C. DeLores Tucker, and Carl T. Rowan, called for Gibson's removal as chairman. Disgruntled staff members, angered that they were being dismissed while top advisers were receiving generous consulting contracts, provided many of the expense reports and other internal documents that were used in an exposé on Gibson that aired on *60 Minutes* in 1994.

Before Gibson received a vote of no confidence at the NAACP membership meeting in February, 1995, the Detroit branch of the NAACP announced that it was launching a class-action suit against the board of directors at NAACP national headquarters in an effort to obtain a full accounting of the organization's past expenses. As the largest branch of the NAACP, the Detroit chapter had contributed some $2.5 million to the national organization in the decade before 1995, and Detroit treasurer Sharon McPhail announced that she and other Detroit officers wanted their lawsuit to prompt a thorough reform of the organization's national leadership.

In February of 1995, NAACP board members voted Gibson out of office. By a narrow margin of 30 to 29, they elected Myrlie Evers-Williams, widow of slain civil rights activist Medgar EVERS, to succeed Gibson. Evers-Williams became the first woman to serve as chair of the NAACP board of directors. She was sworn into office during an elaborate ceremony held on Mother's Day in 1995 that was attended by many prominent civil rights leaders. Among her first moves upon taking office, Evers-Williams appointed Wall Street financial manager Francisco Borges to serve as national treasurer and named Earl T. Shinhoster to serve as acting executive director until a replacement for Chavis was selected. Evers-Williams also announced her intention to lead the NAACP in placing pressure on Congress regarding issues that affect the African American community, including AFFIRMATIVE ACTION and welfare reform.

In January of 1996, former MARYLAND congressman Caucus Kweisi MFUME was sworn in as president and executive director of the NAACP. President Bill Clinton was among the figures who attended the ceremony, which was held in the Great Hall of the Justice Department in Washington, D.C. As a former chair of the CONGRESSIONAL BLACK CAUCUS, Mfume had established a strong network of contacts in Washington, D.C., and was expected to use his political influence to help further the NAACP's ongoing fight for racial justice.

Mfume faced a daunting situation, with the NAACP in debt, torn by internal squabbling, and seen by many outsiders as irrelevant, but he attacked the problems diligently. He managed to reduce the debt by $2 million within four months, and by early 1997 the debt had been cleared, a result of both cost cutting and increased contributions. He set as the next priority the problem of attracting younger members to the NAACP and bridging the generation gap between older and younger members.

In 1998 Julian Bond was named chairman of the board, and both he and Mfume sought to refocus the organization on advocating equal rights and fighting discrimination, a focus that would mean deemphasizing the NAACP's service work. The NAACP would remain involved in such areas as small-business loans, scholarships, and anti-drug efforts but would arrange for most of the actual work to be done by other organizations. Mfume, Bond, and other NAACP leaders also reaffirmed the group's commitment to fighting for affirmative action.

—Gerald Horne
—Updated by Wendy Sacket

Suggested Readings:

Avery, Sheldon. *Up from Washington: William Pickens and the Negro Struggle for Equality, 1900-1954.* Newark: University of Delaware Press, 1989.

Factor, Robert L. *The Black Response to America: Men, Ideals, and Organizations from Frederick Douglass to the NAACP.* Reading, Mass.: Addison-Wesley, 1970.

Jack, Robert L. *History of the National Association for the Advancement of Colored People.* Boston: Meador, 1943.

Ovington, Mary W. *Black and White Sat Down Together: The Reminiscences of an NAACP Founder.* Edited by Ralph Luker. New York: Feminist Press at the City University of New York, 1995.

Ross, Barbara J. *J. E. Spingarn and the Rise of the NAACP, 1911-1939.* New York: Atheneum, 1972.

Tushnet, Mark V. *The NAACP's Legal Strategy Against Segregated Education, 1925-1950.* Chapel Hill: University of North Carolina Press, 1987.

Wilson, Sondra K., ed. *In Search of Democracy: The NAACP Writings of James Weldon Johnson, Walter White, and Roy Wilkins (1920-1977).* New York: Oxford University, 1999.

Wedin, Carolyn. *Inheritors of the Spirit: Mary White Ovington and the Founding of the NAACP.* New York: John Wiley & Sons, 1998.